I0475302

Where To Find Your Warehouse Income Sources & Expense Reduction Ideas

By

David E. Mulcahy

10/1/2010

Using this book, you will learn about numerous ideas for income sources, expense reduction, employee productivity improvement, enhanced space utilization, measurement techniques and other ideas that, if applied, will justify the book purchase many times over.

Table of Contents

INTRODUCTION

THE OBJECTIVE OF THIS BOOK

Using this book, you will learn about numerous ideas for income source, expense reduction, employee productivity improvement, enhanced space utilization, measurement techniques and other ideas that, if applied, will justify the book purchase many times over. Our main objective is to provide a book that contains a wide range of methods and strategies for income source, expense reduction, for increasing completed Customer Orders (COs), for improving employee productivity, measurement techniques & space utilization, as well as insights & tips for a warehouse manager to make his warehouse more efficient with a higher throughput & more cost effective with a lower cost per unit (CPU). With ideas to increase source, reduce reduction, increase employee productivity, increase completed CO numbers , measure your warehouse activity& improve space utilization, a warehouse manager can convert his operation into a lean operation with minimal operational expenses.

Implementing the book's ideas, a warehouse manager can (1) increase source and reduce reduction & make budget, (2) can get a cost reduction incentive bonus, (3) can handle volume increases with lowest expenses & higher levels of complete COs and customer return process in the shortest time, (4) can make your operation lean with minimal operational expenses and measurement techniques and (5) can change from a pick cartons operation to a pick eaches/pieces operation.

While, looking at any one income increase or expense reduction idea for a specific warehouse activity may only have a minimal impact on a your warehouse budget detail line or individual activity expense, when you add several warehouse activities with expense reduction ideas together, there is a significant impact on your total warehouse expenses that brings your total operation expenses back within or below budget.

HOW TO USE THE BOOK

Many of the book's income source or expense reduction, throughput improvement, space utilization or employee productivity improvement and measurement techniques ideas require a minimal cost. Each chapter covers a general area of warehouse activity and associated expense reduction ideas, insights or tips that are considered for implementation in your operation whether your warehouse is large, medium or small and regardless of whether your operation handles carton, GOH or small eaches/pieces. The book contains ideas that assist you in turning your warehouse into a lean operation by (1) increasing income and reducing operating expenses, improving profits & lowering handling costs, (2) increasing completed orders, employee productivity and units per hour (UPH), (3) improving customer service, (4) enhancing sku, and return sku flows, (5) improving space utilization, (6) maintaining on-schedule shipments & deliveries, (7) reducing sku damage (8) improving employee safety, (9) assuring asset protection and (10) measuring your warehouse activities.

THE AUTHOR'S INTENTION

The author's wrote this book for people involved in the industry. As such it contains numerous abbreviations, terms and even slang used by managers, journeymen and vendors to the industry. In writing this book, The Author's intention is to help develop the reader's skill and knowledge with specific application of ideas and concepts to increase income and reduce expenses and lower costs, increase completed orders processing, increase employee productivity and/or improve space utilization. Since the warehouse profession is constantly changing, the book may not include the very latest changes in the 'state of the art' and references to all the newest warehouse ideas, equipment applications & technologies. It is also necessary to recognize that a book can not cover all ideas, equipment & technologies in the warehouse field. The book can however, assist in staff training and in quickly obtaining the benefits of years of practical experience that has no substitute. It is important for a reader to use the collection of ideas and touch points as a guide. Prior to implementing any idea, insight and tip in your existing or new warehouse activity, if you want to be able to measure and document the improvements, it is essential that you first measure or develop & project accurate activity expenses, sku, customer returns & CO transactions data, equipment layout, sku, CO & returns flows, employee & customer acceptance & design factors. Due to the actuality that the factors are the design bases for your proposed warehouse operation income increase or expense reduction idea, it is prudent for you to gather & review your existing and proposed change to a warehouse activity with your staff & employees, read vendor literature and visit existing facilities that utilize the suggested idea, insight or tip. The research permits you, your staff and employees to become familiar with operational characteristics of a proposed change or improvement idea that is under consideration for implementation in your facility. Any activity performance specifications, physical design and installation characteristics are subject to redesign, improvement, modification & are required to meet vendor, local governmental standards & specifications.

HOW THE BOOK IS ORGANIZED

Each chapter in the book deals with a key warehouse activity and the associated income source or expense reduction ideas. The book chapters are sequenced to mirror a vendor delivered sku as it flows through the various potential warehouse activities, from stocking, to picking, to shipping, to return. To assist you in more easily achieving your warehouse objectives, each book chapter is focused on one warehouse activity & associated income source or expense reduction ideas. This permits a manager & his staff to locate and focus on the most relevant or appropriate ideas, tips & insights for each warehouse. Each idea has a title, which allows readers to focus their attention on the specific warehouse activity over which they have budget expense & operational responsibility. If a reader is assigned to increase income or reduce expenses, improve customer service or increase the number of completed Customer Orders (CO), the book with its income source or expense reduction, completed CO number increase, customer service improvement, employee productivity increase and space utilization enhancement ideas for each warehouse activity does assist a reader to develop ideas to achieve an expense reduction or lower CPU, customer service or increase CO & UPH objectives. Some expense reduction ideas are directed to warehouse equipment layout, sku, order, customer returns flows, employee productivity, when to use the 80/20 rule, where to locate your power 'A' moving skus, how to route your CO pickers, how to organize employee work for the best productivity & that your most important opportunities are the activities with the highest warehouse employee count and budget expense numbers.

Warehouse income isource or expense reductions, completed order increases, space utilization or employee productivity improvement ideas also impact the operations to increase accurate and on-time COs & improve profits. By implementing multiple expense reductions, throughput increases, space utilization or employee productivity improvement ideas, as outlined in the book, you can dramatically lower existing or new warehouse cost, increase productivity and minimizes new construction cost per sq. ft and techniques to measure your warehouse and activities.. Regardless to the quality of any combination of warehouse operation improvements, in order to achieve major operations income source and expense reductions, dramatic space utilization improvements or employee productivity improvements, may require capital investments in new equipment, new construction or changing from a manual operation to a mechanized or automated operation.

THE AUTHOR'S OTHER REFERENCE BOOKS

The author's other reference books include
Warehouse Distribution & Operations Handbook
Materials Handling Management
Order Fulfillment And Across The Dock Operations Concepts, Designs And Operations Handbook
Eaches And Pieces Order Fulfillment Design And Operations Handbook
A Supply Chain Logistics Program For Warehouse Management

Reduce Your Warehouse Expenses

The author would like to express thanks to all the warehouse, distribution, logistics, plant and IT or WMS program professionals with whom they have had an association with at various companies, as fellow managers, as clients, as a speakers at seminars and as publishers.

CHAPTER   1   YOUR POTENTIAL WAREHOUSE OPERATION INCOME SOURCES

Introduction

Your potential income sources from your warehouse operation create income to your operation that creates income to your operation and reduces your cost per unit (CPU). In most operations, income results from a normal warehouse operation that has your employee complete additional value added activity or collects sku secure/filler material for a recycle/green program. If an income item is a repetitive activity, you have a line item on your annual operation budget to reduce your company total annual operation expense or bottom dollar line.

Bale Cardboard & Paper Program

Bale cardboard & paper program collects filler material, slip sheets or empty cartons for your recycle program. Bale cardboard or paper program occurs in many warehouse operations and results from a used slip sheet board, empty master carton or filler material that are created from your operation. If you do not bale cardboard (employee fill/operated or mechanical fill/automated operated), your operation expenses are (1) your labor handling expense for cardboard transport to your trash compactor or bin, (2) less maximum internal compactor or bin space utilization due as a ram returns, it creates some open space within a compactor or bin does not allow compaction that creates low space utilization, (3) with one compactor, on-site trash queue in your facility and additional labor trash double handling expense, (4) with two compactors, no trash queue but additional dock area/doors allocated to trash handling and (5) trash compactor or bin haul expense. With a bale cardboard concept your warehouse expenses are (1) cardboard employee or mechanical transport expense and with a manual bale fill concept to assure cardboard is placed into a baler cavity, (2) assure that a baler has ties, (3) employee controlled or photo-eye controlled baler, (4) baler provides maximum space utilization as a compact item and (5) employee controlled forklift bale transport to truck or storage position. A baled cardboard concept, no trash compactor or bin rental or haul expenses, in most situation one year depreciation expense, with compactor same electrical expense and your company becomes involved in a recycle or green program.

COMPARTIVE CARDBOARD TRASH HANDLING FORM

COST FACTOR	COMPACTOR/BIN TRASH HANDLING	BALE TRASH HANDLING
Lease/Rental $		
Haul $		
One Unit		
Two Unit		
Building Space & Door		
Employee Hours $		
Income		

Bale Or Box Plastic Program

Bale or box plastic paper program collects pallet or slip sheet plastic sheet secure material for your recycle program. Bale or box plastic program occurs in many warehouse operations and results from a used plastic wrap from a storage pallet or slip sheet board that is created from your operation. A plastic wrap is removed from a pallet or slip sheet and transferred to a trash container. A full container is transported to a trash compacter, bin or manual baler. For features and benefits, we refer a reader to a cardboard bale program. For a comparative form use Comparative Cardboard Trash Handling Form Format.

Extra Storage Positions

If your storage operation has a facility with a 5 year peak storage position design factor and your are in year 1 to 3, your storage area has potential for a high number of vacant storage positions. Per your storage philosophy, your storage area has potential rack rows with a high vacant position number or your rack rows rear positions from your ship docks are vacant. Per your local code, insurance company and company policy, your operation has an opportunity to become a third party storage operation that rents storage positions to other companies or if your operation is part of a chain, you have storage positions available for your company hedge purchases.

Manufacturer Sku Stuffers Placed Into Your Customer Order Package

Your manufacturer sku stuffers placed inside your CO package has your pack activity at fee to place a manufacturer stuffer (advertisement) into your CO package. For this activity your manufacturer pays your company a fee or reduction in a sku purchase price. For maximum efficiency, a packer or picker or machine transfers a stuffer into a CO container. For an employee activity, a shelf is placed at an elevation for your most frequent carton height with flaps up for easy and quick employee transfer.

Gift Wrap

Gift wrap sku handling is a value added activity for any sku. After a customer order is received for a gift wrap activity sku your WMS computer processes a CO as a single line/single sku. A picker completes a sku pick transaction and a picked sku is sent to a gift wrap activity station. At a gift wrap station, an employee verifies that a sku is per a CO & specific gift wrap type. After a sku is gift wrapped, a gift wrapped sku is packaged & sent to the ship conveyor.

Mono-Gram

Mono-gram sku handling is a value added activity for GOH or flat-wear skus. After a CO is received for a mono-gram added to a flat-wear or GOH sku, your WMS computer processes a CO as a single line/single sku. A picker completes a sku pick transaction and a picked sku is sent to a mono-gram activity station. At a mono-gram station, an employee verifies that a sku is per a CO and request mono-gram. After a mono-gram is added to a sku, a sku is package and sent to the ship conveyor.

Lay-Away Program

Lay-away program is a value added activity in your catalog, e-mail, TV marketing or retail store business to increase COs and increase sales, an opportunity is to develop/modify your CO lay-away or dated delivery sku program. Your CO lay-away or dated delivery sku program is your game plan to assure that your customer desired sku is available at your retail store or at your CO delivery location for a major holiday event, birthday, special occasion or other important date. An on-time sku delivery at your CO delivery location or at your retail store for CO pick-up creates a satisfied customer who has high potential for a repeat customer and a customer to network their satisfaction with friends who are potential new customers. Your CO lay-away or dated delivery sku program requires your business to decide your CO lay-away or dated delivery sku inventory (resident) location that is at a distribution facility or your retail store back room. Your selected option provides storage space at a sku resident location for sku storage/access, assure sku/inventory control and tracking for a pre-determined time period and at your retail store for customer pick-up or assure sku on-time freight delivery for availability at a CO delivery location.

Your distribution facility or retail store back room CO lay-away or dated delivery sku storage components are arranged to have a cost effective and efficient operation for sku storage activities and sku transfer from your storage area for transport to your retail store or delivery to a customer preferred delivery location. Your design team objective is to understand, design, develop and implement a cost effective and efficient distribution facility or retail store back room operation to handle your CO lay-away or dated delivery skus. Your team designs a CO lay-away or dated delivery sku storage distribution facility or back room storage equipment layout that includes cost justification/implementation, maintains/improves employee productivity, increases space utilization, assures sku proper storage environment and assures CO pick-up/on-time delivery. Lay-away is an idea that improves customer satisfaction. Lay-away has a customer pre-order a sku and your operation is not required to ship a lay-away sku for several weeks or months such as Christmas Gifts that are to be reserved by your company. With your WMS computer inventory program your options are (1) for a sku in WMS ID storage position, to place a sku quantity on hold as 'not available for sale status' and schedule for release on a specific date and (2) to pick & transfer sku to a special temporary hold position and place sku quantity on hold as 'not available for sale status' & (3) to pick & pack a sku and place in a temporary hold position and place sku quantity on 'hold as not available for sale status'. The approaches delete your sku quantity available for sale and on an appropriate date to have skus status changed and complete a CO pick and pack activities.

Specific Delivery Date

Specific delivery date is a value added activity that improves your customer satisfaction by assuring that a sku is delivered to a customer on specific date such as birthday or anniversary. With your WMS computer CO process program and CO pool classifications, your options are (1) to hold a CO in your CO pool and have your staff include a specific delivery date CO as part of a CO wave or (2) to pick and pack a CO and place CO container in a temporary hold position and place skus on hold and 'not available for sale' status. On a specific delivery date, your staff changes a sku status to available for sale, completes a CO identification & sku scan transaction & manifest activity.

Backhaul Concept

Backhaul concept is a transport/warehouse concept that has your company purchase and trucking departments arrange with a vendor for your company or contracted empty truck to pick-up your company purchase order at a vendor location & deliver vendor skus to your warehouse. For a vendor sku pick-up & delivery activity your company receives compensation. In some companies, a backhaul occurs after your truck completes a delivery at a customer location and is empty. With an empty truck, a truck travels from your warehouse to a vendor location, picks-up your purchase order & with purchase order returns to your warehouse. If your co delivery location is within a short travel distance to a vendor location, your warehouse realizes good cost savings due to a large mile percentage was incurred as your delivery miles to your customer order location. A backhaul compensation or freight charge lowers your warehouse delivery costs.

CHAPTER 2 YOUR POTENTIAL EXPENSE REDUCTION OR LABOR PRODUCTIVITY IMPROVEMENT IDEAS

Introduction

Your potential operation expense reduction or labor productivity improvement source lowers your (CPU) or improves labor handling units per hour (UPH). In most operations, your expense control reduces your sku/equipment damage, employee injury and handling/shipping expenses or employee work/activity control/productivity improvement reduces an employee time to complete an activity or (CO) transaction.

General & Administrative Activities To Ideas (GA1 – GA8)

GA 1. Daily Labor Productivity Detail Or Total Man-Hours

Daily labor warehouse productivity is bases for your manager to allocate his available or call-in labor to match an actual or I T department CO volume. With your actual CO pieces & labor productivity rates, a manager improves his control labor allocation to work/activity stations & daily labor expenses & assures CO service matches a company standard. Labor allocation approaches are (1) detail or budgeted labor activity productivity. With your actual CO volume & budgeted productivity rates, your staff determines an employee number that is required for each work/activity station. With an insight and before your e start-up, your manager allocates employee number to each activity with-out non-productive employee change work/activity station time and to call in part-time employees & (2) total man-hour or total operation productivity. A total man-hour or total operation productivity has your daily CO volume divided by your budgeted total operation productivity rate. The approach provides you with required total employee to complete work, but does not consider different volumes for each warehouse activity. For your day's volume, if one activity station has a low volume, an employee has insufficient work to match your budgeted productivity rate and if another activity has a high volume an employee hours are insufficient to handle your actual volume. During a workday, your supervisor detects a situation & allocates labor to another work/activity station with some non-productive employee change activity station time.

TOTAL MAN-HOUR DAY LABOR PROJECTION

$$\frac{\text{DAILY PIECES OR UNITS}}{\text{WAREHOUSE PRODUCTIVITY RATE}} = \text{TOTAL EMPLOYEE NUMBER}$$

DETAIL MAN-HOUR DAY LABOR PROJECTION

$$\frac{\text{PICK ACTIVITY DAILY PIECES OR UNITS}}{\text{PICKER PRODUCTIVITY RATE}} = \text{PICKER EMPLOYEE NUMBER}$$

$$\frac{\text{PACK ACTIVITY DAILY PIECES OR UNITS}}{\text{PACKER PRODUCTIVITY RATE}} = \text{PACKER EMPLOYEE NUMBER}$$

$$\frac{\text{FORKLIFT TRUCK UNLOAD/PUT-AWAY DAILY UNITS}}{\text{FORKLIFT TRUCK DRIVER PRODUCTIVITY RATE}} = \text{FORKLIFT TRUCK EMPLOYEE NUMBER}$$

$$\frac{\text{FORKLIFT TRUCK LOAD/WITHDRAWAL DAILY UNITS}}{\text{FORKLIFT TRUCK DRIVER PRODUCTIVITY RATE}} = \text{FORKLIFT TRUCK EMPLOYEE NUMBER}$$

GA 2. Warehouse Expense Budget Tied To Your Labor Productivity

To plan and control your operation requires your man-hour and operational item expense budget that is based on your company's sku sale forecast and anticipated employee productivity rate for each activity. Each expense budget activity line has an expense. Labor expense is related to a forecasted skus that is divided by anticipated employee productivity rate. Your staff & other operational item expenses are based on last year's staff & item expense with a percent increase for volume & inflation. The approach helps your manager plan employee number, explain an actual expense that is over or under a budgeted expense occurrence & allows a company to account for new equipment or a change in an activity performance.

GA 3. How Does It Impact Your Warehouse

How does it impact your total warehouse is a reference to a change in one warehouse activity & its impact on your other activities. During your idea or design phase, you determine your activity savings & impact on your sku & CO flows. As part of your project justification & evaluation, you determine your proposed sku & CO flow change impact on upstream & downstream activities. If you do not consider an activity change impact on other activities, there is potential to have uncontrolled sku & CO surges, employee down time or travel path jams that reduce your activity benefits & return on cost.

GA 4. Cancel Customer Order Before Customer Order Wave Creation Or Pick Activity

In your warehouse, there is potential for a canceled CO. If a CO is canceled in your host computer, you do not incur CO process labor and ship supply expenses. If a CO is canceled after release to your activity & canceled at a pack or manifest station, you incur CO I T department process expense, CO sku replenishment, pick, check and pack labor expense & WMS identified sku re-stock expenses.

GA 5. Biggest Bang For Your Investment Dollars

Most warehouses have a limited capital investment budget to purchase new equipment or to change employee work methods. With limited available capital funds and prior to purchase, companies require a capital project economic justification, your manager completes an annual budget, potential labor costs with associated expense savings, space savings & CO volume increase as capital justification factors. Your manager ranks potential projects based on each capital project lowest cost & economic justifications for highest labor & expense savings, space utilization improvement or CO increase. With a ranking concept, your manager places a capital project with lowest cost & highest economic justification in first position due to your manager gets a biggest bang for your investment dollars.

GA 6. Look At Your Expense Numbers & Employees

When reviewing your expense reduction or customer service improvement opportunities, you look at your e numbers or employees. Your numbers are (1) activities that have greatest employee number. An improvement in your activities or UPH reduces your employee number & wage expense & (2) activities that have a re-occurrence of errors such as overs, shorts, damages or late delivery. Improvement activity has greatest impact on your labor expense or customer service standard.

PROJECT RANKING FORM

Project Description	Dollar Cost		Savings	
Warehouse Activity	$	Description	$	Employee #

GA 7. Look At Today But Prepare For Tomorrow

To design your sku & CO flows, equipment layout and activity stations, your design team attains a balance to satisfy today's sku & CO requirements but prepares for your future volumes. With a flexible design, your design is modified to satisfy today's volumes & tomorrow sku & CO volumes with minimal interruption to your existing sku & CO flows.

GA 8. Lights/Conveyor On/Off

No skus or COs (after a pre-determined time period) on a powered conveyor travel path is an opportunity for your powered conveyor travel path shutdown. If your have a powered conveyor travel path, electric powered motors that use electricity move a conveyor travel path. Powered conveyor travels paths are used in several activities such as transport, pick, pack, ship & customer returns activities. Since electricity is an expense, a warehouse objective is to control or minimize expenses and to incur an expense as employees or equipment handle a sku or CO. A powered conveyor travel path turn on or turn off options are (1) *At A Work Day Start Time*, to turn all powered conveyor travel path sections on and leave electric drive motors on all day. With an 8 to 12 hour workday, the feature has high electric power usage & associated expense. During a workday, there are time periods (nothing available, breaks or lunches) or occasions with no sku or COs moving on a conveyor travel path. The situation means that you have an expense with no sku or CO being handled that incurs an expense with no sku or CO to account for an expense or (2) *When Skus Or COs Are Scheduled To Move Over A Powered Conveyor Travel Path*, your staff turns on a powered conveyor travel path. If no sku or CO (after a pre-determined time period) is on a powered conveyor travel path, powered conveyor travel path sensing devices and controls turn off electric drive motors for a powered conveyor travel path and with a sku or customer order on a powered conveyor travel path, sensing devices and controls turn on electric drive motors for a powered conveyor travel path. The situation means that your warehouse only incurs an expense when skus or COs are being handled that means a CPU with skus or COs to account for an expense. Your powered conveyor manufacturer or electric company projects your electric expense savings that are based on your electric cost & hours not being used. Your powered conveyor sensing device/control options are (1) a supervisor who turns on/off a switch with no cost or (2) electric/micro-computer type with a cost.

Lights on/off (after a pre-determined time period) in a warehouse activity section or workstation are an idea to save electric power expense. Each activity requires lights to illuminate an aisle or work station area that allows an employee complete an activity or transaction, powered vehicle travel over a travel path or an employee to walk through an aisle or area. Local codes & company policy set illumination standards for each activity aisle, work area or work station such as minimal light fixtures on, safety lights or single-phase lights. Some activity areas are (1) receiving dock area that includes dock lights, (2) storage vehicle aisles & best opportunity is with carton or pallet AS/RS crane concept, (2) single item, carton, GOH or pallet pick sections or aisles, (3) check & sort/pack stations, (4) manifest, sort & loading dock areas that includes dock lights & (5) customer returns dock area that includes light and process areas. Since electricity is an expense, a business objective is to control or minimize expenses and to incur an expense that is associated with the handling for a sku or CO. Light turn on or turn off options are (1) at you open time, to turn all activity lights on & leave lights on all day. With an 8 to 12 hour workday, the feature has high electric power usage & associated expense. During a workday, there are time periods (nothing available, breaks or lunches) occasions with no employees or powered vehicles in an aisle or work area. The situation means that you have an expense with no employee handling a sku or CO. This means a CPU with no sku or CO to account for an expense or (2) when an activity is scheduled for area or a vehicle or employee moves into an area, your warehouse turns on aisle or work area lights and lights remain on for a pre-determined time period or as an employee or powered vehicle remains in motion or creates a noise that has lights remain on. If powered vehicle or employee (after a pre-determined time period) is working in an area, area motion sensing devices/controls turn off lights & as required turning on lights. The situation means that your warehouse has an expense with skus or COs being handled that means a CPU with skus or COs to account for an expense. Your electric contractor or electric company projects your electric expense savings that are based on your electric cost & hours not being used as a percentage for total work day hours. Example is your work hour day is 9 hours with 30 minute lunch and 2 each 15 minute breaks. This means that 60 minutes in a work day or 11% of your total work day, you have no employees in a work area & by turning lights off you could realize an 11% savings on your electric expense that is associated with lights. It is noted that best quick turn on lights are fluorescent tube. Per your activity area light turn on/off sensing devices/controls are (a) supervisor who turns on/off a light switch that has no cost or (2) motion or noise electric/micro-computer type that has a cost.

After a pre-determined time period) in your cafeteria or break room's lights on/off is an idea to save electric power expense. Each activity requires lights to illuminate a cafeteria, break room or restroom that allows an employee use or enjoy the area. Local codes & company policy set illumination standards for each activity area such as minimal light fixtures on, safety lights or single-phase lights. It is noted that best quick turn on lights are fluorescent tube. If you leave a cafeteria, break room or restroom lights remain on for an entire work-day, your warehouse incurs an expense with no return or benefit to an employee or operation. Per you cafeteria or break room light turn on/off sensing devices & controls are (a) a supervisor who turns on/off a light switch that has no cost or (2) with a restroom area motion or noise electric/micro-computer type that has a cost. The situation means that you have an expense with an employee is using or enjoying the area and accounts for an expense. Your electric contractor or electric company can project your electric expense savings that are based on your electric cost & hours not being used as a percentage for total work day hours.

Employee Control & Scheduling Ideas (ECS 1 – ECS 4)

ECS 1. Look For Your Slowest Activity & Balance Your Customer Order Wave Number

Look for your slowest activity or know and balance your pick, sort and pack productivity rates and employee number is a plan that has a direct impact to assure your continuous CO flow and high completed CO number. Your pick, sort and pack activity rates are your budgeted productivity rate that were based on a projected sku volume and used to project your annual expense budget. With CO wave volume and activity productivity rates you determine your required employee work stations. From your day employee work schedule, you know your picker, sorter and packer number that is compared to your projected employee picker, sorter and packer number. For an on-budget operation, you assure your actual projected picker, sorter and packer number matches your budgeted picker, sorter and packer. If one operation activity has an employee number that exceeds your required employee number, there is potential for your CO flow to have uncontrolled queue or low completed CO number. With a CO wave plan, you have an opportunity to provide on-time customer service at the lowest cost. Your entire pick and pack activities completed CO number is based on your slowest pick or pack activity. For you to increase your sku flow and completed CO number, for your slowest activity you add work stations, change your work method or add mechanization. You slowest activity identification methods are (1) to look for uncontrolled queues and (2) low employee productivity.

ECS 2. Establish A Call-In List

A call-in list has a manager complete a list for part-time employees who are available to work for a day or with a short notice. With a call-in employee list, your manager determines a requirement (based on a projected sku or CO volume) for part-time employees, you call-in part time employees. For best results, your staff assures sufficient work for part-time employees with a lower wage rate.

ECS 3. Use Part Time Employees & Make Your Schedule Fit Their Time

If your have an opportunity to use part-time employees, you potential to lower your CPU. Since most part-time employees are available at specific hours for work and hours in most cases do not match normal hours (8 hour day). The situation means that part-time employees cannot work in your normal work hours or for a complete work day. With a complete knowledge of available skus for pre-pack activity & CO types such as slapper label or fast pack activities, your manager assures that sku & CO volume is available and activity is set-up (warm start) for part-time employee hours, assures a sufficient work for your part-time employee hours, training or skills & makes your work schedule fit your part-time employee schedule.

ECS 4. Plan Your Over-Time

Since your over-time is for your regular employee, your considerations are (1) Regular employee over-time hours & cost at & 1 ½ pay per hour cost that exceeds part-time employee pay with a lower wage rate & minimal benefits, (2) Requires minimal additional work stations, equipment & employee support Items and (3) Over-time or longer work hours increases employee fatigue, lower productivity rates & increased potential for errors. Your over-time options are (1) *Pre-Standard Start-Time* that has work day prior your next work day forecasted volume exceeds your budget volume & you request employees to start early. With set-up employee over-time assures warm start for fast pack & pack activity and assures maximum completed COs shipped or (2) *Post Work-Day End Time* that has no work day forecast work day volume exceeds your budgeted productivity rates, results from an electric, mechanical or I T/computer problems or down time unexpected employee sickness or injury creates an employee number short fall. With an early employee number short fall indication, you have potential to call-in part-time employees or re-assign employees from non-critical activities. Some completed COs do not arrive at your freight company for sort time.

ECS 5. Forecast Pick & Pack Employee Over-Time

After you develop your CO wave/work day volume/pieces your determine your ability to complete COs on-time by dividing your volume/piece by your latest productivity rate that equals your required employee number & is compared to your budgeted employee number. If a minus, you call-in or add part-time employees or your existing employees have over-time.

ECS 6. Cold Or Warm Start

Your manual pick concept has CO pick activities & your daily pick/pack employee start work options are

Cold Start has your manual pick activity concept & pack activities start-up with no completed CO transactions. With a manual pick activity concept, a cold start has your manual pick activity concept start and wait for your skus set-up/replenishment to pick positions, your pack employees are assigned to other warehouse activities. After your position replenishment completion, your packer employees are transferred to your pick activity and after X number of CO completion for a CO queue, your packers are transferred to your pack stations. Employee relocation represents non-productive walk distance & time.

Warm Start assures higher bulk, sort and final picker productivity and increases your completed CO number. For a warm start, your 'A'/fast moving skus set-up/replenishment to pick positions occurs the day before or on the same day prior to your pick activity starts. Your warm start options are (1) if your manual pick employees start work at one time, your pack employees are assigned to start as a pick person or to another warehouse activity & at a specific time move to your pack activities. Feature is some low employee productivity due to non-productive walk time to complete activity changes and shut-down that a previous activity and start-up new activity or (2) your sku set-up/replenishment activity employees complete a day before or on the same day start prior to your sort and final pick activity, your pick and sort employees start prior to your pack activity employees start time. As soon as possible, skus are in pick positions and COs are moving from your pick area to your pack area. Your COs flow is from your pick area to your pack work stations & on your travel path COs queue prior to your pack stations. In conclusion, a final sort & pick concept with at least your promotional, special, advertised or seasonal or 'A'/fast moving skus (20% of your skus based on Pareto's Law 80/20) in pick positions is considered a warm start. If your WMS computer sequences your pick positions sku set-up/replenishment transactions for skus with the maximum picks first, next highest second and so on, your pick activity has a warm start. For maximum efficiency and high CO completion, your operation assures a pick concept warm start with your pick position set-up/replenishment employees start before your other pickers.

ECS 7. Picker Short Interval Schedule

Requires separated & identified CO cube, picker identification, picker productivity rate & based on a picker aisle, PC adjusts for travel time/distance & staff member to complete PC entries. On a short interval schedule form, you indicate a picker dispatch time & aisle location & computer projected return time. After a picker completes a CO pick activity & returns to the dispatch desk, on a short interval schedule form, you indicate a picker return time. A picker variance between a computer projected return time & actual picker return time shows each picker's real-time poor, above or average picker productivity.

ECS 8. Pick & Pack Activity Monitor

Requires your CO wave/work day COs separated by single line/single piece, single line/multiple pieces, multi-line & combination that are entered into a warehouse computer by CO classification & total COs. Requires a manifest reader/scanner that reads CO IDs are sent to a warehouse computer for adjustment to show each CO completion or decrease to each CO classification & total number. On-time micro & macro pick & pack activity productivity for each CO classification & total CO actual completion number to your computer projected CO completion to show your pick & pack activity is on schedule. Productivity data allows a manager to make labor adjustments & relocation for maximum CO completion number & good employee productivity

Sku & Inventory Control Ideas (SIC 1 – SIC 4)

SIC 1. Average Inventory Or Moving Average Inventory Projection

Average inventory projection or X month moving average inventory projection are your manager's options to project a design year sku/pallet inventory. Your design year sku/pallet inventory projection has a direct impact on your proposed facility sq. ft. or cubic ft. area, storage rack type, forklift truck type and required cost. An average inventory project is calculated by dividing 12 (months) into your annual sku/pallet inventory & the result is multiplied by your required months of inventory on-hand such as annual pallet inventory/12 months = average inventory.

A moving average inventory projection has several steps. First: you determined your company's each months sku/pallet inventory. Next: you determined a number of months (time period such as 3 months) for your proposed operation on-hand inventory & you calculate each 3 months inventory such as (1) Jan, Feb & Mar, (2) Feb, Mar & Apr, (3) Mar, Apr & May, (4) Apr, May & June, (5) May, June & July, (6) June, July & Aug, (7) July, Aug & Sept, (8) Aug, Sept & Oct, (9) Sept, Oct & Nov, (10) Oct, Nov & Dec & (11) Nov, Dec & Jan. A 3 month period with a highest sku inventory is used to project your design year pallet inventory. Using a moving average projection method provides you with a more accurate inventory for your peak business & if you use an average inventory, it could be understated.

SIC 2. Sku Life Cycle

Sku life cycle is a chart or percentage presentation that shows your sku's historical movement over a time period that is 1 week, month or season. A sku life cycle shows after a sku has a sales promotion, TV presentation or advertisement that a sku sales are very high or 'A' or 'B' moving sku. Each additional day, week or month, a sku sales volume declines until a sku becomes a 'C' or 'D' mover with very few sales. A sku life cycle indicates a time period that a sku remains in a prime storage/pick position as an 'A' or 'B' moving sku and the time that a sku is relocated from an 'A' or 'B' moving sku storage/pick position to a 'C' or 'D' moving sku storage/pick position. Features are improved employee productivity & enhance storage utilization. If a sku life cycle is considered for a sku with similar characteristics, it indicates the date that a sku has low sales & is a candidate for transfer from a prime storage/pick position. Feature is that your sku moves are completed on low volume days or an off-shift.

SKU LIFE CYCLE
Days Or Months After Advertisement Or TV Presentation

	Day/Month	Day/Month	Day/Month	Day/Month	Day/Month	Day/Month
Sku /Volume 95782	88407	5976	2402	1311	978	798
100%	88%	6%	3%	1%	1%	1%
Time In Days/Months	1	2	3	4	5	6

SIC 3. Smaller Is Sometimes Better

Smaller is sometimes better is a phrase that means when you offer a same item as a carton sku & as an individual sku, a smaller piece quantity per carton is a strategy to have your purchase department, I T, customer service & your review of each skus sales to determine a best sku quantity per carton. In many industries, a smaller sku quantity per carton has a carton that is picked for a CO improves picker & packer employee productivity with fewer replenishment activities for broken cartons, less sku damage & where a carton is opened less trash handling. If your review shows a sku number for a carton & there is positive customer response, your team reviews a new carton sku quantity with your vendor to determine any economic impact on a sku cost. Your team considers potential for a sku with a smaller carton quantity to become a vendor ready to ship sku, I T department to have a WMS computer program for COs to separate skus as single sku or carton & receive associated employee productivity improvements.

SIC 4. How To Handle Your High Volume Ready To Ship Skus

High volume vendor ready to ship skus are transferred to a scan station, you complete sku ID & CO ID scan transactions. Each scanned CO pack slip/invoice is placed with sale literature into a slapper envelop. Each slapper envelop has a CO delivery address window, CO ID, sku ID & pick position number. Envelop options are (a) self-adhesive backing, (b) plain envelop sent through a glue pot or (c) plain envelop on a carton with a plastic sheet is sent heat tunnel. After skus are bulk picked to a slapper envelop station, an employee places an envelop onto a carton that is transferred to a completed CO take-away conveyor.

SIC 5. How To Handle Your Low Volume Ready To Ship Skus

Low volume ready to ship skus have CO pack slip/invoice & sales literature insert into an envelop bulk picked per skus and at a pick position and transferred onto a take-away conveyor. Features are high picker & packer productivity, large completed CO number, eliminates ship carton, tape & filler material expense but has slapper label expense, improves customer returns process & minimal trash handling expense, when compared to a regular pack activity lower labor cost, with minimal employees your have an early start activity and potential for future robatic pick activity with glue spray & slapper envelop stuff & apply machine that operates 24 X 7 with minimal employees.

SIC 6. How To Increase Your Ready To Ship Carton Volume

To increase your ready to ship carton volume, you consider create separate CO waves with 1 CO wave for no sales literature and 1 CO wave for sales literature, review past CO number for your existing vendor ready to ship cartons from high to low volume, a sku sale volume is for a pre-determined time period such as ½ or 1 year, identify past COs for single line/single piece/sku as non-ready to ship cartons from high to low volume. Sku sale volume is for a pre-determined time period such as ½ or 1 year, assure your slapper envelop size (length & width) match your non-ready to ship carton length & width dimensions, review each sku & determine what has to done to convert a sku to a vendor ready to ship carton, add carton side wall, top or bottom structural strength, eliminate printed & advertising on a carton exterior surface, add filler or sku interior protection material and increase carton size & add interior protection material, know your potential savings & costs that are no ship carton, tape & filler material expense, customer returns process labor savings & trash handling expenses, picker & packer employee productivity increase & savings, slapper envelop expense, stuff slapper envelop expense & propose your idea to your vendors with sharing in potential cost savings.

SIC 7. How To Maximize Your Ready To Ship Carton Activity

To maximize your ready to ship carton activity, your vendor ready to ship carton has side wall, top & bottom structural strength & filler material & exterior surface to be shipped as an individual carton (not in a carton), identify your CO ready to ship carton skus from high volume to low volume. Sku sale volume is for a pre-determined time period such as ½ or 1 year, Look at how your vendor delivers your vendor ready to ship cartons & estimate your employee time to prepare vendor ready to ship cartons for slapper envelop activity such as cutting a carton & trash handling an empty carton. A vendor ready to ship carton that is received in a corrugated carton is the least preferred concept due to your high preparation labor & trash handling. Plastic or paper wrap or plastic bands is preferred concept due to minimal preparation labor & trash handling. Sku Hi & Ti is the most preferred concept due to no preparation labor & trash handling costs.

SIC 8. Your Vendor Wraps Your Vendor Ready To Ship Deliveries

Your vendor wraps your vendor ready to ship carton deliveries is an option for a single line sku that involves your purchase & warehouse departments. If you are receiving vendor ready to ship cartons in a carton (encased in another large cardboard carton) & a sku is sold as a single line sku, you have an opportunity to improve picker & packer productivity, increase CO handling volume a lower trash handling expenses. Since a sku is packaged in a vendor ready to ship carton & you send it to a customer as a vendor ready to ship carton, a sku carton has structural cardboard strength, quality, interior filler material to protect a sku & exterior surface to meet your CO deliver quality standards. Your opportunity is to have your vendor wrap same sku quantity in plastic wrap, paper or plastic bands that during vendor delivery is a secure method to hold skus on a pallet & a vendor ready to ship carton protects a sku quality. With a plastic wrap concept & during your fast pack activity, to remove a smaller carton from a plastic wrap is less labor tense than cutting open a large & bulky cardboard carton or trying to pull a smal carton from a large carton. After a plastic wrap sku quantity depletion, plastic wrap is easier for an employee to place into a recycle bin, requires less space than a large cardboard carton & reduces your trash expenses.

Internal Storage Ideas (IS1 – IS3)

IS 1. What Is Your Storage, Pick Or Returns Position Occupancy Rate

What is your storage, pick or returns position occupancy rate is your existing storage, pick or returns position survey. Your storage, pick or returns position occupancy rate indicates how full are your storage, pick or returns positions that provides you with an opportunity to improve your space utilization and employee productivity. To calculate your storage , pick or returns position occupancy rate is a multiple step process. First step: you establish your storage, pick or returns position occupancy factor. Factors are full, ¾ full, ½ full, ¼ full and 1 carton layer or less. Second: you inventory your storage, pick or returns positions and identify each position by its factor that determines your total position number and each factor storage, pick or returns position number. To calculate your total storage, pick or returns area occupancy rate, you divide each storage, pick or returns position factor position number by your total storage, pick or returns position number. If your results show that your storage, pick or returns area has a high percentage for ¼ full or less occupied storage, pick or returns positions, you have an opportunity to improve your space utilization. If your storage, pick or returns rack posts are capable to support additional load beam levels, your ¼ full storage, pick or returns positions have load beams added to create two ¼ storage positions and vacate storage, pick or returns position is full height storage, pick or returns position. When designing a new storage, pick or returns area or remodeling an existing storage area, you match your storage, pick or returns position heights to match your storage position occupancy rate that has a sku height match a storage, pick or returns position height. The results are you increase your sku and skus per sq. ft due to less unused open space in full height pallet positions with less than full high pallets & improves your employee productivity due to hit concentration and hit density per aisle.

TOTAL STORAGE, PICK OR RETURN AREA OCCUPANCY FORM

Storage, Pick Or Returns Aisle Position Identification	¼	½	¾	Full	Vacant	Total

IS 2. What Is Your Total Storage, Pick Or Returns Area Position Occupancy Rate

What is your total storage, pick or returns area position occupancy rate is your existing total storage, pick or returns position study that indicates an opportunity to improve your storage, pick or returns position space utilization. To calculate your total storage, pick or returns position occupancy rate is a multiple step process. First step: you determine your total storage, pick or returns positions. Second step: is to count your occupied storage, pick or returns positions. Your total storage, pick or returns area occupancy rate is calculated by dividing your total storage, pick or returns position number into your occupied storage, pick or returns position number. Your total storage, pick or returns position occupancy rate helps you to develop plans for improved storage, pick or returns position occupancy.

TOTAL STORAGE, PICK OR RETURNS AREA OCCUPANCY FORM

Storage, Pick Or Returns Aisle Identification	Position Number Full	Vacant	Total

$$\frac{\text{Full Occupied Position, Pick Or Returns Number}}{\text{Total Position Number}} = \text{Storage Area Full Position \%}$$

$$\frac{\text{Vacant Occupied Position, Pick Or Returns Number}}{\text{Total Position Number}} = \text{Storage Area Vacant Position \%}$$

IS 3. Dual Commands With Early Receiving Activity

VNA forklift truck single or dual commands are a VNA forklift truck activity commands or instructions to complete a transaction between a storage position and a P/D station. Dual command concept can be implemented with a WA or NA forklift truck operation between a position and dock/drop position. For maximum employee productivity and sku availability, your receiving department has an early start (prior to your pick activity) to assure that a storage deposit transaction is completed & pick area replenishment transaction is available for a forklift truck driver. If drop position is not adjacent to a receiving dock, there is additional forklift truck travel distance & time.

VNA Forklift Truck Single Command Mode is a standard command. A VNA forklift truck single command has a vehicle make an aisle trip from a P/D station into an aisle. Travel command options are (1) with a sku for deposit to a WMS ID storage position and after deposit for a vehicle return empty to a P/D station and (2) empty to a WMS ID storage position and at a storage position after sku withdrawal to return travel with a sku to a P/D station. A single command has a vehicle complete only 1 inbound or 1 outbound WMS ID sku transaction per aisle trip and does not require a work hour balance for inbound skus at a P/D station and outbound CO withdrawal transactions. A VNA forklift truck concept with a WMS program concept a dual command program requires some additional computer programming, sku deposit & withdrawal communications & aisle end P/D station designed with inbound and outbound queue lanes.

VNA Forklift Truck In A Dual Command Mode has a vehicle (1) with a sku travel from a P/D station to a WMS identified position and complete a sku deposit storage activity, (2) from a position travel empty to another WMS ID position for sku withdrawal from another position and (3) with a sku on board travel to a P/D station and transfer a sku to a P/D station. A dual command mode has a vehicle complete both 1 inbound and 1 outbound WMS ID sku transaction per aisle trip and does require a work hour balance for inbound skus & outbound CO withdrawal transactions and P/D stations have inbound and outbound queue lanes. Per aisle trip a dual command mode per aisle almost doubles skus that are handled per hour, but if it is combined in-bound & outbound activities that creates a UPH increase.

Off-Site Storage Ideas (OSS 1 – OSS 24)

OSS 1. Off-Site To Build Or Lease

After your company determines a new warehouse total sq. ft. requirement, your next major decision is to lease or build a building. A leased building option has your company design a storage and pick concept to fit into an existing building. Leased options are to (1) lease an existing facility that has a short start-up time & low cost & (2) 'build to lease' a new facility that has a leasing company constructs a building to your specifications. The approach has a longer start-up time with a medium cost. If your company construct sa new building, it has your company purchase a site & with an architect & construction company to obtain local authority approval and build a facility. During & after building construction, your storage & pick concept is installed in a facility. The own land & build approach has a longer start-up time & higher cost.

OSS 2. Tent On A Slab

Tent on a slab is an outside storage concept that minimizes your building construction costs for low cost storage positions. If a slab is located on your main facility site/property, you have an opportunity to minimize your shuttle costs. A tent on slab concept has a cement slab constructed onto the ground and to have a fabric shell with a door installed on the cement slab. After installation completion, the shell interior cement slab area is ready for rack or floor storage concept. If your local government considers a fabric shell/cement slab as temporary construction, there is potential different code requirements. If employees use your main facility printers, restrooms, break rooms, equipment chargers and other support items, there is a lower building cost and greater storage units per sq. ft. In the future for facility expansion, the cement slab is used for low weight facility support areas such as office, returns process, maintenance and computer area.

OSS 3. Where To Receive Your Off-Site Storage Skus

Where to receive your off-site storage skus options are you receive at your (1) off-site facility with receiving capabilities or (2) at your main facility. If your sku is a big/ugly, overstock or speculative purchase sku that you ship from your off-site facility, you receive skus are your off-site operation. If your sku is a fast pack sku and you ship from your off-site facility, cross-dock or replenish to your main facility, and your know your fast pack projected quantity your options are (a) with two vendor delivery trucks to have one vendor delivery truck received at your main facility and one truck at your off-site facility & (b) with one vendor delivery truck your select one facility to receive skus and transfers your estimated sku quantity to your other facility & (2) main facility with receiving capabilities at your main facility, you receive sku vendor delivery at your main facility & transfer to your off-site facility. Features are low CPU & good inventory control.

OSS 4. Your Off-Site Dock Determines Your Dock Equipment To Bridge Your Dock Edge & Delivery Trucks

Your off-site dock determines your dock equipment to bridge dock edge and unload to assure a safe activity, low cost sku and smooth sku flow. Your dock equipment is a device that bridges your delivery truck end and dock edge and allows a unload/load vehicle to enter and exit a delivery truck. A unload/load vehicle enters and exits a delivery truck with a pallet and transports a pallet to a dock staging area or pallet storage position. Your dock equipment options are based on (1) ground level or no elevated dock with a smooth truck yard and ground level facility entry door that requires (a) dock ramp with a level top that allows a forklift truck to enter and exit a delivery truck. Features are ramp has an additional cost and difficult to use in rainy weather and (b) forklift truck to remove the rear two pallets and a forklift truck to place a human powered pallet truck into a delivery truck for an employee to move a pallet to a delivery truck rear for forklift truck removal and (2) elevated platform dock or dock door that requires (a) with a pallet truck to use a fixed position edge of dock or front of dock device for delivery truck entry/exit. Features are restricted to a pallet truck use and requires delivery in proper dock position and (b) with a pallet truck or forklift truck to use a portable dock plate, portable dock board or in-floor dock leveler. A pallet truck or forklift truck enters and exists a delivery truck and transfer a pallet to a dock staging area or travel to a storage position for deposit. Features are additional cost, used with platform or dock door concept extends into a dock staging area, employee or forklift truck place a portable device in a delivery truck end and has potential damage to your door frame, requires a dock light or forklift truck mast lights and use with a pallet truck or forklift truck. If you receive side load/unload delivery trucks in a smooth truck yard, a forklift truck with proper counterbalance weight & two long forks is used to unload/load a delivery truck and transfers pallets onto a dock or dropped in a staging area.

OSS 5. Off-Site Sku Storage Candidates
Off-site storage candidate is your process to select sku & sku quantity for relocation from a main e facility to an off-site facility. When your position utilization is at 100%, you require additional positions. To create additional positions, your manager has to determine or select sku & sku quantity for off-site or outside storage. Potential candidate skus are (1) aged or 'C'/'D' moving skus, (2) obsolete equipment, (3) extra large quantity buy-ins such as commodities, (4) your heavy & high cube skus that are picked and sent as single line/single sku COs in vendor cartons from an off-site facility to customers, (5) ship supply safety stock & (6) return to vendor skus.

OSS 6. How To Work Off-Site Storage
How to work off-site storage is an objective for an off-site storage activity that combines maximum storage space utilization and lowest annual cost. Most companies use an off-site for seasonal buy-ins with a large pallet number per sku, old/aged skus, damaged/obsolete skus or skus that do not match a main warehouse material handling concept such as high cube/heavy skus that are handled a single sku/single line COs. With the reasons, an off-site storage activity has a dense storage concept and lowest possible operation costs. Most off-site storage buildings has a 20 to 25 ft high ceiling and if your skus are stackable, floor stack (3 to 5 deep and 3 high) provides high storage space utilization, good storage lane flexibility and at a low cost. To optimize an off-site floor stack operation, you have at least a few standard pallet rack rows to handle skus with few pallets. If your skus are non-stackable, standard pallet rack rows or a standard pallet row and floor stack in front storage combination is used for the operation. All off-site storage operations have building columns buried in a floor stack or rack rows. If aisle lighting is problem, an option is to have lights that are attached to a forklift truck's masts.

OSS 7. Fast-Pack In Your Off-Site Facility
Fast pack in your off-site facility is an option that transfers some of your main facility activities to your off-site operation. With an off-site fast pack approach, with a two vendor truck delivery you pre-schedule your one vendor truck delivery to an off-site facility and second truck delivery to your main facility. With one or less sku vendor delivery truck you receive a sku at one facility and for a pre-determined sku quantity, it is transferred to or remains in your off-site facility. After you determine your sku fast pack quantity, you have slapper envelopes prepared at your main facility and delivered to your off-site facility or slapper envelops are prepared at your off-site facility. With a slapper envelop you fast pack, manifest and ship COs from your off-site facility. Features are (1), easy to control WMS computer allocation, (2) low cost activity and (2) allows a main facility controllable sku volume.

OSS 8. Overstock Or Speculative Purchased Skus As An Off-Site Sku Candidate & Send It Direct

From Your Off-Site Or Cross-Dock At Your Main Facility

Overstock or speculative purchase sku as an off-site sku candidate has a sku with very large sku inventory quantity that allows dense or floor stack storage for low cost per storage position. If overstock or speculative purchase sku is stored in a main facility, it allows few positions for regular skus & additional employee time to complete transactions due to travel past positions with no activity. Per your company policy you ship COs direct from an off-site facility, shuttle skus to your main facility for storage activity or shuttle to your main facility for cross dock activity.

OSS 9. 'ABC' Or 'D' Or Obsolete Skus As Off-Site Candidates

A,B C or D obsolete skus are off-site candidates is determined by your CO demand to identify sku candidate that improves employee productivity and space utilization. In most operations, A and B moving skus have good CO demand and remain in your main facility storage positions. C and D moving skus or obsolete skus have very low or no CO demand and require a storage position. If your C, D or obsolete skus are in your main facility positions and during a work day your pick employees travel past a C or D moving sku positions that creates low employee productivity. If you maintain a C and D small sku quantity in your main facility storage position that is hand stacked or half high position, you improve your space utilization and remaining sku quantity is placed in an off-site storage position, your increase your C & D moving sku concentration and density and your other positions have A & B moving skus, your improve storage and pick employee productivity. Features are creates additional main facility positions, improves employee productivity and enhances space utilization.

OSS 10. What Is Scrap & Where To Store It Or Off-Site

You have a possibility to have obsolete or not used material handling equipment. Non-used equipment occupies positions or space that is considered expensive real estate. If you have a requirement for storage space, relocate obsolete equipment to another area. Relocation is an opportunity to increase available space for good skus. To create space for good skus, scrap equipment is placed in a storage position with a longest travel distance from your pick & pack area, in off-set storage, under a cover & elevated on pallets that are outside in a truck yard, placed in your off-site facility or sold.

OSS 11. Once A Sku Is In Out-Side Storage It Remains Out Or Is A Cross-Dock Sku

Once a sku is in out-side storage it remains out or is a cross-dock sku. This is your off-site sku storage strategy that minimizes over-the-road truck shuttle costs, minimizes sku damage & improves employee productivity. With good security, inventory control with random sku counts & off-site facility with capability to print all receiving & ship documents, bar code scan/RF tag read & transfer data to a main warehouse computer, once out stay off-site storage strategy means that after a sku is transferred from your main facility to an off-site facility that a sku remains in an off-site facility. From an off-site facility, a sku is sent direct to a customer or returned direct to a vendor, handled as a palletized single sku or multiple skus as an across-dock CO that is sent from an off-site facility to a main facility or sent as cartons/small quantities for replenishment to a main facility remote storage position.

OSS 12. Ship Supply Sku Safety Inventory In Off-Site Storage

Ship supply sku safety inventory is a storage idea for off-site storage. Ship supply skus (bags, cartons, tape, filler material and other items) safety stock is a sku quantity that is not anticipated for use in your daily or regular pack operation. Safety stock is not track in your WMS computer program and is intended to have a sku supply on-hand to cover for unexpected or more than schedule CO demand situation. Your safety stock position options are in your (1) main facility to occupy storage positions that creates lower forklift truck productivity and no vacate positions for regular skus or ship supply inventory for your CO demand and (2) off-site storage facility that allows you to use dense storage concepts for best storage utilization and does not require shuttle costs.

OSS 13. Single & BIG/UGLY Skus In Off-Site Storage

Single skus and big/ugly skus in off-site storage allows high storage utilization with dense storage concept and improves employee productivity. Single skus permit your operation to bulk pick, pack, slapper label and ship activity. A big/ugly sku has few skus per storage position, permits you to use a slapper label and ship activity. If handled in your main facility, a big/ugly sku is handled on your manual forklift truck concept.

14

OSS 14. Off-Site How To Handle BIG/ULGY Skus

How to handle the big/ugly skus occurs when your have to handle over-sized or long skus that can not fit onto a standard pallet or into a standard position. To handle an extra long sku in a standard rack storage area, your options are (1) use an extra wide pallet that fits into a standard pallet rack bay and with fork opening widths that matches your standard wide aisle forklift set of forks spread (width) that allows a forklift truck to complete storage transactions or (2) use a extra long fork attachment that fits into a 2 deep rack position. After all big/ugly sku transactions are completed, extra long fork attachment is removed and your WA forklift truck completes normal pallet size transactions. If your WA aisle forklift truck requires a 2 wide set of forks or extra long fork attachment, a 2 wide set of forks matches your pallet openings or extra long fork attachments are tested on your WA aisle forklift truck to assure that an existing counterbalance forklift truck has sufficient counter weight. When a wide pallet is placed into a standard pallet position, a deposit scan transaction is made to a first or right hand side position that assures sku and position status in a WMS or inventory control program. Features increases space utilization & improves employee productivity.

OSS 15. Sku Rework Activities In Off-Site Storage

Rework activities completed in your off-site warehouse assure inventory control, controlled sku flow and maximum main facility positions & space used for skus that are available for sale. Rework skus are created from (a) returned skus and quality control sample or (b) vendor delivered skus rejected by QA. Rework skus have an inventory status of 'not available for sale or COs & to meet your company standards some skus require rework labor, material expense and storage positions. With re-work skus in an off-site facility, your main warehouse forklift truck drivers & pickers have higher productivity due no travel past positions with rework skus that do not have possible transactions.

OSS 16. Off-Site Use Single Deep Or Dense Storage

Single deep or dense storage are your basic storage concept options. A single deep stationary or mobile storage concept has each WMS identified sku (carton, pallet or GOH) face an employee, employee controlled forklift truck crane deposit/withdrawal transaction aisle. With a standard WMS computer program and a single deep storage concept, an employee, employee controlled forklift truck has direct access to withdraw a WMS computer program suggested WMS ID sku from a WMS ID storage position.   A dense storage concept has multiple skus deep per storage lane. Dense storage concepts (floor stack, stacking frames/tier racks, drive-in rack, push back racks & 2 deep racks) have a last sku deposited in a storage lane face a storage vehicle transaction aisle (one aisle for both replenishment and withdrawal transactions).   Since dense storage concepts have multiple skus per lane, for an employee, forklift truck to access a specific sku there is no-productive employee time or a WMS computer program requires modification such a WMS ID substitution feature. Dense storage concepts (drive-thru & gravity/air flow rack) have the first deposited sku flows from a deposit aisle, flows through a rack storage lane & ends at a withdrawal transaction aisle. With gravity flow through or drive thru racks, for an employee, forklift truck to access a WMS program suggested WMS ID sku from a WMS ID storage position there is an operation problem to access a suggested WMS computer program ID sku. In most flow through or drive thru rack applications with a pallet riding on a bottom deck boards, a sku bar code label is on a pallet side or sku front that faces a rack. The situation creates some additional non-productive forklift truck time to complete a sku double handling to have a bar code label in a proper orientation for bar code line of sight. With a RF tag symbology a transmission is received in a general area. In conclusion, a single deep storage concept have a low cost, 85% utilization factor, access to any sku, handles a large sku number with any sku quantity & interfaces with a standard WMS computer program. Dense storage concepts have a high cost, 66% utilization factor, with no WMS computer program modifications difficult to access a specific sku or requires additional non-productive to complete a sku scan transaction, handles few skus with a large sku quantity & requires a standard WMS computer program modification.

OSS 17. Off-Site Storage Use Floor Stack Or Standard Pallet Rack Storage

Floor stack or standard pallet rack storage are your storage concept most common options. Floor stack storage concept has 1 sku (master cartons, stacking frames/teir racks or pallets) stacked onto another (3 to 4 high) &

multiple skus (2 to 10) deep. A floor stack concept is used in a warehouse with a 20 to 25 ft high ceiling & wide aisle (WA) or narrow aisle (NA) forklift truck. A standard pallet rack storage concept has upright frames & load beams that have 1 pallet deep rack bay or 1 to 3 pallet positions per rack bay & up to 6 to 7 pallets high. In conclusion, a floor stack storage concept has minimal cost, 66% utilization factor, preferred for a small sku quantity with a large sku number & standard WMS computer program modifications. A standard pallet rack concept has 85% utilization factor, preferred for a large sku & interfaces with a standard WMS computer program.

OSS 18. Off-Site Use A Combined Floor & Rack Storage Concept (6 Pallets Are Better Than 4 Pallets)
Floor and rack storage concept (6 pallets is better than 4 pallets) is a forklift truck storage rack and floor stack concept that is used for a sku with at least 6 pallets and a sku that does not have the structural strength to support a 3 high pallet stack. A standard 4 pallet floor storage concept has 2 deep pallets & 2 high pallets. Features are no cost, medium storage density and low space utilization. A hybrid 2 deep pallet storage rack & floor stack concept has (1) rear pallet positions as a 4 pallet high storage rack row & (2) front pallet positions as 2 high floor stack pallet positions. Concept options are (1) single high front pallet or (2) double stacked pallets with top carton within an employee picker's reach. Your options are (1) one pallet for each storage rack position that 4 high positions or (2) rack floor position with two high stacked pallets. Features are some rack cost, improves storage density and space utilization & both concepts interface with a wide aisle or narrow aisle forklift truck.

OSS 19. Off-Site Use Pyramid Floor Stack
Pyramid floor stack is floor storage that is used for your ship supply items or unstable skus with a dimension that restricts use of a pallet rack storage position & improves space utilization & minimizes sku damage. Most ship supply items are cardboard cartons, sheet paper or filler material, tape or band material, label paper, sheet paper for printers & envelopes. Ship supply skus are not tracked by your WMS/inventory control computer program, usually has a safety stock & with cardboard cartons have an excessive over-hang on a pallet. Palletized collapsed ship cartons have a bowed or concaved top that creates difficulty to stack 3 pallets high due to a forklift truck has difficulty to have a set of forks enter a top pallet fork opening and a 3 high pallet stack has a tendency for tilting to one side. To improve your cube or space utilization & enhance your storage density per aisle, with a same ship carton/sku a pyramid pallet floor stack concept permits 1 to 2 floor stacked pallets that are side by side & become a pyramid base for another pallet that is placed in the middle of a 2 pallet base. In the middle of a 2 pallet base means that 1/2 of a top pallet is setting on 1 bottom pallet half & top pallet other half is setting on another bottom pallet half. With a pyramid stack, a pyramid top pallet is stable, permits a forklift truck set of forks to enter a top pallet fork opening & minimizes sku damage & improves employee productivity.

OSS 20. Off-Site Storage Consider Two High/Tall Pallets On The Floor In Standard Pallet Rack
        Storage Concept
Two high/tall pallets on the floor is a standard pallet storage rack concept that has a bottom (floor level) pallet rack position height set for 2 pallets high (1 pallet stacked on another pallet) & elevated rack positions have an opening for 1 pallet. Two pallets high on a floor rack concept is used palletized skus that have the structural strength to support another full pallet weight. Two pallets on the floor concept requires 1 less load beam pair & one less forklift truck transaction. Prior to implementation, your rack manufacturer assures that your upright post design or structural strength supports a two tall pallet opening or your rack position requires a double upright post design that has an additional cost. Features are increases pallet positions in an aisle, increases storage density, access to all skus, increases space or cube utilization, used with a wide aisle or narrow aisle forklift truck, reduces an overall stacking height by a nomimal 12 ins and reduces your forklift truck replenishment transaction number.

OSS 21. Off-Site Storage With A Wide Aisle (WA) Or Narrow Aisle (NA) Forklift Truck
An off-site storage activity forklift truck requirement is to unload, transport and deposit/withdrawal transactions that has a WA or NA forklift truck complete a sku pick-up at receiving & put-away to a WMS position. When you have long travel distances, a WA forklift truck is preferred. If you have narrow aisles, you prefer a NA forklift truck. With a small storage area and aisles that face a receiving dock & a low sku volume, do it all the way concept has good equipment utilization & good employee productivity. With a wide storage area & aisle that do not face a receiving

dock & a high sku volume, do it all the way concept represents poor forklift truck utilization & low employee productivity. To transport a sku with a high wage rate forklift truck driver & a high equipment cost, it represents a high CPU. An option is to give-away. A give-away concept uses a single or double pallet truck as a transport vehicle with a lower equipment cost, lower wage rate & lower CPU. With a pallet truck transport concept, a storage area requires a wider aisle for a pallet placement at an aisle end & proper pallet placement at an aisle end to have a sku WMS ID face a forklift truck driver.

OSS 22. Off-Site Storage Light Your Aisles Or Forklift Trucks
Light your aisles or forklift trucks are your off-site facility lighting options. To minimize your off-site expenses, the light fixtures remain in an existing ceiling location and a light fixture lighting allows your forklift truck driver to complete a transaction and for transaction instruction to read a paper document or RF device display screen and position ID. Your adjust your position depth and aisle width to have light fixtures located in an aisle or in an aisle middle. If your light fixture lighting is low, your options are to add (1) light fixtures that has additional costs and additional light fixture could exceed your existing KVA that could require additional major electric transformer and (2) lights to your forklift truck masts that are operated from your forklift truck battery that are attached by your forklift truck vendor to illuminate a position and as required operators area. Forklift truck mast lights illuminate positions, aisles and inside a delivery truck. Features are forklift truck lights have a lower cost than additional aisle light fixtures.

OSS 23. Off-Site Facility Use An Overhead/Head Acke Bar, Highway Guard Rail/Post & Wheel Stop
Overhead/head ache bar, highway guard rail/post & wheel-stop are manual controlled powered pallet truck & forklift truck options to minimize equipment & building damage and improve driver productivity. An overhead or head ache bar is a ceiling hung chain with a bar that extends downward or rack bay that is located prior to a facility wall passage way or door frame bottom. If a forklift truck with an elevated sku strikes a head ache bar or rack bay, it is noticed that your forklift driver who should stop a vehicle forward movement & lower an elevated sku & avoid door damage. Highway guard rails are floor anchored & used in a powered pallet truck or forklift truck transport concept along walls, stationary equipment or people paths to prevent a moving vehicle from striking & damaging a wall, equipment or employee injury. Per a sku elevation above a floor, a guard rail bottom, middle or top members are set above a floor. The elevation protects guard rail support post from damage & sku hang-up on a guard member. Guard posts are cement filled floor anchor or sunk post that is placed in front of a door frame. A guard post prevents a moving pallet or forklift truck from striking & damaging a door frame. A wheel stop is an inverted and flatten 'V' shaped harden metal members that is floor anchored in front of a forklift truck transfer to or from a P/D station, flow rack conveyor lane or conveyor travel path. A wheel stop is set at a distance from a material handling equipment to restrict a forklift truck front wheels forward movement and prevent a forklift truck from striking & damaging equipment but permits a forklift truck to complete a sku transfer transaction &assure good employee productivity.

OSS 24. Off-Site Notch Your Man-Down Forklift Truck Mast
Notch your man-down forklift truck mast is a concept to place marks on a man-down controlled (WA), (NA) or (VNA) forklift truck mast that improves employee productivity and minimizes sku damage. Each forklift truck mast mark matches an elevated set of forks for a forklift truck to complete an elevated rack position transaction. At an elevated position, a forklift truck set of forks are withdrawn or inserted into a pallet opening to complete a transaction. Each forklift truck set of forks elevation has a unique color or marks such a 1 mark or red is for level 1 mark or 2 marks or yellow is for level two. Notched masts concept improves man-down forklift productivity, low cost & minimizes sku & rack damage.

Bar Code Scan Ideas (BCS 1 – BCS 13)
BCS 1. Use A Scanner Gun With Depth Of Field & Large/Tall Bar Code
A gun or hand contact scanner is a work station employee or forklift truck driver bar code scanner options. With a gun bar code scanner and from a work station or forklift truck driver's platform, a gun is a device that directs a laser light beam onto a sku or carton, position bar code that completes a scan transaction. Features are (1) slight higher

cost, (2) longer depth of field & (3) improve employee productivity. With a hand contact bar code scanner, a work station or forklift truck driver leaves a forklift truck and walks to a bar code and completes a scan transaction. Features are (1) close to a bar code depth of field, (2) slightly lower cost & (3) lower employee productivity.

BCS 2. Re-Chargeable Battery Or Electric Battery Powered Hand Scanner
Re-chargeable battery or electric battery powered hand held scan/read device are a bar code scanner power options. A rechargeable battery powered scanner receives its power from a re-chargeable battery. If a battery is not full charged, there is a possibility for low employee productivity due to extra scan transaction attempts or a no read means a round trip travel time to battery replacement location & time to transfer batteries. An electric powered vehicle battery powered scanner has a scanner obtain its power source from a vehicle's battery. In most warehouses, an electric rechargeable battery has an electric charge that lasts for one shift that assures power to a scanner & minimizes employee non-productive time. At a fixed work station such as pack station, for minimal scanner down-time and minimal employee effort, a hand scanner has a direct electric power hook-up.

BCS 3. Your Work Station Or Forklift Truck Scanner Has A Short Or Long Cord
Your work station or forklift truck scanner short or long cord are options for an employee hand held bar code scanner cord connection to a storage vehicle battery that allows your work station employee or forklift truck driver to have a mobile scanner device for good bar code line of sight. With WA or NA forklift trucks, a scanner with a short cord restricts an employee mobility to complete a WMS identified sku & position scan transactions. If a powered vehicle is not in proper location, there is a possible to have no scan transaction that means low employee productivity due to no scan transaction & time to relocate a forklift truck. A scanner device with a re-trackable long cord assure maximum employee mobility to complete a scan transaction from a work station employee or forklift truck driver's platform or seat & minimizes cord damage.

BCS 4. Your Scanner Depth Of Field
Your scanner depth of field is a bar code scanner feature that determines distance between a bar code scanner & a WMS identification to complete a good scan transaction. Your WMS ID and scanner with good depth field assures maximum good read number or a scanner device light beam crosses all bar codes within sufficient time to complete a read. A WA forklift truck depth of field is from a work station or forklift truck driver seat to a sku or position WMS ID. Your NA or VNA forklift truck depth of field is from a forklift truck driver's platform or work station to a sku, carton or position WMS ID. Your work station depth field is very short with a short distance between a WMS ID & hand held scanner. Minimum depth of field is longest distance between an employee hand held scanner to a sku or position WMS ID. Hand held scanner device tests determine a scanner device that gives your forklift truck or work station employees a maximum good read number that improves employee productivity.

BCS 5. Your Scanner Has A Default As One
Your work station or forklift truck scanner has a default as one is a storage, pick, pack, returns or activity area idea to improve employee hand held scanning a WMS ID scan productivity. With a WMS program, each sku (piece, carton, pallet, GOH), each position and CO has one WMS ID. This means that each WMS scan transaction has an entry for a quantity of one WMS ID. To complete a WMS ID hand held scan transaction, after a good read an employee enters (presses) one button to complete a WMS ID (sku, position or CO) scan transaction. If a scanner device is programmed to default as one, there is an employee scan productivity increase. Productivity increase results from an employee not looking for & pressing a one button due to the fact that a hand held scanner is programmed with a good scan transaction recognizes it as one.

BCS 6. Delayed Or On-Line Transaction Update
Delayed or on-line work station or transaction update are your options for an employee, employee controlled forklift truck, CO pack or returns transaction completion or data transfer from your warehouse area to WMS or inventory control computer to update a WMS identified sku, position or CO package status in the files. Both concepts assure accurate sku, position, CO or returns transaction transfer and improve employee productivity. A delayed transaction completion transfer concepts are (1) an employee to register transactions on a paper document and requires clerk

to enter data into a WMS or inventory control computer or (2) bar code scanner that sends transaction data to a warehouse computer for later at a pre-determined time (established by your IT & warehouse departments) to transfer data to a WMS or inventory control computer. An employee document & clerk transfer concept is not preferred due to potential errors. A delayed transfer to a computer features requires a warehouse computer that has capacity to handle all data and send message (receive, store and send) activities that means improve employee productivity due to no waiting time to verify data transfer, IT & warehouse departments determine transfer data times, less costly WMS or inventory control computer, some potential extra storage positions, WMS computer to complete other programs & inventory is updated to reflect sku quantity & position status. On-line transaction transfer completion concept after a transaction completion has a bar code scanner/RF tag reader that sends data to a WMS or inventory control computer program. Features are a larger capacity WMS or inventory computer & cost, some situations have slow verification message sent to an employee that creates low productivity & fewer extra positions.

BCS 7. Large Human Readable Symbology
To use a sku WMS human/machine readable symbology with large human readable characters/digits and tall bar code improves employee productivity, provides operation activity flexibility and enhances accurate sku, position and CO package ID reads and on time date transfer. When we compare human readable symbology to a human/machine readable symbology, a machine readable section is added to a human readable label face. A human readable symbology read and data transfer activity has potential for transposition or writing errors, employee & office clerk time to read and write onto a form & delayed data transfer. A human/machine readable symbology read activity has minimal transposition error potential due to complete a transaction, a scanner requires a line of sight to a machine readable symbology that increases an employee sku data collection and transaction productivity accurate & on-time data transfer.

BCS 8. Human Readable Symbology On Top Or Bottom Of Machine Readable Symbology
WMS sku human readable alpha characters/digits or machine readable symbology label locations are on a label bottom or top. A human/machine readable symbology as part of an employee instruction. At a transaction location, an employee reads a sku WMS ID on a GOH, carton, pallet or CO package that directs an employee to complete a WMS identified sku transaction. A sku WMS ID purpose is to assure quick & readable employee line of sight. Human/machine readable ID label locations are a label bottom or top. Human readable alpha characters/digits on a sku WMS label bottom means that human readable alpha characters/digits are above your bar code symbology. Features are (1) assures employee or scanner line of sight & at a lower elevation of a nomimal 2 ins above a conveyor or cart surface. To read a sku WMS, it requires an employee to lift a carton or bend to read a pallet identification that means non-productive time & physical effort, (2) same label print cost & (3) no impact on bar code line of sight. Human readable alpha characters/digits on a sku WMS ID top means that a bar code symbology is below your human readable characters/digits. Features are (1) assures an employee or scanner line of sight, at a higher elevation of a nomimal 8 ins. above a conveyor or cart surface. To read a sku WMS identification, it does not require an employee to lift a carton or deep bend to read a pallet ID that means less physical effort with minimal non-productive time, (2) same label print cost & (3) no impact on bar code line of sight.

BCS 9. Fixed Position Hand Held Scanner At A Pre-Determined Elevation
Fixed position hand held scanner at an employee check, pack station or returns process station is an option to improve employee productivity and accurate scan transaction. A fixed position hand held scanner allows an employee to complete a CO and sku ID scan transactions without moving a hand held scanner. After a CO container arrives at a work station, an employee simply moves a CO pack slip/invoice and sku identifications under a scanner and transfer the skus into a CO container. A fixed position scanner with a default of one for each good read that is in an elevated position for your most frequent sku height allows an employee's two hands to move a sku and complete a scan transaction without reaching or picking up scanner that is non-productive employee time. If required to scan a tall sku a scanner is removed from a stand and an employee completes a scan transaction. Features are improved employee productivity with no hand movement to locate and pick-up a scanner and return a scanner to a pack table and moving a sku with two free hands lowers potential sku drop/damage.

BCS 10. Over Square Bar Code With Quiet Zones

Quiet zones, over-squared and bar code edges are bar code label characteristics that improve good read number and employee productivity. A bar code quiet zones are on a bar code label both sides and is space between a paper edge and first black bar code and a last black bar code and paper edge. Feature assure a break between a metal structure and black bar code. An over-squared bar code label has a total bar code and white space width equal to a black bar code length. Feature allows a laser beam to cross all bar codes and white spaces. Bar edges is a sharp contrast between a white space and black bar code. Feature assures a laser beam reads a bar code proper width.

Vendor & Receiving Activity Ideas (VDS 1 – VDS 6)

VDS 1. Exchange Pallet

Exchange pallet concept has you (purchasing and receiving departments) arrange with your vendor to deliver your skus palletized on pallets that match your pallet quality standards. With a pallet exchange concept, at your warehouse a vendor empty delivery truck picks-up good quality pallets or your backhaul truck takes good quality pallets to a vendor location. To assure pallet accounting, records are maintained to track pallet delivery & receipt. Your delivery options are floor stack or palletized delivery, a pallet exchange program improves employee productivity by a lower receiving department unload time by at least 5 hours for a full 40 ft long trailer & labor expense, improves your receiving dock turns & improves dock space utilization.

VDS 2. How Is Your Sku Delivered (Pallet, Slip Sheet Or Floor Stack)

How is your sku delivered (pallet, slip sheet or floor stack) is important information to your receiving department that assures your receiving department has proper employee number, proper dock equipment, good employee productivity & increases dock turns. In most warehouses, as a receiving clerk is developing a vendor delivery schedule, with a vendor or from a purchase order a receiving clerk verifies a sku type & vendor delivery method. Sku type indicates a sku storage conditions or section. The delivery method determines the required dock time & dock equipment that is required to complete a unload activity such as floor stacked vendor cartons with a long unload time & unitized (pallets or slip sheets) has a shorter unload time.

VDS 3. Why Do You Want Pallets Or Slip Sheet Deliveries

To achieve good carton receiving productivity & increase dock turns, you have vendor skus delivered unitized & wrapped onto a good quality pallet or slip-sheet. A good quality pallet matches your standards. A slip-sheet is corrugated sheet with a lip that permits a slip-sheet equipped forklift truck to unload & on a receiving dock transfer a slip-sheet onto a pallet. Prior slip sheet transfer to a storage position, a slip sheet lip is cut from a slip sheet or is taped to a slip sheet side. When compared to a carton floor stack vendor delivery, a pallet or slip-sheet delivery requires less unloading time.

SKU UNLOAD COMPARATIVE FORM

VENDOR LOAD	COST	UNLOAD TIME	DOCK TURNS
FLOOR STACK	$ 0	2 EMPLOYEES 6 TO 8 HRS	1
PALLET	$15	1 EMPLOYEE 1 TO HRS	3
SLIP SHEET	$2.50 (*)	1 EMPLOYEE 1 TO 2 HRS	3

(*) For maximum efficiency requires a forklift truck slip-sheet device $15,000 & dock slip sheet back board $2,500 that is depreciated or expensed per your accounting department.

VDS 4. Clear Your Receiving Dock Staging Lanes

Clear your docks is a receiving department WMS ID sku flow idea that has a continuous sku flow from your receiving area to a transport concept that improves employee productivity, space utilization & dock turns. Clear the docks concept has a receiving clerk count, verify piece quantity, verify carton/pallet quality and WMS ID each sku. After a sku receives a WMS ID, it is a signal for a transport concept to move a WMS ID sku from a dock area. In a WMS ID storage position, a WMS ID sku is placed in 'not available for sale' status until your QA department inspection approves or rejects a vendor sku delivery. A QA department approval allows your receiving department to change a sku status as available for sale and a rejection has your company hold a sku in 'not available for sale' status for vendor pick-up. A continuous WMS ID sku flow opens a dock staging area, increases dock turn number, improves employee productivity and creates a constant sku flow rather than a surge.

VDS 5. Count By Numbers (Pallets, Cartons & GOH) & Detail Or Piece Count
Count by the numbers is used for small items or GOH that require a detail/piece count and a receiving idea to clear the docks, enhance dock turns, create an accurate sku inventory count and improve inventory control. The idea has your receiving department count a bulk vendor delivered small sku or GOH quantity & if required to send a vendor delivered and bulk received sku quantity to a detail/piece count receiving activity. First receiving activity assures that a vendor delivered small item or GOH total quantity matches a company purchase order quantity. When a bulk delivery has mixed skus on a vendor delivery (such style, color and size), a bulk-received quantity receives a warehouse tracking ID & is sent to a detail/piece receiving/count activity. At a detail count receiving activity, each WMS ID sku (style, color and size) is counted, receives a WMS ID & entered into a WMS program.

VDS 6. Vendor & Dock Schedule Receiving
A receiving truck dock scheduling idea that is designed to improve your receiving department productivity, improve your dock & dock equipment utilization. Dock scheduling is based on your company's purchase order sku delivery date. After your receiving department receives a purchase order, a receiving clerk with a vendor or freight company verifies or confirms a delivery vehicle date & delivery type (floor stack, pallets, slip sheets or containers), estimates unload & document sign times and assigns a truck dock to a vendor delivery. Truck delivery assignment to a truck dock is completed on a manual or PC spread sheet that blocks for a receiving dock for entire unload & document sign time. On a paper or PC sheet, a dock block activity prevents another vendor from delivery being assigned to a dock. For each work day, a dock schedule spread sheet has across a spread sheet top a series of column with each column as a dock door & down a spread sheet side a series of rows that represents a work day time periods. Breaks & lunch each have a row on a spread sheet. Changes to a dock assignment are reviewed & approved by a receiving manager vendor/freight company & made to a manual or PC spread sheet & e-mail/fax confirms a vendor delivery truck change.

RECEIVING DOCK SCHEDULE FORM

Date

Time Of Day	Dock 1	Dock 2	Dock 3	Dock 4	Dock 5	Dock 6
0700						
0800						
0900						
Break						
0915						
1000						
1100						
1200						
Lunch						
1230						
0100						
0200						
0300						
Break						
0315						
0400						
0500						

Receiving Activity Policy & Practice Ideas (RPP 1 – RPP 21)

RPP 1. Do Not Stack Damage Pallets & Do Not Accept Damaged Skus

Damaged or wrong pallet do not double stack onto a good pallet means your receiving department has skus on a pallet that is not acceptable to your standards. A not acceptable pallet has a broken stringer or deck board or has dimensions that do not your specifications. With close clearances (open space) in storage rack positions, there is a potential problem for a manual forklift truck transaction completion to a position. In your pick activity, your picker has additional non-productive time to handle two pallets. For skus entry into your storage concept, your options are (1) manual re-palletize skus that increases your CPU & occupies dock space, (2) mechanical transfer or invert a problem pallet skus onto your captive good pallet that requires equipment cost & some labor cost & (3) stack a problem pallet onto your captive good pallet that has minimal receiving labor cost, with an unstable load, potential problems & if your warehouse is a carton or pieces operation, at pick position a picker has increased non-productive time to remove pallets that has potential to create a pick line back-up.

What to do with a vendor delivered overs, shorts, damage or wrong sku is a receiving procedure to improve sku inventory control & receiving employee productivity. During a bulk (pallet, slip sheet, GOH or carton) receiving activity, a receiving clerk completes a receiving activity by comparing an actual vendor delivered sku quantity to a company purchase order sku quantity. Part of the receiving activity is to separate a sku quantity that is over a purchase order quantity, identify a sku shortage to a purchase order quantity, separate damage & wrong skus. After over, short, damage & wrong skus are identified and counted, a receiving clerk notifies the merchandising department for proper instruction to handle and account for over, short, damage & wrong skus.

RPP 2. One GOH Or 3 To 5 Bundled GOH

One GOH or bundled GOH is a GOH receiving idea that improves employee productivity & inventory control. As GOH is moved through a warehouse, 1 GOH per WMS ID transaction requires 1 WMS scan & employee movement transaction. After a detail receiving activity, a receiving employee with a rubber band or twister creates 3 to 5 GOH per bundle as a bundled GOH moves through your storage/pick activities, an employee increases GOH per transaction. As a bundled GOH is placed into a WMS ID storage or a picker completes a pick transaction, there is an increase GOH number per scan & employee movement transaction that increases productivity. If your GOH operation is for retail stores, your GOH pieces per bundle is based on your historical sku CO quantity. If your GOH warehouse has a bulk pick activity, your GOH pieces per bundle is based on your first time sku bulk pick quantities. With a 3 or 5 bundle concept, an individual GOH piece transaction is completed by entry on a scanner device.

RPP 3. Know Your Carton & Sku Cube (L, W, H & WT)

Know your carton & sku cube (length, width and height) & weight is an important idea that impacts a carton storage space utilization and replenishment & pick employee productivity. Accurate carton & sku data in your WMS program files assures maximum a carton number to fit into any position and accurate sku carton dimensions assures maximum carton number replenished to a pick position. To assure accurate sku information, as a new sku enters to your warehouse or a computer flags sku on a receiving or QA document that indicates to a receiving or QA clerk that an employee is responsible to take a carton or sku cube data & WMS computer data transfer. Cube data collected options are manual measure and scale, 3-dimensional cube platform that has 3 separate colored lines for each ship carton size & scale & cube machine.

RPP 4. WMS Identification (ID) On A Sku Front Or Side

WMS ID on a carton or pallet front or side is determined by your transport & storage transaction requirements and assures sku good scan transaction, accurate sku tracking and good employee productivity. As a sku enters your warehouse, each sku receives a WMS ID. For each storage (deposit) or replenishment transaction and each sku on a powered conveyor transport concept, each sku WMS ID is read by a bar code scanner device that sends an update message to your WMS computer. For maximum good reads with good employee productivity a bar code scanner requires line of sight to a sku bar code. In most storage and replenishment transactions, a front WMS ID is a preferred location due to the fact that a bar code faces an employee and an employee does not have non-productive time to orient a carton for a scan transaction and re-orient a carton to complete a replenishment transaction. With a front sku WMS ID to a match a transport side scanner requirements, a powered conveyor travel path has a device to turn a sku or pulls a gap between 2 skus for a scanner line of sight. On most transport concepts (except a pallet on forklift truck), a side WMS ID is a preferred location due to line of sight and short depth of field (bar code distance from a scanner). Prior to a transport concept discharge station, a sku turning device turns a pallet to have a WMS ID face a forklift truck driver. To minimize material handling equipment cost & assure a storage, replenishment & transport concept bar code line of sight, bar code label options are to use (1) 2 identical WMS IDs on a sku front & other ID on a sku side, 2 bar code location satisfies all your warehouse activity bar code line of sight requirements; but this represent additional print time, 2 labels & potential label control problems or (2) 1 wrap around WMS ID label that ID is 1 long label with 1 WMS ID that faces a sku front & same (other) WMS ID that faces a sku side. Wrap around label configuration satisfies all your activity bar code line of sight requirements, slightly less label print time, one label & minimizes label control problems. It is mentioned that a RF symbology reader to a recognize a WMS ID does not require line of sight but at most warehouse sku replenishment station a human requires line of sight to a RF tag human readable symbology.

RPP 5. Damaged/Wrong Pallet Do Not Double Stack Onto A Good Pallet

With a damaged pallet or wrong pallet, do not double stack a pallet onto a good pallet. At your receiving department a pallet with vendor delivered skus is a 'not acceptable' pallet to your warehouse. A 'not acceptable' pallet has a broken stringer or deck board or dimensions that do not your specifications. With close vertical clearance space between a pallet top and above load beam in a rack position, there is a potential problem for a manual forklift truck storage transaction to a storage position. A standard pallet height is nomimal 6 in. and a double stacked pallet has a nomimal 12 in. height. In your transport activity, there is a potential for an unstable pallet to tip and create a transport concept down-time and in your pick area and when a depleted pallet (double stacked pallet) occurs, a picker has additional non-productive time to handle 2 empty pallets For skus on a damage pallet to enter your storage concept, your options are (1) manual re-palletize skus onto a captive pallet that increases your CPU & occupies dock space or (2) mechanical transfer or invert a problem pallet skus onto your captive good pallet that requires equipment cost & some labor cost.

RPP 6. Signal When A Sku Is Ready For Transport

Signal when ready for transport is a receiving activity idea that improves employee productivity, enhances space utilization & controlled sku flow. After unloaded skus are properly staged on a receiving dock, each pallet sku has a fork opening side & WMS ID face a main aisle. each carton has a direction of travel & WMS ID face a main aisle/conveyor travel path & GOH lead piece & WMS ID face a direction of travel/conveyor travel path. After a sku & a WMS ID is placed in a proper staging location, a sku WMS ID that faces a main vehicle aisle or transport travel path serves as a signal to a transport employee that a sku is ready for transport or a receiving activity has released sku to a transport activity. A sku with no WMS ID means that the receiving process in not complete & a sku remains in a receiving staging area.

RPP 7. Sku Quantity Handled On A Pallet Or As Individual Cartons

Pallet or carton quantity refers to a receiving department idea for ID and handling a less than one pallet WMS ID sku quantity. Receiving options are with a WMS ID on each carton or carton quantity on a WMS ID pallet. To assist a receiving department with a decision to handle a vendor delivered sku quantity as one pallet with several cartons or individual cartons, your manager establishes a standard or procedure to handle (1) X carton number or less as individual cartons and each carton receives a WMS ID. The concept is used for a carton storage area to improve employee productivity, inventory tracking and space utilization and used in only pallet storage. A storage area has ½ high pallet positions to handle a small carton quantity. As a carton quantity becomes depleted in a pallet position, it creates poor position/space utilization.

RPP 8. Small Size Sku Or GOH Detail Count & Pack

Detail count & pack is a receiving activity idea to improve storage & pick employee productivity & enhance inventory control. Detail count receiving activity has a receiving clerk exactly count a vendor delivery by each sku size, color and style. In a warehouse, a detail count occurs with jewelry, GOH, spare parts or very small skus. Detail count options are (1) *Manual Count Activity* that has an employee physically handle each sku or (2) *Scale Count Activity* that has an employee use a scale to weigh a pre-determined sku quantity. After an entire sku quantity is placed onto a scale, a sample weigh count determines a total count. After a detail count activity, a receiving employee transfers a sku quantity into a bag or container. To optimize future storage or pick employee activity, a detail receiving employee places a pre-determined sku number into a re-sealable and re-useable bag or container & writes a sku quantity onto a tag. A tag is placed inside or onto a container with a sku quantity facing the outside. In a GOH warehouse after GOH detail receiving activity, with a rubber band or twister a receiving clerk bundles GOH into quantities of 3 or 5. Feature improves storage & picker future productivity.

RPP 9. Pre-Inspect Vendor Skus

Pre-inspect your vendor manufactured skus at a vendor facility is a receiving & QA idea that increases your receiving dock productivity & receiving dock turns. Pre-inspect at a vendor manufacturing facility concept has a company or third party inspector who your company has qualified to complete your company sku inspection prior to a vendor loading your company purchased skus onto a vendor delivery vehicle. Your vendor site sku inspection assures that a vendor-manufactured skus are per your company purchase order, company standards & government codes. After vendor-site inspector sku approval, a vendor loads skus onto a delivery vehicle for delivery to your warehouse. At a warehouse, your receiving department unloads and receives a vendor sku delivery onto your receiving dock. Per your company receiving & QA policy, as a vendor delivery is unloaded at your warehouse, an on-site QA inspector completes a random sample sku QA quality inspection or check. With a vendor sku delivery that a pre-inspection status, a vendor sku is unloaded, received and placed into a WMS identified storage position with a not available for sale status until QA approval.

RPP 10. Sku Piece Count Is Important

Sku piece count per WMS ID pallet or carton is very important to assure an accurate sku inventory, inventory control & high employee productivity. During a sku flow through a warehouse, an accurate sku pallet & carton piece count that is attached to a WMS ID permits a WMS program to match a WMS ID sku carton to pallet replenishment activity or CO pick transaction. When there is piece count variance for each WMS ID pallet or carton for an employee to match a WMS ID sku transaction quantity requires an employee to handle each pallet or carton & count each carton or pallet WMS ID sku quantity withdrawn instead of counting or handling a WMS ID pallet or carton quantity.

RPP 11. Scale Count Small Size Skus

Scale count is a detail receiving activity that improves receiving, put-away and inventory count employee productivity. When you receives loose very small or small items that are at a receiving dock bulk or carton received, to verify an actual vendor delivered sku quantity, your receiving department completes a detail or specific sku receive or count activity that is entered into your WMS program or inventory program files. If your detail receiving activity uses a scale count concept, when compared to a manual count activity there is a reduction in time to complete a sku count.

RPP 12. Count Small Size Skus Into Identified Bags

During your detail receiving activity, your receiving clerk counts each sku quantity. For maximum receiving efficiency your receiving clerk counts small sizes into manageable quantities such as 25 or 50 pieces. After your receiving clerk count activity, your options are (1) consolidate total sku quantity into one container. Features are (a) for inventory count or return to vendor, low count productivity and preparation, (b) skus are loose in a container that means no additional picker open activity and (c) skus are not protected and (2) each sku count quantity is placed into a bag with count quantity placed into a bag. Features are for inventory count or return to vendor minimal employee effort, (b) additional picker activity to open a bag and (c) skus are protected in a bag.

RPP 13. Vendor Delivered & Unloaded Skus Are 'Available For Sale' Or 'Not Available For Sale'

When a not available for sale concept is compared to available for sale concept, not available for sale concept has a vendor delivered sku unloaded, received and put-away in a constant flow that improves receiving & transport employee productivity & increases receiving dock turns. An available for sale concept has a vendor delivered skus unloaded, received and held in a receiving dock staging lane for QA approval. After QA approval, WMS identified skus are transported from a receiving dock for put-away to a WMS ID storage position. Waiting for the QA approval, available for sale concept requires additional receiving dock staging area & decreases a receiving dock turns. A not available for sale concept has a vendor delivered skus unloaded, received, WMS ID & transported to a WMS ID storage position. During your QA department inspection activity, your receiving docks are cleared & your receiving & QA department places WMS ID skus into a QA hold or not available for sale inventory status. After your QA department sku approval, your QA department notifies your receiving department & with an entry into a WMS or inventory control program your receiving department changes a vendor delivered sku status from not available for sale to available for sale status. The procedure assures that skus are available for sale & your transport/put-away activities have a constant sku flow to a WMS ID positions.

RPP 14. Under-Size Or Over-Size Vendor Carton

When your receiving department unloads a vendor delivery with under-sized or over-sized cartons, your receiving department contacts your purchasing department and advises your purchasing department that a vendor sku delivery requires re-packaging into your standard size cartons. Per a purchasing department direction and after a vendor or your operation re-packages a sku, a vendor sku is received and each package receives a WMS ID. A sku re-packaged into a standard size carton assures accurate replenishment activity and good inventory tracking. To assure vendor compliance with your standard size carton, your purchasing department advises new vendor and periodically e-mails/advises exiting vendors as to your standard carton size.

RPP 15. Hold For Your Re-Work Or Send To Out-Side For Re-Work

After your receiving department has unloaded and received a vendor delivery and your QA department has ID a sku quality or sku carton size problem (not per your company standard, your receiving department notifies your purchasing department about a problem. If your purchasing department is not available, your receiving department WMS IDs a problem sku and in your WMS computer program enters a sku status as 'not available for sale' and is placed into a 'D' sku or remote storage position. After your purchasing department determines a problem sku disposition (re-work with your or vendor labor or send to an out-side re-work company), your storage activity transfers a problem sku to an assigned re-turn to vendor or re-work station.

RPP 16. Cube Carton Or Pieces For Replenishment, Pick, Pack & Truck Load Activity

Know your carton & sku cube (length, width and height) & weight is an important idea that impacts your carton storage space utilization and replenishment & pick employee productivity and truck loading utilization. Accurate carton & sku data in a WMS program files assures maximum a carton number to fit into a storage/pick position and accurate sku carton dimensions assures maximum carton number replenished to a pick position and loaded into a delivery truck. To assure accurate sku information, as a new sku enters to your warehouse computer flags a sku on a receiving/QA document that indicates to a receiving/QA employee who is responsible to obtain a carton or sku cube data & WMS computer data transfer. Cube data collected options are manual measure and scale, 3-dimensional cube platform that has 3 separate colored lines for each ship carton size & scale/cube machine.

RPP 17. Locate Vendor Delivery Trucks For Shortest Travel Distance To Storage

Your receiving activity assures that your skus are unloaded, received, WMS identified and verified quantity and quality with completed receiving documents filed in your system and updated in your inventory control/WMS computer program to close a vendor purchase order. Your receiving dock options are (1) *General Receiving Dock Area* has your vendor delivery truck assigned to any main open receiving dock. The approach has potential for your big/ugly skus unloaded/received at a dock location that is a great travel distance from your big/ugly storage area that requires increase travel distance and time for specific empty pallets moved to your receiving dock and palletized/unitized skus moved from your receiving dock area to your big/ugly storage area and (2) *Special Receiving Dock Area* has your big/ugly skus unloaded/received at a receiving dock that is directly across from your big/ugly storage area. A receiving dock location reduces travel distance & time for specific empty pallets moved to your dock and palletized/unitized skus moved from your receiving dock area to your big/ugly storage area.

RPP 18. Sku Identification Has One Face, Wrap Around Or Hybrid

Sku ID has one face, wrap-around or hybrid bar code label are label design options to assure line of sight for a sku bar code reader or employee that increases maximum good read number. Bar code label line of sight assures good employee or scanner productivity by reducing your bad read number or scan attempts. A one face label on a paper has one bar code per label. One Face Label on a sku (pallet, carton, tote or GOH) faces one direction that is a sku side, top or front. Features are low label paper & ink expense & with some applications to complete a scan transaction requires additional employee time or a mechanical device to turn a sku. Wrap-Around Label has 2 bar codes that face 2 directions and on a sku a wrap-around label faces a sku front and side. Features are minimizes additional employee time or mechanical equipment to turn a sku for a scan transaction, has a higher paper & ink expense. An example has a wrap around label placed onto a sku with 1 bar face a front & second bar code face a side. Hybrid Label has one bar code in two different orientations on one label/face. A hybrid label faces one direction (side, front or top) but your bar code print format has a picket fence orientation & has a ladder orientation. A hybrid label has the same features as a 1 bar code label, but with the same bar code in two different orientations permits scanner light beam flexibility and higher paper & ink expense.

RPP 19. One Identification For All Your Vendor Delivered Skus (Cartons Or Pallets)
One ID for all your vendor delivered skus (cartons or pallets) is a sku ID concept. With 1 for all concept, an entire vendor received sku quantity has 1 sku WMS ID & has an entire sku quantity attached to 1 sku WMS ID. After a sku is received 1 WMS ID is placed onto 1 sku & all skus (X carton or pallet number) are transferred to a storage area. In a storage area all skus are placed into adjacent position or positions behind a sku with a WMS ID & WMS scanned to 1 WMS ID position. WMS scan transactions are sent to a WMS computer. As skus are withdrawn a WMS program indicates a WMS ID storage position & sku quantity. After a withdrawal transaction, a sku with a WMS ID remains in a WMS ID position or a sku WMS ID is transferred to another sku. Features are (1) most pallet applications use a dense floor storage concept that has a 66% utilization factor with low space utilization & small carton situations use a standard pallet or decked rack storage concept, (2) potential for a sku WMS ID to become lost or damaged, (3) difficult to assure good inventory tracking & (4) to assure accurate withdrawal transaction requires an employee to count & add, (5) difficult to use with a WMS program, (6) requires non-productive employee time, (7) as a sku inventory becomes depleted, there is limited flexibility and ability to move a sku with multiple pallets into standard rack positions & (8) limited to use in an employee hand stack or manual controlled forklift truck operation.

RPP 20. One Identification For Each Sku (Carton Or Pallet)
One ID for each sku (carton or pallet) is a sku ID concept. With 1 for 1 concept, a vendor received sku quantity is handled as 1 sku (carton or pallet) & each sku receives 1 WMS ID. After a sku receives a WMS ID, each sku is transferred to a storage area. In a storage area, each WMS ID sku is placed into a WMS ID storage position & WMS scan transactions are sent to a WMS computer. As skus are withdrawn, a WMS program indicates each WMS ID storage position & sku quantity to complete a withdrawal transaction. Features are (1) used in a single deep storage concept that has a 85% utilization factor with good space utilization & small carton situations use a standard pallet or decked rack storage concept, (2) WMS ID remains on a carton or pallet, (3) assures good inventory tracking & with a WMS computer suggesting a WMS ID pallet or carton, accurate withdrawal transaction with good productivity, (4) use with a WMS program, (5) as a WMS ID sku inventory becomes depleted, flexibility & ability to move a sku with multiple pallets into standard rack positions or few cartons to a decked position & (6) used in an employee hand stack, manual controlled forklift truck warehouse.

RPP 21. Sku Identification Is On Your Carton Or Pallet Front Right Side
Sku ID is on your carton or pallet front right side is a carton or pallet storage area idea that improves employee or forklift truck driver WMS ID scan and put-away productivity. To complete a WMS ID sku deposit, WMS IDs are (1) carton or pallet wrap around WMS ID on a pallet right hand stringer or block front and side or on a carton right front and side and (2) carton or pallet WMS ID on a lower right front & (3) storage rack pallet position WMS IDs on a storage position load beam right side. In locations, both sku & storage position WMS IDs face an aisle & assure line of sight for an employee hand held scanner device light beam. With both sku & storage position WMS IDs on a sku & storage position right side, it minimizes an employee time to locate WMS IDs & minimal time to move &

complete sku ID and position WMS scan transactions. It should be noted that most forklift truck drivers are right hand employees that reduces movement to complete WMS scan transactions.

Dock Area Equipment Ideas (DAE 1 – DAE 15)

DAE 1. Light

At a receiving or ship truck dock, lights is phrase for an idea to improve dock safety. A dock safety light device is located on your interior dock wall. When a dock safety device comes in contact with a delivery truck at a truck dock, a proper light is activated. Dock safety lights are (1) red light that means do not enter a delivery truck from a dock, (2) yellow light that means no delivery truck at a dock & (3) green light that means a delivery truck is at a dock and is ready for dock activity. A second receiving light feature is a dock light that shines into a delivery truck body.

DAE 2. Receiving Door Window To View Truck Yard

Windows to a truck yard refers to a receiving door with a window that views your truck yard to improve safety, improve employee productivity and enhance energy conservation. With a closed truck dock door, a truck door window permits a receiving clerk to verify an immediate dock area and determined that a delivery truck is at a dock. With a truck rear door frame is engulfed by a dock seal/shelter, a receiving clerk sees a delivery truck rear & opens a dock door. With the situation, opening a dock door improves dock area safety and security, minimizes controlled air to escape thereby energy conservation, minimizes dust entry into a facility & minimizes bird entry into a facility.

DAE 3. Your Dock Door Has A Seal Or Shelter

Dock door seals or shelters are receiving dock idea that improves your security & energy conservation. Dock seals & shelters are attached to a building exterior wall & from a dock doorframe extend outward on both sides & top. After a delivery truck is parked at a dock, a seal or shelter engulfs a truck opened rear door. A tight delivery vehicle and dock seal/shelter fit has no opening between a truck rear doorframe & a seal/shelter that reduces temperature loss & improves security.

DAE 4. Block Or ICC Bar Hold Your Delivery Truck

Block or ICC bar hold is a receiving dock idea that improves dock area safety and minimizes a delivery truck roll-away. A truck wheel block is a rubber or metal triangle shaped device that is attached to an exterior wall. When a delivery truck is parked at a dock, a delivery truck driver places a block under a rear wheel that restricts a truck forward movement. An ICC bar is a hook shaped dock leveler component. After a delivery truck is parked at a dock, a hook device extends outward & upward to hook a truck ICC bar that secures a delivery truck at a dock.

DAE 5. Protect Your Receiving Dock Door

Protect a dock door frame is a receiving area exterior & interior dock door frame idea to minimize dock door frame damage. At exterior dock door frame, cement filled pipe is secured to the ground to minimize dock door frame damage from a delivery truck accidental striking a dock door frame. At an interior dock door frame, cement filled pipes are secured to a floor in a dock door frame front to minimize dock door fame damage from a pallet or forklift truck hitting a door frame.

DAE 6. Receiving Or Ship Dock Staging Lanes

Your dock receiving or ship staging lanes is a receiving activity idea that reduces sku damage & improves employee productivity. After a receiving or ship dock is assigned to a vendor delivery or freight company truck, 2 staging lanes directly behind an assigned dock door are assigned for a vendor delivered sku staging. With each pallet opening facing a dock door & other pallet opening facing a main traffic aisle & 2 pallets wide on a nominal wide receiving dock of 60 ft depth, there is (1) sufficient space for 2 wide pallet lanes and 10 pallets deep & sufficient space between pallets for a receiving or ship clerk to complete a count, (2) verify no sku damage, (3) verify a pallet is per a company quality standard, (4) WMS identify each sku & (5) minimize employee injury.

DAE 7. Aisles At Your Staging Lane Both Ends

Aisles at a staging lane both ends is an idea that has mobile vehicle turning aisles at receiving or ship staging lanes ends. A front aisle is between a dock leveler edge & staging lane end width that permits a receiving or mobile vehicle to travel between a dock leveler edge & staging area. A rear aisle is between a staging lane end & a wall or rack that permits a transport vehicle to turn, pick-up a sku & travel from your receiving area to your storage area and from your storage area to your ship dock area.

DAE 8. Back-Up Lines Or Guide Rails In Your Truck Dock Front

Back-up lines or guide rails in each truck dock front, maneuvering area or parking area are ideas that improve truck yard safety and truck driver productivity. To assist a truck driver in a delivery truck back-up activity, options are (1) back-up lines that are painted on to a truck yard surface and onto a dock wall front & (2) delivery truck guide rails are metal tubes secured to a truck yard. Width between 2 lines or guide rails assist a truck driver to direct a delivery truck reverse travel into an assigned truck yard location and properly position at a truck dock spot or parking location. Feature minimizes truck back up time, building damage & adjacent delivery truck damage.

DAE 9. Empty Pallet How Many & Where To Locate

Empty pallets how many and where to locate is a receiving activity to assure that there is a sufficient empty pallet quantity at a dock location to handle a vendor delivery. With a floor staging concept, slip sheet load or pallet exchange program, a receiving department requires an empty pallet large number to handle a vendor delivery sku pallet number. When a receiving department completes a dock schedule appointment with a vendor or freight company, a receiving clerk reviews a vendor delivery type such as floor stack, slip sheet or palletized load. With the information, for each dock position, a receiving department knows a required empty pallet number. For good receiving productivity & truck dock turns, no empty vendor delivery truck departure delays, an empty pallet quantity is readily available to the receiving clerk. Empty pallet location options are (1) floor stack pallets between two dock doors. To minimize building damage, protection posts are located in-front of dock door frames and wall, (2) floor stacked in one empty staging lane, (3) with standard rack staging to use elevated rack positions, (4) with push back rack staging concept to use elevated rack positions & (5) with gravity flow rack concept, use pre-determined reverse flow lanes that flow pallets from a storage area to a receiving dock.

DAE 10. Your Truck Yard Side Unload With One, Two Wide Or Two Long Set Of Forks

Two long or 2 wide forks is a WA forklift truck pallet-unload concept for your side loaded delivery trucks when compared to employee unload cartons improves unload productivity & receiving dock turns. The concept allows your receiving activity to unload your side loaded delivery truck in less time & increases receiving dock turns. A properly designed WA forklift truck that has counterweight, wheels, & a set of 2 long forks or two sets of short forks that handles 2 pallets per unload transaction. After removing 2 pallets from a delivery truck, a forklift truck travels over a truck yard to an assigned delivery door and places 2 pallets into an open receiving dock door. From an open receiving dock door, a mobile receiving dock pallet vehicle moves a pallet into a staging lane. When compared to a WA forklift truck handling 1 pallet per transaction, a set of 2 long forks or a set of 2 wide forks improves employee productivity & increases receiving dock turns with an additional one time cost for a heavy WA forklift truck, additional hydraulics to a lift two pallets with 2 wide or 2 long forks.

DAE 11. Side Unload A Delivery Truck With A Forklift Truck In A Truck Yard

Siide unload with a forklift truck in your truck yard is receiving safety, employee productivity & space utilization idea. If your vendor truck delivery on a side load/unload vehicle that does not occur frequently, you unload a vendor delivery vehicle in your truck yard with a forklift truck is unload option. With a WA forklift truck with normal forks, one pallet is handled per trip between a delivery truck and dock. With long forks or double wide forks on a heavy WA forklift truck 2 pallets are handled per trip that unloads a delivery truck in half the time. After a pallet is removed from a delivery truck, your forklift truck travels from a delivery truck to your dock & places a pallet in an assigned dock door. Inside your facility another pallet truck transfers a pallet to an assigned staging lane. To handle a random but scheduled side unload vendor truck delivery, the approach increases a receiving dock capacity with minimal equipment & building cost. When compared to a manual carton unload activity, there is employee productivity increase. Truck yard safety factors are (1) your truck yard is extended beyond the first or last dock location to accommodate a delivery truck & allow a forklift truck to complete a unload turn and transaction & (2) first or last dock door is assigned to a delivery vehicle that minimizes a potential forklift truck & delivery truck accidents.

DAE 12. Slip Sheet Back Stop

Slip-sheet backstop is a receiving dock device that is used in a slip-sheet unload activity to improve forklift truck driver productivity and lower slip sheet handling costs. A vendor slip-sheet delivery has your vendor place cartons onto a kraft corrugated or plastic slip-sheet. Each slip-sheet has a 6 in. lip that extends outward and is clamped by a forklift truck slip-sheet device. In a delivery truck, a forklift truck pulls a slip-sheet onto slip-sheet device and exists a vendor delivery truck. With a slip sheet back stop, as a forklift truck with a slip sheet load exists a deliver truck & arrives onto a receiving dock, a forklift truck with a slip sheet travels to a slip sheet back stop for slip sheet transfer onto a pallet. At a slip sheet back stop is a pallet stack on a two sided 90 degree metal device that is secured to a warehouse floor & building column. Above a pallet top, a forklift truck places a slip-sheet load & pushes a slip-sheet load forward from a slip-sheet device onto a pallet top. A 2-sided metal backstop device assures proper slip-sheet alignment on a pallet & permits a forklift truck to transfer a slip sheet onto a pallet.

DAE 13. Canopy Stops The Rain

A canopy stops the rain is a truck dock safety and employee unload/load productivity improvement idea. Stop the rain idea has a 6 ft long & truck door width canopy that is attached to each building wall and extends outward from a building wall above each truck dock door. Some building canopies are installed on an entire building front that covers all dock doors & open space between 2 dock doors. A canopy elevation assures that delivery trucks travel unobstructed under a canopy & properly nest against a truck dock. A canopy outward extension & solid surface directs rain or water from a building wall side onto a truck body top & away from a dock leveler. A canopy provides a dry dock leveler that improves dock safety & improves employee unload/load productivity. If a truck dock maneuvering front or area is under an elevated building floor, an elevated floor stops the rain but consideration is given to additional lighting, fire safety & fire sprinkler protection & building column protection.

DAE 14. Painted Lines On Your Receiving Or Ship Dock Floor

A receiving or ship dock floor with painted lines is idea that reduces sku damage & improves employee productivity. Line control on a receiving or ship dock has 6 in wide painted lines on a receiving or ship dock floor surface. Parallel white painted lines on your floor start at each staging lane start that is opposite a dock turning aisle & extend to a staging lane end or main traffic aisle side. For each sku staging lane there are two 6 in. wide lines that means 2 staging lanes has 3 painted lines. Space between 2 parallel painted lines has the width for a pallet and is consider a sku staging lane.

DAE 15. Bridge Your Above Your Dock Doors

If you require storage space, bridge your dock door that is an opportunity to provide additional single deep pallet rack positions. If your dock leveler to door open travel path does not interfere with the rack, a bridge single deep rack bay upright posts and load beams are installed in a dock door. The posts are anchored to the floor and protected with guards. Load beams have front to rear members with a clear space between your floor surface and load beam bottom for a forklift truck travel under. Storage positions are used empty pallets and if potential skus falling to the floor is a potential problem, plastic wrap pallets or add a removable barrier to a pallet position front.

Transport Activity Ideas
Travel Path Ideas (TPD 1 - TPD 8)
TPD 1. Fewer Travel Path Horizontal Curves
Fewer travel path horizontal curves on a transport concept means a lower transport concept one-time cost & lower electric cost. To avoid a building or work station a transport concept horizontal travel path makes a turn/curve.

TPD 2. Transport Concept Is Closed Loop/Round Trip Or One-Way Trip

Closed loop/round trip or one-way trip are your transport concept options. Your selected option impacts your warehouse smooth & constant sku flow, assures on-time and accurate deliveries and enhances dual cycles (handles an in-bound pallet and handles an outbound pallet) to improve productivity. One-way sku transport concept is used in a large warehouse that has a powered conveyor transport concept for sku delivery to a AS/RS crane or GOH storage concept. During a WMS identified sku travel on an one-way travel path, a WMS ID scanner devices & transport concept computer and diverters assure that a WMS ID sku is diverted to an assigned aisle for a storage put-away transaction. If a sku divert transaction is not completed, a transport along a GOH or AS/RS storage area front has a re-circulation travel path or a did not divert sku travel path that is a decline travel path to the floor. A closed loop/round trip sku transport concept is used to handle cartons, pallets or GOH. With a VNA or GOH storage concept, a transport concept travel path is a closed loop travel path that has a transport concept pick-up a pallet from a receiving area for transport to a storage area and in the storage area pick-up an outbound sku for transport to a pick area or ship area. With a human controlled powered sku carrying vehicle, an employee follows a fixed or variable travel path to a storage/delivery aisle & returns over a fixed or variable travel path to a receiving/pick area. Per a warehouse type, a sku transport vehicle moves an outbound sku from a storage area to a pick area, ship or receiving area. With ability to pick-up & transport an outbound sku, a transport concept has an opportunity to complete dual cycles that improves employee productivity & lower sku cost. A conveyor closed loop travel path has additional conveyor, I T one time cost and requires your inbound transport transactions to equal (occur at the same time) your outbound transactions. If a sku divert transaction is not completed, a transport concept handles a did not divert sku with a re-circulation conveyor that has a did not divert sku re-introduced to a scanner or diverts it to a did not divert sku spot.

TPD 3. Transport Travel Path Is Fixed Or Variable Path

Fixed or variable travel path are a transport concept travel path options to assure continuous sku flow and on-time activity completion. A fixed transport travel path concept is common with a computer controlled powered transport concept. With a fixed travel path carrier or conveyor, a sku is moved with a constant travel speed over one travel that assures a constant & scheduled flow. The concept handles a high volume, high 1-time fixed costs with minimal on-going labor costs, requires a free & clear travel path & at a delivery or pick-up station, sku transfers are an unassisted or assisted activity. An assisted activity has a higher (CPU). A variable travel path concept is most common in warehouse that uses an employee controlled vehicle. With a variable travel path concept, an employee controls a vehicle travel speed over an employee selected travel path between 2 locations & at a pick-up or delivery location, an employee controlled vehicle completes an unassisted sku transfer & has a lower CPU.

TPD 4. Your Transport Straight Aisle & Turning Aisle Width Dimensions

Your transport carrier straight aisle width and turning aisle width allows a transport carrier to move over a travel path & to travel from one aisle to another aisle. A straight aisle width has sufficient clearance between a carrier & sku or rack to improve space utilization and minimize sku, building or equipment damage. A turning aisle width is used at an aisle end or in a cross/middle aisle that allows a carrier to transfer from one aisle to another aisle. If a travel path straight or turning aisle width is narrower than a transport concept manufacturer allowance, there is potential sku, building or equipment damage. If a travel path aisle width is wider than a manufacturer allowance, there is poor space utilization with potential for re-design or adjustment.

TPD 5. One-Way Wide Or Two-Way Wide Vehicle Travel Path

One-way or two-way wide vehicle travel path are carrier travel path design options. One-way travel path design has all carriers move skus in a forward direction. Forward direction is from a dispatch/pick-up station, over a travel path and to a destination/delivery station. A 1-way travel path design has a narrower travel path window width due one carrier is on your travel path. A 2-way travel path design has all carriers move sku in a (1) forward direction from a dispatch/pick-up station, over a travel path and to a destination/delivery station and (2) after sku discharge at a delivery station, a carrier return travel is from a delivery station over a travel path and to a dispatch/pick-up station. In a travel path window, your outbound carrier travel path is parallel and in the same window as your return carrier travel path. A 2-way travel path has carriers traveling in different directions and requires additional clearance that creates a wider travel path window. In most applications, a 2-way travel path design has better space utilization & potential equipment savings.

TPD 6. People Path & Vehicle Travel Path Colors
People path is a floor or transport concept travel path option that permits an employee to walk parallel to a powered in-house carrier or conveyor travel path entire length from a dispatch/pick-up station to a destination/delivery station. People path colored floor markings are easily identified and used in most applications. People path & vehicle travel path colors are important transport concept design features. When a people path is adjacent to a manual or powered vehicle/carrier travel path & to assure minimum potential for employee injury, a people travel path is painted with parallel and diagonal lines in a local approved safety color & a vehicle or carrier travel path is painted with parallel & diagonal lines in the a local approved safety color. To assure maximum awareness, human readable & symbol signs are posted at key locations & along both travel paths.

TPD 7. At Intersecting Aisle Use Safety Mirrors
Safety mirrors are a powered mobile manual controlled vehicle transport concept option that improves your operation safety. At blind or right angle turns with high employee & vehicle 2-way traffic, a safety mirror at a proper location shows on-coming traffic. With proper employee training, an employee walking or driving a vehicle approaching a turn or intersection looks into a mirror & assures an on-ward travel path is clear.

TPD 8. Aisle Identification Location
Aisle ID location is a manual storage concept that has an ID at an aisle entrance. Proper aisle ID improves employee productivity & enhances inventory control. With a suggested sku deposit or withdrawal transaction concept, an aisle ID indicates to an employee or employee controlled forklift truck a sku assigned aisle. An aisle ID has each aisle discreet ID in a location for an employee or employee controlled forklift truck clear view. In a manual controlled forklift truck operation, an aisle ID is a nomimal 6 ft above a floor surface or at height that minimizes any forklift truck damage. An aisle ID has alpha characters or digits that have contrast colors between alpha characters/digits and background surface, have sufficient height & width for clear view & understanding from a main traffic aisle middle & 6 ft above a floor surface and at an aisle entrance extends outward from a rack row end into a main aisle. Aisle ID options are (1) one surface that is attached flat against a rack frame & adjacent to an aisle entrance, (2) two surfaces that are attached to both rack row end rack posts, extend outward into a main traffic aisle & adjacent to an aisle entrance that is used for a manual controlled forklift truck operation & (3) three surfaces in a triangle shaped format that is ceiling hung in a main aisle slightly, at an aisle entrance & higher than a WA or NA truck highest component and is used for a WA or NA forklift truck operation with floor stack & rack storage.

Transport Vehicle Ideas (TVC 1 - TVC 13)
TVC 1. Employee Powered Pallet Truck Is Better Pulled Than Pushed
Employee powered pallet truck is better pulled than pushed are a manual powered pallet truck direction of travel options. A pallet truck push concept has an employee push a manual pallet truck forward over a floor. As a pallet truck moves over a travel path when a pallet truck makes a right turn, a pallet truck handle is turned to the left that is no automotive steering. Other features are (1) to start moving a loaded pallet truck, it requires additional physical effort, (2) employee had limited travel path view due to a pallet blocks an employee view that potential for a pallet truck wheel hang-up in a crack or on debris & (3) when to make a quick stop there is potential sku damage from a sku falls to the floor & non-productive clean-up time due to no protection from a back-rest. A pallet truck pull option has an employee pull on a pallet truck over a floor. When required to make a right turn, an employee turns a pallet truck handle to the right (automatic steering). Features are (1) to start moving a full pallet truck requires less physical effort, (2) employee has complete travel path view that minimizes a pallet truck wheel hang-up in a crack or on debris & (3) when to make a quick stop with a back-rest on a pallet truck, lower potential sku damage from falling to a floor & non-productive clean-up time due to back-rest restricting sku movement.

TVC 2. Use A Tugger/WA Forklift Truck With A Cart Train Or Double Pallet Truck

Use a tugger/WA forklift truck with a cart train or a double pallet truck are manual controlled sku transport options. Both concepts with skus for one destination, you improve employee productivity for each trip over a long travel distance. A powered tugger or WA forklift truck with a cart train or double pallet truck are transport concepts that require at a delivery location, a forklift truck to complete a storage put-away transaction. When compared to a single pallet truck concept, an electric powered double pallet truck increases capacity and improves employee productivity by 1 pallet with a slightly higher equipment costs & wider turning aisles. A powered tugger/WA forklift truck with cart train has up to 4 carts in a train. To assure good cart trailing characteristics, each 4-wheel cart has proper steering & hitch/coupler concept. With a tugger and cart concept, at pick-up and delivery locations, a forklift truck is required to transfer a pallet on to a cart & requires a cart train to return carts and empty/outbound pallets to a pick-up location. With a WA forklift truck and cart concept, a forklift that pulls a cart train completes a pallet transfer transaction. To assure maximum employee productivity, on a return trip to a dispatch station, a transport concept backhauls skus or empty pallets.

TVC 3. Powered Vehicle Backrest Is A Must
Backrest is a manual or powered vehicle or carrier option that reduces potential for sku damage from falling to the floor and non-productive employee clean-up & re-palletize time. A backrest has harden metal members that are welded together & attached to a vehicle or carrier base & extend upward. After pallet pick-up, a pallet front or rear rests against a backrest. During travel across a floor & when a vehicle or carrier sudden stop occurs, a backrest prevents one side of a pallet from moving & thereby reducing sku damage from falling to the floor.

TVC 4. Pallet Truck Driver Leads Or Follows A Pallet
Pallet truck driver leads or follows a pallet are a powered walkie or rider pallet truck a transport concept direction of travel options. Proper pallet truck direction of travel improves employee productivity, minimizes sku, equipment & building damage and improves safety. A pallet truck driver lead option has a pallet truck forks in a lead direction of travel & driver on a truck front (ahead of a pallet). When your pallet truck driver turns a pallet truck control handle to the right, a pallet truck turns to the right left. Driver lead features are (1) similar to automotive steering method that results with faster travel speed & low potential damage due to maximum travel path view that has potential for pallet truck wheel to avoid hung-up on cracks or debris & (2) if a pallet truck has a back-rest & with a quick stop, a backrest is protection for a sku to fall onto a floor that creates non-productive clean-up & re-palletize time. A pallet truck driver follow option has a pallet forks/pallet first and a driver follows. With a driver follow option, your driver is behind a pallet/forks and a pallet is in front as a pallet truck moves over travel path. When your driver turns a pallet truck handle to the right, a pallet truck turns to the left. A pallet truck steering method is not similar to driving an automobile (not automotive steering). Driver follow are (1) slower travel speeds & with limited travel path view that increases potential for pallet truck wheel hang-up on cracks or debris & if a pallet truck makes a quick stop back-rest, there is no sku protection that increases potential for a sku falling to a floor.

TVC 5. Walk With Or Ride On A Powered Pallet Truck
Walk with or ride on a powered pallet truck is a basic transport concept option to move a pallet from a receiving area to a storage area. Walk with an electric battery powered pallet truck concept has an employee walks with a pallet truck across a travel path. A walkie electric powered pallet truck moves a pallet over a travel path that minimizes an employee physical effort, a higher cost, human paced concept & with a slower travel speed slightly improves employee productivity. A rider electric powered pallet truck is a machine paced concept that moves a pallet & employee across a travel path. Features are (1) carries a heavier load, (2) higher cost, (3) travels over a long travel path at faster travel speeds and up slight grades and (4) good employee productivity.

TVC 6. Powered Pallet Truck Or Forklift Truck As A Manual Controlled Transport Vehicle
Pallet or forklift truck are a manual controlled pallet truck concepts that move pallets from receiving to your storage area & have a one-time cost difference and improves employee productivity & unit cost. A pallet truck moves a pallet from a receiving dock floor position to a storage floor level delivery position that is at a rack row end but requires a forklift truck to complete a storage transaction. A powered pallet truck concept features are a lower wage rate employee completes a transport activity with a lower cost vehicle and a high wage cost forklift truck driver on a

high cost vehicle remains in a storage area to complete storage transactions. A WA forklift truck moves a pallet from a receiving dock direct to a conventional storage position that completes a storage transaction or to a VNA P/D station. If a forklift truck completes a transport activity, there is increased forklift travel distances that decreases forklift truck productivity that requires additional forklift trucks & drivers that have a higher unit cost.

TVC 7. Transport With One Or Two Pallets
A transport concept two pallet per trip is better than one pallet is a pallet transport idea that improves employee productivity. A storage area with a WA or NA forklift truck requires a wide turning traffic aisle, back to back rack row design and random sku placement into a storage position. Per trip a 2 pallet truck moves 2 pallets from your receiving area to a storage area. When a two-pallet truck drops 2 pallets at a back-to-back flush storage rack row or floor stack row end, each pallet WMS iD faces 1 forklift truck storage aisle that permits a forklift truck driver to complete a sku WMS iD scan transaction. If another aisle forklift truck driver from another storage aisle desires to put-away a pallet in its aisle, to complete a sku WMS ID scan transaction a forklift truck driver is required to complete a forklift truck 360 turn that has lower productivity. If a cart train is used to transport skus, at a delivery station, after carts are dropped-off at an aisle end, an employee arranges a cart at an aisle end to have each pallet WMS ID face a storage aisle or a transport forklift transfers pallets from a cart onto an aisle end position.

A tugger/WA forklift truck with a cart train or a double pallet truck concepts are manual controlled sku transport options. Both concepts with skus for one destination, you improve employee productivity for each trip over a long travel distance. A powered tugger or WA forklift truck with a cart train or double pallet truck are transport concepts that require at a delivery location, a forklift truck to complete a storage put-away transaction. When compared to a single pallet truck concept, an electric powered double pallet truck increases capacity and improves employee productivity by 1 pallet with a slightly higher equipment costs & wider turning aisles. A powered tugger/WA forklift truck with cart train has up to 4 carts in a train. To assure good cart trailing characteristics, each 4-wheel cart has proper steering & hitch/coupler concept. With a tugger and cart concept, at both pick-up and delivery locations, a forklift truck is required to transfer a pallet on to a cart & requires a cart train to return carts and empty/outbound pallets to a pick-up location. With a WA forklift truck and cart concept, a forklift that pulls a cart train and completes pallet transfer or deposit transactions. To assure maximum employee productivity, on a return trip to a dispatch station, a transport concept backhauls skus or empty pallets.

TVC 8. Pallet In Front (Lead) Or Behind (Follow) A WA Or NA Forklift Truck Driver
Pallet In Front (Lead) Or Behind (Follow) A Forklift Truck Driver are forklift truck pallet carrying or direction of travel options. (1) When a WA or NA forklift truck carries a pallet over a travel path with a pallet in the front, a pallet on a set of forks is in the lead. Features are (A) forklift truck driver due to mast & pallet obstruction has limited travel path view, (B) with a standard WA or NA forklift truck, a forklift truck steering method is automotive that is common to most forklift truck drivers. Automotive steering means as a driver turns a steering wheel to the right a vehicle turns right & (C) when to make a quick stop due to no protection from a back-rest there is potential sku damage from a sku falls to the floor & non-productive clean-up time & (2) *When A Forklift Truck Travels With A Driver Faces Rear (Chassis End) Or NA Forklift Truck Driver Faces A Lead Direction Of Travel (Chassis End)*, a pallet or set of forks is in a trail. Features are (A) driver has complete travel path view but with a standard forklift truck, (B) forklift steering is non-automotive that means as a driver turns a steering wheel to the right & a vehicle turns left & (C3) when to make a quick stop with a back-rest on a forklift truck, there is lower potential sku damage from falling to a floor & non-productive clean-up time.

TVC 9. Use An Overhead/Head Acke Bar, Highway Guard Rail/Post & Wheel-Stop (See OSS-23 Page 17)

TVC 10. WA Or NA Forklift Truck Take A Pallet Into A Storage Aisle Or Leave It A Rack Row End
With a WA or NA forklift truck storage activity your transport vehicle pallet drop-off options are (1) *Take A Pallet Into A Storage Aisle*. With a small storage area, a few forklift truck transactions & aisles that perpendicular to a receiving dock, take a pallet into an aisle concept has good equipment utilization & employee productivity. A warehouse with a large storage area & aisles that are parallel to your receiving dock and high forklift truck transactions, take a pallet into an aisle represents poor forklift truck utilization & low employee productivity. To

transport a sku with a high wage rate forklift truck driver and a high equipment cost, it represents a high CPU or (2) *Leave A Pallet At A Rack Row End* option has your transport vehicle deposit a pallet at an rack end. Leave or deposit a pallet at a rack row end with a single or double pallet truck as a transport vehicle has a lower equipment cost, lower truck driver wage rate & lower CPU. With a pallet truck transport concept, a storage area main travel aisle requires a wider aisle that permits pallet placement at a rack row end floor level drop station & to have a sku WMS ID face a forklift truck driver proper pallet placement at a rack row end.

TVC 11. VNA Forklift Truck Take A Pallet Into An Aisle Or Leave It At A Rack Row End P/D Station

With a VNA forklift truck storage activity your pallet transport vehicle pallet drop-off options impact your transport employee productivity, VNA forklift truck driver put-away productivity, potential rack post damage & potential sku WMS scan low productivity. *Take A Pallet Into A Storage Aisle* option has a transport vehicle travel into a VNA aisle, deposit a sku in an aisle & exist from a VNA aisle. Features are (1) to complete a take a pallet into an aisle concept, a transport vehicle travels in a VNA with a pallet truck travel in both lead and driver trail directions that has potential for low pallet truck driver travel speed & potential rack post damage, (2) if a VNA forklift truck is in an aisle, a sku WMS ID has potential to face a wrong direction for a WMS scan transaction. When an employee is in an aisle, for safety reasons an alarm or yellow chain is drawn and hooked across an aisle entrance that is considered a safe activity & (3) if a VNA forklift truck is not in an aisle, a sku WMS ID faces a proper direction for a WMS scan transaction, but a forklift truck driver has to wait for a pallet truck to clear an aisle that is low forklift truck driver productivity. *Leave A Pallet At An Aisle End P/D station* has a transport pallet or forklift truck deposit a sku at an aisle end pick-up & delivery (P/D) station. With leave a pallet at an aisle end P/D station, a saw-tooth P/D station design assures adequate in-house transport vehicle turning aisle to have a sku placed into a P/D station with a sku WMS ID facing an aisle.

TVC 12. Fewer Travel Path Horizontal Curves

Fewer travel path elevation changes & horizontal curves on a transport concept means a lower transport concept one-time cost, minimizes sku jams & lower electric cost. For a powered carrier or conveyor travel path to service a work/activity station on a different elevation a transport concept travel path makes an elevation change. When a travel path makes an elevation change, your sku travel path requires (1) at both charge & discharge ends a horizontal run-out, (2) sloped travel path with side guards, (3) underside protection and penetration through a floor with employee & fire barrier protection & (4) additional electric drive motors. To avoid a building or work station a transport concept horizontal travel path makes a turn/curve. When a sku travel path makes a turn/curve, for minimal sku damage, continuous flow and to have proper travel dimension, skus are singulated on a straight conveyor and a curve has a faster travel speed. Many curves have tapered or special rollers that require an additional electric motor. When a powered conveyor travel paths make an elevation change or curve, a sku powered travel path requires an additional drive motor & controls that increases the electrical expense.

TVC 13. Transport Concept Is Closed Loop/Round Trip Or One-Way Trip

A closed loop/round trip or one-way trip are your transport concept options. Your selected option impacts your sku smooth & constant sku flow, assures on-time and accurate deliveries and enhances dual cycles (handles an in-bound pallet and handles an outbound pallet) to improve productivity. *One-Way Sku Transport* concept is used in a large warehouse that has a powered conveyor transport concept for sku delivery to a AS/RS crane or GOH storage concept. During a WMS identified sku travel on an one-way travel path, a WMS ID scanner devices & transport concept computer and diverters assure that a WMS ID sku is diverted to an assigned aisle for a storage put-away transaction. If a sku divert transaction is not completed, a transport along a GOH or AS/RS storage area front has a re-circulation travel path or a did not divert sku travel path that is a decline travel path to the floor. *Closed Loop/Round Trip Sku Transport* concept is used in a warehouse that handles cartons, pallets or GOH. With a VNA carton or pallet AS/RS or GOH concept, a transport concept travel path is a closed loop travel path that has a transport concept pick-up a pallet from a receiving area for transport to a storage area and in a storage area pick-up an outbound sku for transport to a pick area or ship area. With a human controlled powered sku carrying vehicle, an employee follows a fixed or variable travel path to a storage/delivery aisle & returns over a fixed or variable travel path to a receiving/pick area. Per a warehouse type, a sku transport vehicle moves an outbound sku from a storage area to a pick area, ship or receiving area. With ability to pick-up & transport an outbound sku, a transport concept has an opportunity to complete dual cycles that improves employee productivity & lower sku cost. A conveyor closed loop travel path has additional conveyor, I T 1 time cost and requires your inbound transport transactions to equal (occur in the same time period) your outbound transactions. If a sku divert transaction is not completed, an in-house transport concept handles a did not divert sku with a re-circulation conveyor that has a did not divert sku re-introduced to a scanner/reader or diverts a did not divert sku to the floor.

Storage Activity Ideas
General (SG1 – SG 17)
SG 1. Wide Aisle (WA), Narrow Aisle (NA) & Very Narrow Aisle (VNA) Forklift Trucks
WA, NA or VNA forklift trucks are your employee controlled forklift truck options. A WA forklift truck features are (1) 3 or 4 wheel, (2) employee seats, (3) lift to a 20 ft height in a 10 to 13 ft wide aisle, (4) electric battery powered or internal combustion engine, (5) notched mast or level finder assist to complete an elevated storage transaction and (6) complete transport activities and handles most accessories. A NA forklift truck features are (1) employee stands, (2) lift to 25 ft in a 7 to 8 ft wide aisle with a bottom storage on floor level or load beams, (3) electric battery powered, (4) notched mast/level finder assists to complete an elevated storage transaction and (5) engulfs a pallet between two out-riggers. A VNA forklift truck features are (1) employee seats, (2) lift to 35 ft in a 6 to 6 ft 6 in guided wide aisle with a bottom storage on floor level or load beams, (3) electric battery powered, (4) man-up minimizes transaction problems, (5) best performance with a P/D station and (6) used as a pick vehicle.

SG 2. Average Inventory Or Moving Average Inventory
Average inventory projection or X month moving average inventory projection are a manager's options to project a design year sku/pallet inventory. Your design year sku/pallet inventory projection has a direct impact on your proposed facility sq. ft. or cubic ft. area, storage rack type, forklift truck type and required cost. An average inventory project is calculated by dividing 12 (months) into your annual sku/pallet inventory & the result is multiplied by your required months of inventory on-hand such as annual pallet inventory/12 months = average inventory.

A moving average inventory projection has several steps. First your determined your company's each months sku/pallet inventory. Next, you determined a number of months (time period such as 3 months) for your proposed operation on-hand inventory & you calculate each 3 months inventory such as (1) Jan, Feb & Mar, (2) Feb, Mar & Apr, (3) Mar, Apr & May, (4) Apr, May & June, (5) May, June & July, (6) June, July & Aug, (7) July, Aug & Sept, (8) Aug, Sept & Oct, (9) Sept, Oct & Nov, (10) Oct, Nov & Dec & (11) Nov, Dec & Jan. A time period (3 month period) with a highest sku inventory is used to project your design year sku/pallet inventory. Using a moving average projection method provides you with a more accurate inventory for your peak business season & if you use an average inventory, it could be understated.

SG 3. How To Handle Your Average Sku Storage
How to handle your average sku storage is a storage concept to handle 80% of your skus & 20% of your volume. Most average 'B' & 'C'/moving skus have a medium to small sku inventory that has 1 to 2 cartons, pallets or few GOH ln. ft. A storage concept for an average inventory are (1) carton quantity is single deep storage position that is a decked pallet rack position, (2) pallet quantity is a single deep, ½ high or normal high standard pallet rack position & (3) GOH is static rail. For best results, sku storage positions are located at an aisle rear or in 1 aisle. The concept improves your storage space utilization, position occupancy & employee productivity.

SG 4. How To Handle Your Promotional Sku Storage
How to handle your promotional sku storage is a storage concept to handle 20% of your skus & 80% of your volume. Most promotional or 'A'/fast moving skus have a large sku inventory (many pallets or large GOH ln. ft). A storage concept for a promotional sku inventory is a dense storage position (flow rack, drive-in/drive thru, floor stack or 2 deep) or a VNA forklift truck one deep position. For best results, 'A'/fast moving sku storage positions are located near at an aisle exist or located with a short travel distance to your pick area. The concept improves your storage space utilization, position occupancy & employee productivity.

SG 5. Where Are Your Remote & Ready Reserve Positions

Where are your remote or ready reserve storage positions are a sku storage positions in a WMS or inventory control program that assure on-time replenishment to a pick position for maximum completed CO number. A remote storage position is in your main storage area, has a large pallet storage position number and has forklift trucks to complete sku deposit and withdrawal transactions. In a remote storage position, a sku is held until required for a pick position replenishment transaction. In most warehouses and when compared to other main facility ready reserve storage position, a remote storage position holds a sku for a longer period of time. After a sku quantity from a remote reserve position exceeds a pick position sku quantity, your over-flow sku quantity is placed into a pick area ready reserve position. Until required for replenishment to a pick position, a sku is held in a ready reserve storage position. A ready reserve position is above, adjacent or behind a pick position. In some manual carton or pieces warehouses, sku remote storage positions are pallet positions above pick positions.

SG 6. All Storage Rack Openings With Same Height Or Different Opening Heights

Your storage rack opening options are (1) *All Storage Rack Openings With The Same Height* is a storage area that has all rack pallet position set at the same height and assures maximum storage area position flexibility. All positions set at the same height means that an open space between 2 standard rack load beams have same dimension. With a full pallet in & out operation, all rack positions at same height provide best space utilization, maximum pallets per sq. ft. & maximum flexibility. In a pick operation, all pallet storage rack positions at same elevation has some limitations. The limitations are less than a full pallet in a position means low position utilization, difficult to store maximum sku number & lower employee productivity. In a GOH warehouse, all positions set for a long GOH dimension permits maximum position flexibility but with a short GOH in a long position means low position utilization & low employee productivity & (2) *Different Opening Heights* for your racks means that racks have at least 2 rack opening heights, there is great potential for a storage area to have less than full pallets or to have 'C' or 'D' moving sku with a small carton quantity. When a less than full pallet occupies a full high rack position, there is unused space in a position that creates poor position and space utilization, low skus per sq. ft. or storage area and low employee productivity. If a storage area has a percentage of rack positions that are less than full or high (based on your position occupancy rate), results are improves storage position and space utilization, improved productivity with improved hit density & hit concentration per aisle, increased skus per sq. ft. & additional load beam cost & maybe new upright post to support a heavier load.

SG 7. Separate Storage & Pick Positions Or All Storage Positions Are Pick-able

Your position in your computer program options are (1) *Separate Storage & Pick Positions* means that a carton or GOH warehouse has separate sku WMS ID storage & pick positions. If all inbound or new skus are assigned to a WMS ID storage or pick position and a storage position is accessed by a forklift truck & a pick position is accessed by an employee. As COs deplete skus from a WMS ID pick position, a WMS computer program advises an employee or forklift truck to complete a WMS ID sku replenishment activity. A replenishment activity has an employee or forklift truck move a WMS ID sku from a storage position to a sku same pick position or different pick position. WMS ID sku quantity & pick position scanned and sent to a WMS computer for update. Features are that it requires a replenishment activity & improves picker productivity & (2) *All Storage Positions Are Pick-able* it means that a carton or GOH warehouse sku positions are pick-able. A pick position means that a picker has to access a sku quantity from a WMS ID position to complete a CO. All pick-able position concept means that received and WMS ID skus are placed into any position. Position & sku WMS IDs are scanned and sent to a WMS computer for update. Feature means if a sku quantity becomes depleted in a pick position and to complete a CO for additional skus from an elevated WMS ID storage position, your employee accesses a WMS ID storage position. Your picker has non-productive time to locate forklift truck to access skus from an elevated WMS ID position but no replenishment activity.

SG 8. Tall Or Short Storage Position Location

Tall or short position location is a storage rack design with 2 sku heights and locates a specific dimensioned position at an upright post top or bottom. With a human controlled WA, NA or VNA forklift truck, a set of forks has a load back rest. When completing a transaction with a short at a top position and a back rest height exceeds a pallet height, to complete a transaction you require a tall position for backrest clearance. To assure access to high positions, have maximum space utilization & rack structural strength, your rack design has short positions at a upright post base (floor level) & tall positions at a upright post top (highest level). Most tall pallets have a light load weight & most pallets have heavy load weight, that matches a forklift truck load weight reduction at maximum elevation above the floor.

SG 9. Decked Pallet Rack Row Design

Decked standard pallet rack or slotted angled rack row is a warehouse carton storage design for 'C'/'D' sku movers that increases sku facings per aisle, space utilization and permits access to all pick positions. Decked standard pallet rack or slotted angled rack designs are similar with upright posts, load beams & deck material (wood, wire mesh, metal sheet, conveyor or particle board) but an exception is that a standard pallet rack height design can exceed an angle iron rack height design. With standard pallet rack, above your human accessible positions, additional storage positions are designed for cartons or pallets. Rack row design options are (1) *Single Rack Row With One Carton With An Aisle On Both Sides*. Features are (a) provides maximum sku facings, (b) 85% highest space utilization, (c) easy sku access, (d) easy to have FIFO rotation & (e) mid-deck divider that is wood, pipe or rope restricts carton moving another carton into the opposite aisle & (2) *Back To Back Rack Row With 2 Deep Cartons Per Rack Row With An Aisle On Each Rack Row Side*. Features are (a) provides maximum carton storage, (b) good utilization with a rear position at 85% utilization & front position at 66% utilization, difficult to access a sku, (c) difficult to have FIFO rotation & (d) to maintain a flue space, it requires rear deck stop.

SG 10. Your Highest Storage Position Gets Warm & Is A Secured Position

Your storage position characteristics are (1) *Your Highest Storage Position Gets Warm* is a storage area situation that occurs at your highest rack positions. In all storage concepts, a storage area warm air rises to a ceiling that causes internal temperature to increase at your highest rack positions. Temperature increase occurs in a low warehouse building (20 to 25 ft high ceiling) and is especially true for a VNA forklift truck tall rack facility (40 to at least 80 ft high ceiling). To protect your temperature sensitive skus in your storage area, for your temperature sensitive skus your WMS computer or inventory control program has a flag that suggests to a receiving clerk to direct a sku deposit transaction to a low (floor level) pallet rack position. The approach protects your sku quality with minimal cost. An example is chocolate skus & (2) *Your Highest Storage Position Is A Secured Position*. In all storage concepts, in a storage area your highest rack positions increase an employee difficulty to access positions. A tall pallet position security feature occurs in a conventional warehouse building and is especially true for a VNA forklift truck tall rack warehouse with least a 40 ft high ceiling & requires a VNA forklift truck to access your highest positions. To protect your high value skus in your storage area, for your high value skus your WMS computer or inventory control program has a flag that suggests for a receiving clerk to direct a sku deposit transaction to a high pallet rack position. Features are high value sku security with a minimal cost.

SG 11. How Your Carton Or Pallet Faces In A Storage Position

How your carton, pallet & GOH faces in a storage position (sku orientation) is a major position and vehicle design consideration. Most cartons, pallets & GOH have a rectangle shape with a long & short dimension. When a carton, GOH or pallet sku is placed in a position with a rectangle short side facing an aisle, there is an increase sku positions per ln. ft., easy to complete a WMS scan transaction with a wrap around label that faces an aisle, with a short travel distance & time between two skus, improves employee productivity & with a short load beam length, less potential for carton or pallet deflection with a lower rack cost. When a sku isn in a position with a long dimension facing an aisle, the results are longer travel distance & time to complete a storage transaction, fewer positions per aisle ln ft & longer load beam length, greater potential for carton or pallet deflection & higher rack cost.

SG 12. Lock Your Pallet Onto A Storage Position Load Beams

Lock your pallet onto your storage rack load beams concept is a storage rack & pallet bottom deck board concept that locks a pallet onto your rack load beams. In a medium or high seismic zone, if you desire to secure your pallets in a rack position & permit a forklift truck to complete a transaction, lock a pallet onto rack load beams concept is a consideration. Lock your pallet onto a rack load beam concept has your pallet bottom deck board

37

designed at both fork openings (ends) an open space between the first & second deck boards. The open space has sufficient width for a storage rack front load beam to set in a pallet front deck board opening & a storage rack rear load beam to set in a pallet rear deck board opening. Second design factor is your rack upright post span is design to have front & rear load beams to fit between in a pallet bottom deck board opening. Since a pallet bottom deck board is a nomimal ¼ thick, a 2 pallet bottom deck boards secure a pallet between load beams that restricts a pallet forward or reverse movement & a pallet stringers rest on the load beams. Since a lock pallet stringer rests on your load beams, a lock a pallet onto a rack load beams concept does not diminish a pallet fork opening dimensions. It assures a forklift truck set of forks completes a storage transaction from a pallet position.

SG 13. Two Tall Pallet, Two Pallets Or Slip Sheets On The Floor
Two high pallets, two pallets or two slip sheets on the floor is a floor stack or standard pallet rack concept that has a bottom (floor level) pallet rack position with height for 2 pallets high (1 pallet stacked on another pallet) & elevated pallet rack positions have an opening for 1 pallet. Two pallets high on a floor rack concept is used with palletized skus that have the structural strength to support another full pallet weight. Two pallets on the floor concept requires 1 less load beam pair with clearances and 1 less forklift truck replenishment transaction. For an outside storage concept, it is considered an good rack concept due to lower rack cost (fewer load beams and less installation labor) and for excellent density. Prior to implementation, your rack manufacturer assures that your upright post design or structural strength (additional upright post) supports a 2 tall pallet opening or rack position requires a double upright post design that has an additional cost. If you have pick activity, you assure that your employee picker can access a double stacked pallet top carton. During a forklift truck deposit transaction to a position, the first pallet is set on the floor and your driver completes a WMS scan transaction (100A) and second pallet is set onto the pallet top and your driver completes a WMS scan transaction (100A). Features are (1) with a pick operation, one less forklift truck pallet replenishment transaction, (2) standard pallet rack upright post structural strength to support the additional height that could require an additional upright support structural member, anchored posts and is approved by your rack manufacturer, (3) with one less load beam level, lower rack cost, (4) improved space utilization and in an aisle, increases storage density, (5) used with a WA or NA forklift truck & standard pallet rack, reduces an overall stacking height by a nomimal 12 in., & (6) for pallet WMS identification tracking some WMS computer program modification.

SG 14. Tall (Full Height) Or Short (1/2 High Height) Storage Position Heights
Tall (full height) or short (1/2 high height) pallet position height is a storage rack design with two different rack bay opening heights and locates a specific dimensioned position as the top or bottom position. With a human controlled WA, NA or VNA forklift truck, a set of forks has a load back rest. When handling a short pallet and a back rest height exceeds a pallet height, you require a tall pallet position for a clearance to complete a transaction. When your full high pallet becomes a ½ high pallet and to improve your storage space utilization, your forklift truck driver transfers a ½ pallet from a full high rack position to a ½ high pallet position. To assure access to high pallet positions with maximum space utilization & rack structural strength, your rack design has your short positions at the base (floor level) & tall positions the top (highest level). Tall pallets have a light load weight & most short pallets have heavy load weight that matches a forklift truck load weight reduction at maximum elevation above the floor.

SG 15. Stack Your Non-Stackables
Stack your non-stackables is a concept that is used to allow your to contain your fragile, crushable or non-supportable skus in a stackable container. With your non-stackable skus in a stackable container, your storage area has similar operational features as a 3 or 4 high & 3 or 4 deep floor stack concept. Your stackable container options are (1) *Tier Rack Or Metal Frames* that are connected at the top & set on a pallet. For best results a nail secures each tier rack leg to a pallet (2) *Four-Wall & Bottom Wire Mesh Container With Fork Openings* & (3) *Stacking Frames* with four upward extending legs connect at a top & fork opening on the bottom that permits hand stack cartons or to place a full pallet into a stacking frame. Stacking frame options are (a) full length fork sleeves to minimize a metal frame sliding on a metal set of forks, (b) when not being used nestable frames & (c) plastic wrapped or rubber bands to secure skus onto a pallet. Features are improves your space & cube utilization,

minimizes sku damage especially with a container wrapped in plastic, increased storage density per aisle, interfaces with a WA or NA forklift truck & difficult to use with a WMS computer program.

SG 16. 1, 2 Or 3 Pallets Wide
1, 2, or 3 pallets wide is a standard pallet rack option with 3 pallets in a rack bay. When you have low or medium volume skus, an option is to have a sku palletized onto 40 long (stringer) by 32 wide (fork opening) with your rack bay load beam length for 3 pallets. Features are increases sku hit concentration and density, improves space utilization and enhances position occupancy.

SG 17. Narrow Aisle (NA) Forklift Truck Bottom Level Storage Position Is Floor Level Or Up & Over
A NA forklift truck bottom storage position has two options. With a floor level concept, bottom position pallets are set on a floor. *Floor Level* pallet concept with a straddle forklift truck requires 5 to 6 ins open space between 2 pallets & pallet and upright post. An open space permits a forklift truck straddles to enter a bottom level position and complete a storage transaction. Features are (1) adds 15 to 18 ins to each rack bay horizontal dimension, (2) longer rack load beam length that creates low space utilization and due to open space in each rack bay and a forklift truck driver assures a truck straddles engulf a floor level pallet lower employee productivity & (3) creates a long rack row. *Up & Over* concept has a bottom position pallets set on a load beam pair that have a 6 in open space between a floor & load beam bottom. With the concept, to complete a transaction a NA forklift truck straddles go under load beams. An open space & bottom storage position load beam adds 12 ins to a rack vertical stack dimension. Features are (1) due minimal space in a rack bay and short load beam length improves employee productivity, (2) creates a long rack row, (3) additional 12 ins per rack level that creates low vertical space utilization & (4) additional load beam cost.

Storage Positions Ideas (SP 1 – SP 18)
SP 1. Single Deep Or Dense Storage Position Concepts are your two basic storage concepts are (1) *Single Storage Position* is a storage concept with one deep position that has all WMS identified pallets in a WMS identified rack position face an aisle. With a one deep concept, at a WMS identified position an employee, forklift truck completes WMS identified pallet transaction. One deep concept has 85% utilization, forklift truck direct access to all WMS identified pallets, assures FIFO sku rotation, good storage density per aisle & with ability to enclose a rack bay in a wire meshed or solid enclosure, it is frequently used in flammable or pressurized sku storage areas. Single deep features are pallet rack position that is in a single deep rack row with an aisle on one side/both sides, an aisle on one side and wall or back to back single deep rack rows with an aisle on each rack row front and are serviced by an employee controlled forklift truck. In a building with at least a 20 ft. high clear ceiling, you use a WA forklift truck, in a building with a 20 to 40 ft. clear ceiling, you use a NA forklift truck and in a building with a 40- to 60-ft. high clear ceiling, your use a VNA forklift truck. A single deep rack row provides access to all pallets, low density (i.e., fewer skus per sq. ft,), FIFO sku rotation, a large sq. ft. facility, uses a basic WMS program & it easy to complete a specific pallet deposit & withdrawal transactions & (2) *Dense Storage Position* concept is a storage concept with 2 or more deep pallet positions per lane that increases density and fire sprinkler cost. To complete a transaction, it requires additional forklift truck driver time. There is one position in the front & additional positions behind the front pallet. An employee controlled forklift truck completes a pallet first transaction to a first/interior position and additional transactions are made to the other positions. With most dense storage operations, pallets in a dense concept lane/bay are the same pallets/skus. To track a pallet/sku WMS ID most WMS programs require modification such as a WMS ID substitution or position directory. Floor stack, drive-in & drive-through, push-back, gravity/air flow, mobile rack dense concepts are serviced by a WA forklift truck or NA forklift truck. A double reach NA forklift truck services a two-deep rack concept. A VNA forklift truck services two deep or gravity/air flow rack concepts. With most dense applications a position (lane or bay) has lower utilization factor due to over time an increase of vacate positions that are created from fewer pallets in a lane positions. It is difficult to achieve a FIFO rotation. Some concepts require one deposit and withdrawal transaction aisle or two aisles for separate deposit and withdrawal aisles. Dense concept has high sq. ft. or space utilization with fewer aisles.

SP 2. Single Deep Pallet Rack Positions

A standard pallet storage rack is a single deep design that has 1, 2, or 3 pallets in a rack opening, level or bay. Pallet number per rack bay is determined by a pallet width and load-beam length. In most operations, the lowest pallet in a vertical bay is placed on the floor and other pallets in a vertical rack bay are placed on a pair of load beams. In all forklift truck operations, your single deep layout has (1) *One Standard Pallet Rack Row* with one side that faces an aisle for transaction completion and other side faces a wall or has netting due to an adjacent aisle or (2) *Back To Back Standard Pallet Rack Rows* with a 8 to 12 in. flue space between each row back side and front side faces an aisle for transaction completion. In a WA or NA forklift truck operation, there is a 3 to 6 in. clearance between a pallet and an upright post, between two pallets and between a pallet top and next level load beam bottom. If a NA forklift truck is used with a pallet 40 ft. opening facing the aisle is placed on the floor, at least 5 in. is allowed between a pallet and rack upright post, between 2 pallets and between a pallet top and next level load beam bottom. An option with a NA forklift is to place the lowest pallet level onto a pair of load beams that allows a NA forklift truck straddles to travel under the load beam. The feature reduces 5 in. to a standard clearance space. With a VNA forklift truck rack design, a rack bay has two vertical upright frames, each rack bay has two load beams support pallets and are attached to upright frames that reduces potential damage to upright post base plates and anchor bolts. In all pallet rack operations, to provide good stability, there is a minimum of one pair of load beams on the first level and a second pair on an upright frame top. Many conventional rack installations are 3 or 4 pallet bays high. With tall racks, rack bays are at least 4 or 6 levels high.

In a WA or NA forklift truck operation with standard pallet racks, to assist highest position forklift truck transaction, your rack design allows upright post/frame height to extend 3 to 4 in. above the load beam top. During a forklift truck transaction, the upright post extension serves as a forklift driver guide for proper pallet placement onto the top load beams.

With a standard pallet rack, WMS program, and a WA, NA or VNA man-up forklift truck position ID locations are on a load beam that supports a position. A position ID on a load beam ensures forklift truck driver or bar code scanner line-of-sight and with a man-down forklift truck operation for load-beam levels above a forklift truck driver's line-of-sight, position IDs are stacked on a load beam under rack pallet right side or upright frame post and are within a forklift truck driver or hand-held bar code scanner line-of-sight. With a man-up VNA forklift truck, each position ID is on a load beam that supports a pallet.

SP 3. Cantilever Rack
Cantilever rack is single deep position that is designed to handle long pallets with skus, such as pipe. A cantilever rack is designed as a single-arm row or double-arm rows. Arms extend outward from an upright post and create pallet positions. Cantilever pallet positions are serviced by a WA or NA forklift truck. Cantilever racks permit a FIFO sku rotation, excellent storage density, sku accessibility, and 85% position utilization. A cantilever rack design ensures WA/NA forklift truck line-of-sight for pallet position identifications. Employee or bar code reading of pallet and position IDs, a forklift truck driver uses the same procedure as standard pallet racks.

SP 4. Bridge Rack Above Doors & Main Traffic Aisles
Bridge rack is a single deep rack concept that is used over your receiving/ship dock and storage area passage-way doors and main traffic aisles. If you require additional space, a rack bridge is an opportunity to provide additional single deep pallet rack positions. If your floor to ceiling clearance and door open travel path does not interfere with a rack bridge (single deep rack bay upright posts and load beams) is installed in a door bay. The posts are anchored to the floor and protected with guards and load beams have front to rear members with a clear space between your floor surface and load beam bottom for a forklift truck entry/exit between your dock and vendor truck. If you desire a wider aisle than your standard load beam, with your pallet weight and aisle width specifications, your rack manufacturer calculates the preferred standard load beam. The positions are used for empty pallets, ship supply items or obsolete skus. If potential skus falling to the floor is a potential problem, plastic wrap pallets or add a removable barrier to a pallet position front.

SP 5. Floor Stack Or Block Storage
Floor Stack or Block Storage Design is a dense concept that has pallet that are placed directly on the floor or onto another pallet. A floor-stacked design provides a maximum of 6 –10 pallets deep per storage lane. A lane is a single

lane or back-to-back lanes.   Due to pallets leaning and forklift truck pallet placement variance on the floor and on top of another pallet, longer or deeper lanes reduce WA or NA forklift truck's ability to complete transactions with good employee productivity. To utilize air space, additional pallets are stacked on other pallets to a maximum of 3 to 4 pallet height. To ensure good WA or NA forklift truck driver productivity and minimal sku damage, 3 to 5 in. of open space is allowed between two lanes. To ensure accurate pallet placement in a floor stack lane, open space is painted with white or yellow paint line full lane depth to guide a forklift truck driver. If a slip sheet on a pallet is used in a floor stack design and a slip sheet lip remains on a unit load, at least 6 in. is allowed between two lanes. A floor stack pallet has cartons with capability to support a stacked weight and a pallet/sku at an aisle position is the same pallet/sku for an entire floor stack lane. A full a floor stack concept provides the highest density with lowest cost but poor pallet accessibility. A 60% utilization factor is used to determine a pallet lane and position number and is used due to honeycombing (vacant positions in a vertical stack) and vacant positions in a lane depth. This is due to normal WA or NA forklift truck transaction activity. In a floor stack design, to make a pallet transaction a forklift truck enters a lane from aisle 'A', travels to a position, completes a transaction and backs out from a lane to the same aisle 'A'. When a floor stack area is designed, pallet number per lane is varied to bury building columns or between lanes and pallet fork opening and pallet identification faces a main aisle.   Floor stack has a LIFO sku rotation, handles a high through-put volume, and with a wide stacking aisle, interfaces with WA or NA forklift trucks.

Floor stack options are (1) 90-degree floor stack pallets with pallet fork opening face perpendicular to a main aisle and with a 10 or more pallets deep and (2) 45-degree floor stack pallets that are set at a slight angle to a main aisle with 3 to 4 pallets deep, allows a minimum right-angle forklift truck turning aisle, one-way forklift truck traffic and fewer pallet openings per aisle.

To track a WMS identified pallet in a floor stacked location, as a WMS identified pallet is placed into a position, a forklift truck driver scans WMS pallet and position IDs. Scans are sent on-line or delayed to your WMS computer program for inventory file update. In a floor stack concept, WMS identified pallet considerations are (1) How to ensure that a floor stack lane has proper ID and (2) To complete a WMS computer program suggested WMS identified pallet withdrawal transaction.

WMS identified pallets in a floor stack lane do not have the same sequence that are suggested for withdrawal by a WMS computer program.   WMS identified pallet deposit and actual pallet sequence in a floor stack lane has the first WMS identified pallet that is a pallet on the floor level and in a floor stack deepest pallet position from a main aisle. In a floor stack lane, the last pallet is the highest pallet on a floor stack adjacent to an aisle. In a standard WMS computer program, when a WMS computer program suggests a withdrawal of a pallet from a floor stack lane, a pallet that is adjacent to a main aisle is the first pallet accessed by forklift truck driver. A driver scans the first pallet's ID but it is not the corresponding WMS pallet ID that was suggested by a WMS computer program.

To comply with a WMS computer program and floor stack design, floor stack pallet position ID options are to have pallet lane position IDs that are (1) ceiling hung above each lane with limits to a floor stack height, (2) embedded in the floor in the front of each lane middle and (3) attached to an upright post between two floor stack lanes that corresponds with the open space between two lanes.

SP 6. How To Reduce Honey Comb Or Poor Dense Storage Utilization
Honey comb occurs in floor stack, drive-in rack, drive through rack, push pack rack and gravity/air flow rack dense concepts. When your pallet quantity is less than your dense lane position number, you have potential for honey comb or poor lane utilization that is due to vacate position number in a lane. In a floor stack dense position concept, *Honey Comb* occurs in a vertical stack due vacate positions such as only 3 pallets high in a 4 pallet high position. With or without (employee suggested pallet put-away) a WMS computer program to reduce honey comb or poor dense utilization, you have a pallet number that matches your dense lane pallet number.   For a pallet quantity that exceeds or less than your dense lane number, you have your WMS computer program or employee placed pallets into a single deep rack position. When you have withdrawal transactions, you withdraw pallets from a dense concept. At a sales program end , any residual pallet quantity is transferred from a dense concept (partial full lane) to a single deep pallet positions.

SP 7. Standard Pallet Rack Row Behind One Deep Pallet Floor Stack (5/6 Plts Is Better Than 4 Plts)

Standard pallet rack row behind one deep floor stack concept is used in a WA or NA forklift truck rack and floor stack concept that is used for a sku with at least 6 pallets and a sku that does not have the structural strength to support a 3 high pallet stack. A standard 4 pallet floor concept has 2 deep pallets & 2 high pallets. Features are no cost, medium density and low space utilization. A hybrid one deep pallet rack behind a floor stack concept has (1) rear positions as a 3/4 pallet high one deep rack row & (2) front positions as 2 high floor stack positions. Concept options are (a) single high front pallet or (b) double stacked pallets with top carton within an employee picker's reach. Your options are (A) one pallet for each rack position that 4 high positions or (B) rack floor position with two high stacked pallets. Features are some rack cost, improves sdensity and space utilization & both concepts interface with a WA or NA forklift truck.

SP 8. Pyramid Floor Stack
Pyramid floor stack is a floor stack concept that is used for your ship supply items or unstable skus with a pallet dimension that restricts pallet rack position use, improves space utilization & minimizes sku damage. Most ship supply items are cardboard cartons, sheet paper or filler material, tape or band material, label paper, sheet paper for printers & envelopes. In most operations, ship supply skus are not tracked by your WMS/inventory control program, usually have a safety stock & with cardboard cartons with an excessive over-hang on a pallet. Palletized collapsed ship cartons have a bowed or concaved top that creates difficulty to stack 3 pallets high due to a forklift truck difficulty to have a set of forks enter a top pallet fork opening and a 3 high pallet stack has a tendency for tilting to one side. To improve your cube or space utilization & enhance your density per aisle, with a same ship carton/sku a pyramid pallet floor stack concept permits 1 to 2 floor stacked pallets that are side by side & becomes a pyramid base for another pallet that is placed in the middle of a 2 pallet base. In the middle of a 2 pallet base means that 1/2 of a top pallet is setting on 1 bottom pallet half & top pallet other half is setting on another bottom pallet half. With a pyramid arrangement, a pyramid top pallet is stable & permits a forklift truck set of forks to enter a top pallet fork opening that minimize sku damage and improves employee productivity.

SP 9. Portable Containers, Tier Racks & Stack Frames
A dense design uses portable containers, tier racks or a stack frames for non-stack-able skus. If vendor delivered cartons are placed in a floor stack design are crushable or are not square, a container, tier rack, or stack frame design optimizes cube space by making a uniform unit load. All the devices have fork openings with a tier rack placed (nailed for security) on a standard wood pallet and with a stack frame you consider two full length fork sleeves that during a transport activity to reduce a metal frame sliding on a metal set of forks. It is common practice to have one sku per pallet storage lane & stack. In a storage design with a WMS computer program, a pallet ID is attached (permanently/temporarily) with a sleeve, tape, or adhesive label to a container, stacking frame or tier rack structural member. During a put-away transaction, a forklift truck driver requires additional time to assure a container, tier rack or a stack frame has proper alignment for deposit on a base container, tier rack or stack frame. In a lane, each sku ID faces a main aisle; forklift truck practices & scan transactions are the same as those with a floor stack & WMS program.

SP 10. Double-Deep Or Two Deep Reach
A two-deep or double-deep pallet rack design is a dense storage design that is used with a two-deep NA forklift truck design. With few exceptions, a two-deep pallet rack components & design characteristics are similar for a standard pallet rack design. A rack upright frame and load beam structural strength is determined by pallet weight and desired flexibility (for reusing upright frames at another location) and are floor anchored. Two-deep rack options are (1) long frame with four load beams & two upright frames or (2) standard upright frame with four standard load beams & four upright frames. With both two-deep rack concepts, your interior position is determined by your NA deep reach forklift truck set of forks extension or stroke. Double deep rack concept options are *Up-&-Over* (bottom/floor pallet level is raised on load beams above the floor) design for transaction completion has an open space (5 to 6 in.) permits forklift truck straddles to pass under bottom load beams and to turn in a narrow aisle. An aisle allows easy pallet transactions at any rack level because the straddles are not required to straddle a floor-level pallet. The up & over design handles pallets with narrow widths or pallet widths that exceed the distance between forklift truck straddles. When compared to a standard two deep design, up & over rack design has a

narrower rack opening that increases positions per rack row but increases rack cost with additional rack upright post height and highest pallet is 12 in. higher building height due to first level load beam and open space & *Bottom Pallets Set On The Floor* design has the bottom pallet set on the floor and all pallets in elevated rack positions are directly aligned with a floor pallet. This reduces forklift truck driver productivity because additional time is required to line up a forklift truck straddles between floor-level pallets. When compared to up & over concept, standard two deep concept requires additional forklift straddle space in a rack bay that means a wider load beam with fewer positions per rack row and top pallet is 12 in. lower due to bottom pallet sets on the floor.

A two-deep pallet design is a dense design that stores the same sku in interior and exterior positions. To ensure proper position ID, position labels are placed on load beams or upright posts. To complete position ID and pallet ID scans, a forklift truck driver uses a substitute method or floor stack design and pallet iID directory design. For additional approaches & information on ID or location directory design, please see the section on floor stack.

SP 11. Drive-In Racks

A drive in-rack dense storage design is used for non-self-supporting cartons on a pallet. A drive-in rack has pallet rack lanes and is a dense pallet design. Drive-in rack lane pallet positions are used for a single sku. Rack components are upright frames, upright posts, support arms, guide rails, support rails, and side, top, and back bracing. A drive-in rack bottom lane has bottom pallets (one sku) set on the floor and elevated lane pallets (same sku) set on rack structural members. Each elevated pallet position level has two support arms and rails. Support arms are attached to each upright post. A drive rack lane is 2 –10 positions deep and 3 – 4 pallets high. A drive-in rack layout provides medium to good density but poor pallet accessibility; sku rotation is LIFO. A drive-in rack is designed as either a single row or back-to-back rows. Drive-in rack design allows distance between a rack second level lane/structural members (support arms and rails) and floor height that permits a WA or NA forklift truck overhead guard/collapsed mast and as required NA straddles to enter and exit a floor-level lane. A second drive-in deep rack design parameter is that a forklift truck mast is able to travel through the open distance between an elevated drive-in rack lane two pallet support arms & rails and open space between two rack upright posts allow forklift truck travel in a drive-in rack lane. During a storage transaction, a drive-in rack position rail serves as a pallet guide and assures a pallet is placed properly in a position.

Drive-in rack lanes are best designed between two building columns. The number of pallets is varied to place building columns within a flue space that is between back-to-back drive-in rack rows. When a drive-in rack design requires fire sprinklers and a forklift truck mast, overhead guard and straddle clearances. Most drive-in rack designs are designed with each pallet fork opening sides facing an aisle. To complete a pallet transaction in a drive-in rack design, a forklift truck enters a floor-level lane from aisle 'A', completes a transaction and backs out into the same aisle 'A'. Due to this operational characteristic, a drive-in rack design handles a medium volume and has a LIFO sku rotation. In a drive-in rack concept with a WMS program, position IDs are placed on upright posts and have same ID design as floor stack and pallet ID location directory designs. The design also permits a forklift truck driver to use pallet ID substitution. As a truck driver faces a rack bay, a right hand upright frame has a pallet position ID a pallet on an upright frame left side.

SP 12. Drive-Through or Drive Thru-Racks

A drive-through or drive thru-rack design is a dense design that handles non-self-supporting cartons on a pallet. Drive-through racks and storage lanes are used for a single sku with same rack components and design characteristics as a drive-in rack design with a 66% utilization factor. One rack component difference is that drive-through racks use top bracing rather than back bracing. Drive-through racks are designed as stand-alone rack rows with forklift truck aisles on a rack structure both sides. There are no back-to-back rack rows designs. Drive-through racks handle a medium volume & sku rotation is LIFO or FIFO. With a LIFO sku rotation, a warehouse and WMS computer program has pallet deposits that are made from aisle 'A' and pallet withdrawals are made from aisle 'B'. With a LIFO sku rotation and WMS computer program features are the same as a drive-in rack that has a forklift truck complete storage transaction from aisle 'A'.

With a FIFO sku rotation, a forklift truck enters a drive-through rack lane from aisle 'A', completes a transaction to an elevated lane and drives-through a rack lane into aisle 'B'. After all elevated pallet lanes are full, a floor-level lane is handled as a drive-in rack lane. An alternative procedure in a FIFO sku rotation is to exit a storage lane by driving without a sku through a drive-through lane and to exit into aisle 'B'. To retrieve a pallet, a forklift truck enters a rack lane from aisle 'B', retrieves an sku and backs out from a drive-through lane into aisle 'B'. Drive-through racks have medium density and poor pallet accessibility. In a a drive-through rack design with a WMS computer program, position identifications are placed on upright posts. With a 'LIFO' transaction, a WMS computer program suggests an sku for withdrawal from a drive-thru rack, a forklift truck driver uses a pallet identification substitution method. Drive-through pallet withdrawal transaction creates non-productive forklift truck driver time because a driver walks to a pallet front to scan a label.

SP 13. Gravity/Air-Flow Racks

A gravity ('flow-through' or 'air-flow') rack design is a stand-alone rack design that uses aisle 'A' for pallet deposit and aisle 'B' for pallet withdrawal. Per your pallet quantity, each flow lane is allocated to one sku or one sku is allocated to multiple lanes. Thus, in a 4-level pallet gravity rack, the options are (1) one sku per each pallet flow lane in a stack means a 3-high flow rack design has one sku per flow-rack lane or 3 different skus and (2) one sku in all pallet flow lanes in a stack.

A gravity flow rack design has upright frames, upright posts, braces, brakes, end stops, and skate wheel or roller conveyors that make up the individual pallet flow storage lanes. With WA or NA forklift truck, pallet flow lanes are 3 or 4 levels high. In a VNA forklift truck warehouse, pallet lanes are designed 5 to 8 pallet lanes high. Pallet weight and height determines pallet flow rack lane slope and pitch. A pallet height and length ratio is 3:1. If pallets exceed this ratio, there is a potential for uneven pallet flow through or hang-ups in a flow lane. A gravity flow design is designed with 3–20 pallets per lane. In most flow rack designs, a pallet is placed on a slave pallet to ensure smooth flow through a lane. In some designs, pallet flow lanes have entry guides and forklift truck wheel inverted 'V' shaped stop, conveyor rollers have flanged wheels that act as guides for pallet flow through a rack and roller stop device to have controlled pallet flow/travel speed through a flow lane. To prevent rack damage, lane entry guides, upright post protectors, forklift truck stops, and sufficient turning aisle widths are designed for entry and exit position has a device to pull a gap between a discharge pallet and next pallet in the flow lane.

A flow rack design uses a forklift truck for access to a deposit side. After a forklift truck in aisle 'A' places a pallet onto a conveyor, gravity/air and a pallet weight move a pallet through a flow lane to an end of a lane. Pallets/skus are withdrawn by forklift trucks in aisle 'B' from a flow lane end and next pallet in a lane flows index to a withdrawal position. In a long pallet flow rack design, pallet brakes and a sku separator (at an exit position) are installed in a flow lane to reduce line pressure and sku damage. A pallet flow design that indexes pallet movement from a deposit position to a withdrawal position allows each flow lane to accommodate one sku per lane. Features are permits flow racks with two aisles, high density & fair pallet accessibility. In a gravity flow design with a WMS program, as a pallet is transferred to a flow lane, a forklift truck driver has line-of-sight to a pallet WMS ID. Flow rack pallet position IDs are placed on upright posts and have the same pallet position ID arrangement as a floor stack. Because a WMS computer program suggests skus for withdrawal, a forklift truck driver uses a pallet ID substitution method for withdrawals as outlined in the floor stack section. Unfortunately, a gravity rack pallet withdrawal transaction causes nonproductive forklift truck driver time: To obtain pallet ID, a driver walks to front of a pallet.

SP 14. Push-Back Racks

A push-back rack design is a stand-alone dense rack design with a single aisle. A push-back pallet rack design has the same components and design characteristics as a gravity flow rack with some exceptions. A push-back rack design is designed as a single rack row that is installed along a building wall, in a location that allows for an aisle (for a forklift truck to perform entry and withdrawal transactions) or as back-to-back rack rows. A push-back design is 3 to 4 pallets deep and 3 to 4 pallets high with one sku per all lanes or 3 to 4 different skus per push-back rack bay. To complete a deposit, a forklift truck places a pallet against an existing pallet in a push-back position. When an existing pallet is sufficiently pushed back into a lane, it creates a required new pallet space for a forklift truck to lower a pallet onto a flow lane. To withdraw a pallet, a WA/NA forklift truck raises a discharge pallet 2 to 3 in. above a push-back conveyor and backs out a pallet from the lane. As a pallet is removed from a flow lane, gravity moves the next pallet into a flow lane exit/aisle position. The design permits 66% lane utilization & a LIFO sku rotation. A push-back rack provides good density, fair accessibility, handles a low to a medium volume, and each lane handles one sku. A push-back rack design has two options (1) *Standard Conveyor Push-Back* rack design does not require brakes but requires end stops on both ends of flow lanes & (2) *Telescoping Push-Back Rack* design has 3 carriages that ride on a set of tracks. After a forklift truck places a pallet on a carriage, a forklift truck pushes a carriage forward that has a carriage travel on tracks into an interior pallet position. With no pallet on a carriage, by gravity force a deepest empty carriage moves forward and nests over a carriage that is adjacent to an aisle.

In a push-back design, position IDs are placed upright posts and has the same ID arrangement as a gravity-flow rack design and ID location directory design. It also permits a forklift truck driver use an ID substitution design. Because a WMS computer program suggests skus for withdrawal, a forklift truck driver has to use an ID substitution method for withdrawals as outlined in the floor stack section. A push-back rack pallet withdrawal transaction permits line-of-sight for pallet ID.

SP 15. Mobile/Sliding Racks
A mobile or sliding rack design is similar to a standard rack design, except that (a) it is a dense design, (b) it has fewer forklift truck aisles and rack rows & (c) aisles and rack rows move to create forklift truck transaction aisles. Mobile racks are standard single deep-pallet rack rows or back-to-back rack rows on moveable bases. A mobile rack design has two ends positions as fixed single deep rack rows that do not move. Interior rack rows are mobile rack rows that move to create a forklift truck transaction aisle. All rack rows are placed in an arrangement that is 90 degrees or perpendicular to a main traffic aisle. A mobile rack is designed with nominal 6 back-to-back moveable rows, 1 forklift truck aisle and at each end is a single deep rack row. Mobile racks are 4/5 pallets high with 1 pallet deep. If sprinklers are required in the racks, this is added by your rack vendor.

For access to a position, a mobile rack moves to a side and creates a WA/NA forklift truck transaction aisle between 2 rack rows. A forklift truck enters an aisle, performs a required transaction and exists into a main traffic aisle. After a transaction completion, mobile rack sections are moved to create a new aisle between 2 different rack rows. Sensing devices on moveable rack base bottom section sense an object or employee in a mobile rack section travel path & if there is an object, a rack section stops. The feature prevents equipment damage and employee injuries. With one access aisle, mobile racks provide high position density and good accessibility. A mobile rack design has a 85% utilization factor and handles low to medium volume due to slow rack movement. A WMS computer program and batched transactions for each row improves forklift truck transaction productivity. In a mobile rack design with a WMS computer program to ensure WA or NA forklift truck line-of-sight, pallet position IDs and pallet IDs have the same arrangement and scan procedures as standard racks. For maximum forklift truck driver productivity and minimal mobile rack movement to complete deposit transactions, a WMS computer program assigns one sku to mobile rack row vacate positions that face one aisle. When required to withdraw pallets, your WMS computer program suggests pallets for an aisle with mobile rack faces on both sides that minimizes mobile rack movement, maximum access to suggested skus and high employee productivity.

SP 18. An Aisle Between A Dense Storage Row & Single Deep Rack Row
Mix Single Deep & Dense Storage Positions
For maximum storage area flexibility, your 'A'/fast moving sku storage area has a mix of single deep and dense storage positions. With an aisle between your single deep rack rowtions and dense storage row options are
Aisle & Rack Design With A Short Travel Distance To Your Pick/Ship Dock Area With Dense Storage Positions On One Aisle Side & Single Deep Pallet Rack Position On An Aisle Other Side Features are maximum storage position flexibility to handle few pallets that exceed you dense storage positions, short travel distance to complete customer orders and short travel distance to re-organize 'A' moving sku at a sku life cycle end from a dense storage concept to single deep pallet rack positions.
An Aisle With A Short Travel Distance To Your Pick/Ship Dock Area With Dense Storage Positions On An Aisle Both Sides Features dense storage positions are short travel distance to your pick/ship area, creates potential for high honey comb occurrences in dense storage lanes and when required to re-organize 'A' moving sku at a sku life cycle end long travel distances to move a sku from dense storage positions to a single deep pallet position.

Pallet & Slip Sheet Ideas (PSS 1 – PSS6)
PSS 1. Sku Over-Hang A Pallet

Sku over-hang a pallet is carton or bag that extends beyond a pallet top deck boards. In most concepts, a pallet floor or rack concept design parameter allows for a carton or bag to extend 2 ins beyond each deck board side. When designing a pallet position for a 40 in wide pallet deck with an over-hang allowance, a pallet floor stack lane or rack position is 44 ins wide. No sku over-hang and an over-hang allowance assure good forklift truck productivity, good space utilization & minimal sku damage. If a carton or bag over-hangs or extends beyond your pallet over-hang allowance, there is potential for low forklift truck productivity, sku damage & with 1 pallet in a position & unable to use an adjacent position, poor space utilization. Prior to your storage area floor stack or rack position design, complete a pallet survey to determine your sku over-hang dimensions.

PSS 2. Employee Reach Height Or Vendor Pallet Height

Employee reach height or vendor pallet height are pallet height options. If a carton on a pallet bottom layer has sufficient structural strength to support a carton pallet TI (cartons per layer) & HI (carton layers high) & a delivery trailer has weight capacity to handle a heavier pallet, a tall carton stacked pallet is an option. An employee reach height (easily handle a carton) has a range from 5 ft 6 ins to 6 ft high. When compared to an average vendor pallet height of 4 ft 6 ins, an employee reach pallet height is 18 ins or above an average vendor pallet height. An employee reach pallet height results are for same sku inventory quantity are (1) fewer pallets, (2) fewer transactions, (3) improved employee productivity, (4) fewer positions, (5) less clearance space & (6) improved space utilization. For a new or remodel operation, pallet height & weight are rack structural member, forklift truck & building floor design facts.

PSS 3. How To Handle Your Slip Sheet Lip

How to handle your slip sheet lip is a concept to remove from or secure a slip sheet lip to a sku side that minimizes sku damage & improves space utilization. If a slip sheet is received at your dock, your slip sheet lip options are (1) slip sheet with a lip requires a wider lane or position due to a slip sheet lip is considered pallet over-hang. Features are poor space utilization, lowers employee productivity & increases potential sku damage or (2) for storage, with tape a slip sheet lip is secured to a sku side and after withdrawal for a CO in your ship area, the tape is removed that allows a slip sheet lip to used in a ship activity. If a slip sheet is not used for another transaction, in a receiving lane, an employee with a knife cuts a lip from a slip sheet and disposes a removed lip into the trash. A slip sheet sku with no lip requires a narrower position, improves employee productivity & minimizes potential sku damage.

PSS 4. Slip Sheet/Pallets Two High

Floor level slip sheets or pallets two high in a floor stack area has your activity double stack two slip sheets/pallets in all floor positions. Prior to implementation, you assure that your bottom level slip sheet or pallet sku has structural strength to support the additional weight and your double high pallet/slip sheet in a position and allows an employee to complete a pick transaction. During a forklift truck deposit transaction to a position, the first pallet/slip sheet is set on the floor and your forklift truck driver completes a WMS scan transaction (100B) that has your WMS computer program use for a second transaction and second pallet/slip sheet is set onto the floor level pallet and your forklift truck driver completes a WMS scan transaction (100A) that has your WMS computer program use for a second pallet/slip sheet transaction. Features are (1) one less forklift driver truck replenishment transaction, (2) sku has structural strength to support the additional weight that could require additional carton side wall support structural strength, (3) improved space utilization and (4) to track a pallet/slip sheet deposit to a position and to ensure withdrawal of a pallet/slip sheet ID from a position, using two high pallet /slip sheet storage with a WMS program uses pallet/slip sheet ID substitution or directory location program.

PSS 5. Ribbed Pallet

In a pallet operation, a ribbed pallet is a special designed pallet that is used with a slip sheet. A ribbed pallet is designed with basically a standard pallet with a ribbed deck. A ribbed deck has a series or full depth ribs and open spaces between two ribs. The open space permits a slip sheet tines to enter and assure a slip sheet is properly located over a pallet for deposit a slip sheet onto the ribs. When required to complete a transaction, your options are remove a ribbed pallet to a transfer position for a forklift truck with a tine slip sheet device to remove a slip sheet from a ribbed pallet for slip sheet (1) direct transfer onto a delivery vehicle or (2) transfer onto a pallet for placement onto a delivery vehicle. Feature is a forklift truck completes a transaction with no slip sheet lip handling.

PSS 6. Standard Pallet

Standard wood pallet is used in a storage operation with an employee controlled forklift truck and are available as *Throw-Away Pallet* is purchased with your skus from your vendor is sent to your storage operation. After your operation has made effective pallet use, a pallet is thrown in the trash. A throw-away pallet is less expensive and has thin bottom and top deck boards and narrow stringers.

Rental or Exchange Pallet is used by your vendor or customer location & has the same operational specifications as your warehouse. Upon receipt at your warehouse, your warehouse exchanges a good pallet number from your operation that matches your sku delivery pallet quantity & places a pallet quantity onto your vendor delivery truck.

Pallet Dimensions are determined by your (1) forklift truck set of forks length and type, (2) sku dimensions, weight and palletize patterns and (3) storage position dimensions. Your important pallet dimensions are (a) *Length* is a pallet bearer or stringer dimension that is a pallet depth into a storage position and matches your forklift truck set of fork length. In most American storage operations, a common pallet a pallet has a 48 in length, (b) *Width* is deck board dimension that is a pallet width in a storage position and allows you to place one or two pallets into a rack storage position and has a pallet rest on a forklift truck set of forks. In most American storage operations, a common pallet width has a 40 in. wide, (c) *Height* is the overall height between a pallet top and bottom deck boards that is 5 ½ to 6 in. height is determines your storage position opening & (d) *Fork Opening* is a pallet face that allows a forklift truck set of forks to enter a pallet and lift a pallet. In most storage operations, a common pallet opening has two openings with a 5 to 5 ½ in. height.

Most popular standard pallet designs are (1) *Block Pallet* is a four-way pallet with equally spaced blocks along its length and width. Deck boards are attached to blocks; a block provides good a WMS pallet identification location and allows a front-face or wrap-around WMS ID label. In a drive-in or drive-through rack storage concept, a pallet bottom deck boards spans a position two arms or rails. If a block pallet is used in the standard pallet rack storage area, prior to implementation in a floor or rack storage concept, a block pallet tested in a position. The pallet material determines the identification attachment method, which includes self-adhesive glued, sleeve insert, staple, or tape. If a block material does not accept one of the attachment methods during label attachment tests, the identification may be attached to a carton on a pallet bottom layer & (2) *Stringer Pallet* A large width stringer pallet has two exterior stringers and one interior stringer for top and bottom deck board attachment that create a forklift truck set of forks opening. Small-width stringer pallets have only two exterior stringers. Exterior stringers either are solid or have two notches in a stringer side. Notches are additional set of fork entry openings that permit a forklift truck chisel set of forks to handle a pallet from all four sides. A pallet stringer face provides a good location for WMS program ID that accepts a front face or wrap-around ID label. A stringer pallet is used in single deep or dense floor stack or rack storage concepts.

Storage Position Identification & Routing Pattern Ideas (SPI&SRP 1 - SPI&SRP 18)

SPI&RP 1. What Is Your Storage Aisle Route Or Position Number Pattern

What is your aisle route or position number pattern is a storage area position number route, pattern or sequence between 2 rails, shelf or rack rows that direct an employee, employee controlled forklift truck to sku position for a transaction completion. An aisle routing pattern has an arithmetic progression from an aisle first sku position with the lowest possible position number, through an aisle and to an aisle end or last sku position with the highest possible position number. Aisle number sequence options are (1) *Carton Pick Operation*, an aisle routing sequence has positions with odd numbered last digits on an aisle left side positions (01001, 01003 and so on) & with even numbered last digits on an aisle right side positions (01002, 01004 & so on) & (2) *Handles Pallets In/Out* has each rack row positions on an aisle side with a unique prefix. All positions in an aisle on one side progress is from an aisle first/lowest number to an aisle last/highest number & on an aisle other side a rack row positions have a unique prefix. Example: aisle 1 with position numbers as 01001, 01002 & so on is number sequence for an aisle right side positions & aisle 2 with position number 02001, 02022 & so on is number sequence for an aisle left side positions.

SPI&RP 2. Storage Position Identification On A Rack Upright Post

Storage position ID placed on a rack upright post has a position ID that is placed onto a rack post that improves employee productivity and enhance inventory control. To be effective a position ID, an ID width matches or fits onto a rack post width and faces an aisle. With a 1 pallet or 2 pallets wide rack bay, there is consistent association of a post ID to a position. To help with the post ID to a position, directional arrows or colored labels (borders) assist a forklift truck driver. Feature is used when a load beam front or aisle face does not have sufficient space for an ID label or with a man-down forklift truck to complete elevated storage & bar code scan transactions to assure good inventory tracking. In a VNA forklift truck or HROS truck, additional position IDs are attached to a rack post side at a higher elevation than a sku in a position. As a VNA or HROS truck travels in an aisle, a position ID location above a normal pallet height allows an operator clear view.

SPI&RP 3. Storage Position Number Sequence Is Vertical

Storage position number sequence is vertical in an aisle that is required with WA, NA, VNA forklift trucks and in all storage types (floor stack, standard racks, gravity flow racks, drive-in/drive-thru racks or mobile racks). A position number sequence discreetly identifies one position from another position & for a transaction completion IDs a position for a transaction. Features assure good employee productivity & accurate transaction completion for good inventory control. A vertical number sequence has each position number sequence progress from a bottom/floor level position to a top position (an aisle first position number in a rack bay at a bottom that progressively moves up to a top position). An example is in a rack bay, a bottom position number is 01001A, second level is 01002A, third level 01003A & so to a highest position number on next rack bay, a bottom position number is 02001B, second level is 02002B, third level is 02003B & so to a highest position number & progresses for each rack bay and position in an aisle. Features are uses a 5 digit number with first 2 digits as a rack bay, next 3 digits as position in a rack bay and alpha character IDs level & with an alpha character that means it is used for a concept with 26 vertical positions.

SPI&RP 4. With Two Identifications On One Load Beam Use Directional Arrows & Colors

With two IDs on one load beam, you use directional arrows and colors on your position ID label to identify a position. Two IDs on a load beam are used in a WA, NA, VNA forklift truck operation with bottom pallets on the floor to improve employee productivity & enhance inventory control. In most employee controlled forklift truck warehouses, bottom positions are supported by the floor and all elevated positions are supported with a pair of load beams. With a standard 1 in high and normal width, human/machine readable position ID use a load beam front for position ID attachment. A position front load beam surface faces an aisle with sufficient space for 1 or several positions/IDs attachment & each position label is placed onto a load beam in a consistent & repeated configuration. With 1 position label on a load beam, a position ID label refers to a position above a position label. With 2 position labels on one load beam, a bottom ID label refers to a position below a position ID label & a top ID label refers to a position above a position ID label. If a man-down warehouse has 3 to 4 positions in a rack design, required ID labels are placed onto a load beam in a step configuration that is consistent. With a multiple ID label concept, as you travel down aisle in an arithmetic progression, multiple position ID label configuration has (1) First Position ID label adjacent to a first rack post & is a bottom ID label that refers to a bottom position, (2) Seocnd Position ID label is slightly forward of & above a first position ID label that refers to a first elevated or second high (next) position, (3) Third Position ID label is slightly forward & above a second position ID label that refers to a second elevated or third (next) high position & (4) Fourth Position ID label is slightly forward & above a third position ID label & refers to a third elevated or fourth (next) position. To assist a man-down forklift truck driver to determine each position, with a multiple position ID label configuration on one load beam, for each elevated position, each position ID label has a colored border that is consistent on all load beams. An example: (1) Blue for a first position & bottom ID label, (2) Yellow for a second position & second ID label, (3) Green for a third position & third ID label & (4) Brown for a fourth position or fourth ID label. In addition with a 2 or 3 high position rack, directional arrows are attached to each ID label & refer to an ID label & position location. An example is (1) a first ID label directional arrow points down for a first position, (2) in a two high pallet configuration, second ID label directional arrow points up for second a first position (3) in a three high pallet configuration, second ID label directional arrow is level or parallel to the floor & (4) in a three high pallet configuration, third ID label directional arrow points up for a third position. If your rack concept has two pallets per bay & you attach position ID labels to a rack position, your position ID labels are placed onto a rack post in a stacked configuration. The configuration has bottom position ID label refer to a bottom position, second ID label in a stack refers to a first elevated or second position & so on. Since a rack post is between 2 bays & each bay has 2 unique pallet positions, an aisle first rack post has one from rack bay or an aisle first pallet & bottom position ID label 01001. To assure proper forklift truck instruction, a position ID label directional arrow point to an adjacent position. An aisle second rack post has 2 bottom pallet position ID labels (this configuration occurs for each rack bay to an aisle end) that are (1) 01001 or second pallet from rack bay one with a position ID label directional arrow point to an adjacent position & (2) 02001 or first pallet from rack bay two with a position ID label directional arrow point to an adjacent position. If a rack configuration has multiple elevated positions, then you use a color code & arrow combination & on a rack post have each rack bay in a separate group that is identified.

SPI&RP 5. Sku & Storage Position Identification Large Or Small

Sku & position ID large or small label is a position label size options. In most employee or employee controlled forklift truck operations with a WMS computer program, a sku or position label is a human/machine readable label to assure good inventory control, good employee productivity & accurate transaction completion. Each sku & position label has a human readable position ID alpha characters & digits & machine readable bar code or RF tag symbology. As an employee or employee controlled forklift truck travels in an aisle, position labels are an employee instruction that assures an employee arrives at the suggest position & a sku label assures accurate sku tracking. In most aisles, an employee is 2 to 3 ft from a position label face & moving at a good travel speed, thereby a position label human readable alpha characters & digits have sufficient size for an employee to easily & quickly read position number. To assure good employee label read or productivity, most sku & storage position label human readable alpha characters & digits are 1 to 2 ins high and have sufficient width. In most operations with a WMS computer program, for each transaction, an employee with a gun scanner completes a position & sku machine readable symbology scan transaction. A scan transaction or laser light beam crossing all bar codes is completed from an aisle location that has a range from 2 to 3 ft and has to assure a good read. To have a fast good read, an over squared bar code (total bars and white spaces equals tallest bars) assures increase opportunity for an employee direct laser light beam to cross all bar codes for improve employee productivity.

SPI&RP 6. Flat Or Indented Load Beam

Flat or indented standard pallet rack load beam are hand stack or standard pallet rack load beam options. A flat load beam has the entire face/front surface for position ID. When you require two on a load beam, you use a standard ID and with a man-down vehicle minimal difficulty to complete an elevated position scan transaction. An indented load beam has interior section is set-back from top/bottom load beam section that restricts the front/face surface for position ID. When you require two ID positions on a load beam, you could use a narrower ID and with a man-down vehicle potential difficulty to complete an elevated position ID scan transaction.

SPI&RP 7. Storage Position Label Attachment

Storage position label attachment is your position ID placement onto a position load beam or upright post. For maximum employee scan transaction productivity and maximum good read number, your label placement is consistent and assures employee or hand held scanner line sight.

SPI&RP 8. Plain Or Coated Position Identification

Plain or coated position ID are your bar code label options. A plain bar code label is black bar codes that is printed onto a paper surface and placed onto a position. Features are potential black bar code damage from equipment or sku and less expense. A coated bar code label is plain bar code label that a coated surface that covers all black bars and is placed onto a position. Features are (1) slight cost increase and (2) reduces black bar code damage.

SPI&RP 9. Floor Stack Storage Position Identification Location

Floor stack ID location is in a location to assure employee or scanner line of sight and to assure proper floor stack lane ID. Proper floor stack position ID location assures employee productivity, accurate transaction and good inventory control. Floor stack position ID locations are (1) ceiling hung placard that is chain hung from the ceiling and extends downward. The extension permits pallet transactions but the height is difficult to complete a WMS storage position scan transaction, (2) floor embedded is tape, glued or plastic cover that is in each floor stack position from. A ID cover permits a WMS scan transaction and there is potential for position ID damage. Some additional cost & (3) upright post is located at a floor stack front side that is located at a lane clearance space. Directional arrows point to a floor stack lane and assures line of sight. Some potential damage & upright post cost.

SPI&RP 10. Sku WMS Identification Directory Or Substitution For Your WMS Program In A Dense
                       Storage Concept

Dense storage concepts are floor stack, two-deep, drive-in rack, push-back rack. With a dense concept, your WMS program suggests the first sku WMS ID that was WMS scanned and physically deposited to a WMS ID dense position. A first sku WMS ID scanned and deposited to a dense concept is not available for a withdrawal transaction due the last or other sku WMS IDs are at a dense position withdrawal position. For your WMS program, a WMS ID directory or substitution are options for you to track skus in a floor stack or dense concept positions. A directory concept has at your dense concept deposit position a directory that has a WMS ID for each deposit transaction, for each dense lane your WMS program suggests the lowest WMS ID position number, for each transaction your forklift truck driver WMS scans the appropriate WMS position and your WMS computer program considers a WMS ID position is occupied and does not accept another sku WMS ID in a position. Example your first position transaction has your dense position highest number and your last transaction has your highest position number. With a sku WMS ID approach, your WMS program accepts all sku WMS IDs scanned to a e WMS ID. When required to withdraw a sku WMS ID, a WMS computer program suggests a WMS ID and at a dense e concept, forklift truck driver withdraws a sku and scans a sku WMS ID and position WMS ID. As a sku WMS ID scan transaction is sent to a WMS computer program that reviews a position and sku WMS IDs. After a review and match of a sku WMS IDs, a WMS computer program approves a withdrawal transaction and reduces sku WMS ID from a dense storage lane sku WMS IDs.

SPI&RP 11. Quiet Zones, Over-Squared & Bar Code Edge (See BCS 10 Page 17)
SPI&RP 12. Use A Gun Or Hand Held Contact Scanner (See BSC 8 Page 18)
SPI&RP 13. Your Scanner Has A Default As One (See BSC 5 Page 18)
SPI&RP 14. Re-Chargeable Battery Or Electric Battery Powered Hand Scanner (See BSC 2 Page 18)
SPI&RP 15. Your Scanner Depth Of Field (See BSC 4 Page 18)
SPI&RP 16. Delayed Or On-Line Transaction Update (See BSC 6 Page 18)
SPI&RP 17. Large Human Readable Symbology (See BSC 7 Page 19)
SPI&RP 18. Human Readable On Top Or Bottom Of Machine Readable y (See BSC 8 Page 19)

WA & NA Forklift Truck (WA/NA 1 - WA/NA 3)
WA/NA 1. Forklift Truck Notched Mast/Level Finder & Allow Clearance (See OSS 24. Page 27 & PSS 1. Page
                    46)

WA/NA 2. WA Or NA)Forklift Truck Take A Pallet Into A Storage Aisle Or Leave It An Aisle End
With a WA or NA forklift truck storage activity your transport vehicle pallet drop-off options are (1) *Take A Pallet Into An Aisle*. With a small storage area, low forklift truck transactions & few aisles that perpendicular to a receiving dock, take a pallet into an aisle has good equipment utilization & good employee productivity. With a wide storage area & many aisles that are parallel to a receiving dock and high forklift truck transactions, take a pallet into an aisle represents poor forklift truck utilization & low employee productivity. To transport a sku with a high wage rate forklift truck driver and a high equipment cost, it represents a high CPU or (2) *Leave A Pallet An Aisle End* option is to have a transport vehicle deposit a pallet at an aisle end. Leave or deposit a pallet at an aisle end with a single or double pallet truck as a transport vehicle has a lower equipment cost, lower truck driver wage rate & lower cost per unit. With a pallet truck transport concept, a storage area main travel aisle requires a wider aisle that permits pallet placement at an aisle end floor level drop station & proper pallet placement at an aisle end to have a sku WMS ID face a forklift truck driver.

WA/NA 3. WA Or NA Forklift Truck Deposits A Pallet Or Has A Transport Vehicle Drop Pallets At An

50

Aisle End

Do It All The Way Is A Transport & Storage Activity Concept has a WA or NA forklift truck complete a sku pick-up at receiving & put-away to a WMS position. With a small storage area and few aisles that face a receiving dock & a low sku volume, do-it-all-the-way concept has good equipment utilization & good employee productivity. With a wide storage area & many aisles that do not face a receiving dock & a high sku volume, do it all the way concept represents poor forklift truck utilization & low employee productivity. To transport a sku with a high wage rate forklift truck driver & a high equipment cost, it represents a high CPU. *Give Away Concept* uses a single or double pallet truck as a transport vehicle with a lower equipment cost, lower wage rate & lower CPU. With a pallet truck transport concept, a storage area requires a wider aisle for a pallet placement at an aisle end & proper pallet placement at an aisle end to have a sku WMS ID face a forklift truck driver.

VNA Or HROS Forklift Truck Ideas (VNA 1 - VNA 14)

VNA 1. HROS/VNA Travel In A Tunnel With UPS, Line Driver, Off-Guidance Stop & On-Board Lighting

HROS or VNA forklift truck aisle or a tunnel is a concept that has a vehicle driver travel horizontal and vertical in a very narrow aisle between to tall shelf or rack rows. When a HROS or VNA vehicle travels in an aisle it resembles travel in a tunnel. To maintain your employee productivity and reduce damage, if your VNA or HROS vehicle is wire guided you have a (1) *UPS Or Battery Back-Up* that provides sufficient electric power for a vehicle to exit and aisle, (2) *Line Driver* that sends an electric impulse through a guide wire to guide a vehicle, (3) *Off-Guidance Stop* that if a vehicles goes off-line in an aisle, it stops vehicle travel and (4) *On-Board Lighting* that has spot lights added to your vehicle that provides additional in aisle light.

VNA 2. Restrict Employee From A VNA Aisle

Restrict employees from an aisle is VNA or HROS safety procedure. After an employee (such as inventory clerk) enters a VNA aisle, at an aisle entrance an employee extends a yellow, orange or bright green chain across an aisle and hooks the chain onto a rack post. When a chain is across an aisle entrance, it is sign to a powered VNA or HROS vehicle driver that an aisle is occupied with an employee.

VNA 3. Very Narrow Aisle Forklift Truck (VNA) P/D Station Aisle Width

A VNA pick-up and delivery (P/D) station aisle width options are determined by your VNA P/D station design. A VNA forklift truck P/D station design assures a transport vehicle & VNA forklift truck sku drop or queue location, easy sku pick-up & delivery location and assures WMS ID has proper orientation. In most 'turn a load' in an aisle VNA forklift truck applications, a rack to rack aisle width is 6'-6" wide. With a 'do not turn' a load in an aisle VNA forklift truck application, a rack to rack aisle width is 6'-0" wide. If we consider a 2 in pallet overhang of each rack load beam, an aisle width shrink to 6'-2" and 5'-8" wide aisle. Your VNA P/D station design affects your transport vehicle selection, VNA forklift truck driver productivity and sku/rack damage. VNA P/D station options are (1) flush VNA forklift truck P/D station design has both rack rows end even and between 2 rack rows an aisle width is to narrow for a transport vehicle truck to complete a right angle turn for a P/D transaction or (2) saw-tooth drop or delivery VNA forklift truck P/D station aisle width includes at both ends, 2 exterior rack rows that extend by one rack bay toward a main aisle, 2 VNA forklift truck aisles & 2 interior rack rows that one bay less than 2 exterior rack rows. An aisle width is more than sufficient for a transport vehicle to complete a right angle turn for a P/D transaction. With saw-tooth P/D station design, above P/D stations you have positions that increases your position number.

VNA 4. VNA Forklift Truck Take A Pallet Into An Aisle Or Leave At A Rack Row P/D Station

With a VNA forklift truck storage activity your pallet transport vehicle pallet drop-off options impact your transport employee productivity, VNA forklift truck driver put-away productivity, potential rack post damage & potential sku WMS scan low productivity. Your options are (1) *Take A Pallet Into A Storage Aisle* option has a transport vehicle travel into a VNA aisle, deposit a sku in an aisle & exist from a VNA aisle. Features are (A) to complete a take a pallet into a storage aisle concept, a transport vehicle travels into a very narrow aisle with a pallet truck travel in both lead and driver trail directions that has potential for low pallet truck driver travel speed & potential rack post damage, (B) if a VNA forklift truck is in an aisle, a sku WMS ID has potential to face a wrong direction for a WMS scan transaction. In many operations, when an employee is in an aisle, for safety reasons an alarm or yellow chain

51

is drawn and hooked across an aisle entrance that is considered a safe activity & (C) if a VNA forklift truck is not in an aisle, a sku WMS ID faces a proper direction for a WMS scan transaction, but a forklift truck driver has to wait for a pallet truck to clear an aisle that is low forklift truck driver productivity or (2) *Leave A Pallet At An Aisle End (P/D) Station* has a transport pallet or forklift truck deposit a sku at an aisle end (P/D) station. With leave a pallet at an aisle end P/D station, a saw-tooth P/D station design assures adequate transport vehicle turning aisle to have a sku placed into a P/D station with a sku WMS ID facing an aisle.

VNA 5. VNA Forklift Truck P/D Station With A Flush, Jaggered Saw-Tooth Or Saw-Tooth Design

Flush, jaggered saw-tooth or saw-tooth VNA forklift truck (P/D) station design assures that a sku is available for a transport vehicle sku drop-off (delivery) or pick-up (outbound) & a sku is properly oriented for VNA forklift truck pick-up with a sku WMS ID line of sight. *A Flush P/D Station* design has a pallet truck complete a right angle turn for a pick-up or delivery transaction. Aisle width is an aisle width that is between 2 rack rows. In most VNA applications with a flush P/D station design, a P/D station aisle width has a narrow width that limits good pallet transport productivity, creates potential sku and equipment damage & no additional storage positions above P/D stations. But it does provide a sku in proper orientation for a good VNA deposit & pick-up productivity. *A Jaggered Saw-Tooth P/D Station* is a modified flush or saw-tooth P/D station that has a VNA aisle & 1 rack row (not 2 rack rows) that creates a P/D station aisle width has a nomimal 10'-6" aisle width between 2 jaggered P/D station rack rows. Aisle width has sufficient aisle width for a pallet truck & most WA forklift truck to complete a right angle turn for a pallet pick-up or delivery transaction with good employee productivity & minimal sku & equipment damage. With 1 P/D station side there is limited sku queue, fewer positions above a P/D station & with 2 pallets in a P/D station, potential confusion as to what pallet is outbound or inbound but can be minimized with each P/D station pallet position properly ID for inbound or outbound. A saw-tooth P/D stations design has 2 VNA forklift truck aisles & 4 rack rows. 2 interior rack rows are flush & 2 exterior rack rows extend 1 rack bay beyond the flush rack rows. *A Saw-Tooth P/D Station* provides a P/D station aisle width with sufficient aisle width for a pallet truck & most WA or NA forklift trucks to complete a right angle turn for a pick-up or delivery transaction with good employee productivity & minimal sku and equipment damage. With 1 P/D station side there is limited sku queue, fewer storage positions above a P/D station & with 2 pallets in a P/D station, potential confusion as to what pallet is outbound or inbound but can be minimized with each P/D station pallet position properly IDed.

VNA 6. Above Your Saw-Tooth P/D Station Use For Storage Positions

Above your saw-tooth P/D station use run-out space for positions is a VNA forklift truck end front aisle rack options that increase your pallet position number & transaction productivity. With a VNA forklift truck rack P/D station concept, a VNA forklift truck has to complete a pallet P/D station transaction to each P/D station pallet position. With pallet rack positions above a P/D station position a VNA forklift truck is able to complete a transaction to positions. The concept requires a P/D station upright posts to extend up above a P/D station & increases position number that are considered prime pallet positions. To complete a transaction to positions above a P/D station does not require VNA forklift truck to travel that represents an employee productivity increase. The concept increases a position number by positions above each P/D station on an aisle both sides.

VNA 7. VNA P/D Station Rub Bar & Back Stop

A VNA forklift truck P/D station rub bas and back stop are P/D station design options that minimize rack damage & assure proper pallet orientation for good VNA truck pick-up productivity. A rub bar is a harden metal member that is attached full length between a P/D station rack posts depth. If a P/D station rack has a side anchor bolt, a rub bar coverage includes a rack post side anchor bolt. A rub bar height assures that a deposit pallet will not become hung-up on a rub bar. As a pallet truck or WA or NA forklift truck completes a P/D station deposit or pick-up transaction, a rub bar assures that a pallet does become hung-up on a rack post. A back stop is a harden metal right angle member that is anchored to a P/D station floor rear with an angle iron flush side facing a P/D station aisle. A back stop height assures that a pallet deposit does not become hung-up on a back stop. Most powered pallet trucks & forklift trucks do not have fork tips extend beyond a pallet deck board. As a pallet truck for forklift truck completes a pallet deposit into a P/D station, pallet deck board comes in contact with a back stop flush front. Feature assures that a sku is in a proper orientation with a WMS ID facing an employee and alignment for exact pallet pick-up. Exact pallet placement on a VNA set of forks means proper placement into a rack position with minimal pallet put-away problems.

VNA 8. VNA Forklift Truck Or HROS Vehicle Guided Or Non-Guided Aisle Travel
Your VNA forklift or HROS vehicle has guided or non-guided aisle travel are your vehicle in aisle travel options. A VNA forklift & HROS truck travel is in a very narrow aisle between 2 rack rows (an estimated 3 to 6 in clearance between truck & rack) to complete a sku deposit or withdrawal transaction at a floor level or elevated position. During aisle travel or at a position, a VNA forklift or HROS truck inclines or declines to have an employee or a set of forks complete a transaction at an elevated position. To assure maximum travel speed for good employee productivity with minimal vehicle steering & minimal rack, vehicle and sku damage, a VNA forklift or HROS truck has an aisle guidance concept to guide truck travel in an aisle. In an elevated travel path, a VNA forklift & HROS truck aisle guidance is a must. Aisle guidance permits a VNA forklift or HROS truck as it travels in an aisle to travel horizontal & vertical (incline/decline an employee or set of forks) to have proper elevation to complete a transaction at an elevated position or aisle end P/D station. The horizontal & vertical travel feature increases employee productivity. Guidance options are rail or electronic guidance concepts.

VNA 9. When To Use Rail Or Electronic Guidance
When to use rail or electronic VNA forklift or HROS truck guidance concept is a basic question that is determined by your storage aisle number, vendor equipment & floor features. A Rail Guidance Concept has entry guides & single or double rail (angle iron) with each iron section connection joint is ground smooth. Guide rail is secured to an aisle floor surface, built up floor section side or rack bay for full aisle length that allows a VNA forklift or HROS truck multiple guide wheel device to ride along or connect onto a guide rail. When your warehouse has few aisles or a captive vehicle to an aisle, rail guidance is a consideration. Electronic Guidance options are (1) wire guidance that has (a) a closed loop wire embedded in your floor. An impulse driver sends out an electric impulse, sent through all aisles and sent back to an impulse driver & (b) vehicle underside sensor device that picks-up an electric impulse from a wire. As long as a truck under side sensor receives an electric impulse, a truck travel is guided through an aisle. If a truck under side sensor does not receive an electric impulse, a truck emergency stop concept halts truck travel in an aisle & (2) laser beam guidance that has light beam targets strategically located in an aisle. A light beam is transmitted from a truck & hits a target that reflects a light beam back to a truck receiver. As long as a truck receiver has a light beam, a truck travel is guided through an aisle. If a truck receiver does not receive a light beam, a truck emergency stop concept halts truck travel in an aisle. If your new storage area has multiple aisles & at least several trucks, an electronic guidance is a consideration. If remodel an existing operation with high metal content in the floor that has potential to prevent an electric impulse transmission or an uneven floor surface that breaks a truck sensor connection to an impulse transmission, before a wire guidance concept selection you have your truck manufacturer warranty a wire guidance concept & if no warranty consider rail or laser beam guidance.

VNA 10. How To Slow Down VNA Forklift Truck Or HROS Vehicle Aisle End Travel Speed
How to slow down a VNA forklift or HROS vehicle aisle end travel speed truck is a manual or electro-magnetic concept to slow down a vehicle travel speed prior to main aisle entry or to halt a vehicle travel at a dead end aisle end. When a VNA forklift or HROS truck enters a main aisle at slow travel speed or to stop at a dead end aisle end, it enhances safety and minimizes potential vehicle damage & employee injury. Manual Slow Down Concept options are (1) for entry to a main aisle, painted rack upright posts & load beams such as yellow & red colors & (2) at a dead end aisle, colored racks and a floor anchored bumper full aisle width at a distance from your last storage position to allow storage transaction at a rack row last position. A manual slow down concept is most frequently used with a rail guidance concept, requires employee training & is low cost. An Electro-Magnetic Slow Down Concept has a sensor device on a truck underside & magnetic devices embedded in an aisle floor. Magnetic devices are set at pre-determined distances from an aisle end. As a vehicle travels over magnetic devices, a signal is picked-up by a vehicle sensor that sends a command to automatically slow down a vehicle travel speed.

VNA 11. VNA Forklift Truck Man-Down Or Man-Up

VNA forklift truck man-down or man-up are to complete a transaction a VNA forklift truck operator location options. *With A Man-Down VNA Forklift Truck* to complete a transaction has an operator platform remain stationary at the floor level. To complete an elevated transaction, an operator eye-balls or uses a range/position level finder to assure that a VNA forklift truck set of forks are at the proper elevation. When storage positions are in a low bay building, if a man-down VNA forklift truck has a lower cost combined with low operator productivity & potential sku/rack damage are important considerations. *With A Man-Up VNA Forklift Truck* to complete a transaction, an operator platform moves up with a set of forks to an elevated level that permits an operator to have view of a transaction. In a low building or a 40 ft high building with tall racks, a man-up VNA forklift truck has the same cost as a man-down VNA forklift truck, your increased employee productivity & low sku/rack damage are considerations.

VNA 12. Improve Pallet Pick-Up, Paint Strips On Your VNA Forklift Truck Forks & Position Load Beams
To improve pallet pick-up, paint stripes on your VNA forklift truck set of forks are options to improve employee productivity. During a pallet pick-up transaction at a P/D station, painted stripes on a set of forks helps an operator to assure that a pallet is properly aligned on a set of forks for exact put-away or deposit onto a rack position load beams. At a P/D station & after a pallet is on a set of forks, a driver moves a pallet carrier to a position for an operator to view a set of fork painted stripes. With paint stripes in view, it means that a pallet is in a proper location for exact position deposit. An exact position deposit has a pallet 2 bottom deck boards evenly placed on a rack position front & rear load beams. With a pallet properly placed in a position, it reduces potential for sku damage from a misaligned pallet & assures good employee productivity for pallet withdrawal from a position & deposit at a P/D station.

For improved pallet deposit in a tall rack position, paint stripes on your VNA forklift rack bay front load beam 2 pallet positions. Paint stripes for each rack bay pallet position improves forklift truck driver put-away/deposit productivity & minimizes sku damage. During a VNA forklift truck deposit to a rack bay with 2 pallet positions, an operator uses the nearest or adjacent upright position as a guide for a pallet deposit to a position. With a pallet in the nearest or adjacent position, pallet deposit to a vacant or far position is difficult transaction for a VNA forklift truck driver to assure proper pallet alignment in a position. If you look at a VNA forklift truck full rack bays, most pallets that are deposited to a position that are adjacent to an upright post are very close to an upright post due to a VNA forklift driver used an upright post as a deposit transaction or pallet alignment guide. Two paint stripes sets (1 set for each pallet or outside to outside distance between two pallet exterior stringers or blocks) on a rack bay front load beam are in a driver's view and serve as a guide for a forklift driver to complete a transaction. Paint stripes or two tape strands on a load beam improve driver deposit productivity & minimizes sku damage.

VNA 13. How Your VNA Forklift Truck Or HROS Vehicle Enters & Travels In An Aisle
How your VNA forklift or HROS vehicle driver enters and travels in an aisle enhances safety, improves employee productivity and minimizes vehicle damage. A VNA or HROS concept has an aisle between two tall shelf/rack rows and a vehicle travel is guided by a rail or electric concept. Per your company policy, no other vehicle or employee has access to an aisle. As your driver enters a VNA or HROS aisle, a driver is facing your main aisle that assures complete main aisle vision and as entering a main aisle minimizes vehicle accidents. With your driver in this position, your shelf/rack number pattern directs an employee to assigned position.

VNA 14. VNA Forklift Truck Single Or Dual Commands
VNA forklift truck single or dual commands are a VNA forklift truck activity commands or instructions to complete a storage transaction. A VNA forklift truck single command is a standard command. *A VNA Forklift Truck Single Command* has a vehicle make an aisle trip from a P/D station into a storage aisle. Travel command options are (1) with a sku for deposit to a WMS ID position and after deposit for a vehicle return empty to a P/D station and (2) empty to a WMS ID position and at a position after sku withdrawal to return travel with a sku to a P/D station. In conclusion, a single command has a vehicle complete only 1 inbound or 1 outbound WMS ID sku transaction per aisle trip and does not require a work hour balance for inbound skus at a P/D station and outbound CO withdrawal transactions. *A VNA Forklift Truck Dual Command* with a WMS program concept a dual command program requires some additional computer programming costs, sku deposit & withdrawal communications & aisle end P/D station designed with inbound and outbound queue lanes. A VNA forklift truck in a dual command mode has a

vehicle (1) with a sku travel from a P/D station to a WMS identified position and complete a sku deposit activity, (2) from a position travel empty to another WMS ID position for sku withdrawal from another position and (3) with a sku on board travel to a P/D station and transfer a sku to a P/D station. In conclusion, a dual command mode has a vehicle complete both 1 inbound and 1 outbound WMS ID sku transaction per aisle trip and does require a work hour balance for inbound skus & outbound CO withdrawal transactions and P/D stations have inbound and outbound queue lanes. Per aisle trip a dual command mode per aisle almost doubles skus that are handled per hour, but it is combined in-bound & outbound activities that create a UPH increase.

Storage Philosophy & Ideas (SP 1 – SP 2)
SP 1. Your Storage Philosophy
Your storage philosophy determines a sku location in your storage aisle. Your storage philosophy is based on your sku's historical sales, estimated sales such as a promotional sku and is implemented through your WMS computer program with computer program directed transactions. A sku storage location has an impact your employee productivity and space utilization. Various storage philosophies are (1) *ABC & D Philosophy* has from your skus historical movement usually 6 to 12 months separated into 4 groups that is based on Pareto's Law. 'A'/fast moving skus that account for 85% of your picks and have few sku number. Preferred storage locations are dense storage or single deep positions that are close as possible to your pick section with the shortest travel distance to your pick section. 'B' & 'C' slow to medium moving skus that account for an estimated 15 % of your picks and are old 'A' skus that have lower sales. Skus have a large number with typical medium to small inventory and are assigned to standard pallet rack positions that have a medium travel distance to your pick section. 'D'/very slow moving or obsolete sku that account for an estimated 5 % of your picks. Skus have a large number with a small inventory and are assigned to remote ½ high or hand stacked standard pallet positions that have a longest travel distance to your pick section, (2) *Power Allocation* that is based on your merchandising department promotional sku and account for 85% of your picks. Your promotional skus are few sku number with a large inventory. Preferred locations are dense or single deep positions that are close as possible to your pick section with a short travel distance to your pick section, (3) *Seasonal Skus* that have specific life cycle for a pre-determined number of months. Preferred locations are dense or single deep positions that are close as possible to your pick section, (4) *Family Sku Group or Pairs* that are skus used to produce one sku, language specific nationality that have a large to medium inventory and are assigned to standard pallet rack positions that have a medium travel distance to your pick section or unique skus that a sale of sku creates sale for another sku such as salt and pepper shakers and toy and electric battery. Skus are assigned to standard rack positions that have a medium travel distance to your pick section, (5) *Sku Size* that are separated by a sku overall height. When you have a pallet or carton storage area, your standard rack positions have two heights for your positions that are one full high position and one half high position, (6) *FIFO Sku* that requires that your oldest sku is the first withdrawn for replenishment or CO. Standard position & gravity/air flow are preferred positions, (7) *Flammable Skus* are required storage in a containment chamber and standard pallet rack is preferred, (8) *Toxic Skus* that require storage in a meshed area that during a fire restricts air pressurized can flight & (9) *Random* approach that has an employee select the first vacate position. In most operations, it does not improve employee productivity due to increased travel distances to your pick area.

SP 2. Promotional Skus Located In Your Front Positions
Promotional or sales skus are located in your front or prime real estate position. A promotional or sale sku has a high sales volume, large sku inventory & have a short sku life cycle. To improve employee productivity & space utilization, with a WA or NA forklift truck, skus are assigned to an aisle exist end or as close as possible to an exist end & in 1 storage area or aisle. With a VNA forklift truck operation, skus are spread over aisles to positions that are at a P/D station end or as close as possible to a P/D station. With promotional skus located to positions at an aisle exit end approach, there is less travel time to complete VNA forklift truck sku put-away & withdrawal transactions. After sku promotion there are vacant positions for new skus, minimizes non-productive forklift truck travel past positions with medium 'B' or slow moving 'C'/'D' skus & residual sku inventory is transferred to another position.

Storage Activity Transaction Ideas (SAT 1 - SAT 3)

SAT 1. What Are Your Storage Area Transaction Numbers

What are your transaction numbers refers to your design year peak sku deposit and withdrawal transaction number. Your concept design year peak deposit & withdrawal transaction number impacts your storage transaction employee or vehicle (employee, WA, NA or VNA forklift) number & P/D station number with associated queue capacity, bar code scanners/RF readers and transaction communication network. In an employee or manual controlled WA or NA forklift truck operation each sku deposit transaction is 1 transaction per aisle trip & each sku withdrawal transaction is 1 transaction per aisle trip. An example has 500 deposit transactions & 500 withdrawal transactions that equals 1000 single transactions. If an employee or vehicle completes 20 single transactions per hour, with a 7 hour work day, 7 to 8 vehicles or employees are required for your storage area. In most VNA forklift truck crane operations with P/D station queue positions/lanes, a warehouse attempts to have deposit & withdrawal transactions occur within the same work day time period. When deposits and withdrawal transactions occur within a work day same time period, a VNA forklift truck completes dual command transactions. With an aisle trip, a vehicle travels from a P/D station with a sku & completes a deposit transaction, continues empty aisle travel to a position and completes a sku withdrawal transaction and travels with a sku to a P/D station. With a balance for deposits and withdrawals per hour, a dual command completes 2 transactions per aisle trip. A storage area P/D station pallet position queue with vendor delivery scheduling & CO sku profile helps to obtain a balance for deposits & withdrawals. It is noted with additional aisle travel time, that a dual command mode increases transactions per trip by an estimated 50% to 80%. An example has 500 deposit transactions & 500 withdrawal transactions that equals 1000 single commands. If a vehicle completes 30 dual commands/transactions per hour, with a 7 hour work day, 5 vehicles are required for your operation. Knowing your transaction number allows you to determine an accurate employee, vehicle and scanner number.

SAT 2. Employee Directed Or Computer Directed Withdrawal Transaction

Who directs a withdrawal transaction options are (1) *Employee Directed* withdrawal transaction is used with an employee controlled forklift truck concept & has an employee determine from what position to withdraw a sku. Features are transaction position potentially does not match your storage philosophy or FIFO rotation, in most applications there is a delayed transaction completion data transfer & for good inventory management, requires a forklift truck driver to write each sku ID & position onto a paper document & have a clerk complete book entry that increases potential for errors or (2) *Computer Suggested* withdrawal transaction is used in an employee controlled forklift truck operation that has a WMS program program to identify a specific or WMS ID position & associated sku quantity. Features are withdrawal transaction matches your storage philosophy or FIFO rotation, transaction is delayed or on-line transferred to a computer via paper document or RF device for computer update & with a RF device a transaction data transfer is more accurate and faster.

SAT 3. Computer Directed Sku Put-Away/Deposit Or Employee Directed Sku Put-Away/Deposit

Your put-away/deposit transactions are (1) *Computer Directed* sku put-away transaction is a WMS ID sku deposit to a WMS ID position that was suggested by an inventory control or WMS computer program. With a computer directed deposit an employee, employee controlled forklift truck travels in an aisle to a suggested WMS ID position and completes a sku (carton, pallet or GOH) deposit transaction. To assure accurate inventory, sku & position WMS IDs are scanned & sent to a WMS computer that minimizes any sku inventory tracking or position status problems. Features are maintains your storage philosophy & improves productivity and (2) *Employee Directed Sku Put-Away Or Deposit Employee* directed deposit transaction is a WMS identified sku deposit to a WMS ID position that is determined by an employee controlled forklift truck. After an employee controlled forklift truck enters a storage area, an employee controlled forklift truck places a sku into a vacant WMS ID position. To assure accurate inventory control, sku & position WMS IDs are scanned & sent to a WMS computer that minimizes any sku inventory tracking problems. Features are difficult to maintain your storage area philosophy & low employee productivity.

Storage Area Aisles Lights & Building Column Location Ideas (SAA 1 - SAA 10)
SAA 1. Parallel Or Perpendicular Storage Rack Rows & Aisles Flow To Your Pick Area

Parallel or perpendicular rack rows and aisles flow to your pick area are rack & forklift truck aisle direction of travel options. In a rectangle shaped building, *Parallel Rack Row* and forklift truck aisle direction of travel has e rack rows & aisles parallel to your next warehouse activity. For a forklift truck to drop pallets at a next warehouse activity, you add a middle aisle or your forklift truck uses end turning aisles. Features are increased transport time, distance & cost. *Perpendicular Rack Row* & forklift truck aisle direction of travel has a storage rear turning aisle adjacent to a next warehouse activity. For best operational results, your end turning aisles have additional width due to one aisle interfaces with your receiving activity & other aisle interfaces with your pick activity.

SAA 2. What Is Your Forklift Truck Storage & Turning Aisle Width

What is your forklift truck storage & turning aisle width is a WA or NA forklift truck right angle/stacking turn requirement to complete a transaction that improves employee productivity & minimizes sku & rack damage. With most WA or NA forklift trucks, rack to rack plus 12 in is a manufacturer's recommended stacking aisle width. If a stacking or turning aisle width is narrower than a manufacturer's stated dimension, there is potential sku & rack post damage. If a stacking or turning aisle width is wider than a manufacturer's stated dimension, your storage area has wide aisle that has low space utilization.

SAA 3. Turning Aisles In A Storage Area

Turning aisles in a storage area is a manual controlled forklift truck design factor that increases employee productivity. Aisle number per storage area design options are (1) front turning aisle is common with a WA, NA forklift truck & VNA forklift truck, (2) front & rear turning aisle concept is used with a WA or NA or VNA forklift truck concept. In a manual controlled forklift truck operation, front & rear turning aisles allow a forklift truck transfer from one aisle to another aisle. Features are reduces forklift truck travel time & distance that improves employee productivity & provides a lower pallet position number & (3) front, rear & middle aisle concept is common in a large pallet position e concept with very long rack rows and aisle & has a WA or NA employee controlled forklift truck. Front, rear & middle aisle widths permit forklift trucks transfer from one aisle to another aisle & transport vehicles to complete sku P/D transaction that improves employee productivity & provide fewer pallet positions.

SAA 4. Building Column Locations

Building columns locations are a rack row & aisle layout design factor that affects your position number, your space utilization and employee productivity. Your building column location options are (1) *In A Back To Back Rack Row Flue* space is a common building column location. With a standard 8 in wide building column & an allowable 2 in open space on a column both sides, a back to back rack flue space is a 12 in space for an entire rack row. For a 150 ft long rack row with 40 ft building column spacing, a flue space occupies 150 sq. ft. (1 X 150) & provides 128 t positions (16 rack bays X 2 plts wide X 4 plts high = 128 positions). If your facility is in a high seismic location, a building column increases to 3 ft. wide with 450 sq. ft of unused space, (2) *Building Columns In A Rack Bay* has a rack bay position arranged to have a building occupy 1 position. A typical position is 4 ft X 4 ft. Based on a 150 ft. long rack row, your unused building column space is 36 sq. ft. (4 X 4 X 3 columns = 36) & provides 116 positions (128 – 12 (3 columns X 4 plts), (3) *Rack Around A Building Has A Rack Row Arranged In Between 2 Building Columns*. With a 32 ft building span, there are 4 rack bays with 2 pallets wide & 1 rack bay with 1 pallet wide. Based on a 150 ft. long rack row, your unused building column space is 64 sq. ft. (4 X 4 X 4 columns = 64) and provides 126 positions (3.5 bays X 2 plts wide X 4 plts high X 4.5 sections = 126 positions. With the concept there is some additional rack costs for additional posts & load beams & (4) *Building Columns In A Forklift Truck Aisle* is a least preferred location. With a building column in an aisle there is 148 sq. ft. of unused space (1 ft X 150 ft plus 33 sq. ft. blocked positions that are blocked by building columns & provides 116 position (128 - 12 blocked) and there is an increase for potential building damage & accidents. Space savings with a WA forklift truck & 18 back to back rack rows allows you to add 2 rack rows & 1 WA forklift truck aisle. Space savings with a NA forklift truck & 16 back to back rack rows allows you to add 2 rack rows & 1 NA forklift truck aisle.

SAA 5. Where Are Your Light Fixtures

Your light fixtures in your storage area improve safety, reduce sku damage and improve employee productivity. A storage area has aisles between two pallets, rails, shelves or rack rows. Rails, shelves, pallets and rack rows are positions & aisles allow employees, employee controlled forklift trucks travel to a position & complete a transaction. When your light fixtures hang above your rails, shelves, pallets or rack rows, your top sku & light beam angle minimizes light in an aisle and minimizes an employee vision to a sku or position IDs. Feature lowers your employee productivity, increases potential for sku & rack damage & creates safety concerns. When your light fixtures hang above your aisle middle, a light beam is proper & provides light to easily see a sku or position ID. Feature enhances your employee productivity, decreases potential for sku & rack damage & minimizes safety concerns.

SAA 6. When To Turn Your Storage Aisle Lights On & Off

When to turn your aisle lights on/off is a storage concept that is used with fluorescent light fixtures or fast illumination light fixtures that reduces your energy or electrical cost. An aisle light turn on/off options are (1) *All Aisle Lights Remain Turned* whether an employee or forklift truck is traveling in an aisle or not traveling in an aisle. Feature is that your operation incurs an expense with no employee productivity to off-set the expense & (2) *All Aisle Lights Remain Off Except For A Main Aisle Lights* and as an employee or employee controlled forklift enters an aisle, an aisle motion detector senses or a light beam is broken by an employee or forklift truck aisle travel & activates an aisle lights. For a pre-determined time or as long as employee or forklift truck moves in an aisle, lights remain on.

SAA 7. Sprinklers Are In The Ceiling &/Or Racks

Sprinklers are in a ceiling and/or racks and the final determination is per local code or insurance underwriter requirement for fire sprinklers in your new or existing storage facility. In most storage concepts above 20 ft, fire sprinkler systems require a water holding tank that is above ground or buried in the ground or pond, pump to assure per-determined cubic ft of water per minute or water pressure, sprinkler heads, piping & alarm system. A storage concept fire sprinkler locations are (1) in a rack bay opening top under a rack bay fire barrier, (2) in a flue space between back to back rack rows or rack row & wall, (3) extending downward from a ceiling at a pre-determined height above your highest sku & (4) under solid walkways.

SAA 8. Control Your Liquid Run-Off

Control your liquid run-off is a storage concept with a storage area that during a fire is designed to restrict liquid run-off from burning sku containers in your facility or onto local grounds. Your local government or insurance company suggests skus for assignment to a restricted liquid run-off storage area. A containment chamber & building wall siding has cubic capacity to contain your liquid sku run-off and sprinkler water amount. Restrict run-off concepts are (1) storage area perimeter that is at an approved height with a drain that directs liquid flow to a containment chamber or (2) along a storage area wall, there is leak proof siding, but the siding is design to allow forklift truck entry & exist.

SAA 9. Stop The Missiles

Stop the missiles is a storage concept with storage positions that during a fire are designed to restrict air pressured cans with flames from being propelled from one location to another location & spread a fire to a new location. Restriction concepts are (1) with a very large inventory quantity, enclosed storage rack rows & aisles, (2) for a medium inventory quantity, storage bay has solid wood, solid metal sheets, small wire mesh or planks that are securely attached to rack posts & load beams & (3) for a small inventory quantity, a solid sheet metal cabinet with doors. Stop the missiles concept lowers your insurance costs.

SAA 10. Nets

Nets are plastic or fabric meshed is option to improve employee safety and reduce sku damage. After a net is attached to a single pallet rack row upright post, the net covers positions with exposure to an aisle (employee walk aisle). The net meshed opening size prevents a small sku falling from a pallet into an aisle.

GOH Ideas (GOH 1 - GOH 14)

GOH 1. Your Vendor Or You Cut & Tie Your GOH Bag Bottom

Your vendor or employee cut or tie your GOH bag bottom has your GOH vendor or an employee assure that a GOH plastic bag extends 1 to 2 ins beyond a GOH length. Most vendors send GOH with a plastic bag that extends 12 to 18 ins beyond a GOH bottom and with multi level GOH storage positions, a lower GOH ID is blocked by the above GOH plastic bag extension. GOH with 1 to 2 in length permits at least 2 GOH rails high and an elevated GOH bag does not block a lower level GOH ID. If your GOH vendor cuts or ties each GOH bag, there is minimal cost. If your employee cuts or ties a GOH bag, there is a small additional labor cost. Features are (1) dust barrier, (2) shorten a GOH overall length & (3) in a vertical GOH storage stack line of sight to a lower position WMS ID.

GOH 2. Short Or Tall GOH Storage Position
Short or tall GOH positions are your two basic GOH positions. Each GOH position matches a GOH length that means a short length GOH fits into a short position or if all short positions are full, a short GOH fits into a tall GOH position. Only tall GOH fits into a tall GOH position. To maximize your GOH storage area utilization, your important position design facts are (1) employee reach height, (2) your short & long GOH sku number and inventory quantity, (3) number of summer GOH skus & winter skus & GOH per linear ft, (4) ability to have 2 deep static positions & (5) to have unassisted access to (a) 2 or 3 short GOH levels, (b) 1 long and 1 short GOH levels & (c) elevated walkway with GOH hanging below a walkway in a fire and employee protected well.

GOH 3. One Deep Or Two Deep GOH Storage Rails
One deep or 2 deep GOH storage rails are floor level static rail GOH storage options improves employee productivity and increase density. *One Deep Floor* level static rail GOH storage concept has 1 rail that is adjacent to an aisle & is full aisle length. After GOH is deposited onto a rail, a GOH position WMS ID is fixed or slides over a rail. GOH occupies as many ln. ft. that is required for a vendor delivery. Features are (A) with 1 GOH sku that occupies a large ln. ft length in one aisle, there is additional travel & distance to access other GOH positions & to complete a transaction, creates low employee productivity, (B) low density per aisle ln. ft. & (C) few skus per aisle. *Two Deep Floor* level static GOH rail concept has a front rail that is adjacent to an aisle & is full aisle length. A second GOH floor level static rail is full aisle length & directly behind the front rail. In a GOH storage module, there is sufficient space for GOH transfer equally onto both front & rear rails. When a new WMS ID GOH is evenly divided between both front and rear static rails, a WMS ID position is attached to both rails & slides over both rails that allows a position WMS ID to match a GOH sku quantity. To assure a GOH quantity is even on both rails & both rails have the same WMS ID GOH sku, after GOH withdrawal transactions have depleted a front GOH rail quantity, an employee notices a large open space on a front rail. Since a WMS ID GOH was WMS scanned to a 1 WMS ID storage position that included both front and rear rails, an employee moves a GOH sku quantity from a rear rail to a front rail & slides a storage WMS ID from a large space to a smaller space. Features are (A) increases sku facings per ln. ft that increases space utilization, (B) increases sku density per aisle, (C) some additional employee effort to consolidate skus from a rear rail to a front rail & move a position identifier & (D) with short employee travel time & distance to complete a transaction, increases employee productivity.

GOH 4. GOH Hangs In A Hole
GOH hangs in a hole or cavity is a GOH storage concept that improves employee productivity, increases space/cube utilization and enhances density per aisle. A GOH hang in a hole/cavity concept options are (1) in a multiple level standard rack or structural pipe storage concept, there are walkways between two static rail rows and GOH rails are set at a pre-determined elevation to a walkway. In relation to a walkway, a GOH rail is above a cavity that allows for GOH to hang into cavity. Rails above a cavity improves employee access to (a) 3 short GOH storage levels or (b) 1 long GOH storage level with 1 short GOH storage level & (2) in a floor level GOH storage area, an elevated walkway is installed between 2 static rail rows and GOH rails are set at a pre-determined elevation to a walkway. A walkway elevates an employee to a GOH rail. With an employee elevated to GOH rails, it improves employee access to (a) 3 short GOH storage levels or (b) 1 long GOH storage level with 1 short GOH storage level. Prior to an in-rack or pipe structure cavity concept or elevated walkway concept, you review your local codes & insurance company for walkway handrails, kick-plates, required steps & cavity material and structural strength to support an employee load and fire barrier & sprinkler requirements.

GOH 5. Convert Your Shelf Or Hand Stack Pallet Rack Storage Position To GOH Storage Position

Convert your standard shelf or hand stack pallet rack position to GOH storage is a concept that permits a your manager to convert a carton hand stack standard pallet rack or shelf concept to a GOH rail storage/pick concept. During peak GOH season a standard shelf concept middle 2 to 3 shelves are removed from a shelf bay and top and bottom shelves remain. The 2 to 3 removed shelves are stacked onto the bottom shelf. Below the top shelf by 1 to 2 ins, you add a hang bar support devices to each side post & a hang bar is placed into support members. To convert decked standard pallet rack or angle iron hand stack bay to a GOH storage position, your options are (1) use eyebolts, nuts & washers. After 2 eyebolts are inserted through deck material (wood, wire mesh or sheet metal) adjacent at a rack bay ends or next to load beam cross members and each top is secured with a washer and nut. Through eyebolts an employee inserts a GOH hang bar & (2) in a standard rack bay to add special designed cross or front to rear members to load beams. In a front to rear member middle are two drilled holes for an inverted 'U' shape bolt attachment. Through each inverted 'U' bolt you insert a hang bar and add nuts to the threaded inverted 'U' bolt ends. With secured bolts, your position is ready for GOH. A flipped shelf or rack bay has capacity for (a) 1 long GOH & (b) 2 short GOH. Feature increases your GOH storage capacity with minimal equipment, labor cost & storage flexibility due to a shelf/rack bay is converted to carton or GOH storage.

GOH 6. GOH Skus Slide To A Storage Row Rear Or Front

GOH skus slide to a storage row rear or front is a GOH static rail storage concept for a single side employee routing pattern that increases employee put-away & pick productivity, enhances rail utilization & rail occupancy. With GOH slide to a rear or front concept, at an aisle entrance that is nearest a pack area an employee transfers GOH onto a rail. As GOH is transferred onto a rail, an employee pushes GOH forward over a rail. After a last GOH is transferred onto a rail, an employee places a sliding position WMS ID onto a rail at a GOH lead end. Features are reduces a put-away employee walk distance to complete a put-away transaction and new skus are closest to your pack area. As another GOH is added to a rail, an employee repeats an old GOH push forward & adds a new sliding position WMS ID onto a rail at a GOH lead end and adds a new GOH to a sliding rail. The concept moves GOH closer to an aisle exist to a pack location thereby to complete a pick reduces an employee walk distance to complete a pick transaction, sliding GOH improves rail utilization.

GOH 7. Hang GOH In A Cavity

Hang in a cavity is a GOH static storage concept that has GOH hang from an elevated rail into a cavity or below an employee walkway. The concept increases GOH storage capacity by adding another short GOH rail (increase from 2 rails to 3 rails or have 1 long GOH rail below 1 short GOH rail) & improves an employee's productivity due to elevated GOH rail is within an easy reach. Cavity design that allows lowest rail level GOH to hang into a cavity options are created from a rack or pipe structural members to support GOH rails & elevated walkway loads and on a floor to build an elevated walkway to support an employee. Walkway steps, kick-plates & handrails are per your local codes & company policy.

GOH 8. How To Handle Winter, Spring, Summer Or Fall (Promotional) GOH Skus

Winter, spring, summer and fall are a year 4 major seasons and promotional GOH skus has an impact on your GOH sku mix. For a particular season, your company purchase department issues POs to bring skus in your warehouse for a season & skus have a sale promotion. In most cases, a season 20% skus account for 80% of your warehouse activities. With this high specific sku volume or high hit concentration & hit density to improve your employee put-away & pick productivity, space utilization & position occupancy, your GOH storage philosophy & layout is planned with 4 sections and each section has skus for each season. Each section is designed to handle your sku peak inventory volume for one season and consideration is given for winter skus that have few GOH skus per ln. ft. & summer skus with many GOH number per ln. ft. If at the completion of a season, residual GOH sku quantity is allocated to an aisle remote rail area or consolidated into one aisle with the season section.

GOH 9. GOH SCAP Handling

GOH SCAP is a term that describes a concept to place GOH in a temporary position in a GOH SCAP (sort, count & pick area). When compared to a GOH manual transport & transfer to a static rail storage position, a GOH SCAP concept improves employee productivity due to less employee walking distances & lower GOH transfer to a position transaction. GOH SCAP equipment options are (1) 4-wheel cart with a hang bar & (2) overhead non-powered trolley with a load bar. With both options, there are 3 cart lanes or trolley travel paths. Two exterior lanes/paths are used for inbound GOH & middle lane/path is for detailed received GOH. GOH SCAP area has two design options. The first is after GOH is bulk received onto a middle lane or path carts/trolleys, GOH remains in lanes/paths, WMS scanned to a temporary position and is ready for withdrawal. A second option has carts/trolleys moved from the detail receiving area to another area lanes/paths, WMS scanned to a temporary storage/pick position and is ready for withdrawal. You design your GOH SCAP area on your GOH sku quantity that is sold after a sku sales promotion or historical sku sales data (based on a vendor delivered quantity, a sku percentage that was sold). After allocating a pre-determined GOH quantity to a SCAP area, a residual quantity is sent to static rail area.

GOH 10. What Is Your GOH Hanger Type

What is your GOH hanger type is a very important design factor for your automatic GOH storage/pick concept. Your GOH hanger design and material selection are determined by (1) your customer preference such as your retail sales floor, (2) how is your GOH is shipped to your customer such as on delivery truck rope loop, hanger box or GOH on a cardboard fold, (3) hanger cost and (4) machine vendor requirement such as metal, wood or plastic.

GOH 11. What Are Your GOH Static Storage Rail Types

Your GOH static storage galvanized rail diameter matches your hanger neck, position identifier and provides a GOH storage/pick position. GOH static rail allows hanger material flexibility. GOH static position types are (1) manual concept with 1 deep and 1 high or 2 levels high, (2) with a manual concept two deep and 1 high or 2 levels high, (3) with an employee elevating concept 6 to 8 levels high HROS vehicle, (4) with GOH hanging in a cavity 2 to 3 levels high, (5) manual push back trolley lanes, (6) dynamic or trolley gravity flow lanes and (6) with an elevated employee walkway 2 to 3 levels high.

GOH 12. GOH Aisle Dust Barrier

GOH aisle dust barrier is a solid cardboard or sheet metal barrier with evenly spaced support members that are anchored to the floor and upright posts. As an employee or vehicle travels in an aisle, a solid barrier prevents dust and dirt moving from an aisle onto the floor below your GOH. Feature are (1) reduces dust collection on to GOH and (2) reduce housekeeping time.

GOH 13. GOH Storage Position Identification

GOH position ID assure employee or hand held scanner line of sight that provides good employee productivity and inventory control. For an effective GOH ID, above GOH does extend downward and cover a below GOH ID and each GOH position ID upward extension is above your GOH. GOH ID options are (1) plastic placards, (2) large cardboard doughnuts, (3) rectangle shaped placards, (4) clip on, (5) cardboard triangles & (6) 'Z' shaped holder. A preferred GOH position ID holder is a cardboard holder that has a GOH position ID upward extension or height above GOH on a rail height to assure easy and quick employee or hand held scanner line of sight.

GOH 14. What Are Your GOH Mechanized Or Automatic Storage Concepts

Your GOH mechanized or automatic storage concepts require that your hanger material matches your equipment manufacturer's specifications. A mechanical GOH concept has at a transfer station an employee completed a transaction. Mechanized concepts computer controlled are (1) powered horizontal carousel that requires horizontal space. Options are (a) single unit and (b) multiple units in a horse-shoe layout and (2) powered vertical carousel that requires vertical space. Automatic concepts require GOH on a standard hanger that matches your automatic storage/pick machine specifications. Automatic machine options are (1) Promech, (2) 200 GOH trolley-less storage/pick and (3) MTS trolley-less storage/pick.

Old Inventory Ideas (OI 1 – O7)
OI 1. Small Sku Quantity & Old Sku Consolidation

Small sku quantity & old sku consolidation is a sku profile strategy that consolidates your small sku quantity and old skus into one pick zone or pick aisle that improves your picker productivity, space utilization and enhances inventory control. A small sku quantity and old sku situation occurs in a catalog, direct marketing or TV marketing warehouse that has a requirement for a minimum on-hand sku quantity to be advertised and old/out of season skus on COs. When a sku with a small inventory quantity (less than allowed to appear in a catalog or TV program) or an old skus are prime positions that are adjacent to positions with 'A' & 'B' moving skus, it creates low sku set-up/replenishment & pick productivity due to additional travel distance between two transactions and low position/space utilization. To improve your picker productivity and space utilization, you relocate your small sku quantity & old skus from prime positions to a pick zone or aisle positions in a non-prime area.

OI 2. What Is Old Inventory & How To Store Your Old Inventory
What is the old inventory stored is a term that describes a dated (old) inventory or skus and how to store your old inventory have several options. With an ABC & D sku inventory classification, old inventory skus have a 'C' & 'D' classification that have few or very few COs and have a receiving date (tag) that is at least several months old. In most warehouses, 'C' & 'D' sku types have a medium sku number & few skus per sku. If you consolidate your 'C' & 'D' skus into 1 aisle or at an aisle remote positions (hand stack onto decked rack bays or with additional load beams create additional short pallet positions) increases sku facings, enhances space utilization and provides a good sku hit density & concentration that improves employee productivity.

OI 3. When To Move & Where To Move A Sku
When & where to move a sku are storage activity decisions that focus on when & where to relocate a sku from its present/prime storage position to a less prime storage position. If a sku has low demand or sales, a sku relocation from a prime storage (dense or standard rack near an aisle exist) position to a less prime storage (rail, decked rack, ½ high or standard rack position in an aisle rear) position improves employee withdrawal productivity due to a reduction in travel time and distance to complete a high volume transaction. When skus are ready for relocation to a less than prime position, in most cases a sku has a small sku inventory. With a small inventory in a less than prime position, it provides storage space improvement & increases position utilization. To answer when to move or relocate question, you look at a sku life cycle or a storage computer program print-out that shows each sku present storage position or just skus in prime positions, age & historical movement (demand or sales) for a specific time period such as 6 months.

OI 4. How To Identify Your Old Inventory
How to identify your old sku inventory is an activity that has an employee or computer program to identify your out-of-date or 'C' & 'D' skus. An out-of-date sku has a sku life or date that has expired & can not be sold to customers. 'C' & 'D' inventory class sku is a sku that has very few or no COs due to lack of customer interest or sku inventory quantity is below your company inventory quantity criteria to qualify as a sku for CO sales. In most operations, 'C' & 'D' skus have few skus/cartons but some skus could have a pallet quantity on a pallet in a storage position that is consider in a prime real estate or high rent area (near an aisle entrance/exit). If your company has an inventory control or WMS computer program, your manager has a computer program print a sku list that lists from oldest received sku sequence that shows each sku position and quantity to your latest sku received date. If your company has a sku receiving & inventory tag with a color code or printed receiving date, an employee is assigned to walk aisles & for each sku with a color code/received printed date to list each sku and sku number, position & quantity. A second old sku ID concept is to notice accumulated dust on a sku exterior surface that indicates an old sku. To consolidate your 'C' & 'D' skus into 1 aisle or remote positions, hand stack onto decked rack positions or place in short positions increases sku facings, provides a good sku 'C' & 'D' hit density & concentration that improves employee productivity & enhances space utilization. If your old skus have a pallet quantity, a few skus/cartons are placed in an aisle with other old skus & a full/partial pallet quantity is placed in a most remote or off-site storage.

OI 5. 'D' Skus Are In An Aisle Rear Or In One Storage Aisle
'D' skus are consolidated in an aisle rear or in one aisle positions is a storage philosophy for your slow moving skus that have very few COs or have 'not available for sale' status. When you consolidate your slow moving 'D' skus in

one area, you have increased your sku hit concentration & density & with a small carton quantity improves your space utilization. Increase in your sku hit concentration & density improves your employee productivity due to (1) in your storage aisle, if your fast ('A') & medium ('B' & 'C') moving skus are adjacent to each other it means less employee travel time & distance to complete a transaction & (2) with 'D' skus in one area, if there are several carton transactions there is less travel time & distance to complete transactions. Since a 'D' sku has relatively no movement & if a 'D' sku has a large carton inventory, a small carton quantity is a hand stacked position & large pallet inventory is placed into a very remote or off-site position that improves your space utilization.

OI 6. How To Scrap Your Old Inventory
How to scrap your old inventory is an activity that has old or aged sku inventory removed from a position and donated to charity, sold to another company or disposed in trash. An old inventory scrap program objective to remove old skus from a position & create vacant positions for new sku inventory. After a manager has received authorization to scrap old or aged sku inventory, you are required to select skus for your scrap inventory activity. With the same age, your sku scrap selection options are (1) *By Age* that scraps oldest sku first, (2) *Random Sku* selection that scraps skus, (3) *Book Inventory Or Sku Value* that scraps highest valued skus first & (4) *SILO or Small-In & Large-Out* that scraps skus by size. With a limited dollar inventory scrap amount by scrapping high cube skus first, a SILO scrap program creates greatest vacate position number in a warehouse that increases sku facings, enhances space utilization & with no traveling past positions with old skus improves employee productivity.

OI 7. Where To Place Skus With Small Inventory Quantity & Aged Skus
Where to place skus with a small inventory quantity or aged skus are skus that occupy a position, do not have many COs ('C' or 'D' skus) and have a small inventory quantity that does not permit advertisements. Most operations have 'C' and 'D' skus mixed with high & medium volume 'A' or 'B' moving skus in 1 aisle positions that creates non-productive storage put-away or withdrawal employee travel past your small inventory or aged skus. When skus with a small inventory quantity or aged skus with a 'C' or 'D' classification are grouped in 1 aisle or at an aisle rear positions, the approach improves sku hit concentration & hit density that improves forklift truck driver withdrawal productivity & permits.

Pick Position Replenishment Activity Ideas
General Replenishment (GR 1 – GR 18)
GR 1. Must Be Occupied Or Skus In Pick Positions
Must be occupied is a small item, GOH or carton replenishment that improves picker productivity and increases completed CO number. Must be occupied replenishment concept has a replenishment employee transfer and WMS scan a sku quantity to a WMS identified position and scan transactions are sent to a WMS computer program to update the status. After a sku quantity and position update, a WMS computer program releases a CO number that matches a sku replenishment quantity. Features are (1) for 'A' moving skus in a position increases hit concentration & density that improves picker productivity, (2) minimizes 'no stock' or stock and requires on-line replenishment transaction transfer to a WMS computer.

GR 2. What & Where Are Your Replenishment Tools
What & where are replenishment tools that are required for proper carton presentation and transfer to a position. In a small item warehouse, replenishment tools are (1) for employee safety, safety rubber tip gloves, (2) for productivity, a knife with a replaceable rigid blade, (3) tool holder on a cart or employee belt that has a knife, pencil, scanner & other items sleeves/holsters, (4) sku symbology faces a replenishment employee, (5) use a cart or pallet as a work surface & (6) access to trash removal device.

GR 3. Know Your Cubes
Know your cube (carton/tote & position) is a small item or carton factor that impacts your position set-up/replenishment employee productivity and position utilization. Cube information includes your carton/tote exterior dimensions (length, width & height) & your position dimensions (length, width & height). When considering a position height you allow sufficient open space from a carton/tote in a position to the above position structural

member bottom. The space permits a replenishment employee to easily transfer a carton/tote to a position and a picker to easily remove a sku from a carton/tote. Each carton/tote and position dimensions (length, width and height) determines a carton/tote number per position. With accurate carton/tote and position cube data in the computer files and your CO sku demand, your computer suggested replenishment transaction carton/tote number matches your position capacity to assure 100% utilization and minimizes ready reserve positions in a pick area.

GR 4. What Is Your Replenishment Signal
What is your replenishment signal is an idea that is used to improve replenishment employee productivity and enhance position utilization. After a position has a sku quantity set-up or WMS scanned and physically transferred to a position, a sku quantity and position and sku WMS IDs are sent to a WMS computer for CO release. Completed COs deplete skus from a position and depleted sku quantity is sent to a WMS computer. If a sku set-up quantity is less than a CO sku quantity, a sku replenishment is required at a position. With a WMS program (computer suggested), as a position require a replenishment a WMS program sends a message as a paper document or paper less message on a RF device. With a manual operation (employee suggested), as a position requires a replenishment, an employee recognizes that a position has capacity for a carton/tote or a colored mark appears on a sleeve/lane. A mark indicates that an average carton/tote quantity fits into a position.

GR 5. One Or Double Slot
One or double slot is a small item pick line/aisle strategy that is used to increase your completed CO number and reduce ready reserve requirement and replenishment transactions to 1 position. *One Slot* concept has a sku assigned to one pick position. *Double Slot* concept has a sku scanned and placed into 2 WMS ID pick positions. To control your pick activity, your pick instruction computer program directs a pick to the first scanned position. After a sku quantity is depleted, a computer directs the next pick transaction to the second scanned position.

GR 6. Multiple Fronts/Zones
Multiple fronts/zones is a small item, GOH or carton pick area design that separates a fast moving/'A' sku into multiple pick front/zones in separate pick sections to improve picker productivity and increase your completed CO number. When your CO wave sku quantity exceeds your budgeted picker productivity, a sku in one position creates good picker productivity but your picker completes a CO wave sku pick requirements. Multiple pick fronts/zones for your 'A' moving skus (sku demand exceeds picker productivity) has you creates two 'A' moving pick fronts/zones/sections that are entered into your WMS computer program as separate WMS identified pick activity area. With 2 separate WMS identified pick activity areas with the same 'A' moving skus allows your WMS computer program to direct COs to two pick areas that from both pick areas assures good picker productivity and higher completed CO number.

GR 7. Sku Set-Up Or Replenishment Before Or During Your Pick Activity
Sku position set-up or replenishment before or during your pick activity is a small item or carton issue or when does your set-up or replenishment employee transfer a carton to a position. If your WMS program requires a sku quantity in a position to match a CO wave sku quantity for a CO release to a pick concept, you require an entire CO demand for a sku quantity that is WMS scanned and physically transferred to a position. Features are (1) creates good pick productivity, (2) minimizes stock outs and (3) with one aisle for both replenishment and pick activities, reduces aisle congestion and assures good productivity. If your warehouse has a sku replenishment activity occur during your pick activity means that your replenishment activity is human controlled or CO wave requirement exceed a pick position capacity. To assure on-time CO completion and as a sku quantity is depleted, a WMS program suggests a replenishment activity prior to additional CO release to a pick concept or prior to a zero quantity in a position. Features are (1) slow completed COs, (2) potential stock outs & (3) with one aisle for both replenishment & pick activities, increase potential aisle congestion & low productivity.

GR 8. Who Determines Your Customer Order Wave Or Pieces
Who determines your CO wave or work day piece quantity is an issue for a small item or carton that determines your replenishment employee number that is based on their productivity. A CO wave or piece quantity is

determined by your staff and is based on your picker budgeted productivity rate that determines your picker number. From a CO wave, a WMS computer allocates in inventory files and sends your warehouse moves messages for a sku quantity transferred (set-up/replenishment) from a storage area to a position. Each sku set-up/replenishment transaction assures sufficient sku quantity in a position to satisfy a CO wave sku demand and based on your set-up/replenishment productivity rates it determines your employee number.

GR 9. Employee Or Computer Directed Replenishment

Employee or computer directed replenishment is a small item or carton concept that has an employee complete a replenishment transaction to improve replenishment productivity and increase completed CO number. A dynamic catalog, direct mail, TV marketing or retail store pick concept with a very large sku number that requires numerous aisles and positions and covers a large area requires on time and accurate replenishment transactions. *Employee Directed Replenishment Activity* has a replenishment or picker look at a sku quantity in a position, determine a replenishment quantity and transfer a sku quantity from a reserve position to a position. Features are (1) sku selected for replenishment could have potential for no picks and if a picker completes a replenishment transaction means lower picker productivity and lower completed CO number. *Computer Suggested Replenishment Activity*, for a CO wave your WMS computer identifies each sku with each sku quantity that requires replenishment. Features are (1) due to CO demand, only skus that require a replenishment are listed, (2) if a replenishment activity starts before a pick activity, improved picker productivity due to available skus in a position, (3) improved replenishment productivity due less aisle congestion & (4) with a replenishment activity sequenced by pick zones/aisles from highest to lowest sku number & time due to complete COs, increased completed CO number.

GR 10. Pick Clean

Pick clean is a small item or carton pick activity that improves your picker and replenishment employee productivity and enhances your 'A' or fast moving sku inventory control. Pick clean is used when you group your 'A' or fast moving skus in one pick zone or aisle and occurs when your pick activity depletes a sku quantity in a position to zero. After a position sku quantity has been depleted to zero, prior to a sku replenishment to a position a zero WMS scan transaction is completed and sent to a WMS computer to assure that old sku is depleted from a position. After zero scan transaction, a new sku is WMS scanned & physically set-up/replenished to a position. When a CO wave sku quantity exceeds a position capacity for a CO wave sku quantity to assure a sku quantity is available in a pick area, a second position has sku quantity to assure a CO wave completion.

GR 11. Do Not Oversize

Do not oversize is a small item and carton idea assures a carton size and sku quantity matches your position requirements to assure replenishment productivity and enhance inventory control. Do not oversize has your purchasing department request vendor to package skus into a carton size that matches your pick concept design features & are easily handled by an employee. With a small item pick concept, this means that your carton size fits into your position that assures good replenishment productivity, carton sku quantity permits accurate replenishment to an automatic pick machine that assure good inventory control and a carton is travels on a powered conveyor travel path that assures maximum picker productivity and is not picked as a manual picked carton.

GR 12. Your 'A' Skus Are Fixed/Remain Or Rotated

'A's are fixed or remain is a small item or carton strategy that has for all your CO waves your 'A' moving skus are assigned to one pick zone or aisle position. With skus remaining in one pick zone or aisle, a sku set-up or replenishment strategy that lowers picker productivity and enhances sku inventory control. With a fixed or remain sku allocation to pick zone or pick aisle concept, after sku quantity becomes depleted in a position, a WMS/inventory control program directs a sku quantity replenishment transaction to move a sku from a storage area to the same position. If new 'A' or fast moving skus are allocated to positions that are adjacent to slower moving skus, your pick productivity is lower due to additional travel distance between two picks. A fixed or remain sku position strategy is preferred for your B, C & D moving skus.

Rotate your 'A' skus is used in a small item or carton idea and has your 'A' skus assigned to one pick zone or pick aisle strategy that improves your replenishment and picker productivity and enhances sku inventory control.

The concept has for day 1 CO wave all your 'A' or fast moving skus assigned to one pick zone or pick aisle that minimizes a picker walk distance between two picks. At a CO wave end from all your 'A' positions any residual sku quantity is transferred to another pick zone or pick aisle. After a position zero scan transaction completion, 'A' sku rotation creates vacate positions for day 2 CO wave 'A' or fast moving skus. Features are (1) additional employee activity to relocate skus that is minimized with rounded down cartons, (2) requires a zero scan transaction to assure sku inventory control, (3) requires position profile and set-up for hit concentration & density for high picker productivity & (4) preferred for your 'A' or fast moving skus.

GR 13. Re-Organize Or Re-Profile Your 'A' Skus
Re-organize or re-profile your 'A' skus is small item or carton strategy that improves your picker productivity and increases your completed CO number. A re-organize or re-profile strategy requires your set-up or replenishment employee to allocate 'A' or fast moving skus to one pick zone or aisle and as required to relocate 'B' or medium moving skus to another pick zone or aisle. With your 'A' or fast moving skus in one pick zone or aisle, it increases your sku hit concentration & density that improves your picker & replenishment employee productivity due to short travel distances between two positions.

GR 14. Profile Or Pick Line/Aisle Set-Up (See PAP 6 Page 96)

GR 15. No Stock
A "no stock" condition occurs when a sku physical inventory is physically in a position but a WMS computer inventory file does not reflect sku inventory in a position. When a situation occurs with a CO, a WMS computer does not release COs to print a CO pick transaction instruction for a picker or pick machine. It creates a low mark for CO service and an inventory control problem that requires a sku count & allocation to another position.

GR 16. Stock Out
A "stock out" or "out of stock" condition occurs when an sku inventory file shows inventory in a position when there is none. A "stock out" or "out of stock" condition creates non-productive picker/pick machine activity because the picker/pick device traveled to a position but could not complete a transaction.

GR 17. Loose, Bagged/Boxed/Binned Or Carton Skus
Loose, bagged, boxed/bin or carton skus are a small item sku characteristics and replenishment options to improve replenishment productivity and enhance inventory control. Sku replenishment characteristics are determined by your (1) CO wave sku quantity, (2) position capacity & type, (3) WMS identified sku quantity per bag, box/bin or carton & (4) sku handling concept. A loose sku replenishment features are (1) has an employee physically count a sku quantity, (2) sku is placed into a captive position bin or is stackable in a shelf or decked rack, (3) potential for sku damage or lose & (4) low replenishment employee productivity. Bagged, boxed or binned small sku replenishment quantity uses repacked skus that have a WMS ID in your computer program. When required to complete a replenishment transaction, a bagged/boxed/binned is transferred from a storage position to a pick position. Features are (1) requires a repack activity and labor, (2) bag/box/bin is placed into a position, (3) minimal replenishment employee count activity, (4) minimal sku damage and lose & (5) good employee productivity. Carton replenishment quantity uses a vendor carton with a WMS ID in your computer program. Features are the same as bag/box/bin replenishment sku concept except no re-pack activity and labor.

GR 18. Know Your Pairs Or Family Group
Know your pairs or family group is a small item, GOH or carton replenishment concept that improves pick & replenishment productivity & increases completed CO number. Pairs or family group replenishment means that 1 sku creates sales for another sku (salt and pepper items), common components for an end product or several skus with a common language. When pairs or family group skus are profiled or assigned to pick positions in one aisle, pick zone or pick cell, it creates (1) multiple sku replenishment transactions to one pick aisle, zone or cell that means less time to set-up a pick line and faster CO release, (2) hit sku hit concentration and density to improve picker productivity & (3) less picker travel distance and time that increases your completed CO.

Replenishment Quantity Ideas (RQ 1 – RQ 6)

RQ 1. Human Or Computer Suggested Replenishment Quantity

Human or computer suggested replenishment quantity is the basic question in a small item warehouse for a sku quantity for set-up or replenishment to a position. When a human determines a sku replenishment quantity, there is potential for a sku quantity not to match a position capacity. If a human replenishment sku quantity is less than a pick position capacity or CO requirement and to satisfy a CO wave it requires another sku replenishment transaction. Additional transaction lowers your employee productivity. If a human replenishment sku quantity exceeds a position capacity or CO wave requirement, it requires an extra sku quantity WMS scanned and physically transferred to a ready reserve position. Features are additional employee activity that lowers productivity and additional reserve position that has low space utilization. A computer suggested sku replenishment quantity matches a position capacity. With one replenishment transaction, it means good employee productivity and enhanced position space utilization & minimal ready reserve position for enhanced space utilization.

RQ 2. How To Replenish

How much is small item or carton pick position set-up or replenishment sku transfer quantity that improves employee productivity and enhances sku inventory control. Sku quantity options are (1) CO wave requirement. When a total CO wave sku requirement is transferred and fits into a position, with one replenishment activity it assures good replenishment employee productivity, inventory control and high completed CO number. If a total CO wave sku requirement exceeds a position capacity, it requires your replenishment employee to locate & transfer a sku quantity to a ready reserve location that lowers your productivity and requires additional space and (2) position capacity. Features are minimizes your ready reserve position requirement, improves space utilization, maintains your employee productivity.

RQ 3. Round-Up, Round-Down Or Exact

Round-up, round-down or exact are a small item carton replenishment quantity options that are calculated by your WMS computer program to improve replenishment productivity and enhance inventory control. Per your CO wave (sku demand), a WMS computer program determines each WMS identified sku quantity and from each sku quantity a WMS program calculates each sku rounded-up, rounded-down or exact sku (full and partial full cartons) carton quantity. *Rounded-Up Carton Sku Quantity*, if a WMS ID sku quantity exceeds a CO wave sku demand, full carton is transferred from your storage area to your pick position. It is anticipated that a your CO wave end that a position has a residual sku quantity. For your next CO wave a residual sku quantity in a prime position options are (1) to relocate a residual sku quantity from one position to another position in different pick zone that creates vacate positions in your prime pick zone. For your next CO wave, the approach assures good sku hit concentration and density for good picker productivity but requires additional replenishment labor and a second pick zone (2) to have a sku remain in a prime zone position and profile your new skus around existing skus. For your next CO wave, the approach creates additional walk distance and time between two picks that creates lower picker productivity but does not require additional replenishment labor. With a rounded-down carton concept, for a CO wave skus your WMS computer program calculates only full cartons are sent to your prime pick zone and 1 full carton sent to a second pick zone that at a CO wave end would contain your residual sku quantity. *Rounded-Down Approach*, your prime pick zone positions are picked clean and with zero scan transactions are ready to receive your next CO wave skus, assures good prime zone pick line profile for good picker productivity, no relocate/replenishment labor, with skus in a second pick zone completion of all CO. *Exact Sku Quantity* is a carton replenishment concept that has your storage area employee in transfer full cartons and in a storage position to open, count and transfer a required sku from a carton into a carton for replenishment to a position. With exact sku approach, all prime pick zone pick positions are picked clean & with zero scan transactions are ready to receive your next CO wave skus, assures good prime zone pick line profile for good picker productivity, no relocate or replenishment labor, but low replenishment labor due to open and count activity, trash (empty carton) in a storage area & open carton in a position that means potential sku damage or lose.

RQ 4. All At Once Or In Sections

All at once or in sections is a small item, carton or pallet CO wave WMS identified sku replenishment strategy that improves replenishment productivity and enhances inventory control. When a high volume or high cube sku is a replenishment sku, there is potential for a CO wave sku replenishment quantity to exceed a position capacity. *Send All Or Entire Sku Replenishment Quantity* to a pick area, features are (1) extra sku quantity removes a ready reserve position and physical transfer and scan transaction & (2) additional sku quantity and potential queue on a transport concept that delays an entire pick line set-up and in an early pick time fewer WMS computer released and completed CO number. *Send A Sku Replenishment Quantity In Sections Or Quantity That Fits Into A Position*, features are (1) minimal ready reserve position and transfer/scan transactions, (2) your replenishment labor focuses on a pick line set-up, (3) minimal queues on a transport concept & (4) greater sku set-up number on a pick line means a greater WMS computer release and completed CO number in a short time.

RQ 5. What Is The Capacity

What is the capacity is a small item, GOH or carton concept that identifies your position small item, GOH, carton or pallet sku number that fits in each position and assures maximum space utilization and enhances inventory control. Your position capacity is determined by (1) cube space or sku number that fits into each position, (2) residual sku quantity or cube in each position & (3) your computer program calculates a sku replenishment quantity that is rounded-up, rounded-down or exact piece number. To have an efficient replenishment activity, your computer replenishment program calculates your sku replenishment quantity for full cartons, partial or full pallet that satisfies your CO wave sku demand & minimizes sku handlings/scan transactions.

RQ 6. Partial Or Full Pallet First

Partial or full pallet first is a small item or carton flow rack that has a WMS computer program suggests a sku pallet quantity for replenishment to a position. To complete a CO wave, a sku requires multiple pallets and in a storage area there are at least 1 partial full pallet and full pallets. Your pallet replenishment options are (1) *First Pallet Replenishment Is A Partial Pallet* option has a move transaction for a WA, NA or VNA forklift to withdraw from a storage both a partial pallet and full pallets. In a standard WMS program, a sku allocation sequence is based on a pallet received date, the oldest sku is allocate first, regarding of whether a pallet is partial or full. In most warehouses, partial pallet is the most frequent occurrence. When a partial pallet arrives first at a transfer station, an employee completes an sku move and either transfers cartons to another pallet or places a label on each carton for transfer to transport or transfer a partial pallet to a temporary hold position. When a full pallet arrives at a transfer station, an employee either completes an sku move and transfers cartons from a full pallet to a temporary hold position or onto a partial pallet; or transfers each carton to a transport concept. Features are (a) standard WMS program, with minimal computer calculations, (b) FIFO sku rotation, (c) at an early time, picker handles an empty pallet, (d) at an early time, an other replenishment activity is required at a position & (e) at a CO wave completion, partial pallet is returned to a storage area & (2) *First Withdraw A Full Pallet & Withdraw A Partial Pallet As Required* option has your WMS program determine a skus that require a full pallet quantity and matches a full pallet quantity to sku pallet. In response to a CO wave needs, a full pallet is allocated and is withdrawn from a storage area. If a CO wave requires a partial pallet quantity, a WMS program allocates an existing partial pallet. A partial pallet is a last pallet withdrawn from a storage area and sent to a transfer station. At a transfer station or replenishment position, a full pallet is handled as described above. Features are (a) dynamic WMS program with some additional WMS computer processing time, (b) accurate pallet carton quantity, (c) at an early start, picker handles a minimal empty pallet number, (d) at an early start, other positions are set-up due to one less replenishment at a pallet position, (e) at an early start, a transport concept handles full pallets & (f) CO wave end, a partial pallet has minimal cartons.

Replenishment Position Identification Ideas (RPI 1 – RP 2)

RPI 1. Replenishment Position Identification

Replenishment position ID is a small item, carton, GOH or pallet ID on a position structural member that IDs a position replenishment location to improve replenishment productivity and enhance inventory control. Each replenishment position ID is a human or human/machine readable symbology that allows an employee to match an employee or computer directed replenishment activity to an appropriate position. With a shelf, decked rack, standard rack, carousel basket, GOH rail, drive-in rack, slide, peg board, stacking frame and floor stack rack a position ID is a replenishment position ID that is placed onto a shelf, load beam, rail or post that is above, below or adjacent to a position. Whenever possible an ID is placed in the middle of a position and for all positions in a consistent location. With some IDs, directional arrows or colored labels assure proper pick/replenishment position ID. With some small item automatic pick machines, a replenishment ID is attached to a sleeve or lane structural member and a shelf or flow rack ready reserve position is related to each sleeve or lane ID. In a carton or pallet AS/RS crane concept, all replenishment transactions are completed by a computer controlled crane that requires all replenishment/pick position IDs entered in a computer program. With a carton or pallet flow rack and drive thru concept, there is a pick aisle with position IDs that a progression along a pick zone front and a replenishment aisle with replenishment IDs along a same front. During replenishment position ID attachment you make sure that each pick and replenishment position IDs match.

RP 2. Mark Your Lane/Sleeve/Basket/Shelf

Mark your sku lane/sleeve/shelf or basket is used in small item automatic pick machine or horizontal carousel pick concepts to improve replenishment employee productivity. After you determine a carton sku quantity that fits into an automatic pick machine sleeve/lane or horizontal basket, from a pick machine sleeve/lane or carousel basket top you place a mark. Space between a pick machine sleeve/lane to carousel basket top & mark represents one carton sku quantity. As a mark appears, it is a signal for a replenishment employee to complete a carton transfer. If a carton quantity exceeds a reasonable length, ¼ or ½ is written onto a lane/sleeve or basket mark.

Replenishment Position Routing Ideas (RPR 1)

RPR 1. Replenishment position routing is a small item, GOH, carton or pallet pick area concept that is used to sequentially direct a replenishment employee through a pick aisle or zone, arrive at a position and complete replenishment to a correct position. A routing concept improves replenishment productivity due to minimal double walking past positions and is easy to understand.

Carton & Position Preparation Ideas (MCPP 1 – MCPP 8)

MCPP 1. Save & Reuse A Carton Top/Front

Save & reuse a carton top/front is a small item idea that has your replenishment employee cut a carton top or front (smiley face). After a carton has a cut top or front and is transferred to a position, there is potential for skus to fall from a carton to the floor. To reduce falling sku potential, your replenishment employee transfers as carton cut top/front that serves as a sku barrier to retain skus in a carton. After a carton is in a position and skus become depleted, as required a picker removes a cut top/front.

MCPP 2. No Flaps

No flaps is a small item idea that improves replenishment and picker productivity and reduces sku damage. A carton with no top flaps transferred means that your replenishment employee remove a carton top flaps. Features are (1) improved picker productivity due clear and unobstructed access to a carton, (2) minimal potential for carton hang-up in a flow lane, (3) standard width clearance in a position, (4) during a replenishment activity, minimizes potential carton flap hang-up on a pick position structural member and (5) on a trash conveyor or in a trash wagon lower trash master carton cube that increases a carton per ln ft or per wagon.

MCPP 3. When To Cut Your Carton Or Who Opens

When to cut your carton or who opens a carton in a pick position is a small item question to assure good replenishment and picker productivity. As a sku flows through your activities some activities are pre-pick activities that are less time critical and pick activities that are time critical. Your carton cut options are (1) *Picker Employee concept* has a picker focus their attention on a pick instruction that is a position, pick quantity, CO container and to transfer a sku into a CO container that is in a cart, on a conveyor or in a basket. A non-open carton in a position has minimal clearances that could require additional time to handle a carton and dispose of a carton top into the trash. For a picker to open a carton, it is considered a non-repetitive activity for one carton that requires additional non-productive picker time to locate a knife and open a carton or tear open a carton or (2) *Replenishment*

Employee concept in most situations a carton is on a conveyor travel path, pallet or cart deck that has solid, flat and smooth surface with sufficient clear space to handle a carton. A replenishment employee open carton activity is a repetitive activity that most frequently involves several cartons and is considered simply activity with protective gloves. If you complete a carton open time study, a carton open activity requires from a picker to notice an empty carton in a pick position & to place a cut open a carton in a position requires at least 1 minute. With a pick/pass concept, 1 minute of picker non-productive time can congest a pick line & lower your completed CO number. A replenishment employee open carton activity involves 30 to 40 seconds per carton with no pick line down time. If we accept that customer on-time service & high completed CO number is an objective, your replenishment employee cuts a carton as part of a replenishment activity.

MCPP 4. Remove Filler Material

Remove the filler is replenishment activity in a small item idea to improve picker productivity that results from easy access to skus in a carton. Remove a carton filler material occurs as replenishment employee opens a carton and after a carton top is removed to remove any filler material such as padding, sheets, cardboard, chipboard or other items from a carton. In a replenishment aisle, removed filler is transferred to a trash container. If filler material remains in a carton, it becomes difficult (obstruction) to pick skus & trash in a pick aisle. Features lower picker productivity & decreases your completed CO number.

MCPP 5. Zero Scan

Zero scan is a WMS identified position scan transaction that enhances inventory control and assures good position management. After a pick position is picked clean (skus are depleted) and prior to a new WMS ID sku transferred and scanned to a position, your set-up employee completes a zero scan transaction. A zero scan transaction is sent to a WMS computer that updates a WMS ID sku quantity in a position as zero. Per your pick area design, a zero scan transaction assures that in a WMS computer that there are not two WMS ID skus in one position. The situation creates pick errors due to a CO pick was completed for a sku that was not a CO.

MCPP 6. Narrow Carton Width

Narrow carton width is a small item or carton idea that has your carton placed into your position with narrow carton width facing a picker to improve picker productivity, space utilization and reduce sku damage/lost. With a carton dimension facing a picker aisle, it provides potential for the greatest sku number between 2 position posts that increases (1) hit concentration and density to improve picker productivity with a shortest walk distance between two picks,(2) enhances space utilization with the greatest sku number per ln ft and (3) in a carton flow rack lane, carton bottom flaps run in a carton long dimension that assure smooth carton travel.

MCPP 7. Smile Or No Smile

Smile or no smile are a small item carton replenishment to a position feature that improves picker productivity and increase your completed CO number. *No Smile Face Carton* in a position means that a carton has a solid front/top and requires a picker to cut/rip open a carton front/top. *Smile Face Carton* has top flaps removed and the front has a 'V' or half circle cut front. A carton open activity is a non-productive activity that lowers your completed CO number and on a pick/pass line can create congestion. When compared to a replenishment employee opening a carton requires additional time due a more difficult time to access a carton front/top which is more difficult in a carton flow rack position. When a replenishment employee creates a smile face carton or removes a carton top, it adds time to a replenishment activity. But the additional time is offset by increased picker productivity, replenishment employee has a solid work surface, safety gloves and quality knife, easier to handle carton trash and remove filler material and with multiple cartons per position is consider a repetitive activity. To minimize potential of skus falling from an open carton, a removed front section can be inserted into a carton front and serve a sku retainer and top flaps placed on the top to retain skus.

MCPP 8. Pick Position Divider

Pick position dividers/separators are used in a small item idea to separate skus in a position bay that improves picker productivity, space utilization and enhances inventory control. A position divider is used in a shelf, decked rack or carton flow rack position. When your skus are difficult to stack or are loose full depth dividers are used to restrict sku mix in a wide position. To create multiple positions or skus in a bin/tote for very small skus, dividers are placed into a bin/tote interior. To assure cartons in a flow rack lane remain in a lane, a divider is placed full length between two carton flow rack positions.

MCPP 9. Mark Your Carton Flow Lane Width

Mark your carton flow lane width is an idea that is used in a small item activity to separate skus in a carton flow rack position to improve picker productivity, space utilization and enhance inventory control. Mark your carton flow rack lane has an employee place colored tape onto a flow rack impact bar or structural support member. The distance between two marks is width for a position and is set for widest carton width. If your flow rack lane has guides or no guides, for a replenishment employee to mark identify a position width. With narrow cartons, it could allow two cartons wide in a position.

Extra Replenishment Quantity Ideas (ERQ 1 – ERQ 2)

ERQ 1. Where To Put It

Where to put it. It is a small item or carton set-up or replenishment employee idea that improves employee productivity and enhances sku inventory control. If a sku replenishment quantity exceeds a pick position capacity extra sku quantity is placed into a ready reserve position. With a shelf or decked rack pick concept, reserve positions are above a top (highest) or bottom (pigeon hole) pick positions or at another shelf/decked rack position location. With flow rack pick concept, reserve positions are decked positions on a flow rack top structural members and below a bottom flow rack lane on decked positions. With an automatic pick machine or carousel pick concept, the reserve positions are shelves or flow racks along the replenishment aisle.

ERQ 2. When Your Position Sku Quantity Runs Over

When your position runs over describes a computer suggested sku replenishment quantity that is based on a CO withdrawal and exceeds a WMS ID pick position capacity. In a pick area, a sku replenishment quantity requires a ready reserve position and physical deposit and scan transactions are sent to a WMS computer for sku update. To assure accurate sku inventory control and CO completion, a position sku quantity is scanned and sent to a WMS computer for sku update.

Carton & Pallet Flow Rack Ideas (CPFR 1 – CPFR 6)

CPFR 1. Carton Flow Rack Impact Bar

A carton flow rack impact bar is a small item activity with a carton flow rack pick position idea that improves your replenishment employee productivity and reduces flow lane wheel damage. A carton flow rack impact bar option are (1) horizontal structural member that is a flow rack bay full width, 4 to 8 ins depth and installed on a flow rack change end or (2) solid metal member that is structural attached to the flow rack end and extends 12 ins into a flow rack. A replenishment employee transfers cartons to a flow rack lane, it provides a solid surface for a carton and allows a master carton to be push gently onto a flow rack wheels. Features are protects the flow lane wheels from damage as a replenishment employee transfers a carton into a carton flow lane, serves as the location for replenishment (pick position) identification and location for you to apply to indicate flow lane width.

CPFR 2. Sheppard Hook

A sheppard hook is a small item idea that improves picker/replenishment employee productivity & minimizes sku damage. As cartons are transferred onto a carton flow lane, gravity force & replenishment employee forward pressure on the last carton moves all cartons through a flow lane. On some occasions, a carton can become hung-up in the flow lane and does not arrive at the pick position. To move a hung-up carton in a flow lane, a replenishment or picker uses a Sheppard hook or pole to push or pull a carton forward in a flow lane to a position end. When not in use on a replenishment or pick side, a hook shaped pole is hung on a flow rack member.

CPFR 3. Look For Jams Or Hang-Ups

Look out for jams or hang-ups is a small item, carton, GOH or pallet flow rack situation occurs as a tote/carton, GOH or pallet does not travel/move over a flow lane. When a carton/tote, GOH or pallet does not travel over a gravity flow travel path it is considered a jam or hang-up that is resolved by a pick or replenishment employee. Resolution time is non-productive picker time and lowers your completed CO number due to a sku was not available in a pick position. To minimize future hang-ups or jams in a carton flow rack, you should quantify reasons and take corrective action. Some reasons are (1) poor quality carton bottom surface or bowed carton, (2) carton length was to narrow for flow lane, (3) flap hang-up, (4) carton edge in one flow lane hangs-up/jams on an adjacent carton or flow rack member, (5) carton weight was to low, (6) carton weight was to heavy and cause sku damage & (7) skus fall from a carton. GOH flow rail potential problems are (1) trolley wheels are not on a rail, (2) trolley load was to low and (3) trolley load was to heavy. Pallet flow lane potential jam/hang-up reasons are (1) pallet bottom deck board missing, (2) bottom deck board nails extend beyond wood, (3) pallet not square on flow lane, (4) wheel or roller hangs-up in open space between 2 bottom deck boards & (5) wrong pallet.

CPFR 4. Carton Flow Rack Lane Guides
Carton flow rack lane guides are an option that is used in a small item activity with carton flow rack positions to improve picker productivity, space utilization and enhances sku inventory control. Carton flow rack guides are used full length in a flow rack bay and extend an estimate 1/8 in above a flow lane wheels to create a lane between two positions or a position and side structural members. The open space between 2 guides is 1 in wider than your widest carton width that sets your carton width characteristics. As gravity moves a carton over a flow lane wheels, guides direct carton travel from a flow rack charge end to a pick position. If a carton width exceeds an open space between 2 guides, it is extremely difficult to move a carton through a flow lane and requires a wide carton assigned to another position type or skus transferred into a standard flow rack carton/tote. Also, space between 2 guides serves as a replenishment identification location on a flow rack impact bar or structural support member.

CPFR 5. Three Skate-Wheels Or Rollers Under Your Shortest Carton
Three skate-wheels or rollers are under a shortest carton length is a small item idea for carton flow through a flow lane that minimizes sku damage/lost and improves picker productivity. To assure carton travel over your flow lane travel, a flow lane requires at least 3 wheels under your shortest carton.

CPFR 6. Pallet Flow Lane Entry Guides & Forklift Truck Stop
Pallet flow lane entry guides & forklift truck stop is used on a pallet flow lane entrance to improve your forklift truck pallet transfer productivity and to minimize flow lane damage. Pallet flow lane entry guide are harden metal angled shaped members on both flow lane sides. Each angle is pitched toward a flow lane and serves as a guide to assure a pallet is easily and properly placed onto a flow lane wheels. A forklift truck stop is an inverted 'V' shaped metal member that is anchored to the floor with an inverted 'V' shaped member crown extending upward. In this position as a WA forklift truck is completing a pallet transfer to a pallet flow lane, an inverted 'V' serves as a stop for a WA forklift front wheels. Features are assure proper placement onto a flow lane & minimizes flow lane damage.

Replenishment Position Height Ideas (RPH 1 – RPH 2)
RPH 1. Replenishment Top Position
Your replenishment top position is a concern for a small item or carton activity to assure that your replenishment employee can complete a replenishment transaction to a top position above a floor surface that improves employee productivity and enhances space utilization. To complete a carton or GOH replenishment transaction, an employee is required to lift a full carton or GOH to an elevation above the floor surface and push a carton onto a shelf, conveyor or basket or GOH onto rail. In most applications, a top shelf, conveyor, basket or GOH rail is above an employee's head, a carton has a smiley face and a replenishment transaction is completed with no skus falling to the floor. When you design a shelf, decked rack, horizontal carousel basket or static GOH rail your pick position height has the same replenishment height above the floor surface. If you have a 5'-6" employee and your top position is 6'-0" to 6'-1" above the floor surface, a mobile cart with a safety step ladder, safety stool, safety step ladder permits your employee to complete a top position replenishment transaction. If a work assist or HROS vehicle is used, your pick area has restricted aisle travel or replenishments are made from a separate aisle. With

carton gravity flow rack or sloped conveyor pick concepts, replenishment top position elevation is a nomimal 8 ins higher that a top position elevation. The situation could require a concept to increase a replenishment elevation above the floor.

RPH 2. How To Reach Your Replenishment Top Position
How to reach your top replenishment positions is a question that a small item activity must answer to your shelf, decked rack or horizontal replenishment position to improve employee productivity, enhance space utilization and minimize equipment damage and employee injury. When we consider positions for your 'C' & 'D' skus, we must assure a replenishment employee can quickly, easily and safely complete a sku set-up or replenishment transaction. Various concepts to increase a replenishment employee ability to complete a transaction above an employee normal reach are several. These are (1) *Mobile Stool* with safety pads is a low cost item but an elevation change is 8 ins, requires additional employee time to locate and transfer to required location and used in a pick aisle, (2) *Cart With Safety Step Ladder* has 24 in elevation change additional cart counterweight cost that reduces an employee time to use and used in a pick aisle, (3) *Mobile Safety Step Ladder* with permanent or collapsible top or attached to a position top structural member have an added cost, requires time to relocate and has an elevation change to a top position and used in a pick aisle, (4) *Work Assist or HROS Vehicle* has a high cost and separate aisle or when being used in a pick aisle for maximum safety pickers are restrict from an aisle, (5) *Shelf Or Deck Rack Positions With A Step* along the front that has a higher cost, wider aisle, 12 in elevation change but no relocation time, (6) *Re-Enforced Lower Shelf Position* that has a higher shelf cost, 12 in elevation change but no relocation time, (7) *GOH Static Rail Concept With An Elevated Walkway* or GOH hangs into a cavity that has structural capacity to hold an employee. Both have safety rails, kick-plates and increase an employee ability to reach top rails & (8) *Automatic Pick Machine Platform* in a replenishment aisle allows an employee to easily reach a sleeve or lane top.

Replenishment To Your Pick Position Ideas (RTPP 1 – RTPP 7)
RTPP 1. Human Or Machine Position Set-Up/Replenishment
Human or machine sku set-up or replenishment is a carton/tote replenishment options to carton flow rack or horizontal carousel that improves productivity, enhances space utilization and enhances inventory control. *Human Set-up/Replenishment* concept has an employee complete a sku transfers to a flow rack or carousel position and with a paper document or RF device for replenishment transaction transfer to a WMS computer program. With an 'A' moving sku rotation to a pick concept allows an employee to determine a position, employee activity and handles all sku container types. *Machine Replenishment* concept has a carton AS/RS crane complete a replenishment from a storage position/conveyor to a flow rack position. With an AS/RS crane carrier your opened carton sku is handled by itself or in a tray/tote. With a horizontal carousel pick concept, a robatic and elevating sku carrier receives a sku opened carton/tray/tote from a conveyor travel path. Per a computer suggested pick position elevates a sku to a position elevation for transfer into carousel position. A pallet AS/RS crane has the ability to complete a sku replenishment transaction direct to a position or onto a carrier for transfer to a pallet position. Machine replenishment concept features are (1) crane communicates replenishment transaction (sku and pick position) direct to a WMS computer program, (2) accurate and on-time replenishment transaction communication, (3) sku set-up/replenishment occurs 24 X 7 that allows a pick activity warm start, (4) higher capital cost, (5) high employee productivity & (6) additional employee safety features such as meshed fence area.

RTPP 2. Carton Replenishment From A Pallet
For high volume carton replenishment from a pallet to a flow rack position improves employee productivity, reduces damage and improves safety. Cartons on a pallet provide a smooth flat surface for a replenishment employee to open a carton and allow easy/quick open carton transfer to a position.

RTPP 3. Replenishment To An Automatic Pick Machine
Replenishment to an automatic pick machine is a small item or carton activity that assures good productivity and enhances inventory control but requires on-time replenishment transactions to assure maximum completed CO number. A small item automatic pick machine requires an employee from a replenishment aisle to transfer an

individual sku quantity from a carton into a automatic pick machine pick sleeve or lane. To have an effective, cost efficient and on-time replenishment to a pick position your replenishment activity is computer program suggested, for some 'A' moving skus you use the floating slot concept and a non-powered conveyor is along a pick machine replenishment side to serve a work surface and back-up pick lane. With some pick machines that have an elevated base, a replenishment aisle is and elevated platform that increases an employee ability to reach a sleeve or lane top. For easy and quick empty carton & filler material removal, a replenishment aisle has an elevated powered trash conveyor concept. Small item automatic pick machine replenishments are made from an aisle that is between a pick machine & carton flow rack and shelf ready reserve positions. Reserve position front configurations are (1) *Parallel To A Replenishment Aisle* that provides the fewest fronts per aisle but less employee walk distance and time to complete a replenishment transaction and (2) *Perpendicular Flow Rack & Shelf Bays To A Replenishment Aisle* that provides the greatest fronts per replenishment aisle but additional employee walk distance and time to complete a replenishment transaction. A pallet automatic pick machine replenishment options are (1) with a S. I. Ordermatic are (a) pallet concept that has standard pallet racks with meshed walkways between a pallet position and automatic pick machine. Features are few positions, requires under pallet position safety netting, requires on-time forklift truck pallet transfer to a replenishment position and difficult to handle fast moving skus unless the fast moving skus have a floating position arrangement & (b) conveyor replenishment with a pick lane loader that receives carton from a mechanical or human de-palletize station that has multiple transfer station. Features are fast moving skus require a floating position arrangement, multiple transfer stations and on-time forklift truck transfer to a transfer station & (2) Vertique pick machine that has conveyor replenishment with a pick lane loader that receives carton from a mechanical or human de-palletize station that has multiple transfer station. Features are fast moving skus require a floating position arrangement, multiple transfer stations and on-time forklift truck transfer to a transfer station.

RTPP 4. Replenishment To Carton Flow Rack

Replenishment to carton flow racks is a small item activity that assures sufficient sku quantity in a position to improve replenishment productivity and enhances inventory control. For high picker productivity with minimal travel problems over a flow lane, all cartons have open tops and cut fronts. Your carton replenishment options are (1) replenishment from floor position pallet is made from an aisle between a flow rack and pallet and has all cartons transferred from a pallet to a flow rack. Features are few pallet positions behind a flow rack bay, used for fast moving or high cube skus, requires on-time powered vehicle pallet transfer and for a pallet set-down spot painted lines improve safety and replenishment productivity, (2) for 'A' very fast moving skus replenishment from pallet flow lane is made by an employee who assures that each carton is open and transfer a carton from a flow lane pallet to a carton flow lane positions. Features are a pallet flow lane services one carton position and you require an empty pallet flow lane, (3) for medium moving skus a conveyor transports carton to a replenishment conveyor that is directly behind a flow rack replenishment aisle. As a carton arrives at a replenishment position, an employee assures that a sku is assigned to a position and transfers an open carton into a position. A conveyor travel path serves as a work surface and (4) for slow moving skus or few skus/cartons, replenishment cartons are picked mixed onto a cart or pallet. A cart or pallet is moved a floor position that is directly behind a flow rack. From a replenishment aisle an employee opens and transfers a carton from a cart or pallet into a flow lane. Features are requires on-time replenishment carton pick transactions, a small carrying surface requires several trips and for a pallet or cart set-down spot painted lines improve safety and replenishment productivity.

RTPP 5. Replenishment To Standard Pallet Rack Position

Replenishment to a standard pallet rack position is used in a small item or carton activity that improves replenishment productivity and enhances inventory control. In a small item or carton pick concept from standard pallet rack, nominal positions are 1 and 2 position levels and 3 and 4 pallet rack positions are used for reserve pallets. If replenishment is made to 1 or 2 position levels, any residual cartons are placed into a rack bay between 2 pallets or onto a pallet. With a manual forklift truck replenishment activity to a standard pallet rack position with only one pick level that has extra top open space, any residual cartons in a position from a previous pallet are placed onto a new pallet. Feature extra high position opening reduces employee injury & minimizes potential sku damage.

RTPP 6. Replenishment To Horizontal Carousel

Replenishment to a horizontal carousel small item position (horizontal carousel basket) is a disciplined activity to assure good employee productivity and enhances inventory control. An employee or computer commands a horizontal carousel to revolve a basket to a replenishment station. Replenishment to a horizontal carousel has an ecliptic layout with two ends as possible replenishment locations. A replenishment transaction assures that a sku is secured in a basket position, to access higher positions requires a picker elevating device and fast or 'A' moving skus require a floating slot concept. Replenishment transactions at a station occurs on a separate shift, there is potential for lower picker productivity, potential inbound sku and outbound sku, separate trash handling concepts and minimal requirement for interlock controls. At the other end, replenishment transactions occur on the same shift or separate shift. Interlock controls assure that a carousel basket movement minimizes potential employee injury by allowing one station to access a carousel basket. Replenishment on the same shift concept features are lowers replenishment and picker productivity due to limited access to a carousel and lower completed CO number. Replenishment on a separate shift improves both picker and replenishment productivity due unlimited carousel access, higher completed CO number and lower cost with one trash handling concept.

RTPP 7. Replenishment To Shelf, Decked Rack, Pegboard, Drawer Or Slide Positions

Replenishment to shelf, decked rack, pegboard, drawer or slide pick positions is used in a small item activity assures replenishment productivity & enhances inventory accuracy/control. With the pick concepts, a replenishment activity occurs in the same aisle as your pick activity. In most warehouses, a picker has depleted a position quantity. With a zero sku quantity in a position, to assure accurate inventory control a replenishment employee completes a zero scan transaction that is sent to a WMS computer program for sku and position update. To assure budgeted picker productivity, prior to carton transfer a replenishment employee opens each carton. For maximum replenishment productivity, a 4-wheel cart with a solid surface permits carton opening activity & on a bottom shelf has a trash container.

Replenishment Activity Transaction Communication Ideas (RATC 1 – RATC 2)

RATC 1. Delayed Or On-Line Replenishment Transaction Communication

Delayed or on-line replenishment transaction communications are options to have a sku replenishment transaction sent to a WMS computer program that updates a sku position and quantity status. *Delayed Communication* concept has a sku replenishment transaction sent to a warehouse computer and it groups transaction messages and at a pre-determined time are transferred from a warehouse computer to a WMS computer program. *On-Line Communication* as a WMS identified sku quantity in a WMS identified position updated in a WMS computer program before release of a wave COs, the concept has a potential of adding time to CO order/delivery cycle time but a WMS computer with a lower capacity/cost due to when a computer has free time it handles a batched sku replenishment transactions. When you rotate 'A' skus in pick zones and to maintain a CO service standard an on-line transfer from a position to a WMS computer program allows minimal time for a CO wave release to a pick concept but requires a WMS computer to have a larger capacity/cost to handle multiple transactions.

RATC 2. When & How To Scan

When and how to scan is small item, GOH, carton or pallet employee activity that completes a sku set-up or replenishment transaction to a position by sending a sku quantity & position to a WMS computer. A WMS computer updates a sku quantity and position in a computer program and is ready for CO pick activity. After a sku quantity is in a position, a WMS computer program releases COs to a pick area means higher picker productivity and enhances inventory control. In all position concepts a sku physical transfer to a position have similar activities that have an employee scan a sku symbology, transfer a sku to a position, scan a position symbology & send scan transactions to a WMS computer program. In a position, a sku symbology faces a pick aisle.

Trash Container Or Conveyor Location Ideas (TC 1)

TC 1. Trash container or conveyor location is a small item or carton pick area layout idea that improves replenishment or pick productivity and increases completed CO number. A trash container or conveyor assures a constant trash flow from a pick or replenishment area, employee access and low cost. A replenishment or pick activity creates trash that is carton tops or front sections and filler material. With a shelf and decked rack pick concept, replenishment container locations are on a cart bottom shelf or along a pick aisle. Features are requires an employee to replace full container with empty container, potential to mix cardboard and plastic trash, low capacity and handles a low volume. With a carton flow rack or automatic pick machine concept for 'A' fast moving skus creates a high trash volume. If your flow rack replenishment employee removes a master carton top/front and filler material, a replenishment aisle has a separate container for plastic trash and a replenishment employee accumulates cardboard carton tops/fronts in a large box/tote and transfers cardboard trash onto an elevated trash conveyor. With an automatic pick machine or horizontal carousel concept, a replenishment employee has direct access to a trash conveyor for cardboard trash and a separate container for plastic trash. With a carton warehouse, a pick aisle has trash container in a pick position for pallet plastic wrap trash.

Pick Activity Ideas

General Pick Activity (GPA 1 - GPA 9)

GPA 1. At A Pick Activity Start Have Empty Cart, Trolley & Carton/Tote Queue

At a pick activity start have empty cart, trolley & empty carton/tote queue lanes are used in a small item or GOH pick concept to assure a picker with a new CO has an empty CO container to improve picker productivity. A small item and GOH pick concept designs are (1) at a pick/pass line or automatic pick machine entry have an empty carton or tote queue conveyor prior to a pick line start station or automatic pick machine first pick position and (2) with a small item or GOH pick into/onto a cart/trolley, at a control/dispatch desk has an empty cart/trolley queue. If a cart uses cartons/totes in pick/sort position, at the control/dispatch desk, there are empty carton/tote stacks.

GPA 2. Travel Empty To Your First Pick Position

Travel empty to your first position is a manual small item or GOH activity that has a picker travel with an empty pick tote/carton/cart/trolley from a dispatch desk to a first pick position for improved picker productivity and minimal sku damage. Picker travel with an empty pick tote/carton/cart/trolley to the furthest position concept has a picker with an empty tote/carton/cart/trolley/vehicle to travel from a dispatch desk with a CO pick instructions to the furthest pick position. Feature allows a picker to travel at a fast travel speed with no sku on a tote/carton/cart/trolley. From a furthest pick aisle, each aisle and position routing pattern has an arithmetic progression that leads a picker to a discharge/dispatch desk. During pick activity, as picked skus accumulate in tote/carton/cart/trolley, it minimizes a picker physical effort and minimizes potential sku damage.

GPA 3. Small Item Apron Or Small Carton/Tote With Handles Or Holes

Small item apron or small carton/tote with handles/holes improves picker productivity and minimize sku damage. Using an apron or small carton/tote increases a picker's ability to transfer a multiple picked sku quantity between a pick position and CO container that decreases the walk distance and permits handling a larger sku quantity.

GPA 4. Picker Clipboard

A picker clipboard is used in a small item activity with a paper pick document that improves picker productivity, reduce possible paper pick document damage/lost and reduce sku damage. When picking with a paper document, a clipboard provides a picker with a device to maintain a paper pick document in one location and to have a solid surface for easy and quick picker marking on a document that assures a transaction completion. Also, a clipboard is solid surface that is used to transfer multiple skus from a position to a CO container.

GPA 5. Skus Are Set-Up In Pick Positions

Skus are set-up in positions with sufficient sku quantity for your CO wave number. With a proper sku quantity in all positions, it assures high picker productivity and high completed CO number. After your CO wave creation, your WMS computer program directs your storage activity to transfer skus from your storage area to positions or ready reserve positions. In some operations, after a WMS computer program has received a sku transfer to a position message, it releases COs to a pick concept. As COs deplete a sku quantity from a position, a WMS computer program suggests a sku replenishment transaction from a storage or ready reserve position.

GPA 6. Pick Skus From Mixed Skus In Totes/Trays/Rails

Pick skus from mixed skus in totes/trays/rail is a small item or GOH pick concept that has different skus mixed with no separation in one container or on one GOH rail. When a picker completes a transaction from a mixed skus tote/tray/rail, a picker has non-productive time to search and locate a sku for a transaction completion that lowers a picker productivity and completed CO number. Since your pick activity is a time critical activity & for good customer service, it is more productive for your replenishment employee to physically separate skus in a mixed tote/tray/rail. Mixed skus in a container concept is used to improved space utilization for 'C' and 'D' moving skus, consider one sku per position with a narrower or shorter tote/tray.

GPA 7. Set-Up Your Pick Equipment & Pick Line Skus For Your Next Customer Order Wave

Set-up your pick equipment & pick line skus for your next CO wave is designed to improve your picker productivity and increase your completed CO number. Set-up your pick equipment means that you match your pick position type to your pick volume. With high volume skus, you use pallet flow rack or carton flow rack pick positions with 1 sku per level or 2 skus per level. If your CO wave has medium volume skus, you use carton flow rack position with standard skus per level. If your CO wave has slow moving skus, you use shelf pick positions with 3 skus per level.

GPA 8. Your Replenishment Employee Or Picker Makes A Carton Smiley Face

Your replenishment employee or picker makes a carton smiley face or cuts-off a carton top/front end that is placed in a pick position to improve picker productivity and trash handling. A carton properly opened or with a smiley face permits a manual picker to easily and quickly with minimal sku removal obstruction and complete a transaction or a replenishment transaction to fill an automatic pick machine pick lane/sleeve. An open carton allows an employee to insert a hand into a r carton and remove a sku from a carton without hanging-up on a carton top flaps. Your carton open options are (1) *Picker* that is time critical activity that focuses on completing a manual or mechanized pick transaction or sku transfer to an automatic pick machine or (b) *Replenishment Person* that is not as time critical. In most pick activities with a WMS computer program, after a sku is physically transferred and scanned to a position. After a WMS computer program updates a position status, it releases COs to a pick concept. In all pick concepts, a replenishment employee opens a carton is the preferred activity. This is due to the fact (1) your replenishment activity is less time critical than a picker activity that is more time critical, (2) a replenishment employee is handling a carton and in most replenishment activities a carton is an employee has work station that is level and a solid surface and (3) with most standard WMS programs a carton replenishment quantity is based on your CO wave and after a carton is physically and WMS scanned to a position, a WMS computer program releases COs to your pick concept. Replenishment to an automatic pick machine sleeve/lane, a replenishment employee is not preferred to open cartons but a storage employee who transfers a carton to an automatic pick machine ready reserve position. We preferred that a picker or automatic pick machine pick position replenishment employee does not open cartons is due to the fact that (1) it requires a time critical employee (picker) to remove a carton from a pick or ready reserve position that is extra handling or with limited space leave a carton in a position and open a carton & (2) it is a picker non-productive time that requires a 1 to 1 ½ minutes to open a carton. This time includes aware that a carton is empty, located open knife, remove a knife from a sleeve and open or rip carton top, replace master carton to pick position and place trash in a container. Features are non-productive picker time lowers your picker or productivity, with an automatic pick machine slow CO release to a pick machine and in a pick/pass or pick cell concept potential to create CO container congestion on a pick conveyor or pick zone in-feed conveyor.

GPA 9. Increase Ready To Ship Skus

Convert to vendor ready to ship is an idea that has a large single line sku CO number and increases completed CO number, improves packer productivity and lower ship supply expenses. With your purchase, I T, customer service & warehouse, you review each single line sku that is available for COs. A review process determines (1) single line sku number & sku quantity that had single line COs & structural cardboard strength, quality, interior filler material to protect a sku & exterior surface to quality for a vendor ready to ship sku & (2) single line sku number & quantity that has had single line COs but a cardboard carton does not have structural cardboard strength, quality, interior filler material to protect a sku & exterior surface to quality for a vendor ready to ship sku. If a sku qualifies for a vendor ready to ship carton, your I T, warehouse, purchase & customer service team prepares a slapper label & to introduce vendor ready to ship cartons. If a sku requires a vendor to modify a carton cardboard quality, structural strength, interior filler material or exterior surface, your team meets with a vendor to improve a sku to become a vendor ready to ship carton. For best results or vendor participation, you share some of your savings with a vendor. When a vendor ready to ship carton is compared to a carton repack process, your potential benefits are (1) pack labor savings with a slapper label, (2) no ship supply expenses (tape, carton and filler material), (3) lower customer returns open expense & trash handling (carton and filler material) & (4) opportunity to avoid regular pack stations or divert a volume to a pick activity or mechanize or automatic the activity.

Pick Area Layout Ideas (PAL 1 – PAL 2)

PAL 1. One Pick Section With All Skus Or Multiple Pick Sections With 'A'/Fast Moving Skus

Your pick area options are (1) *One Pick Section With All Skus (A, B, C & D Moving Skus)* in 1 pick section, all COs are completed from 1 pick section. Features are large sq. ft. area with low picker productivity due greater travel distances to complete a CO, potential for pick aisle congestion or pick line CO uncontrolled queues & difficult to obtain good hit concentration & density & develop good pick line profile or (2) *Dual Or Multiple Pick Sections & Both Sections With 'A'/Fast Moving Skus* Based on 80% of your volume is from 20% of your skus, your have dual or multiple pick sections (two pick lines) for 20% sku number & 1 pick section for your 80% sku number & 1 pick position. With all 'A' or fast moving skus are allocated to each pick section high volume pick positions it allows you to complete 80% of your COs that provides good sku hit concentration & density & pick line profile & with short travel distance between two active pick positions means high picker productivity, high completed CO number & low replenishment congestion.

PAL 2. With Dual or Multiple Pick Sections Where To Start Your Customer Orders

Your start CO locations are (1) *Start COs In Your B & C Moving Sku Or Low Volume Pick Section* that accounts for 20 % of your picks & your low volume pick section sends 20 % of your COs to high volume pick section. Features are requires CO scan entry, high pick area requires additional queue to handle all COs. With existing skus (fragile or crushable) in a CO container, there is potential difficulty to add your high volume skus into a CO container and sku damage that lowers your high volume pick area pickers productivity. It requires picker management in two sections with different volumes & potential slow CO completion & CO flow control from your B & C sku pick section with queue entry into the 'A' pick section & (2) *Start COs In Your 'A' Fast Moving Sku Or In A High Volume Pick Section* that accounts for 80 % of your picks. Your high volume pick section sends 20 % of your COs to low volume pick section. Features are requires scan for CO entry, low pick area requires minimal CO container queue to handle all COs. With existing skus (fragile or crushable) in a CO container, there is potential difficulty to add your low volume skus into a CO container and sku damage that lowers your low volume area pickers' productivity. Easier to assign pickers into two pick sections.

Pick Position Ideas (PP 1 – PP 14)

PP 1. Top & Bottom Pick Level Heights

Your pick level heights are (1) *Top Pick Level* is within pickers & replenishment employees reach that permits a picker to physically transfer a sku from a pick position carton/tote to a customer order carton/tote. If above a picker's reach, low productivity due to employee reach or non-productive search to find & climb a ladder. In many situations, a picker uses lower pick position shelf member as a step that has potential shelf damage but is minimized with re-enforced shelf & with a lower level pick to light display in a 'C' channel member and (2) *Pigeon Hole* or lowest pick level requires a picker to bend that creates low productivity due to bending & physical effort.

PP 2. How High Is Your Maximum Sku Pick Position Height

How high is your maximum position height is a manual, mechanized or automatic activity consideration for a position height that impacts your picker reach height and assure good productivity. Your position height is a position with a sku carton or GOH rail above the floor surface. A position height above the floor allows an employee picker or replenishment employee to complete a pick/replenishment transaction without stepping on a shelf or using an elevating device. A pick/replenishment transaction removes a sku from a carton, picks a GOH from a rail or adds a sku to a pick lane. In most pick operations, your pick levels are shelf with 4 to 5 levels, decked rack with 3 levels, standard pallet rack with 2 levels, GOH with 2 to 3 levels and carton flow rack with 4 to 5 levels.

PP 3. Increase Your Picker Reach

Reach higher is used in a small item or GOH activity for a picker ability to reach a pick position above the normal reach. Features are to improve picker productivity and enhance space utilization. Since most skus are classified as A,B,C or D moving skus, to have good picker productivity your 'D' moving skus are assigned to your highest positions or non-Golden Zone positions. Devices to increase a pickers reach height are (1) *Manual Group* that includes (a) mobile one step high stool with safety step, (b) mobile three or four safety step ladder that is attached to a pick cart with safety step, (c) fixed step that is attached to a position front, (d) mobile 4 wheel & 6 or 7 step ladder with a safety step & (e) captive aisle 2 wheel & 6 or 7 steps that is attached on a rail to a pick position top & (2) *Mechanized Group* that includes (a) work assisted vehicle with limited carrying capacity, (b) HROS vehicle with cart or pick cage with an attached GOH bar carry capacity & (c) man-up very narrow aisle vehicle with a pick cage.

PP 4. All Positions Are Pick Positions Or Separate Storage & Pick Positions

Your position options are (1) *All Positions Are Pick Positions* means both employee reachable & elevating vehicle reachable are recognized in your WMS computer as positions. Features are to elevated positions it requires a picker to walk & get an elevating vehicle or device that creates non-productive picker time, difficult to develop a good pick area profile, slow completed CO flow & number, low WMS program cost & small sq ft area pick area & (2) *Separate Storage & Pick Positions* means in a pick area all positions that are employee reachable & elevating vehicle reachable, your WMS computer recognizes all elevated positions as storage positions & all employee reachable positions as pick positions. Features are requires an elevating vehicle & employee to complete sku replenishment transaction from a position to a depleted position that requires a replenishment employee, easy to develop a good pick area profile, easy to obtain good picker productivity, higher completed CO number & standard WMS program cost.

PP 5. One Sku Identification For Total Cartons Or One Sku Identification For Each Sku Carton

Your sku ID options are (1) *One Sku Identification For A Sku Total Cartons* for all cartons and cartons have different piece quantities, it adds to your replenishment activity time to assure exact sku quantity transferred to a pick position. Considerations are (a) to assure exact inventory transfer, all cartons are placed into a position and (b) with a random picking cartons, during a pick transaction, there is potential for a sku shortage and after a CO wave completion, potential for a sku inventory overage in a position. Features are with multiple cartons per sku difficult to obtain a good pick aisle profile & to achieve good hit concentration & density due some skus occupying 2 or more positions, if skus occupy 2 positions, creates additional non-productive picker travel time past positions with no picks, does not require replenishment activity & transaction, new skus require pick area expansion due to few vacate positions, requires 1 label & if a carton with WMS ID is removed in the future additional time to complete sku move transaction & complete a sku inventory count. For best sku inventory control in a storage area, each carton sku quantity has a separate sku ID/pallet and storage location or (2) *One Sku Identification For Each Sku Carton With 1 Sku Identification* for each carton in a storage area. Position replenishment is completed by any cartons that are randomly transferred from a storage position. Features are easy to obtain a good pick aisle profile, with 1 sku per position, picker travels past positions with potential picks, requires replenishment activity with a WMS Identified carton sku quantity that matches, each carton requires a label & your computer suggested sku & quantity, permits extra cartons placed into storage positions with greater active position density & sku occupancy a smaller pick area.

PP 6. One Carton Open Per Sku To Comply With A Vendor Consignment Policy

With a vendor sku on consignment (your company pays a vendor for only sku that are sold and residual/non-sold skus are returned a vendor), most vendors prefer that you pick activity opens one carton due to the fact for a sku quantity that did not sell it is easier to sell non-open cartons to another company. With single deep single high positions, for high picker productivity you have your replenishment employee open 1 carton as it is transferred to a position. With a carton flow lane or multiple cartons per position concept or skus in a captive tote and WMS sku allocation is based on your CO wave, a replenishment employee opens each carton as a carton is transferred to a position. To comply with a vendor consignment policy your WMS computer suggests a carton quantity that is based on your CO wave sku quantity. The approach means that all cartons in a position matches a CO wave sku quantity and are picked in a work day. If you open all cartons & sku quantity does not sell, you have wasted employee carton handling & position preparation cost. To comply with a consignment policy you have additional labor & carton costs.

PP 7. One Sku Per Pick Position Or Mixed Skus In A Pick Position

Your sku number in a position options are (1) *One Sku Per Pick Position* has in a WMS computer 1 sku that is assigned to 1 position. The approach assures maximum picker productivity due to minimal time to match a position & sku quantity to a pick instruction. Features are minimizes potential pick errors & inventory problems. With a standard size position requires a large sq. ft. pick area, preferred for A, B & C moving skus that achieves a pick area profile for good picker productivity and not suggested for D moving skus due non-productive travel time and easier replenishment transactions and (2) *Mixed Skus In A Pick Position* has in a WMS computer several skus that are assigned to 1 position. The approach is preferred for D moving skus that have very low or no sales & in a position each sku is separated by an insert & totally different skus in a position that means no sku skns (skus with same size but different colors or same ring design with different sizes). Features are low picker productivity due to non-productive time to search & match a pick instruction to sku, small sq. ft. pick area & not suggested for A, B & C moving skus. When D moving skus are placed into a mixed carton/tote position, each sku is separated by a barrier and when bulk picked good picker productivity.

PP 8. Fixed Pick Position Or Floating Sku Slot Or Pick Position

Your position and sku assignment options are (1) *Fixed Pick Position* after a position quantity is depleted, for additional CO pick transactions a sku replenishment is made from a storage position to a pick position. Features are easy to achieve good hit concentration & density & obtain good pick line/aisle profile for good picker productivity that means minimal travel distance between 2 active positions, easy to maintain family group or hit philosophy, minimal pick position number & small sq. ft. pick area & requires a replenishment activity & labor or (2) *Floating Sku Slot Or Pick Position* concept in 1 pick section or area, 'A' or fast moving sku is placed into 2 positions (100 & 425). After CO picks deplete sku quantity in position (100) for a next CO, your computer has a transaction from position 425. Features are (a) difficult to achieve good hit concentration & density, (b) difficult to obtain good pick line/aisle profile, (c) due to increased travel distance between 2 active pick positions that means lower picker productivity, (d) difficult to maintain family group philosophy, (e) requires additional position number or larger sq. ft. pick area & with very fast moving sku requires a replenishment activity & labor.

PP 9. Your Picker Or Replenishment Head Height Is Your Pick Position Maximum Height

Head high is a manual or mechanized small item or GOH position maximum elevation above your floor to assure good picker productivity. Head high is an elevation with no employee restriction or difficulty to transfer a sku from a shelf, decked rack, standard pallet rack, GOH rail or horizontal carousel basket position into a CO container/cart rail/vehicle carrying surface. Above a head high, a picker productivity is lower due to increased picker physical effort to reach a sku position or obtain a device to elevate a picker. If 'C' or 'D' moving skus are allocate to above head high positions, means less potential for lower picker productivity due to few picks.

PP 10. Your Lowest Or Pigeon Hole Lower Picker Productivity

No squats or pigeon hole positions is not good in a manual small item position location. A pigeon hole is lowest pick level (3 in) above the floor that lowers picker productivity. To access a sku from a pigeon hole position, a picker squats or bends that is difficult to transfer a sku from a position into a CO container or vehicle carrying surface. A picker time and physical effort to complete a pick transaction creates lower picker productivity. If 'C' or 'D' moving skus are allocate to above head high positions, there is less potential to lower picker productivity due to few picks.

PP 11. Pick Position Types

A position is a pick area position that holds a sku quantity and assures picker access to skus for transfer from a position into a CO container.

(1) *Floor Stack* carton or pallet pick position is preferred for fast 'A' moving skus with large inventory per sku that is in self-supporting cart & best for vendor ready to ship & very large cartons. With few positions per aisle, there are nominal 20 to 25 skus per pick aisle. Whenever possible have 2 high pallets that allows a picker to reach/pick a top carton & your pallet height matches pallet rack opening height that allows easy/quick residual sku transfer to a pallet position. Floor stack pick area design with a fork lift truck wide aisle between 2 floor stack rows & allow 6 ins between pallets minimizes damage & improves deposit productivity. Floor stack is used with paper, RF device & voice directed pick instruction concepts & has no one-time cost except painted lines on a floor. During forklift truck activity, painted lines on a floor minimize sku damage & assure a straight floor stack lane. A picker handles empty pallet, if required picker opens cartons that decreases picker productivity & position identification is hung from a ceiling, embedded in a floor or on a post between 2 lanes.

(2) *Bin Pick Positions* are used for skus that your receiving department transfers from a vendor transport device (plastic bag or odd shaped carton) that does not match your position design or your loose 'D' moving sku inventory quantity is mixed in a position. A bin is basically a performed cardboard, plastic corrugated, solid plastic, wood or metal 4 sides and bottom container with structural strong bottom & side wall/lip structural strength that in a position permits a stack, 1 level high or wall attachment. Performed corrugated plastic or cardboard bin is supported by position bottom full width. A bin has a small sku inventory quantity or small size sku. When placed onto a cart shelf, shelf or decked rack, bin depth matches position depth. A bin front has sufficient space for position or sku IDs, front opening permits a picker hand to complete a transaction & retains skus in a bin. In most operations, a bin interior/clear front width is 5 to 6 ins with a 5 ¼ to 6 ¼ in overall/exterior width. Narrow bin fronts (5 ins exterior to exterior wall) increase hit concentration & density with 10 bins in a 5f ft wide shelf & wide bin fronts with 18 to 20 ins wide has 3 bins in a 5 ft wide shelf. With 10 pick levels high in shelves, your (a) Golden Zone is pick levels 3. 4, 5, 6, 7 & 8, (b) Pigeon holes are pick levels 1 & 2 & (c) top pick levels 9 & 10 could require a picker reach effort or elevating device. A bin concept is used with all pick instruction concepts. Features are with low volume very small skus or 'D' moving skus with low inventory separators in a bin depth increases position number & permits position ID attachment, allow for clear shelf space to transfer bins between shelf or other bins in a position, measure a bin exterior dimensions to determine bin number per shelf bay, when attached to wall with a bin lip allow 4 to 5 ins between 2 vertical position bins for a picker to complete a transaction & remove an empty bin, replenishment & pick activities occur in same aisle, an aisle has sufficient width for 2 cart traffic, one-time cost & captive bin to a position has a lower structural strength design & cost when compared to a bin that is moved by a powered conveyor concept. Most bin n applications are use a fixed shelf or mobile cart position concept.

(3) *Fixed Shelf Pick Position* has metal or plastic structural members (posts & braces or side walls), solid or meshed shelves and connecting devices that form a rectangle/squared shaped position. An open shelf concept has braces & posts that increases light & air circulation but requires skus in stackable containers. A closed shelf concept has solid side & back walls that decreases light & air circulation but is able to handle loose skus or most frequently skus in bins. Skus are contained in a carton, bin or tote and a carton, bin or tote depth matches shelf depth. A position ID is attached to shelf lip & to minimize damage a bottom shelf level ID has a cover or coating. Shelf opening elevation & open space between carton/tote top & above shelf member permits a picker to easy complete a transaction. A shelf concept is used with paper, RF device, voice directed & pick to light pick instruction concepts and employee walk or ride pick concept. Within a shelf bay, most picker routing patterns for a shelf level use a horizontal picker pattern. Sku, bin, tote or carton size determines inventory quantity in a position & positions per shelf level. For easy sku transfer to shelf position allow 1/8 In between 2 cartons, totes, bins & posts. With very small skus, features are high position number per aisle (10 per shelf & 10 levels high), average skus medium position number per aisle (3 per shelf & 5 levels high) & a 5 pick level shelf concept requires 6 shelves with top shelf used for ready reserve positions. With a 5 pick level shelf concept, your Golden zone is pick levels 2, 3 & 4, Pigeon hole is bottom pick level 1 & top pick level 5 that requires a reach effort and with 10 pick level shelf concept, your Golden zone is pick levels 3, 4, 5 & 6, Pigeon hole is bottom pick level 0, 1 & 2 & top pick level 7, 8 & 9 that requires a reach effort. Other features are good profile means minimal picker walk distance between 2 picks & high hit pick concentration & density, when used for very small size skus such as jewelry or 'D' moving skus with very small inventory a short shelf depth with short bins or normal shelf depth with separators provides good space

utilization. Open cartons by replenishment employee improves picker productivity & pick & replenishment activities occur in same aisle. When a shelf post width is compared to a decked pallet rack post width there is 1 to 2 ins width reduction per post that means a greater position number per aisle & a lower cost.

(4) *Mobile Shelf Pick Positions* are basically fixed shelf positions on a mobile base or posts with wheels/casters that permit a picker to parallel move a front mobile shelf position bay to access a rear fixed shelf position or to manual or mechanical parallel move a shelf row to create a aisle for position access. One concept has 4 fixed rear shelf bays that are anchored to a floor & 2 mobile front shelf bays are parallel to main aisle. Your picker routing pattern compensates for both front & rear shelf bays. Additional cost are to floor anchor rear shelves & front shelves in-floor guidance concept. Second option, front shelf bays are overhead guided through a rail that is attached to rear shelf posts. Your picker routing pattern compensates for both front & rear shelf bays. With the concept, there is additional cost to floor anchor rear shelves & top rail guidance. Manual or mechanical concept moves shelves horizontal perpendicular to a main aisle over a floor level guided travel path to create access aisle to shelf pick positions. The concept has 2 fixed position shelf rows with 4 to 6 mobile rows (3 to 4 bays long) & a picker access aisle. For 'D' moving skus, mobile shelf concept increases hit concentration & density, high position number with minimal aisle space with standard routing pattern & some additional cost.

(5) *Decked Standard Pallet Rack & Slotted Angle Pick Position* has upright frames/posts, load beams & deck material to create 3 to 4 k levels high on an aisle both sides. The concept is used for low volume, heavy, large cube & ready to ship skus. Each level has a medium position number for a pick position with a 12 in wide carton, tote or bin with 1/8 in open between 2 cartons. Per aisle there are 14 to 15 rack bays at 113 ins C/C. Based on 7 positions per level in a rack bay & provides medium sku inventory quantity in a position. With 3 levels in a rack bay, it provides good pick aisle profile & hit concentration & density. Used with most routing patterns. Per decked level a horizontal picker pattern. Decked rack opening elevation & open space between top carton/tote top & above load beam permits a picker to easily complete a transaction. Used with paper, RF device, pick to light & voice directed pick instruction concepts. Each position ID faces a pick aisle. When your lowest load beam has position IDs for a floor and first elevated deck level are on a load beam position IDs have a step configuration with lower ID for a floor level position and higher ID for a decked level position. For picker awareness each position level has a unique colored border & associated directional arrows. Attached to an end rack bay post is an aisle ID that extends outward into a main aisle. Pick & replenishment activities occur in same aisle & open cartons by replenishment person improves picker productivity.

 (5A) *Deck Your Bottom Hand Stacked/Decked Pallet Rack Level* has your bottom (floor) level skus hand stacked onto a deck instead of 2 pallets.   A deck is a solid wood, harden plastic or metal member with 1 or 2 in high bottom full depth runners evenly spaced to assure minimal deck bow. When compared to hand stack on 2 pallets, a deck increases vertical open space by a nomimal 4 ins and allows a rack bay entire area used for skus that increases usable space by 8 to 12 ins or 1 standard carton width. Deck & runner cost is equal to 2 pallets cost.

(6) *Standard Pallet Rack Pick Position* has upright frames/posts & load beams to create 1 to 2 pick levels high on an   aisle one side or both sides.   Standard rack is used for high volume/'A', heavy, large cube & ready to ship skus,   Used for palletized self supporting skus, vendor ready to ship carton, very large cartons or fast 'A' moving skus with requirement for a large sku inventory quantity in a position. With 2 pick levels, medium position number per aisle means medium hit concentration & density. Position height or load beam elevation matches pallet height & picker reach height but it is difficult to reach a rear carton on bottom & second level that is minimized with a pallet short dimension into a rack opening. Rack opening elevation & open space between carton/tote top & above load beam level permits a picker to easily complete a transaction. Used with paper, RF device or voice directed pick instructions. With skus depleted from a pallet, a picker handles empty pallet from a position. Aisle width is for forklift truck stacking requirement & pick & replenishment activities occur in same aisle that creates some additional picker walk distance & time. If required to open cartons, a picker has low productivity. If your levels above positions are used for storage, trash conveyor support or elevated pick area support, your upright frame structural strength & anchor & aisle width is approved by a rack manufacturer. Pallet placement in a rack bay options are (a) 1, 2 or 3 pallets wide in a position pallet is determined by your building column span & pallet dimension, (b) pallet dimension options are (*) 40 in short dimension is placed into a rack & 48 in long dimension faces a pick aisle that means a short picker reach for rear carton & fewer positions per aisle with a longer load beam and solid stringer pallet forklift truck double handling or (*) 40 in short dimension faces a pick aisle & 48 in long dimension is in a rack

that means no lift truck double handling & long picker reach for rear carton & greater position number per aisle, (c) 3 narrow pallets (32 in X 48 in) per rack bay with 32 in dimension facing pick aisle narrow dimension faces pick aisle. The approach could require additional labor to stack or transfer skus from a in-correct dimension pallet onto a proper size pallet, (d) 1 or 2 high position concept is determined by your required sku quantity in a position, picker reach height & desire to have fewer forklift truck replenishment transactions, (*) 2 high positions has the lowest pick level set on a floor with lower picker reach & second level is set on load beams with higher picker reach & (*) 1 high pick lowest pick level that has double high pallets that has upright frame matches requirement or possible double post at a frame front. Provides a large sku quantity in a position & easy to match WMS program requirements.

(7) *Push Back Carton Flow Rack Pick Position Push Back Rack* is a special carton flow rack with standard carton flow rack components that is design with an aisle between 2 push back rows or 1 aisle with 1 push back row. A push back pick position means that a position holds several cartons deep. First carton is placed onto a flow lane & a second carton pushes a first carton deeper into a position. A second carton is at a position front & picks made from a second carton that means no FIFO rotation. A pick aisle is the replenishment aisle. Lowest pick level is 3 ins above a floor. With 3 to 4 positions high & conveyor pitch or slope assures carton/tote flow. A horizontal picker routing pattern for each bay provides medium hit concentration & density & easy to complete good profile. Open space between carton/tote top & above conveyor lane bottom permits a picker to complete a transaction. With 2 to 3 18 in long cartons deep, it has a medium sku inventory quantity in a position. All cartons/totes require a good conveyable bottom, 3 wheels/rollers under each carton/tote & front & rear end stop. A standard push back rack has a 5 ft long conveyor. Guide rails are between 2 pick lanes minimizes hang-ups. If a carton/tote hang-up use a Sheppard hook pipe to pull a hung-up carton/tote forward. Used with a picker walk or rider pick concept, not used with a pick/pass or elevating vehicle pick concept and used for all pick instruction types. Flow rail front end has a pick and replenishment position ID & bay support member between 2 upright post holds bay IDs. Front end is tilted, slanted or straight frames with front end as solid sheet metal or conveyor. A replenishment employee opens all cartons to improve picker productivity. Building column located is between 2 push back bays. If a building column is placed inside a rack bay, it requires potential frame cut & weld.

(8) *Slide Or Chute Pick Position* has a solid bottom surface & side walls & is designed to handle loose skus or cartons with poor conveyable bottom. An aisle is between 2 slide/chute rows or slide/chute row has 1 aisle that is a pick & replenishment aisle. With 3 to 4 pick positions high, it is easy to complete good profile & medium hit concentration & density. Used with a horizontal pick bay routing pattern & all pick instruction concepts. Bay support member between 2 upright post holds bay ID. Building column is located between 2 slide/chute bays. If a building column is placed inside a rack bay, it requires potential frame cut & weld.

(9) *Pegboard Pick Position* has pegs that extend outward from a fixed wall or solid side wall on a mobile cart with 1 or 2 sides. Each sku requires a hook that maintains sku quality such as chain jewelry or loose skus. A position holds small inventory quantity. Hanging skus creates minimal number sku high but large number sku wide, a small sku number & easy to profile. Position requires position ID above hook. Pick & replenishment aisle is same aisle.

(10) *Drawer Pick Position* is a metal cabinet with several drawers. When required to complete a transaction, a drawer is pulled outward into an aisle. Aisle width permits 1 picker or 2 picker travel & with drawer open or closed. Sku is required to fit into drawer space. Lockable drawer improves security. To increase sku position number, each drawer has separators for very small size 'D' moving skus. Each drawer cabinet, each drawer & each position has an ID. Each position holds loose small sku with a sku small inventory quantity. Use a front to rear picker routing pattern. Easy to profile for high sku hit concentration & density. Design or layout options are installed in floor, in a rack bays or mobile.

PP 12. Pick/Pass Concept Pick Positions

Pick/Pass Pick Position is a pick concept that has a CO container travel on a conveyor travel path past ll positions and is used for a high volume pick activity. Most common position types are shelf, pallet, decked pallet/angle iron or carton flow rack positions. A sku cube and volume determineds pick position type. Most pick/pass concepts have position mix. For maximum picker productivity & accuracy, a pick/pass line is separated into picker zones. Pick/pass pallet, carton flow rack & shelf pick zone lengths are (1) high volume & high cube 'A' moving skus with a volume that match your budgeted productivity rate. 1 or 2 pallets wide with a pick conveyor stop & empty pallet return lane for sku (1 pallet = 4 ft wide), (2) high volume & medium cube 'A' moving skus with a volume to match your budgeted productivity rate. 2 carton flow rack bays wide & a pick conveyor stop at a last bay end (1 bay = 5 to 6 ft wide) & (3) low volume & any cube 'A' slow moving skus with a volume to match your budgeted pick rate. Shelf design options are (a) 3 parallel shelf bays wide & pick conveyor stop at a last bay end (1 bay = 3 ft wide) or (b) 6 perpendicular shelf rows & aisles with a pick conveyor stop at a last row (2 rows & 1 aisle = 6ft). Each pick zone has flags/banners to identify pick zone start & and positions. Pallet & carton flow rack pick face a pick aisle. A pick aisle is 30 to 36 ins wide between conveyor and position, In an aisle, a picker transfers CO skus from a position into a CO container. For best picker productivity, cartons are open by a replenishment employee. Non-open cartons in a position are not preferred due to non-productive picker time to open cartons & that creates potential pick line congestion & low completed CO number.

PP 13. Skus As Separate Or Mixed In Pick Positions
Skus as separate or mixed skus in positions is a small item/GOH position set-up or relocation strategy for your 'C', "D" & obsolete/very slow moving skus to improve picker productivity and enhance space utilization. Skus in separate positions is based on a philosophy that your pick activity is time critical, most of your COs have multiple lines/multiple skus and your pick aisle/line profile minimizes a pickers walk distance between two picks. With 'C', 'D' & obsolete/very slow moving skus, to improve sku hit concentration and density, allocate the skus to one pick aisle in narrow positions. If your one pick aisle is considered in your WMS computer program as one pick section and where your multiple lines/multiple skus CO starts. your transport concept moves a partial completed CO from your slowing sku section to your 'A' fasting moving section. Features are you maintain your budgeted 'A' fast moving picker productivity and assure good space utilization. When you mix 'C', 'D' & obsolete/very slow moving skus skus into a carton/tote or GOH on rail with no sku separation, you improve your sku re-location or set-up/replenishment employee productivity and space utilization but lowers your picker productivity due to non-productive time to search and locate a sku in a carton/tote on a rail. If you mix 'C', 'D' & obsolete/very slow moving skus skus into a carton/tote or GOH on rail with sku separation, you maintain your sku re-location or set-up/replenishment employee productivity and space utilization but slightly lower your picker productivity due to minimal time to search and located a sku in a carton/tote on a rail.

PP 14. Too Much Of One Sku In One Pick Zone Creates Pick Line Congestion Or Shut-Down
To much of one sku (pick volume) in one pick zone/position creates pick line congestion or shut down is not good and lowers your picker productivity and space utilization. This statement refers to a pick concept that has for one sku with a very high pick volume that exceeds your standard position front or budgeted picker productivity. If your have one position with a high pick volume. it creates pick line or CO container congestion that has one picker achieve good productivity but lowers other pickers productivity. To remedy a situation, in your WMS computer program and in your operation you have two separate pick sections or dual pick lines. Another too much situation occurs with your vendor carton exceeds your standard shelf or decked rack position front and your over-sized carton extends from one position into an adjacent position. The situation creates low picker productivity due to a vacate position (vendor carton extends into adjacent position) that increases a picker walk distance between two picks. To remedy the situation, you have skus transferred from a vendor oversize carton into a standard size carton for a position and sku quantity per new carton ID are updated in your WMS computer program and in the future your purchasing department advises your vendor to use a standard size carton.

Pick Area Aisle Ideas (PAA 1)
PAA 1. Do Not Liter In A Pick Or Replenishment Aisle
Do not liter in a pick or replenishment aisle has a picker or replenishment employee transfer an empty carton or filler material into a trash container or trash conveyor travel path to assure clear aisles that improves picker productivity and safety. To assure maximum picker productivity, a sku in a pick position has minimal residual liter. With a small item pick concept, a replenishment employee opens a carton and removes filler material that is transferred to a trash container or trash conveyor. After carton depletion, a picker transfers an empty carton to trash container or conveyor. With an empty plastic tote in a pick position, a picker turns an empty plastic tote upside down that is a signal for replenishment employee to remove an empty tote. During a pallet replenishment

activity to a pick position, a forklift truck driver or replenishment employee removes all plastic wrap that is transferred to a container and empty pallets are transferred onto an empty pallet return lane.

Cube Ideas (C 1)
C 1. Cube Your Sku Exterior, Ship Carton Interior & Pick Position
Cube your sku exterior, ship carton interior and pick position means that you have entered in your (1) CO processing program, each sku's exterior length, width and height dimensions, (2) CO processing program, each ship carton's interior dimensions, (3) in your replenishment program you have entered each vendor carton's exterior length, width and height dimensions and (4) in your replenishment program each position's interior dimensions. When your CO computer program cubes a CO small item or GOH skus cube to a ship container cube, your have improved picker productivity due to each CO sku quantity fits into a computer suggested ship container. Cube your small item pick activity has your CO computer program that takes each CO sku quantity cube, ship carton utilization, filler material factor and matches it your pick vehicle capacity or one of your pick/ship containers. With a GOH pick activity, it determines GOH number per trolley hang bar that assures a full trolley per pick trip. With your carton and position cube information, it determines a carton number that fills your position to capacity with no overflow and assures maximum space utilization.

Start Pick Activity Ideas (PA 1)
PA 1. Your Pick Or Pack Activity Warm Or Cold Start
Warm or cold start is a small item or GOH activity strategy to have sku quantity for a CO wave in positions that assures good picker/packer productivity and constant CO flow. *Cold Start* has your replenishment, pick and pack activities start at the same time. Features are delayed pick activity start due to skus are replenished and scanned to a pick position that is updated in your WMS computer program. Time that is required to complete these activities, delays CO release to a pick area and low employee productivity due to non-productive waiting time or time to change an employee activity from replenishment to picker. *Warm Start* has your set-up employee start at an early time to assure that skus are physically transferred and scanned to positions that allows a WMS computer program to on-time release COs to a pick concept. Feature is your 'A' moving skus are in pick positions that allows a pick activity warm start-up with a high completed CO number. After your pick activity has completed COs, COs are queued on your transport concept, packers start at a later time to assure a warm start-up with COs ready for your pack activity.

Customer Order Ideas (CO 1 - CO 10)
CO 1. Your Customer Order Service Standard
Your CO service standard is a company policy that a work day COs/CO wave are completed and CO packages on a freight delivery truck to assures customer service. To assure good customer service and on-time delivery, a catalog, direct mail or TV marketing warehouse determines a CO wave/work day COs based on several factors. The factors are (1) time require to complete all I T computer CO processing or time that COs as pick instructions are on your pick floor or available for your pick and pack activity, (2) your pick and pack employee budgeted productivity and actual employee number and (3) time for a delivery truck to travel from your operation to a freight terminal and arrive for freight company sort time.

CO 2. Accurate Picks Reduces Problems Orders
Accurate picks reduces problem COs. A problems CO package is sent to a customer with a damaged, wrong sku, short sku or extra sku quantity. The situation occurs in a small item or GOH warehouse and when a CO is received at a delivery address it creates a dis-satisfied customer. To minimize problem COs, a pick activity objective has your pickers pick correct and quality skus in the correct quantity from a pick position into a CO container. In other words, for your warehouse to maintain your customer service standard, it starts at your pick position or pick activity.

CO 3. Customer Order Carry-Over
CO carry-over is Day 1 CO wave COs that are not completed in Day 1 due to low productivity from unexpected volume increase with no additional employees, employee sickness, pick electrical/mechanical or I T computer

process problems. If you rotate skus in positions, Day 1 CO carry-over is picked before Day 2 CO wave sku set-up in positions & Day 2 CO release to pick concept. This is due to Day 1 sku residual is in a position, Day 2 sku position set-up to same position that is scanned/sent to a WMS computer that have potential mis picks. If skus remain in positions, Day 2 CO wave sku set-up is in same position with same sku & Day 2 CO release to pick concept with potential pick & replenishment activity occurring together.

CO 4. Customer Order Pool

CO pool equals existing COs in a WMS computer that are not released to a previous work day/CO wave & new COs that are sent from a Host computer to a WMS computer and are not included a previous CO wave. CO pool has COs available to a warehouse staff for creation of a CO wave.

CO 5. What Customer Orders Are First In Your Customer Order Pool

What COs are first in your CO pool is an idea with an existing CO pool (COs not been released to your pick activity) and can have an impact on your customer service standard. As new COs are received by your warehouse, after CO processing and approval new COs are added to your CO pool. To achieve your company customer service objectives from your CO pool & per your company criteria your warehouse staff creates a CO wave/work day CO number. Per your employee number, productivity rates & CO pool, CO type, your CO wave selection factors are (1) single line/single sku that includes pre-packed & if you use a slapper label, vendor ready to ship cartons & single line/multiple pieces that assures your highest completed CO number, (2) age/oldest CO to assure customer service, (3) new customers to retain customers, (4) promotional/special value for high volume, (5) carton size, (6) delivery company or CO delivery address, (7) multiple lines/single or multiple skus & (8) combination.

CO 6. Your Customer Order Wave

A CO wave is a small item or GOH staff activity that has your staff selects COs from an existing CO pool in your WMS program computer for an operation work day COs. Based on your company CO priority and your budgeted picker/sorter/packer productivity, your warehouse staff selects COs for a work day/wave and sends it your WMS computer. Your WMS computer allocates skus and suggests WMS ID sku moves to satisfy your CO wave. After skus are physically placed and scanned in positions, scan messages are sent to a WMS computer that releases COs to your pick concept. The arrangement assures CO control, due to only a wave's COs that can be completed are issued to a warehouse.

CO 7. What Are Your Customer Order Types

What are your CO types are important to a small item or GOH activity and has an impact on your picker productivity. In a warehouse your CO types are single line/single piece, single line/multiple pieces, multiple lines/single or multiple pieces or combination. If your CO computer program has the ability to separate your COs into CO waves for each group, you have potential to improve your picker/packer productivity, reduce sku damage and increase completed CO number. With single line/single sku COs, you have an opportunity to set-up fast pack lines with a sku bulk pick activity. With multiple line/multiple sku COs, you have an opportunity to bulk pick sku for sort to a temporary hold position and final CO assembly.

CO 8. Pick Single Customer Orders

Pick singles has one picker or pick machine pick one CO's total sku number. A single CO pick approach has good picker accountability, easy to identify problem pickers, handles a small CO number, minimal computer program requirement and low picker productivity. Single CO pick activity has one picker complete all picks for a CO. A manual single CO pick concept has good picker accountability but low picker productivity due to greatest travel distances and is not preferred in a warehouse.

CO 9. Bulk Or Batch Pick Customer Orders

Batch pick is a small item or GOH pick concept that has your CO computer program separate COs into pre-determined groups. After your CO skus are picked as a group, later your CO picked skus are sorted to a CO holding position that increases picker productivity & your CO number. Picker productivity increase is due to at one

86

position a picker has potential to pick multiple skus and off-sets your sort activity. Each sku has a sku or CO ID that is used in a sort area to separate skus to CO collection/hold positions. Batch pick concepts are (1) small item or GOH pick/sort activity completed at a position that has a picked sku sorted to a CO hold position on a cart/trolley/tote. Each cart/trolley/tote capacity determines your batch size, (2) small item or GOH bulk pick, transport, sort and final pick activity that has in a separate area, skus sorted to temporary sort/hold position. From skus temporary hold positions, a final CO picker with a CO pack slip/invoice completes a final CO transaction. A separate sku bulk pick document and CO pack slip/invoice minimizes a computer program cost, (3) small item or GOH bulk pick, transport, sort and final sort activity that has in a separate area, picked skus sorted to CO temporary hold positions. Each batch has a separate sort area/lane and picked skus are transported on a belt conveyor or in totes. After sort, a packer with a CO pack slip/invoice verifies a CO accurate completion & (4) small item or carton bulk pick, transport, sort and final sort activity that has a pre-determined CO group small item skus sorted to a CO temporary hold position. Per position has a nominal 50 piece quantity. With a CO pack slip/invoice, a packer completes a final CO sort. To handle a high pick volume, a powered conveyor moves skus loose or in totes to an induction location for sku transfer onto a powered/mechanized scan and sort concept. To assure maximum completed CO number, you assure a constant sku flow that is based on your picker/packer budgeted productivity rates and available employee number at each work station.

CO 10. Your Customer Orders Are Separated By Sku
Your COs are separated by sku is a small item final pick and CO pack slip/invoice preparation concept for a sku that is used in a bulk pick, transport, sort and final CO pick that improves picker productivity and increases completed CO number. To have a cost effective, efficient, accurate and good employee productivity for your final pick activity, you have (1) your WMS computer program arrange your CO wave CO pack slips/invoices for print by a first or last sku digit and (2) sort your bulk pick skus by WMS sku ID. Sku sort options are by (a) first and last digit and first digit that IDs a shelf or rack bay and last digit IDs a shelf level, (b) last and next to last digit and last digit that IDs a shelf or rack bay & next to last digit IDs a shelf level or to first & (c) first and second digit and first digit that IDs a shelf or rack bay & second digit IDs a shelf level. When your WMS computer program groups/prints your CO pack slips/invoices by your selected sku digit sequence and your printed CO pack slips/invoices as group are placed into a shelf or rack bay & level for the corresponding sku digit sequence, your final picker productivity is high due to a picker first CO pick transaction is at a shelf/rack bay position with no non-productive walk time.

Pack Slip Ideas (PS 1)
PS 1. Your Customer Order Pack Slips/Invoices Go Onto Your Pick Floor
Your CO pack slips/invoices go onto your pick floor means that your WMS computer program printed CO pack slips/invoices are used by your picker/sorter or final picker. With a bulk pick/sort to a CO carton/tote, a CO pack slip/invoice is placed into a CO carton/tote that is in a cart sort position. After your picker pick/sort activity completion, a completed pick/sort cart with picked skus and CO pack slips/invoices are delivered to a pack station. With a bulk pick, sort and final pick concept, a CO pack slips/invoices are printed and sorted by sort position sequence (first digit, last digit) and each CO pack slip/invoice group is distributed to each sort position number. From each sort position, a final picker with a CO pack slip/invoice a CO completes final pick. A completed CO in a carton/tote with picked skus and CO pack slip/invoice are sent to a check/pack station. To assure all CO pack slips/invoices are accounted, your WMS computer program has your CO pack slip/invoice total that is compared to a manifested CO pack slip/invoice. If there is a variance, your pick and pack activities search for a missing CO pack slip/invoice. Features are (1) improves packer productivity, (2) with pick, sort and final pick lowers pick instruction cost, (3) with pick, sort and final pick concept that has CO pack slips/invoices separated by sort location improves picker productivity & (4) for accountablility, alcomputer compares printed total to manifested total.

Pick Container Ideas (PC 1 - PC 6)
PC 1. Pick Into A Ship Carton Or Tote
Pick & sort or pick/pass pick into a ship carton or tote are your pick container options. (1) *Pick into a carton* concept requires carton pre-made-up as an employee or machine activity with required space and carton queue to a pick line entry. For best productivity, computer program cubes CO skus to carton size & CO carton entrance to a pick

line is sequenced by carton size. If a CO sku cube exceeds your largest ship carton cube, your computer cube program creates 2 cartons for a CO. Prior to a first pick position, each carton receives a CO ID on an exterior near side wall or interior far side wall/flap. Used with carton with sealed bottom flaps, pop-out or 2 piece carton. In pick into a carton concepts, on a pick line have no bottom fill, empty cartons & wide carton size mix on a pick conveyor has potential travel path problems such as jams and cartons jumping from a conveyor travel path. Flaps-up require picker to lift sku over a flap to deposit into carton & a tall travel path window. Flaps-down with an additional employee effort at a pick line entrance, requires paper CO IDon a carton far interior side and before carton fill/seal requires additional employee effort. A disposal CO ID is attached with side scanning to near side wall or with top scanning to near side flap or use a peel-off label that has an employee transfer a CO ID from a label front to a proper carton location for manifest/ship & (2) *Pick into a tote concept* has your computer program cube your CO skus to tote interior cube. If you transfer skus from a tote into ship in a carton, a computer program cubes your CO skus to a carton size (not to exceed tote cube) & requires permanent tote IDs on a pick tote both interior & exterior sides that face a picker. Prior to a pick line entry and with a scan transaction, each tote permanent ID is associated to a WMS co ID. If you pick into a ship tote, a tote exterior near side or picker side requires a disposal CO ID. If a CO sku cube exceeds your largest ship carton or tote cube, your computer cube program creates 2 pick totes and ship cartons/totes for a CO. Tote side wall permits CO ID line or sight, minimal travel path problems & you verify tote is empty/clean. Handles/holes are preferred for employee handling. At a pack station, a zero scan transaction of a permanent tote ID breaks a WMS CO ID association and allows tote with a permanent ID used for another CO. A pack station, an employee transfers picked skus from a tote into a ship carton & with a scan transaction prints-on demand CO pack slip/invoice & delivery labels. A tote is an one- time tote cost.

PC 2. Your Pick/Ship Carton WMS Customer Order Identification Location

Your pick/ship carton WMS CO ID location is used in a small item pick/pass, pick/sort or automatic pick machine to assure a picker or automatic pick machine bar code scanner has CO ID line of sight. Feature is to improve picker productivity, no tote cost and minimize errors. After an employee or machine applies a WMS CO ID to pick/ship carton/tote, it enters your pick area and travels through your pick/sort area. On a pick/pass line or on your automatic pick machine conveyor travel path it is considered a CO container. A pick/ship carton/tote WMS CO ID and location is consider part of your picker or automatic pick machine instruction component that allows a picker to match a pick/ship CO ID with a paper document printed CO ID, CO ID on a zone display light or causes a message sent to your automatic pick machine computer to have a sku released for a CO. A basic pick/ship WMS CO ID rule is in a pick area that a pick/ship CO ID faces a picker or automatic pick machine bar code scanner. Each pick/ship has one CO ID location. WMS CO ID objectives are (1) in your pick activity to have clear employee and bar code scanner line of sight, (2) in your CO seal activity, have tape strands applied to a carton top that do not reduce a CO ID readability and (3) by your freight delivery company as your CO package delivery label. With a pick/sort concept, in a pick/sort position a pick/ship carton CO ID is on a carton side or flap that faces a picker. With an automatic pick machine concept, on an automatic pick machine conveyor travel path a CO ID is on a carton side that faces a bar code scanner. In a pick/pass concept, on a pick conveyor travel path a pick/ship carton a CO ID is on a carton side or flap that faces a picker. It is noted a pick/ship carton WMS CO ID is a disposal ID that is used by your freight company for CO package address. At a CO picked sku pack station or machine tape station, your employee or machine applies tape to secure a carton top flaps and tape strands do not reduce a CO ID readability. After a complete CO package, a pick/ship carton WMS CO ID is manifest scanned (scan message sent to your WMS computer) and is sent from your warehouse to a CO package delivery address. This means that a pick/ship carton WMS CO ID is not reused in your warehouse and does not require a zero scan transaction.

PC 3. Your Customer Order Captive Tote Warehouse Identification Locations

Your captive tote warehouse IDs is a small item pick/pass activity with a pick to light or automatic pick machine to have a captive pick tote ID in multiple locations that are quickly and easily reader by your pickers or bar code scanners. Feature improves picker productivity and minimizes errors. At your pick line or automatic pick machine entry, an employee or mechanical scanner attaches a WMS CO ID to your captive (warehouse) ID. After your pick computer relates a captive tote warehouse ID to a WMS CO ID, a warehouse ID tote travels through your pick/pass line or on your automatic pick machine conveyor travel path it is considered a CO container. A captive pick tote warehouse ID and location is consider part of your picker or automatic pick machine instruction component that allows a picker to match a captive tote warehouse ID to a CO ID on a zone light or causes a message sent to your automatic pick machine computer to have a sku released for a CO. A basic captive tote warehouse ID rule is in a pick area that a captive tote warehouse ID faces a picker or automatic pick machine bar code scanner. To have maximum tote flexibility and readability, a tote warehouse ID is preferred on all 4 tote exterior and 2 interior sides. Each tote warehouse ID location has clear employee and bar code scanner line of sight. With a pick/pass concept, a captive tote warehouse IDs are located at the highest possible location on a tote 4 exterior sides and on a rectangle shaped tote long 2 interior sides. On a pick/pass conveyor, warehouse ID locations assure picker line of sight as a tote moves on a conveyor travel path and when a picker is directly in front of a tote, an interior warehouse ID is easily read. It is noted a captive tote warehouse ID is a permanent ID that is related to a WMS CO ID. At a CO pack station or transfer station, your employee or bar code scanner zero scans a captive tote warehouse ID. A zero scan transaction is sent to your WMS computer that breaks the relationship between a captive tote warehouse (permanent) ID and WMS CO ID and allows a captive tote warehouse ID used for another WMS CO ID.

PC 4. One Or Multiple Customer Orders Per Pick Tote (See GC 1 Page 122)

PC 5. Pick By Ship Carton Size
Pick by carton size is a small item activiy option to release COs to a pick/sort or pick/pass pick concept to improve picker/packer productivity, allows a picker to easily read a container CO ID, increase completed COs number and minimized conveyor travel path or cart pick position handling problems. A pick/pass concept has a picker physically or powered queue conveyor travel path moves COs cartons over a pick zone and onto the next pick zone or onto a take-away conveyor. To have your COs arranged to enter a pick/pass pick conveyor by carton size you have your computer cube program determine each CO carton size and to release one carton size CO to your pick line (computer). At a pick line entry or a pick cart preparation station, you have your computer suggested carton size pre-made and available for pick concept entry. Features improves your employee or machine carton make-up activity and easier to control collapse carton in-feed to your carton make-up station. Your pick line computer assures that your COs are sequenced by carton size. Features are requires accurate sku and ship carton cube data and additional computer process time.

PC 6. How To Pick Into A Small Size Customer Order Ship Carton
How to pick into a small size CO ship carton is a pick & sort, pick/pack or pick/pass concept that has your pickers transfer picked skus into a computer suggested CO small size carton. Picking into a CO ship carton improves your picker and packer productivity and increases your completed CO number. With a wide ship carton mixed in a pick/sort cart or on a powered conveyor or on a pick conveyor travel path, there are potential small size carton handling travel problems/jams or carton tipping that creates lost skus with non-productive employee to assure carton stays in a pick/sort position or travels on a conveyor and to correct a lost sku problem. Small size carton conveyor travel path options are (1) *Skew Rollers* that direct all carton travel onto one conveyor side for carton travel along a 'C' channel guard rail (s) and if possible have WMS computer program release CO as a group by carton size. Features are potential travel path problems that are minimized when pick by carton size, requires additional costs but each carton has CO ID and after all pick transactions completion, captive tote/large carton goes to your next activity station (check, pack or seal station), (2) *Place Each Small Made-Up Carton Onto A Captive Tray*. Features are minimal travel path problems, requires additional employee time to handle/relocate empty trays and tray cost but each carton has CO ID and after all pick transactions completion, captive tote/large carton goes to your next activity station (check, pack or seal station), (3) *Pick Into A Captive Tote/Large Carton With A Peel-Off Label* (WMS CO ID) and after all pick transactions completion, captive tote/large carton goes to your next activity station (check, pack or seal station). Features are minimal travel path problems, requires WMS CO ID relocated from captive tote/large carton onto a small size carton, additional tote/carton handling, pack station employee requires small cartons and carton make-up time or small size carton is picked into your captive tote/large carton & (4) *Pick Into A Captive Tote/Large Carton With A Warehouse ID* that is associated to a WMS CO ID and (a) at a special carton/filler material pick station to have a collapsed or made-up small carton transferred into a captive tote/large carton or (b) pack station has small carton size & after all pick transactions completion, captive tote/large

carton that goes to your next activity (check, pack or seal station). Features are requires WMS CO ID related to a warehouse ID, additional tote/carton handling, prior to captive tote/large carton reuse, zero scan a warehouse ID, high pack station employee productivity with minimal carton make-up time & less required space. A small size carton side wall options are (1) fold onto inside walls, (2) place with flaps-up & (3) fold to outside wall & secured with rubber band.

Pick Transaction Communication Ideas (PTC 1)

PTC 1. How To Communicate A Pick Transaction To Your Computer

How to communicate a pick transaction to your WMS computer is an activity that has a picker send a sku pick transaction completion message to your WMS computer program that assures good picker productivity, enhances sku inventory control and depletes a sku quantity from a position. Picked sku depletion from a pick position assures accurate inventory count in a position and WMS computer program on-time replenishment transaction. Picked sku communication options are (1) *Paper Pick Instruction* that is printed by your warehouse computer and occurs after pick instruction preparation but does not assure on-time sku replenishment and accurate pick transaction, (2) *Pick To Light Pick Instruction*, after your pick light pick button is pressed or laser beam is broken, your warehouse computer sends a pick completion message to your WMS computer program & (3) *Automatic Pick Machine* sku release, your warehouse computer sends a pick completion message to your WMS computer program. Features are (1) on-line communication, (2) requires a communication network and (3) with any pick concept between your pick and pack areas, on a travel path or at a pack station you have an employee or machine complete a picked sku check scan transaction for each CO picked sku that is sent on-line to your WMS computer program.

Pick Instructions Ideas (PL 1 - PL 10)

PL 1. What Are Your Pick Instruction Components

What are your pick instruction components is your pick instruction format that is used to direct an employee or pick machine for sku transfer from a pick position into a picker hands, container or onto a conveyor belt. A clear and understandable pick instruction assures good picker productivity and accurate picks. Your pick instruction components identifies your pick aisle, in an aisle a shelf/rack bay, in a shelf/rack bay a level and on a shelf/bay level a pick position. With an employee picker concept your options are (1) alpha characters, (2) digits or (3) combination of both. Alpha characters and digits combination option features are unlimited pick position identifications, easy to print, easy to read due to an employee deals with numbers in their everyday life, easy to have an arithmetic progression &matches most picker routing patterns. Most automatic pick machines use a numeric pick instruction.

PL 2. Paper Or Paperless (Pick To Light) Pick Instruction

Paper or paperless pick instruction are your options to direct a picker to a pick position and complete a pick transaction to assure your picker productivity and minimize errors. *Paper Pick Instruction* options are (A) *Paper Document Pick Instruction* that requires your computer program to print a document and your picker to read. A paper document preferred print sequence has pick position first, pick quantity second, sku description and other company information. Features are a picker carries a pick document, print has clear and large as possible printed digits & characters, associated print paper/ink expenses and requires a printer & (B) *Paper Labels* that are used in a pick, transport and sort CO concept with one label equals one pick transaction. On each label is printed a sku pick position, human/machine readable CO ID, sku description and other company information. When compared to a paper document, labels are printed in pick position sequence as a roll or paper sheets that are difficult to handle, minimal reading requirement and for sort activity requires human/machine readable CO ID & (2) *Paper-Less Pick Instruction* options are (A) a display screen (pick to light) above or below a pick position or finger, wrist or hand held RF device with a display that has an employee read a CO sku pick quantity. With a paper-less instruction and pick concepts an employee walks to a pick position, transfers a sku from a pick position to a CO container and presses a pick to light button, breaks a laser beam or presses a RF device button to register a pick transaction completion. Features are increase picker productivity and accuracy and high cost or (B) computer controlled message to activate a mechanical device to release a small item or GOH for a CO pick transaction. After a pick transaction completion, a small item or GOH pick machine release device computer sends a message to WMS computer that register a completed pick transaction. A picked sku is transferred into a carton/tote or loose onto a conveyor for travel to a pack station. Features are increased picker productivity, with outbound queue works on a 24 X 7 schedule, requires a conveyor in-feed and out-feed concept and highest cost.

PL 3. Your Pick Document Printer Capacity
Printer capacity is a warehouse computer controlled printer ability to print a CO wave/work day pick/pack/ship documents. A computer controlled printer's ability (memory and capacity) to print your CO wave line numbers assures on-time CO pick instructions on your pick floor and pack slips/invoices with delivery labels at your pack stations. If a printer capacity an not handle a memory or print requirement, there is potential for printer problem, late start-up, low employee productivity and poor customer service. Possible solutions are additional printers, new printer or earlier print time that could be difficult due to a time critical factor between a host computer final process time and COs available for print and your operation required start-up time.

PL 4. Pick Labels As A Roll Or Sheets In A Dispenser
Pick labels as a roll or sheets in a dispenser are used in a batched pick concept that is designed to increase picker productivity to off-set your sort labor expense and increase your completed CO number. All pick labels are printed in pick position sequence to assure minimal picker walk distance. A label fits onto a sku and a label adhesive secures a label onto a sku. During a batch pick activity that uses a CO ID as a sort instruction, each sku receives a label. With labels as a roll or sheets, during a pick activity there is potential for labels to become lost, misplaced, damaged or out-of-sequence and to re-group creates picker non-productive time. To assure good picker productivity and minimize potential label problems, a label roll is placed into a dispenser or label sheets are placed into pouch. The devices are attached to a picker belt and assure that labels are readily available to a picker. To assure a clean pick area, a picker has a trash pouch for a label self- adhesive back.

PL 5. Paper Pick Document Have Fast Skus At A Page Top
Paper pick document fast skus at a page top has your 'A' moving sku assignment to pick positions that are first in your pick area/routing pattern. The arrangement has your printer print your CO 'A' moving skus as first picks. Features are improves your picker productivity and accuracy due to minimal reading requirement, easy reading at a page top and increases your completed CO number.

PL 6. Paper Pick Document Sku Number
Paper pick document sku number is the sku number that is printed each picker page. The sku number determination factors are (1) printer ability, (2) page length, (3) skus required to cube a ship carton and (4) print size. To assure picker productivity, your print lines per page are usually 15 to 20 and most catalog COs have 1 to 5 skus/lines. Features are easily read and handled by an employee.

PL 7. Pick Label Holder
Pick label holder is used in a pick activity that applies a label to a picked sku that improves picker productivity and minimizes damaged/lost labels. In any pick concept, a label stack or label sheets are difficult to handle as a picker or a pick line start employee. To complete a label pick activity, a picker arrives at a pick position, sets a label stack in one hand, removes a label, removes a self-adhesive back and places a label onto a sku, transfers a labeled sku into a tote or onto a conveyor and a backing that is placed into a trash holder. Most situations, a picker sets a label stack in a pick position that provides two hands to complete a pick activity. Features are potential for labels to fall and become out-of-pick sequence or become damaged/lost that creates non-productive picker time. For a label roll, a label holder is attached to a picker belt and as a picker removes a label from a holder a label self adhesive back is removed and a picker has 2 hands to complete a pick transaction. A pick/pass concept with a disposal CO label on a CO carton, at your pick line start station an employee adds a CO ID label to a pick/ship carton. If your pick/pass computer CO sequence is the same as your printed label sequence, at your pick line start station you assure that your CO labels are in sequence. With a high volume pick line labels in a stack, there is potential for a label stack to fall that creates pick line down time. A label holder minimizes labels out-of sequence problem.

PL 8. Pre-Labeled Skus

Pre-labeled or non-labeled sku are a small item or GOH (vendor ready to ship) warehouse sku ID that increases your picker/sorter/returns process employee productivity & enhances inventory control. It is clearly understood for good sku inventory control that each sku requires a discreet WMS ID that is attached to a sku by your vendor, your receiving department or picker. With a pick & sort concept, a pre-labeled sku inventory ID serves as part of your sort instruction. In a small item or GOH batched pick, transport, sort & final sort concept, each sku requires a CO ID that is applied by a picker. Feature is additional print time and label/ink expense but handles a large volume.

PL 9. Kiss It Pick Instruction

Kiss it pick instruction is a term to describe a picker transaction instruction. To assure good picker productivity, your pick transaction instruction approach is to keep it simple that decreases your picker non-productive time.

PL 10. Before Skus Sales How To Identify Or Tell Your 'A'/Fast Moving Skus

Before skus sales how to identify or tell your 'A'/fast moving skus is a key factor to assure good hit concentration and density & picker productivity. Your 'A' fast moving sku ID options are (1) advise from your merchandising department, (2) reviewing your TV programmed skus, (3) advertisement copy that show your skus, (4) if special offer is mailed or enclosed in a CO package & (5) seasonal or holiday sku.

Pick Position Identification Ideas (PPI 1 - PPI 2)

PPI 1. Large Or Small Pick Position Identification Human & Machine Readable Symbologies

Large or small pick position ID human readable symbology or machine readable symbology are a small item, GOH manual, mechanized or automatic pick machine replenishment pick concept pick position ID options. To complete a pick transaction, a pick position ID allows a picker to read and identify a pick position. A pick position ID has human (alpha characters and digits) or human/machine readable (bar code) symbologies that are considered part of a picker CO pick instruction. To complete a human pick transaction, from an aisle or pick station an employee reads pick position ID that is attached to a shelf, decked rack, standard pallet rack, carousel basket or carton flow rack member. To read or scan a small human/machine readable pick position ID, a picker walks from an aisle middle next to a pick position that creates non-productive time. To read or scan a large human/machine readable pick position ID, a picker remains in an aisle middle that minimizes non-productive time. Your pick position ID size is determined by your pick position member dimension and your pick position ID label/light.

PPI 2. On A Pick Bay Where Is Each Pick Position Identification Location

On a pick bay where is each pick position ID is used to identify a pick position and is a factor that affects your picker productivity by reducing a picker non-productive time to have line of sight and read a pick position ID. In a decked standard pallet rack concept, as you face a decked pallet rack bay a pick position ID is located for each pick position in a decked rack bay and is under each pick position. If there are two pick position IDs on one load beam, a top ID refers to the above pick position and lower ID refers to the below pick position. In a GOH static rail concept, as you walk in an aisle and face a GOH rail, a moveable (slides or employee moved clip) pick position ID is on a rail in front of a GOH. In a small item shelf pick concept with 3 to 10 shelves. Carton flow racks with 4 to 5 levels high or a horizontal carousel basket, as you face a pick bay, pick position IDs are attached to a shelf/flow lane end member/basket and are located directly below a pick position. With shelf. flow rack and carousel basket concepts to improve line of sight your options are (1) bottom shelf, flow rack lane or basket ID upward and for protection is enclosed in a harden plastic/metal low profile 'C' member & (2) top two flow rack levels are angled downward. With a pegboard or drawer pick concept, position ID locations are same as a shelf position ID features.

Pick Activity Layout Ideas (PAL 1 - PAL 8)

PAL 1. Increase Travel Distance Decreases Your Picker Productivity

Travel distance is an important pick concept factor that impacts your picker productivity. With a manual push cart pick concept, your travel distance factors are walk distance and time (1) between two pick positions and (2) between your pick area and pack/sort area. With a multiple horizontal carousel pick concept your travel distance/time is the time that is required to rotate a basket to your pick station. To improve your manual picker, you minimize a manual picker non-productivity walk distance and time or horizontal basket rotation time. To minimize the distance between two pick positions or horizontal basket rotation time, you consider an 'ABCD' sku moving profile strategy that consolidates 'A'/fast moving skus with 'B'/medium moving skus in few pick aisles/zones, one horizontal carousel or prime real estate that completes 85% of your COs and 'C' & 'D' moving skus in your other pick aisles/zone, a second horizontal carousel or low value real estate that completes 15% of your COs. Features are to increase hit concentration & density that improves your picker productivity. With a manual pick concept to minimize your picker travel distance/time & physical effort, after a picker receives pick instructions you start your picker first pick position most distant from your pack/sort area. Features are (1) to start a picker pushes an empty pick vehicle to the first pick position that requires minimal employee physical effort, (2) picker routing pattern directs a picker toward your pack/sort area that reduces complete CO or full cart travel distance from a pick area to a pack/sort area & (3) with a completed CO or full cart travel distance to pack/sort area is short but requires a picker physical effort to push a cart.

PAL 2. Edible Sku Allocation To Pick Positions
Edible skus allocation to pick positions by some local codes or company policy that require edible skus allocated to separate pick positions from non-edible sku pick positions. With the procedure, you basically assign non-edible skus to separate pick positions.

PAL 3. Flammable Sku Allocation To Pick Positions
Flammable skus allocation to pick positions by some local codes or company policy that require flammable skus allocated to separate pick positions that are in a solid enclosed area with a drain and any liquid run-off flows to a containment chamber. During a fire, a solid wall minimizes potential sku flow and a drain directs sku flow to a containment chamber. For your pick activity skus are assigned to specific pick zones or a cell pick concept that is designed for flammable skus. With the approach a picker or CO carton/tote sent to the specific positions or cell.

PAL 4. Prime Real Estate Or Pick Positions
Prime real estate is a pick position strategy that focuses on your positions that are nearest your pack or sort area that are considered prime real estate & the most distance pick positions are low real estate. When you allocate your 'A'/fast moving skus to prime real estate positions and you consider that 80% of your COs are completed from 20% of your skus, it improves your picker productivity & increases your completed CO number due to a short non-productive distance between 2 pick positions & short travel distance from pick area to pack/sort area.

PAL 5. Pick Area Pick Position Rows & Aisles Have A Parallel Or Perpendicular Layout
Pick area pick position rows and aisles with a parallel or perpendicular layout are small item or GOH pick area layout options that have completed COs flow from a pick area to a pack area to improve picker productivity. Your selected pick position row and aisle layout is determined by your facility shape/sq. ft. area, position number and pick concept. *Parallel Pick Position Row & Aisle Layout* has turning aisles at both row and aisle ends that face a wall. With a parallel pick position row and aisle layout, a picker with a full pick cart/trolley has additional travel time and walk distance to move from a pick aisle to a pack area. Feature is lower picker productivity due to increased walk distance and time. *Perpendicular Pick Position Row & Aisle Layout* has turning aisles at both row and aisle ends. One turning aisle is adjacent to your pack station area. A picker with a full pick cart/trolley has minimal travel time and walk distance to move from a pick aisle to your pack station area. Feature is higher picker productivity due to decreased walk distance and time.

PAL 6. In A Pick Area Have A Cross Aisle
In a pick area a cross aisle is a manual small item or GOH pick area design to improve your picker productivity and increase your completed CO number. If we consider Pareto's law applies to most warehouses that has 80% of your picks are from 20% of your skus/'A' moving skus, after an 'A' fast moving sku pick section, your have few picks and there is a great walk distance between picks. With a long pick aisle that has your 'A' fast moving skus in a front pick section and 'B', 'C' & 'D' medium to slow moving skus in your rear pick section and for your pick aisle a progressive/arithmetic picker routing pattern, there is a need for a cross aisle that permits an employee with no

93

picks in the present or adjacent aisles' 'B', 'C' & 'D' section to transfer from one pick aisle to another pick aisle without walking/traveling to an aisle end. The arrangement allows a picker to complete all picks from both aisles' 'A' fast moving section with the shortest travel distance. For maximum picker travel efficiency and minimal aisle congestion, your pick and cross aisle widths allows two vehicles per aisle.

PAL 7. Light Fixture Location In A Pick Aisle

Lights fixture location in your pick aisle is reference to where are your small item or GOH pick aisle light fixtures hung and to meet local code lighting. Most codes require X lumen number for 30 ins above the floor surface. Properly hung light fixtures in an aisle with proper lighting level improves picker productivity and accuracy. A paper document or label pick concept with a forklift truck activity, aisle light fixtures are chain hung from a ceiling in an aisle middle. With non-forklift truck activity or GOH aisle, light fixtures are chain hung from a ceiling or shelf/rack structural members to provide sufficient light to read a pick instruction. With a small item or GOH pick to light concept, light fixtures are ceiling hung by a chain or shelf/rack structural members and are at a minimum level due to your picker instruction is displayed on a lighted screen.

PAL 8. Clear Pick Aisles

Clear pick aisles is a pick aisle situation with no obstructions in a pick aisle between two pick rows and assures good picker productivity and minimizes equipment/sku damage. No obstructions in a pick aisle means there is no trash, empty carton/tote or debris that causes a picker or pick vehicle to stop travel or non-productive picker time to remove an obstruction from an aisle.

Pick Area/Line Profile Ideas (PAP 1 - PAP 20)

PAP 1. Random Sku Assignment Or No Profile Strategy

Random sku assignment or no profile strategy to a pick position means that your sku is placed in any pick position. With seasonal, catalog, TV marketing or special promotion skus, the approach has potential to mix 'A'/fast moving skus with 'B' or 'C' medium moving skus. Features are low picker productivity due to low hit concentration and density, increased non-productive walk distances and low completed CO number.

PAP 2. Sku Hit Concentration & Density

Hit concentration and density is a small item or GOH pick area factor that groups your 'A' fast moving skus in one pick aisle/zone to improve your picker productivity sku and increase completed CO number. Good hit concentration is a high sku pick number per aisle/zone/pick machine and good hit density is a high sku pieces picked per pick position. With good hit concentration and density, you minimize a picker non-productive travel distance between two picks and within one pick aisle/zone/pick machine, you increase the potential for completed COs.

PAP 3. Pick Area/Line Sku Profile

Profile is a small item, carton or GOH sku allocation to a pick position strategy that assures your skus are in pick positions for your employee, mechanized or automatic pick machine actual pick productivity to match your budgeted productivity. To complete a pick aisle/line/zone, carousel or automatic pick machine profile you require your sku historical sales, estimated sales, sku weight/physical characteristics, your budgeted picker productivity, your selected profile strategy and a spread sheet that shows your positions. Various profile strategies are by budgeted picker productivity, 'A' skus to your Golden Zone or Golden Highway, prime real estate, family group and random. With a PC or paper spread sheet that mirrors your pick concept, you allocate your skus to pick positions. After PC or spread sheet completion, you enter your selected profile strategy into your WMS computer program that directs your sku set-up or replenishment transactions for your pick activity.

PAP 4. What Is Your Pick Area Layout Philosophy

What is your pick area layout philosophy has a major impact on your picker productivity, assures proper sku rotation and increases your completed CO number. Your pick area layout philosophy is how you profiled your skus to pick positions. Whether you have a small item or GOH manual, mechanized or automatic pick machine pick activity, your pick area has a layout philosophy. Pick area philosophies are (1) ABCD or Pareto's Law that groups your

'A'/fast moving skus in one pick aisle/zone to improve hit concentration & density, (2) Pairs, Cell, Kit or Family Group that groups sku with specific characteristics in adjacent pick positions, (3) FIFO Rotation that has your oldest skus picked first & (4) Random that has your skus assigned to pick positions with no discipline.

PAP 5. SKu Value Profile Strategy

Sku value profile strategy assignment to pick position within a specific area/cell by a sku value improves security. With your high value skus in one solid or meshed enclosure and secured area or solid shelves with lockable doors, you have controlled and restricted access to your value sku pick area. To increase security, you have cameras and entrance locks with issued keys/pass cards to listed employees.

PAP 6. Pick Line Or Aisle Profile Sheet

Profile is a small item, carton or GOH sku allocation to a pick position strategy that assures your skus are in pick positions for your employee, mechanized or automatic pick machine actual pick productivity to match your budgeted productivity.   To complete a pick aisle/line/zone, carousel or automatic pick machine profile you require your sku historical sales, estimated sales, sku weight/physical characteristics, your budgeted picker productivity, your selected profile strategy and a spread sheet that shows your pick positions. Various profile strategies are by budgeted picker productivity, 'A' skus to your Golden Zone or Golden Highway, prime real estate, family group and random. With a PC or paper spread sheet that mirrors your pick concept, you allocate your skus to pick positions. After PC or spread sheet completion, you enter your selected profile strategy into your WMS computer program that directs your sku set-up or replenishment transactions for your pick activity.

PICK AISLE OR LINE PROFILE SHEET

CARTON FLOW BAY 1 LANE 1	CARTON FLOW BAY 1 LANE 2	CARTON FLOW BAY 1 LANE 3	CARTON FLOW BAY 1 LANE 4	CARTON FLOW BAY 1 LANE 5	
SKU NUMBER PICK QUANTITY	SKU NUMBER PICK QUANTITY	SKU NUMBER PICK QUANTITY	SKU NUMBER PICK QUANTITY	SKU NUMBER PICK QUANTITY	PICK LEVEL 4
SKU NUMBER PICK QUANTITY	SKU NUMBER PICK QUANTITY	SKU NUMBER PICK QUANTITY	SKU NUMBER PICK QUANTITY	SKU NUMBER PICK QUANTITY	PICK LEVEL 3
SKU NUMBER PICK QUANTITY	SKU NUMBER PICK QUANTITY	SKU NUMBER PICK QUANTITY	SKU NUMBER PICK QUANTITY	SKU NUMBER PICK QUANTITY	PICK LEVEL 2
SKU NUMBER PICK QUANTITY	SKU NUMBER PICK QUANTITY	SKU NUMBER PICK QUANTITY	SKU NUMBER PICK QUANTITY	SKU NUMBER PICK QUANTITY	PICK LEVEL 1

PICKER TRAVEL DIRECTION ⟶

PAP 7. Special, Promotional, Seasonal, Catalog Or TV Sold Sku Location On A Pick Line

Special, promotional, seasonal, catalog or TV sold sku location on a pick is a sku layout strategy with your small item, GOH, or carton skus that are historical or estimated (based on sale promotion) 'A'/fast moving skus in one pick aisle/zone. When you consolidated 'A'/fast moving skus in one pick aisle/zone, you increase your hit concentration and density to improve your picker productivity and density. If your sku profile/assignment to a pick aisle/zone exceeds your picker productivity, you add a second unique ID WMS computer program pick aisle/line that allows your to profile 'A' fasting moving over two pick lines and your computer program to direct your pickers to pick CO skus from two pick line pick positions.

PAP 8. ABCD Or Pareto's Law Profile Strategy

ABCD or Pareto's Law profile strategy is a small item or GOH sku profile strategy that has your skus separated into 4 major groups to improve your picker productivity. Your sku classification groups are established by each sku's historical sales or CO wave/work day sales. When sku is profiled or allocated by sales volume classification to 'A' fast moving pick aisle or pick zone within an aisle (group or adjacent pick positions) it creates high hit concentration and density and reduces travel distance and time between 2 picks that improves picker and replenishment employee productivity. When Pareto's law is applied to sku movement, it means that 85% of your sales are generated from 15% of your skus. In recent study results show that 95% of your sales are generated from 5% of your sales. With the sku movement analysis, your skus are separated into 4 groups. Groups are (1) 'A' fast moving skus (special value or promotional) that have high pick number and few sku number with a high inventory. When consolidated into one pick aisle or required pick zones at a pick aisle/line front that do not exceed your budgeted picker productivity, it creates higher picker productivity and increases completed CO number, (2) 'B' medium moving skus that were last week special or promotional skus or frequently purchased skus. Skus are allocated to a pick aisle middle or required pick zones, (3) 'C' slow moving skus that appear on few CO and skus are allocated to a pick aisle rear and (4) 'D' very slow moving or obsolete skus that appear on fewest COs and skus are allocated to an aisle rear most positions. With your 'B', 'C' & 'D' moving sku consolidation in groups does minimize a picker walk distance & time between 2 picks that improves picker productivity & increases completed CO number.

PAP 9. Pairs, Cell, Kit Or Family Group Profile Strategy

Pairs, cell, kit or family group profile strategy is a small item or GOH sku profile strategy that places skus with similar features to one aisle or pick zone adjacent pick positions and is designed to improve picker productivity and completed CO number. From your sales program you identify pairs, cells, kit or family group skus. With the sku information, your sku pick aisle/line profile assigns skus to adjacent pick positions. If you profile pair skus adjacent to each other, a picker has an increase potential for multiple picks with minimal walk distance that increases picker productivity. Good picker productivity and increased completed CO number results from minimal walk distance and time between 2 picks. Pairs are skus that compliment each other such salt and pepper shakers or battery powered toy & battery. Cell skus are unique skus that are intended for a specific customer group such as a specific language or ethic group. Kit skus are components for one sku that is being manufactured on a production line. Family group skus a retail store aisle minimizes a retail store labor to get a sku onto a retail shelf.

PAP 10. Sku FIFO Rotation

Sku FIFO or first-in first-out sku rotation is used for small item skus with a saleable date on each sku or oldest sku inventory that is sold first. If a company has a criteria for good picker productivity and FIFO sku rotation, your options are (1) with a single deep shelf, decked rack or standard rack pick position use a floating pick position concept that has your computer deplete inventory in one pick position (A100) before have pick transactions occur from pick position (B200). Features are less replenishment activities, lower picker productivity due to increased walk distance between two picks, difficult to profile for high pick concentration and density and additional computer program or (2) with a dense/gravity flow pick position concept that has a replenishment employee transfer the oldest sku first into a flow lane and next transfer another sku. At a pick position, the oldest sku is the first available sku at a pick position. Features are added replenishment activities, higher picker productivity due to minimal walk distance between two picks, easy to profile high pick concentration & density & standard computer program & cost.

PAP 11. Manufacturer Lot Number Registration

Manufacturer lot number registration is very important in some industries (drugs, appliance & medical) that requires a CO picked sku ID (manufacturer lot number) recorded in your files. If you rely on your picker to register a sku manufacturer lot number and WMS CO ID onto a separate document, you have decrease your picker productivity due to additional time for a picker to locate and write a sku lot number and WMS CO ID number onto a separate document. With a pick into a warehouse ID tote, bulk pick or batched pick & sort concept, it is more efficient and cost effective for a packer to register a sku manufacturer lot number onto a separate document with a CO pack slip/invoice number and a packer has table work surface.

PAP 12. 85/15 15/85 Pick Area/Line Profiel Strategy

85/15 15/85 refers to Pareto's Law that states 15% of the population has 85% of the wealth. Pareto's Law means that 15% of your skus account for 85% of your COs. When you profile you 15% of skus ('A' fast moving skus) to a Golden Highway, Golden Zone or prime real estate/front pick positions, you have increase your hit concentration and density that improves your pick productivity and increases your completed CO number. When you profile your skus to one pick zone, your picks must equal your pickers budgeted productivity. If your CO picks exceed your picker budgeted productivity, there is potential congestion and pick line down time. To assure picker budgeted productivity, you design two pick section and your WMS computer spreads your pick volume to each pick section and matches your picker budgeted productivity.

PAP 13. Golden Highway Sku Profile Strategy

A Golden Highway is a small item or GOH profile strategy to assign your 'A'/fast moving skus into one pick aisle/zone to increase your hit concentration and density that improves your picker productivity and increases completed CO number. In a manual, pick/pass, horizontal or automatic pick machine concept you use your historical sales or estimated sales to identify your candidate skus. With your sku movement data, you separate skus into A,B,C & D groups. In most companies, an 'A' moving sku is a promotional sku and 'B' moving sku is a sku with repeat COs. Your Golden Highway options are to allocate (1) all 'A' moving skus to one pick aisle, pick zone, horizontal carousel or automatic pick machine and (2) if your 'A' moving skus do not fill your pick position, you allocate your top moving 'B' moving skus to vacate pick positions. If your profiled Golden Highway sku picks exceed your budgeted picker productivity, in your warehouse or WMS computer you create a second Golden Highway pick section that spreads your sku picks to match your budgeted picker productivity.

PAP 14. Golden Zone Sku Profile Strategy

A Golden Zone is a small item or GOH pick position strategy for sku profile to pick positions above a floor that improves picker productivity and increases completed CO number. For most manual pickers, a Golden Zone is between a picker's knees and shoulders. With pick position elevations above a floor surface, a picker physical requirement (effort & time) to complete a pick transaction is minimal. With a standard high pick position shelf, 4 pick position carton flow rack or 5 basket level high horizontal carousel pick concept, your Golden Zone pick positions are levels 2, 3 & 4. With a 5 level shelf or horizontal carousel pick concept, your Golden Zone pick positions are levels 2, 3 & 4. With a 4 level carton flow rack, your Golden Zone pick positions levels are 2 & 3. With a 3 level decked standard pallet rack with access to both sides pick concept, your Golden Zone pick positions are levels 2 & 3. With a 2 level standard pallet rack pick concept, after partial pallet depletion both levels are not considered a Golden Zone. With a 1 level standard pallet rack pick concept, it is considered a Golden Zone. With a standard 1 long GOH rail and 1 short GOH rail, a long GOH is nearest to the floor and is the Golden Zone. With a standard 3 level short GOH rails, a levels 1 & 2 & are the Golden Zone.

PAP 15. Floating Or Fixed Sku Pick Position Length

Floating or fixed sku pick position length is a term that is used in a manual small item or GOH manual , mechanized or automated warehouse for sku assignment to a pick position. *Floating Pick Position* concept has one sku allocated to two pick positions. Pick positions are adjacent to each other, separated by other skus or in different aisles. With a floating pick position concept, a sku quantity is placed into two positions that are A100 and B290. After CO picks deplete a sku quantity in one position (A100), your computer program has your next CO picked from position (B290). Features are requires additional pick positions, difficult to maintain a pick line/zone profile, requires a computer program, minimizes replenishment transactions and minimizes stock-outs. *Fixed Pick Position* concept has one sku allocated to one position (C250) with additional skus allocated to storage positions. After CO picks deplete a sku quantity in one position (C250), your computer program suggests a replenishment transaction from a storage position to a position (C250). Features are requires minimal positions but additional storage positions, easy to maintain a pick line/zone profile that improves picker productivity, minimizes computer program requirements and requires replenishment transactions.

PAP 16. Your 'A'/Fast Moving Skus Are Fixed Or Remain

If your 'A'/fast moving skus are fixed or remain in one position, it is a small item, GOH or carton strategy for all your CO waves that has your 'A'/fast moving skus assigned to one pick zone or pick aisle pick positions. With all your 'A' fast moving skus in one pick zone or aisle (matches your budgeted picker productivity rate), a sku set-up or replenishment strategy that increases picker productivity and enhances sku inventory control. With a fixed or remain sku allocation to pick zone or pick aisle concept, after sku quantity becomes depleted in a pick position, a WMS/inventory control program directs a sku quantity replenishment transaction to move a sku from a storage area to the same pick position. If a new 'A'/fast moving sku a is allocated to a pick position that is adjacent to a slower moving sku, your pick productivity is lower due to additional travel distance between two picks. A fixed or remain sku pick position strategy is preferred for your B, C & D moving skus.

PAP 17. Re-Organize Or Re-Profile Your 'A' Fast Moving Skus
Re-organize or re-profile your 'A'/fast moving skus is small item, GOH or carton strategy that improves your picker productivity and increases your completed CO number. A re-organize or re-profile strategy requires your set-up or replenishment employee to allocate 'A'/fast moving skus to one pick zone or aisle and as required to relocate 'B' or medium moving skus from your 'A' pick zone/aisle to another pick zone or aisle. With your 'A'/fast moving skus in one pick zone/aisle that matches your budgeted picker productivity, it increases your sku hit concentration & density that improves your picker & replenishment employee productivity due to short travel distances between 2 positions.

PAP 18. Rotate Your 'A'/Fast Moving Skus
Rotate your 'A'/ fast moving skus is used in a small item or GOH concept and has your 'A'/fast moving skus that are assigned to 1 pick zone or pick aisle strategy (matches your budgeted picker productivity rate) that improves your replenishment & picker productivity and enhances sku inventory control. The concept has for DAY 1 CO wave all your 'A'/fast moving skus assigned to 1 pick zone or pick aisle that minimizes a picker walk distance between two picks. At DAY 1 CO wave end from all your 'A' pick positions any residual sku quantity is transferred from your pick zone pick positions to another pick zone or pick aisle. After a pick position zero scan transaction completion, DAY 1 'A'/fast moving sku rotation creates vacate pick positions in your pick zone for DAY 2 CO wave 'A'/fast moving skus. Features are (1) additional employee activity to relocate skus that is minimized with rounded down carton concept and for DAY 1 'A' fast moving sku presence in another pick section pick position (1 carton), (2) requires a zero scan transaction to assure sku inventory control, (3) requires pick position profile and set-up for hit concentration and density & high picker productivity & (4) is preferred for your 'A'/fast moving skus.

PAP 19. If You Daily Rotate Your 'A' Skus With A Skewed 2/4 Day Life Cycle Consider Two Pick Sections
If you daily rotate your 'A' skus with a skewed two/four day life cycle consider two pick sections improves your picker and replenishment productivity and space utilization. With two pick sections, for CO wave on Day 1 you have Day 1 skus in pick section A and pick Day 1 COs and on Day 2 you set-up pick section B with Day 2 skus. With Day 2 your CO wave, your picks are from both pick section A & B. After Day 2 CO wave completion, any residual sku quantity in section A is transferred to regular section and you set-up your Day 3 skus in pick section A.

PAP 20. 'D' Moving Sku Have Few Picks
'D' moving or old sku means that there is low CO demand for a sku. When COs have a 'D' moving skus, due to low pick frequency, it lowers your picker productivity and space utilization. A 'D' moving sku is classified as a seasonal sku, a sku that does not appear in a catalog & TV promotion or a sku inventory level does not satisfy your TV sales sku inventory quantity guide. To identify 'D' moving skus, you have your computer program print a sku historical movement report from high volume to low volume that shows each sku inventory level. With one pick aisle/zone your 'D' moving skus in pick positions mixed with 'A'/fast moving skus in adjacent pick positions, features are (1) low hit concentration and density that means low picker productivity & (2) with a large inventory in a prime pick area means poor space utilization. 'D' moving sku consolidation into one pick aisle with 'D' moving skus in adjacent skus. Features are (1) frees-up prime pick positions for your 'A' moving skus that improves picker productivity, (2) with a few pieces in a short depth & narrow width pick position enhances space utilization or increases pick fronts per bay & (3) with a batch or bulk pick concept, increases 'D' moving sku pick concentration & density.

PAP 21. Your C & D Moving Skus Are Your High Cost Picks

Your 'C' & 'D' moving skus are your high cost picks to complete a CO. With a manual pick concept, your pickers are required to travel the entire pick area. As a picker's travel distance increases, the hourly labor cost increases to complete CO pick transactions. When you consolidate your 'C' & 'D' moving skus with a batched CO pick concept, you lower your 'C' & 'D' CPU.

Manual Pick Skus Ideas (MPS 1)

MPS 1. Manual Pick Small Items

Manual pick small items has your picker push a 4-wheel cart through storage/pick aisles. Manual pick small items requires an employee to have a printed document or RF device that shows a picker each CO sku. Each pick document shows pick position, pick quantity and sku description. A manual pick concept is used to pick single COs, bulk or 'en masse' picked skus for later sort and bulk pick and sort skus. Features are (1) easy to implement, (2) used with various pick concepts and (3) low equipment cost.

Manual Controlled Pick Vehicles Ideas (MCPV 1 - MCPV 11)

MCPV 1. Your Pick Vehicle Matches Your Pick Concept

A pick vehicle matches your pick concept assures good picker productivity. Pick vehicle characteristics are (1) load carrying surface permits picked sku transfer, (2) carries maximum picked sku and CO number, (3) assures skus are retained on the carrying surface, (4) wheel/caster and vehicle permits unobstructed one or two-way vehicle travel in an aisle and accurate steering and (5) allows picked sku transfer onto a pack table.

MCPV 2. Pick Cart Side & Rear Nets

Cart side and rear nets are used in a manual small item bulk or pick/sort pick concept that improves picker productivity, reduces sku damage and increases a cart carrying capacity. With an open shelf cart and a loose sku pick concept, as a cart is pushed through pick aisle with loose skus on a shelf, there is potential for skus to fall from a cart shelf onto the floor. Feature has a picker to have a tendency not transfer a large sku quantity onto a cart. After a plastic or fabric netting is secured to a cart sides and rear, it creates a sku barrier and allows a picker to see and utilize an entire cart shelf.

MCPV 3. Cart Casters/Wheels Types

Cart casters/wheels are an important cart design factor for a small item or GOH manual push cart pick concept that improves picker productivity and reduces equipment damage. Preferred casters/wheels arrangement is swivel in the front and fixed in the rear that improves picker guiding a cart in a straight line and is easy to push a cart through a turn. Other caster/wheel options with difficult to guide/steer features are (1) all swivel casters/wheels with an exception of a 'Z' bottom frame GOH cart that is used to couple 2 cartsr, (2) swivel casters/wheels in rear & fixed casters/wheels in front & (3) fixed casters/wheels on a cart one side & swivel casters/wheels on a cart other side.

MCPV 4. Push Cart Swivel Casters/Wheels In A Cart Front & Fixed In The Rear

Push cart swivel casters/wheels in a cart front and fixed in the rear are a small item or GOH pick cart caster/wheel arrangement that improves picker productivity and assures minimal damage. A cart swivel caster/wheel arrangement with cart push handles make it easier for an employee to steer and turn a cart through pick aisles, travel straight sections and curves. A cart caster/wheel arrangements, swivel casters/wheels in a cart front and fixed in the rear requires less employee effort to turn a cart.

MCPV 5. Push Cart With All Swivel Casters/Wheels

Push cart with all swivel casters/wheels are a cart casters/wheels arrangement on a pick carton that creates a cart steering problems with lower picker productivity and potential damage. A cart with all swivel casters/wheels an employee easily parks a cart adjacent to a work station but it is difficult to steer cart a straight through an aisle or curve and is not preferred for a small item pick cart.

MCPV 6. Shopping Cart As An Employee Pick Cart

Shopping cart as an employee pick cart with a deep cavity and meshed side walls and bottom lowers picker productivity and potential sku damage and is not preferred in a pick activity. Since employees are familiar with a shopping cart, swivel casters/wheels in the front and it is easily pushed through a pick aisle straight sections and curves. Features are low cost, low picker productivity due to a deep cavity requires a picker to bend/reach to complete a sku transfer, potential for skus hung-up on mesh openings & low carrying capacity.

MCPV 7. Multi-Shelf Pick Cart

Multi-shelf pick cart is a manual pick & sort or bulk pick cart that improves picker productivity due to increased carrying capacity or sort locations and reduced pick trips. A multi-shelf cart has 4 to 5 shelf levels that permits sku transfer, each level retains skus on a shelf (shelf lip faces upward or meshed plastic barrier that is secured Velcro and push/steer handles) and allows 3 pick & sort locations per shelf level. Features are when not being used empty carts require a storage area. With one cart per aisle, an aisle width that is 6 ins wider than a cart width or two vehicles per aisle, an aisle width includes two carts & 18 ins for clearance.

MCPV 8. Cart Pick Front Faces A Picker

Cart pick front faces a picker is a small item pick cart design that increases a picker productivity and decreases aisle congestion. A pick cart front is a multi-level shelf cart with 4 wheels and 2 push handles/bar. As a cart with this design is pushed through a pick aisle, a picker is at a cart end. At a pick position, a picker remains at a cart end and is a simple activity for sku transfer from a pick position to a cart shelf. With limited cart width and multiple pickers per aisle, there is minimized aisle congestion. With a 36 in wide and 36 in long carrying surface, for a pick/sort activity there are few CO pick/sort locations but for a bulk pick, sort and final pick activity there is ample space for picked skus. With a pick/sort activity with multiple CO sort locations on a cart, a picker pushes a cart from the rear and from a cart side a picker completes a pick/sort activity.

MCPV 9. Pick Vehicle Aisle Guidance

Pick vehicle aisle guidance is used with a man-up powered HROS vehicle that allows skus picked from very high pick positions and assures good employee productivity, space utilization and minimize damage. A HROS vehicle travels vertically and horizontally in an aisle between 2 shelf/rack rows. Aisle guidance matches your vehicle guidance concept and allows a picker/vehicle to travel at fast speeds with minimal employee effort. Aisle guidance starts at an aisle entrance and stops at an aisle end. Most aisle guidance concepts have entry guides that are harden metal members anchored to the floor and assist employee's vehicle aisle entrance and aisle end slow down/stop devices assure minimal accidents. Aisle guidance options are (1) rail guidance that are (a) single rail on the floor, (b) single rail on rack posts, (c) double rail on the floor, (d) double rail on an elevated floor and (e) double rail on rack posts & (2) electronic guidance that includes (a) wire, (b) magnetic tape, (c) magnetic paint & (d) laser.

MCPV 10. Pick Into Your Man-Up HROS/VNA Vehicle Pick Cart Or Cage

Pick into your man-up HROS or VNA truck pick cart and pack cage are small item, carton or GOH device that improves employee productivity and minimize sku damage. With a HROS or VNA vehicle, your picker and picked sku carrying device vertically and horizontally travels in an aisle to a pick position. At a pick position, a picker transfers a sku from a pick position on a cart shelf/tote or in a cage. A pick cage has a solid three wall pick device with fork openings and open side that faces a picker. After a shelf device is set onto a pallet and a pallet center stringer is secured by a vehicle claw and picked skus are placed onto a shelf level. During vehicle travel, a pick cage side walls restricts shelf and skus falling from a pallet. When picking GOH a hand bar is secured to a pick cage side walls. A pick cart has two long fork sleeves that permit a HROS or VNA vehicle forks to enter and secure a cart to a vehicle with a chain and lock that is used to hold a cart post to a vehicle. You pick skus into totes and mesh netting is placed on a cart two side walls and back side to retain totes on a cart surface that assures sku carrying capacity and minimize skus falling to the floor.

MCPV 11. At An Aisle End Slow Down Your HROS Or VNA Travel

At an aisle end slow down your HROS or VNA vehicle travel is used for a man-up vertical and horizontal travel vehicle to improve employee productivity and minimize equipment damage. When a vehicle travels in a guided aisle between 2 tall shelf/rack pick position rows, your vehicle operator is facing an aisle entrance and not facing an aisle end. During travel to an aisle last pick position an operator has an order picker routing pattern help to determine an aisle location and to calculate the last pick position in a routing pattern. Slow down device is designed to have a vehicle leave a pick aisle and at a slow travel speed enter a main traffic aisle. Slow down devices are (1) manual that are (a) shelf/rack position posts/shelves/load beam painted a different color & (b) anchored barrier across an end aisle & (2) electric magnetic on a vehicle and in the floor.

Pick Position Routing Pattern Ideas (PPRP 1 - MCPV 13)
PPRP 1. Picker Routing Or No Picker Routing
Picker routing or no routing are an employee picker or mechanized picker position sequence options that directs a picker through a pick aisle/line to a pick position or to have a carousel move a basket to a pick station. A pick concept that does not have a picker routing pattern or pick position ID sequence means that a pick position IDs are randomly location in an aisle. Features are low picker productivity due to potential double walking in an aisle, with two pickers in an aisle potential congestion or non-productive conversations and difficult to develop a pick aisle/line profile. A pick concept with a pick position ID routing pattern has an arithmetic progression from a pick aisle/line first pick position, through an aisle/line and to an aisle/line last pick position. Features are minimal potential for double walking, less potential for pick aisle/line congestion and easier to develop a pick aisle/line profile.

PPRP 2. Non-Sequential Routing Or Sequential/Arithmetic Progression Through A Pick Aaisle
Your pick position number pattern options are (1) *Non-Sequential Routing* has pick position IDs that do not follow a pattern as a picker travels through a pick aisle. A non-sequential routing pattern creates low picker productivity due to poor instructions, double walking, walking past pick positions that have been picked and potential high aisle congestion or (2) *Sequential Or Arithmetic Progression* is used in a manual, mechanized or automated pick concept to identify pick positions that improves employee productivity & minimizes aisle congestion. Sequential or arithmetic pick position progression or pattern starts at an aisle entrance/first pick position, progressively each additional pick position ID is increased by one and ends at an aisle last pick position. As an employee travels in an aisle with a pick instruction, it minimizes non-productive double travel (walking) time & with a manual concept reduces potential aisle congestion with other pickers.

PPRP 3. Sku Identification Number Routing Pattern
Sku ID number as your picker routing pattern has each sku inventory ID number as your pick position number. With sku number routing pattern, your picker routing pattern is a random routing pattern. Features are (1) low picker productivity, (2) difficult to obtain a good pick line profile, (3) wide sku mix that are placed into a picker container and (4) difficult to expand.

PPRP 4. Pick Positions That End With Even Numbers & Pick Positions That End With Odd Numbers
Pick positions that end with even numbers and pick positions that end with odd numbers is a manual storage or pick position numerical sequence that improves employee productivity and minimizes employee confusion. An even and odd position numerical sequence has all position IDs that end with odd digits on an aisle left side and all position IDs end with even digits on aisle right side. As an employee travels in an aisle, there is an arithmetic progression from an aisle first pick position ID to an aisle last pick position ID.

PPRP 5. Drawer Pick Position Front To Rear Picker Routing Pattern
Front to rear routing pattern is a small item picker routing pattern that is used with drawer pick positions to improve picker productivity and increase completed CO number. A drawer pick concept is a solid wall container with 10 to 12 drawers per container. Each drawer is separated to make 20 to 30 pick positions. With a same size or different lengths/depths to pick positions, each position has capacity for a 'C' or 'D' moving sku with a very small inventory. With this feature and a front to rear picker pattern, your picker has increased potential for high hit concentration & density to improve picker productivity. A drawer is locked for security for high value skus.

PPRP 6. HROS Routing Pattern

HROS picker vehicle/system routing pattern is an employee controlled vehicle routing pattern that is a specialized picker pattern for picking 'C' or 'D' moving skus from shelf, decked rack or pallet pick positions. A routing pattern is used with a guided vehicle to travel vertical and horizontal in aisle between 2 pick position rows that improves picker productivity, increases completed CO number and minimizes sku/equipment damage. A HROS vehicle routing pattern is an arithmetic progression that starts at a high elevation to access highest pick positions and at the elevation, a pattern directs a vehicle through a pick aisle at an same elevation until all pick transactions completion or arrives at an aisle end. At an aisle end, a HROS vehicle lowers to a next pick level elevation and at the elevation directs a vehicle to an aisle entrance. During a HROS vehicle aisle stop to complete a pick transaction and without vertical or horizontal moving a vehicle, routing pattern has potential to have CO picks from pick positions on an aisle both sides. A HROS pattern has positions that end with even numbers on a pick aisle right side and end with odd numbers on a pick aisle left side. Per your shelf or rack position vertical number, HROS picker patterns are 4, 8, 10 and 12 levels. Features are with good pick aisle profile, it increases picker productivity due to less vertical movement and at the pick activity beginning with a minimal picked sku number on a cart or into a pick cage, there is less potential for sku damage from falling from a cart or pick cage.

PPRP 7. Loop Routing Pattern
Loop routing pattern is a small item, GOH or carton picker pattern that is used for a pick to a powered tugger cart concept in a WA forklift truck aisle from shelf or rack positions on an aisle both sides. With a loop pattern an arithmetic progression positions that end with even numbers on a pick aisle right side and end with odd numbers on a pick aisle left side. As a picker travels through an aisle, picks are made from aisle (A) pick positions on a pick aisle right side and at aisle (A) side completion, a picker enters aisle (B) to complete all picks from aisle (B) right side, returns to aisle (A) to complete all picks from aisle (A) left side, returns to aisle (B) to complete all picks from aisle (B) and enters aisle (C) to complete all pick from aisle (C) right side. With a powered tugger and cart train, in an aisle a picker is between a tugger and pick row. With a remote controlled tugger and cart train in an aisle a picker is between a cart and pick row. Features are with good pick aisle profile and minimal walk distance to complete a pick transaction that improves pick productivity, requires 2 aisle trips that can lower picker productivity and best for a cart CO delivery concept.

PPRP 8. Horse-Shoe Or 'U' Routing Pattern
Horseshoe or 'U' routing pattern is a small item, GOH or carton picker pattern that is used for a pick to a cart or pallet truck concept in a wide or narrow aisle forklift truck aisle. With a 'U' routing pattern has an arithmetic progression positions that end with even numbers on a pick aisle right side and end with odd numbers on a pick aisle left side. As a picker travels through an aisle, at each pre-determined aisle location, a picker stops and completes picks from an aisle right side positions to an aisle left side pick positions. The routing pattern is repeated for an entire aisle. Features are that with good pick aisle profile it requires one aisle trip but requires employee training and potential aisle congestion.

PPRP 9. 'Z' Routing Pattern
'Z' routing pattern is a carton picker pattern that is used for a pick to a cart or pallet truck concept in a WA or NA forklift truck aisle. With a 'Z' routing pattern has an arithmetic progression positions that end with even numbers on a pick aisle right side and end with odd numbers on a pick aisle left side. As a picker travels through an aisle, at each pre-determined aisle location, a picker stops and completes picks from an aisle 3 to 4 bays on right side and picks from an aisle 6 to 8 bays on the left side. The pattern is repeated for the entire aisle. Features are with good pick aisle profile it requires one aisle trip but requires employee training.

PPRP 10. Block Routing Pattern
Block routing pattern is a small item, GOH or carton picker pattern that is used for a pick to a cart or pallet truck concept in a WA or NA forklift truck aisle. With a block pattern has an arithmetic progression positions that end with even numbers on a pick aisle right side and end with odd numbers on a pick aisle left side. As a picker travels through an aisle, at each pre-determined aisle location, a picker stops and completes from an aisle right side 2 bays and from an aisle left side 4 bays and a pattern is repeated for an entire aisle. Features are good pick aisle profile

it requires 1 aisle trip with minimal walk distance between pick position & vehicle & requires some employee training.

MCPV 11. Stitch Routing Pattern

Stitch routing pattern is a small item or GOH picker pattern that is used for a pick to a cart concept in aisle between two shelf or decked rack rows. An aisle width is for a short aisle a minimum width of a cart plus sufficient clearance on a cart both sides or for a long aisle a width for two carts plus sufficient clearance to assure no hang-ups. With an arithmetic progression positions that end with even numbers on a pick aisle right side and end with odd numbers on a pick aisle left side. As a picker travels through an aisle at each pick location there is a minimum distance to transfer a sku from a pick position to a cart. At each pick location, shelf or decked rack pick positions are on an aisle left and right sides with a minimum of 15 skus per side to a maximum of 120 skus per side. Features are with a good pick profile and high hit concentration and density improved picker productivity and one trip through an aisle increases completed CO number.

MCPV 12. From Your Main Aisle Straigth In & Out An Aisle Or Serpentine Through Your Pick Aisles

Travel in an aisle to complete a transaction options are

Straight In-And-Out Through An Aisle for a transaction, an employee completes a s transaction. With a straight in-and-out design, each aisle's lowest position number starts at a main aisle entrance into an aisle (001) and arithmetically progresses to a highest position number at an aisle end. After completing a transaction, an employee turns and travels back through aisle 'A' to a main aisle entrance. Leaving aisle 'A', an employee travels in a main aisle to adjacent aisle ('B') and enters. An employee completes a transaction in 'B' travel to exit aisle 'C' & enters aisle 'C'. Disadvantages are (a) potential double travel in each aisle, (b) low productivity due to traveling past positions that do not have a sku transaction or where an employee has already completed a transaction, (c) aisle width to permit an employee turn in an aisle and (d) potential for meployees traveling in different travel directions in one aisle.

Serpentine Through Aisles Design has an employee travel in first aisle ('A'). During aisle 'A' travel, lowest positions are an entrance to aisle 'A'. After all transactions, an employee exits pick aisle 'A' at an end (highest position number location) & enters aisle 'B' at a lowest position number location. An employee completes a transaction and enters a main aisle. From a main aisle, an employee enters aisle 'C'. With a serpentine design, each aisle lowest position number starts at an aisle entrance and arithmetically progresses to a highest position number at an exit. In a rectangle shaped facility with a main aisle and rear aisle, each aisle has an even number entrance at a main aisle (front) and odd number entrance at a rear aisle. Advantages are (a) one trip through each aisle, b) minimal aisle width and (c) low probability of two drivers in one aisle.

MCPV 13. Single Side Routing Pattern

Single Side Single Pattern starts at an aisle first position & ends at an aisle last position. With an aisle between 2 position rows, each position row has its own number that creates double aisle travel with potential few transactions. Permits positions that end with even numbers on an aisle right side & odd numbers on an aisle left side. Used with all concepts but not preferred for a pick operation due to double picker aisle travel & travel past pick positions that have had picks but a good pick position profile creates good picker productivity.

Pick/Pass Line Ideas (PPL 1 - PPL 26)

PP 1. Pick/Pass Small Item Or GOH Pick Concept

Pick/pass is a small item or GOH pick concept that improves picker productivity and increases completed COs. With a pick/pass concept, skus are picked from flow rack, shelf or rail pick positions that are adjacent to each other and on a pick aisle other side is a pick conveyor. From a 30 to 36 wide pick aisle between a pick/pass line (pick positions) and CO travel path, it minimizes a picker transfer distance for skus from pick positions into a CO carton/tote or onto a cart/trolley hang bar. For maximum productivity, your pick positions are profiled with 'A' moving skus and other skus are separated into pick zones by sku pick quantity that matches your budgeted picker productivity. A pick/pass CO travel path is past each pick zone & assures a minimum distance to transfer a sku from a position to CO container.

PPL 2. Pick/Pass or Pick Line Pick Positions

Your pick/pass or pick line pick positions present skus to your order picker. The pick position options are

(1) *Pallet Flow Lane Pick Position* has entry guides or flanged wheels & at a charge end a fork lift truck stop & roller wheel protection. A pick side has a flat plate end stop. Pick zone length is 1 to 2 pallets wide & pick position ID is in a consistent location to pallet pick face side. A picker handles an empty pallet by tilting & standing an empty pallet onto a guarded roller travel path that flows to a replenishment aisle. Above a pallet flow lane is push back rack or standard pallet rack ready reserve position with overhead ties & for safety above an employee work area safety netting. Preferred CO sequenced is by sku & CO carton size.

(2) *Pick/Pass Carton Flow Lane Pick Position*s are gravity conveyor lanes that face a pick aisle. In most applications, carton flow lanes are in a bay. With average size skus, there are 3 to 4 levels high and 4 to 5 skus wide. A carton flow lane is installed for small size skus in 1 to 2 high flow lanes over & 1 flow lane under a pick conveyor. Carton flow lane concept is used for 'A' or fast moving skus with a large sku inventory quantity in a pick position, single side picker routing pattern, within a rack bay horizontal picker pattern. For a cost effective and efficient carton flow rack pick activity, your pick position width is based on your standard carton size. If you have a smaller carton width, it means a greater carton capacity per pick position. If you have a larger carton width, it means you transfer skus into a standard carton/tote and complete an update in a WMS computer. A pick position width is based on your sku carton width, pick instruction, bay width & sku volume. Carton flow rack concept provides high hit concentration & density for good picker productivity & high completed CO number. Each carton/tote requires a good conveyable bottom & if a tote is used a concept to handle empty totes on a pick side.

Carton Flow Rack Options are (A) high volume & large size sku has 1 sku per flow rack level, (B) high volume & medium size sku has 1 or 2 skus per flow rack level & (C) medium & small size sku has 3 to 7 skus per flow rack level. With 16 to 20 sku average in a flow rack bay, it is easy to complete good profile for good hit concentration & density & picker productivity. Carton flow rack and lane requires a front end stop & flow rail front end that is a location for pick position ID. A bay support member between 2 upright posts on both pick & replenishment sides & holds a bay ID. Conveyor pitch or slope assures carton/tote FIFO rotation or flow with lowest pick level is 3 ins above a floor & replenishment side is higher than pick side & permit an employee to transfer cartons/totes to lane. Open space between carton/tote top & above conveyor lane bottom permits a picker to complete a pick transaction.

Flow Rack Frame Options are (A) titled front end is excellent for pick loose skus from opened cartons/totes and for good picker productivity slant & tilt back front flow racks are preferred, (B) slanted front is excellent for pick loose skus from cartons/totes & (C) straight preferred for full carton picking.

Flow Rack Front End Options are (A) solid sheet metal that minimize sku damage or (B) conveyors with open space between conveyor lanes that increase potential for sku damage.

Pick Position Identification Options are (A) paper attached to each lane front & (B) light display (a) attached to each lane front and (b) 'C' Channel attached to flow rack lane with a pick to light display attached to flow lane. The channel holds & protects pick to light display from damage & shows pick position number & sku quantity & permits display directed to a picker with (*) top pick level angled downward, (*) middle levels face outward & (*) lower level directed upward.

Carton Flow rack is used with paper, RF device, voice directed & pick to light pick instruction concepts.

(3) *Pick/Pass Shelf Pick Positions* are used for B & C slower moving & small size skus. Shelf pick positions are (A) *parallel to a pick conveyor* provides minimal walk distance to complete a pick & provides few pick positions or (B) *perpendicular to your pick conveyor* with each shelf row end faces a pick conveyor with a bay indicator light. An activated bay light shows a pick from a shelf row. The concept has e additional walk distance between pick positions & pick conveyor, provides maximum pick position number & easy to establish pick zones. With a perpendicular concept, each shelf is a pick row. Options are (a) lower pick to light cost & paper pick document in CO carton/tote with bay lamp at shelf row end to indicate a pick transaction in a shelf row & a second bay light indicator on a shelf post for each level to show a pick transaction on a shelf level & (b) each shelf level pick position has a human readable pick position ID is matched to a paper pick document. After a pick transaction, a paper pick document is returned to a CO carton/tote. Carton size & pick position ID size determines pick position number per shelf bay width range from 3 to 5 in a 3 ft wide shelf & pick level number high range from 3 to 5 with standard 12 in high carton.

PPL 3. Pick/Pass Picker Routing Pattern

Your horizontal picker routing pattern options are (1) starts at a top level from shelf bay front top post horizontal to a bay next post & declines to next lowest pick level or (2) starts at a bottom level from shelf bay front top post horizontal to bay next post & inclines to next highest pick level.

PPL 4. Pick By Light Options

Pick by light options are standard shelf and carton flow rack pick to light placed onto pick position to improve picker productivity and lower cost. A pick by light concept has (1) *Horizontal Picker Pattern* in a shelf or carton flow rack bay that starts at each bay upper right pick position, across a horizontal level and to a next lower level right most position & (2) *Computer Activated Pick Position Display Screen* that shows a sku CO quantity. With a standard shelf design, your design options are (1) shelf rows are perpendicular to pick conveyor. Your options are (A) a bay lamp at each shelf row end to indicate a pick transaction in a shelf row & a second bay light indicator on a shelf post for each level to show a pick transaction on a shelf level, (B) a bay lamp at each shelf row end to indicate a pick transaction each shelf bay has a light indicator and each shelf level pick position has a light to show a pick transaction & (C) a bay lamp at each shelf row end to indicate a pick transaction in a shelf row each shelf level pick position has a human readable pick position ID and after a picker removes a pick document from a CO container, a pick position is matched to a paper pick document. After a pick transaction, a paper pick document is returned to a CO carton/tote & (2) shelf row is parallel to pick conveyor that has a bay lamp and each pick position with a pick light. Carton flow rack pick to light options are for (A) high volume & large size sku has 1 sku per carton flow rack level. Your options are to have one pick position with one pick light or to have 4 pick positions with 4 pick lights and your cover three pick lights & three associated replenishment IDs, (B) high volume & medium size sku has 1 or 2 skus per carton flow rack level. Your options are to have 2 pick positions with 2 pick lights or to have 4 pick positions with 4 pick lights and your cover two pick lights and two associated replenishment IDs, & (C) medium & small size sku has 3 to 7 skus per carton flow rack level and each pick position has a pick light and associated replenishment IDs. Carton flow rack bay pick to light displays are attached to each carton flow rack level and improve picker productivity due to a picker quickly and easily reads a pick position display and minimize damage. Each carton flow rack level has a 'C' Channel on each pick level that holds & protects pick to light display from damage & shows pick position number & sku quantity & permits display directed to a picker with (a) top pick level angled downward, (b) middle levels face outward & (c) lower level directed upward. Carton flow rack front end assures that a carton is properly presented to a picker that improves picker productivity and minimizes sku damage. Your carton flow rack end options are (a) solid sheet metal that minimize sku damage or (b) short strand conveyors with open space between conveyor lanes that increase potential for sku damage.

PPL 5. Pick/Pass Design Or Layout

Your pick/pass design or layout options are

(1) *Pick Train* has COs enter a pick line as a pick train. At a first pick position & an employee or powered conveyor moves COs containers over a pick conveyor as a pick train travels past all pick positions within a pick zone. Pallet & carton flow rack pick positions are parallel to a pick conveyor & shelf positions are parallel or perpendicular to a pick conveyor. Completed CO take-away options are

(A) *No Completed CO Take-Away Conveyor Concept* has all COs enter at the first pick position & after all picks in a picker zone. All partial completed COs & completed COs are pushed over a pick conveyor until all COs have past all pick positions. COs are basically queued on a pick conveyor & are moved forward through all pick zones. With no pen space between COs & a pick train is being moved forward by other pickers means (a) lower completed CO number, (b) increased picker physical effort to push a pick train & is more difficult with mixed carton sizes, (c) potential picker transfer sku to wrong CO carton/tote but is minimized with a picker clip, good pick line profile & zone start & end flags/indicators & (d) used meshed skate wheel or roller pick conveyor & less conveyor cost,

(B) *Completed COs Pushed From A Pick Conveyor Onto Powered Low Or Zero Pressure Conveyor Concept* that reduces a pick train length and minimizes a picker push effort. All COs enter at a first pick position & after all picks in a picker zone partial completed COs pushed over a pick conveyor to a next pick zone & completed COs are pushed forward from a pick conveyor onto a completed CO take-away conveyor. Excellent for 'A' or fast moving skus & easy to profile skus to a zone pick positions for high sku concentration & density that means high picker productivity. Pick zone length are adjustable. Features are (a) decreases picker physical effort to move train due to fewer COs, (b) use non-powered or powered roller pick conveyor & completed CO take-away conveyor is low or zero pressure roller conveyor, (c) higher completed CO number, (d) potential picker transfer sku to wrong CO carton/tote but is minimized with picker clip, pick zone conveyor stops, good pick line profile & zone indicators, (e) with completed COs pushed from pick conveyor potential queue space on your pick conveyor & (f) for easy completed CO container transfer, there is a gap plate between pick conveyor and take-away conveyor or a pick conveyor is set high above a take-away &

(C) *Zone Skip COs On Main Conveyor Travel Path* has for each pick section CO ID scanners/readers, diverters & controls after COs sku download to your conveyor computer, per a CO pick requirement, your conveyor computer is controlled to divert a CO from a main conveyor travel path onto a pick section that has a sku on a CO. This means that if a CO has only a pick in pick section 2 that a CO travels on a main conveyor travel path past pick section 1 & is diverted to pick section 2. Features are (a) higher conveyor & systems cost, (b) with a pick train minimizes pickers push effort, (c) increases CO carton flow to required pick positions & in a slower moving pick zone less picker non-productive waiting time & (d) increase CO completion number.

(2) *Pick cell* is a small item pick area configuration with pre-determined sku (language, preferred customer gift) that increases sku hit concentration and density to improve picker productivity and increase completed   CO number. A pick cell is a pick positions that are adjacent to each other and have skus WMS scanned in pick positions for specific CO characteristics such as language, retail store aisle. special catalog or special customers. When a CO has a pick for one sku in a pick cell and with a family sku group in a pick cell a CO has a high potential for other skus to appear on a CO in a pick cell pick position that reduces a picker walk distance and time between 2 picks. Pick cells designs are (1) selected pick aisle or zone, (2) selected carousel, (3) selected automatic pick machine & (4) with a pick/pass concept, options are specific (a) shelves parallel to a pick conveyor, (b) shelves perpendicular to a pick conveyor with open aisle end & (c) shelves perpendicular to pick conveyor with mobile shelf at aisle end. A pick cell pick/pass concept has a series of pick cells that are (A) parallel flow rack or shelf bays or (B) 2 perpendicular shelf rows with 3 to 4 shelf bays long & aisle. After COs are downloaded to a conveyor computer and after a pick cell scanner/reader identifies a CO ID, it is communicated to a conveyor computer that activates a pick cell divert device to divert an identified CO container from a main conveyor travel path onto a pick cell pick line. A pick cell pick line/conveyor directs CO past a pre-determined pick position number. After all pick cell picks, a partial complete or completed CO is pushed forward from a pick cell pick conveyor onto a main travel path for travel to next pick cell or work station. Features are (1) added conveyor costs and (2) difficult to profile or allocate skus to a pick cell that means potential low pick productivity.

PPL 6. Pick/Pass Pick Conveyor Travel Path

Pick/pass pick conveyor travel path assures each CO carton/tote travels past each CO sku pick position. After all completed pick transactions in a pick zone, options are (1) pick zone completed COs are transferred from a pick conveyor onto take-away conveyor for transport to a next pick section or sent to a seal station and partial completed COs are moved on a pick conveyor to a next pick zone or (2) from one pick zone, all completed and partial completed COs are moved on a pick conveyor to a next pick zone. Pick/pass pick conveyor options are

(A) *Non-Powered Conveyor* has human or gravity force move pick cartons/totes over a pick conveyor, handles a low volume due to pick carton/tote in-feed is on a non-powered travel path. Used with a pick train concept that has all COs enter at a pick line start and not in a pick cell concept. Non-powered conveyor options are (a) *Skate Wheel Non-Powered* conveyor is used with a pick conveyor with no take-away conveyor due to it is difficult to push pick cartons/totes across skate-wheel surface, low co-efficient of friction & easier to push a pick train over a pick conveyor, assure sufficient skate-wheel number (at least 3) under your shortest carton. If not there is potential pick carton dumps & able to install manual stops that controls pick train movement through a pick zone. For CO controlled movement over a pick conveyor there is a far side 'C' channel guard rail and picker side pipe guard rail & (b) *Roller Non-Powered Conveyor* is used with a pick conveyor only & pick conveyor with a completed CO take-away conveyor. It is easy to push pick cartons/totes across a roller surface onto a take-away conveyor. There is minimal co-efficient of friction. Minimal picker effort to push a pick train. Assure sufficient roller number (at least 3) under your shortest carton. With minimal potential pick carton dumps & install manual stops that control pick train movement.   If push-off completed CO is used in a pick concept, for controlled CO movement over a pick conveyor picker side has a pipe guard rail and

(B) *Powered Conveyor* has electric motor driven rollers or belt that move pick cartons/totes over a pick conveyor, handles a high volume due to pick carton/tote in-feed is a powered travel path & moves CO pick cartons/totes from pick line entrance over a pick line to last pick position or is employee pushed forward from a pick conveyor onto a completed CO take-away conveyor. With a pick train, there is minimal   employee effort to push/control a pick train & additional cost.   Powered Conveyor options are *(a) Low Pressure Roller Conveyor* motor driven rollers that move a pick carton/tote forward over a pick conveyor, to   stop a pick carton/tote on a pick conveyor at a pick zone a picker applies physical pressure or uses a   manual or mechanical pop-up stop device to stop a carton/tote with some carton/tote forward movement pressure from motor driven rollers. Features are used with a pick cell or pick train concept, allows completed COs pushed forward to take-away conveyor, permits carton/tote queue on a pick conveyor & zone skip concept, requires conveyor travel path sensing device to stop/start conveyor, permits manual flat stops or mechanical pop-up stops & requires electric power & compressed air, (b) *Roller Zero Pressure Conveyor* motor driven rollers move a pick carton/tote forward over a pick conveyor, to stop a CO pick carton/tote on a pick conveyor a picker physically easily stops a carton/tote with no carton/tote forward movement pressure. Features are used with a pick cell or pick train concept, allows completed CO containers pushed forward to take-away conveyor, permits carton/tote queue on a pick conveyor & zone skip concept, requires conveyor travel path sensing device to stop/start conveyor, permits manual flat stops or mechanical pop-up stops, requires electric power & compressed air, higher cost & preferred due to minimal employee effort to stop carton/tote forward movement &

(c) *Belt Conveyor* motor driven belt moves forward it moves a pick carton/tote forward over a pick conveyor. After a CO carton/tote is placed onto a belt conveyor, a carton/tote remains on a belt conveyor position until a completed CO is employee lifted/pushed-off from a smooth belt pick conveyor onto a completed CO take-away conveyor or travels from a belt conveyor discharge end onto another pick section activity. Features are used with a pick train concept with CO carton/tote remains in a same belt conveyor position, no queue on a pick conveyor, requires electric power, requires accurate & fast pickers due to a CO pick carton/tote constantly moves forward & 'E' stop pull cord or push button

PPL 7. Pick/Pass Pick Position Horizontal Or Vertical Sequence/Picker Routing Pattern
Horizontal or vertical are a manual picker routing pattern for pick positions in a shelf bay, decked rack bay, standard pallet rack bat, carousel basket or carton flow rack bay. A picker routing pattern directs a picker to pick skus from pick positions that assures your picker productivity rate. (1) *Vertical Picker Routing Pattern* starts at a bay bottom level pick position & for each pick level progresses (arithmetically) upward. After a reaching the top level, a picker starts at the adjacent bottom pick position and repeats the upward progression. Features are (a) difficult to maintain a Golden Zone, (b) if a Golden Zone sku requires additional space, it is difficult to achieve a Golden Zone and (c) requires additional non-productive time for a picker to review a vertical path for additional picks and (2) *Horizontal Picker Routing Pattern* starts at a bay top level (or bottom level) and progresses horizontal across each pick level. At a pick level end, a picker moves to the next pick level start and repeats horizontal progression. Features are (a) easier to maintain a Golden Zone, (b) easier for a picker to review a level for additional picks & (c) if a fast moving sku requires additional space, a sku occupies additional lanes & remains in your Golden Zone.

PPL 8. Pick Positions Over & Under A Pick/Pass Pick & Take-Away Conveyor
Pick positions over and under a pick/pass pick/take-away conveyor has potential to increase your pick faces along a pick line. Pick positions over and under your pick/pass pick/take-away conveyor are carton flow rack positions that extend over and under your pick and take-away conveyors. The arrangement has one pick level below your pick conveyor frame and with one or two pick levels extended over your take-away conveyor and end above the take-away conveyor frame. In pick positions, you profile light weight & small cube skus. If your have your 'A'/fast moving sku profile (budgeted picker productivity) to carton flow rack position on a pick aisle back, you have potential and additional pick positions over and under your pick conveyor line. Features are (1) lower your picker budgeted productivity due to an additional pick positions to review for 'A' fast moving skus, (2) lowest pick position is a pigeon hole reach & high pick position has a high reach with potential to lower picker productivity, (3) additional

pick position cost & (4) increases pick positions. If your pick/pass line has 'B' & 'C' moving skus that are difficult to profile for picker budgeted productivity, additional pick positions over and under your pick conveyor line are used for 'B' & 'C' skus. Features are (1) increases your pick zone hit concentration and density that improves picker productivity, (2) with fewer COs for 'B' & 'C' skus in a pick zone, minimal CO congestion & (3) increases your pick zone pick faces.

PPL 9. 1, 2 OR 3 Pick/Pass Pick Lines Or Sections
1, 2 or 3 pick lines or sections is a small item pick/pass line layout option that has your 'A'/fast moving skus profiled to multiple pick lines or sections. When your 'A'/fast moving skus pick volume exceeds your budgeted picker productivity rate, your have potential for pick line congestion or CO flow problems. To resolve your pick line situation, spread your 'A' fast moving sku pick volume over multiple pick lines or sections. Each pick line has a unique WMS ID that allows your set-up/replenishment employees to transfer skus to pick positions and for your WMS computer program to release CO to specific pick lines. Features are per shift high picker productivity, continuous CO flow, high completed CO number, sku set-up replenishment to multiple pick lines and easily handles high volume multiple line/multiple skus COs.

PPL 10. Mirrored Pick/Pass Lines
Mirrored pick/pass lines is a small item carton flow rack pick/pass layout with 2 WMS computer identified pick/pass lines that is used to handle a very high pick volume. If your 'A'/fast moving sku pick volume exceeds your one pick/pass line budgeted productivity, a mirrored pick/pass line concept has at least two pick/pass lines and each pick line has skus in the same pick positions. Two pick/pass lines/pick positions assures your picker productivity matches your budgeted productivity, has a simple pick/pass line profile, assures constant CO flow and increases completed CO number. With a mirrored pick/pass line concept your computer program recognizes 2 pick/pass lines and your pick/pass line profile has each sku that is located in both pick lines same pick position. This means that sku 11102 is located in pick line 1 pick position A101 & in pick line 2 pick position A101.

PPL 11. What Is Your Pick Carton/Tote License Plate
What pick a carton/tote license plate (warehouse ID or WMS CO ID tote/carton) to assure picker productivity and accurate transfer transaction. In a pick to light or automatic pick machine pick concept, each pick tote/carton has a unique CO ID. During your pick activity, a pick tote/carton ID is considered a pick instruction component that is read by an employee or automatic pick machine scanner and directs a picker or automatic pick machine to transfer a sku from a pick position into a CO container. A warehouse ID on a CO tote is considered a permanent ID. To be effective, prior to your pick activity each tote warehouse ID is associated with a WMS CO ID that is sent to your WMS computer. As a warehouse ID tote travels through your pick area, a warehouse ID is a pick instruction component. At a pack station, a packer zero scans a tote warehouse ID that breaks a WMS CO ID association to a warehouse tote ID and allows a tote used for another WMS ID CO. Each completed/packed CO ship container receives a WMS CO ID and leaves your warehouse. With a WMS CO ID on a pick/ship carton, a WMS CO ID is a pick instruction component as a CO container travels through your pick area. At a pack station, your packer does not zero scan a WMS CO ID due to it is a disposal CO ID. After a packer completes a CO, a WMS COP ID remains on a CO ship container and leaves your warehouse.

PPL 12. Your Pick Conveyor Is Set High Or Low
Your pick conveyor surface is set high or set low is a pick/pass line conveyor roller location on a conveyor frame to improve picker productivity and assure completed CO flow. Set high roller option has conveyor roller surfaces set at the same elevation as a conveyor frame top surface. Set low roller option has conveyor roller surfaces set below a conveyor frame top surface. A pick/pass pick train concept with only a pick conveyor, a set low roller concept has a pick conveyor frame serve as a guard rail. As a pick train is pushed over a pick conveyor, a conveyor frame retains a pick train cartons/totes on a conveyor. With a pick conveyor and completed CO take-away conveyor on a pick/pass pick train or cell concept, a pick conveyor roller surfaces are set high with a low profile near/picker side guard rail and take-away conveyor roller surfaces are set low with far side high guard rail. With both pick conveyor

and take-away conveyor frames are set at the same elevation above a floor that allows a take-away conveyor frame serve as a guard rail to retain completed customer orders on a conveyor.

PPL 13. Skate-Wheel Or Roller Pick Line

Skate-wheel or roller pick line are a pick/pass conveyor surface options that assure good pick productivity and minimize jams as CO containers are transferred from a pick conveyor onto a take-away conveyor. Both skate-wheel and roller conveyor surfaces assure CO container forward movement over a pick line. If your pick/pass concept does not have completed CO push-off concept, meshed skate-wheel conveyor serves as a pick line conveyor surface and is able to handle narrow cartons/wide carton size mix. If your pick/pass concept has a completed CO push-off concept, a roller conveyor surface with a solid, smooth and continuous surface spans an open distance between a pick conveyor two frames that minimizes a co-efficient of friction as a picker pushes a completed CO from a pick conveyor onto a take-away conveyor. A solid roller surface handles a wide carton size mix. Features improve picker productivity and minimize jams. If a skate-wheel conveyor surface is used on a completed CO push-off concept, skate wheels and open space between skate-wheels creates a co-efficient of friction as a picker pushes a completed CO container from a pick line onto a take-away conveyor. Open space between skate-wheels has potential for CO container hang-up on a skate-wheel or container tipping that means lower picker productivity and potential lost skus.

PPL 14. Pick/Pass Pick Conveyor Frame Edge & Side Guard

Pick/pass pick conveyor frame edge or guard is an option that improves picker productivity and completed CO number. A pick/pass conveyor frame edge or guard serves to guide a pick carton/tote as it is moved over a pick conveyor and assures a pick carton/tote remains on a pick conveyor. A conveyor frame edge means that your pick conveyor roller conveyor surface is below your conveyor frame edge (roller set low). Features are (1) low cost and (2) guides cartons/totes. A pick conveyor guard is a conveyor accessory that is added to your pick conveyor near (picker) frame side and used with a conveyor roller or skate-wheel top surface is above a pick conveyor frame (rollers or skate-wheels set high). Features are (1) additional cost and (2) guides cartons/totes.

PPL 15. Pick/Pass Pick Conveyor Pick Zone Control

Pick/pass pick conveyor pick zone control are options that assure a picker remains in an assigned picker zone (pre-determined shelf bay or carton flow rack bay number). Per your CO wave sku pick number, your pick zone profile (allocated picks) matches your budgeted picker productivity. Your pick zone control options are (1) *Variable Zone* has each pick zone start and end pick positions that vary. For each CO wave, a pick zone bay number is increased or decreased to assure each pick zone pick number matches you picker productivity rate. Features are (a) potential low picker productivity due to a pick zone is long and increases picker non-productive walk distance, (b) requires pick zone profile time, (c) difficult to control CO container travel on a pick conveyor and (d) potential for picked sku transfer errors & (2) *Fixed Zone* has each pick zone start and end pick position that are same pick position for each CO wave. For each CO wave, a pick zone bay number is the same number and does not fluctuate with a different pick volume. With a good pick line profile, you allocate sku picks to assure good picker productivity and some fixed pick zones with high volume picks have 1 or 2 bays and other pick zones with low volume picks have 3 to 4 bays. With a fixed pick zone concept, add banners/flags to identify a pick zone start & finish. Features are (a) potential high picker productivity due to picks matches your budgeted productivity & decreases picker non-productive walk distance, (b) requires pick zone profile time, (c) improves CO container travel on a pick conveyor & (d) reduces picked sku transfer errors.

PPL 16. Completed Customer Is Pushed-Away Or Continues As Part Of A Pick Train

Completed CO is pushed-away or continues as part of a pick train that describes your pick/pass concept completed CO travel path options that impact a picker productivity and accurate picked sku transfer into a CO carton/tote. A pick train option has a completed CO container remain on a pick/pass pick conveyor travel path and after a last pick position to exit. The situation means that each picker pushes a full pick train (CO cartons/totes) through each pick zone. With a great CO container number within a pick zone, it requires additional non-productive time to assure accurate picked sku transfer from a pick position to a proper CO container and potential for increased pick errors.

Continues as part of a pick train board concept has minimal conveyor cost. Completed CO push-away concept has a completed CO take-away powered conveyor travel path that is adjacent and full length to a pick conveyor travel path. The design allows a picker to push a completed CO container from a pick conveyor onto a take-away conveyor travel path. With fewer CO containers on a pick conveyor, it minimizes a picker physical effort to move a pick train over a pick conveyor, lower potential to have a picked sku transfer from a pick position to an incorrect CO container and higher conveyor cost.

PPL 17. Completed Customer Order Push-Off Concept With Gap Plate Or Pick & Take-Away
Conveyors At Different Elevations
With a completed CO push-off concept to permit a picker to easily transfer a completed CO from a pick conveyor onto a completed CO take-away conveyor and on a completed CO travel path to guide completed CO container travel, your require a gap plate between your pick & take-away conveyors or pick conveyor and take-away conveyor travel paths have different elevations. (1) *Gap Plate* is basically a solid sheet metal member with an inverted and flatten 'V' shape with a high middle section. A gap plate low side is attached to a pick conveyor frame far side and high side attached to a take-away conveyor frame near side. A smooth gap plate side permits easy completed CO transfer and high middle serves as a completed CO carton travel guard rail. Features are minimal carton jams and additional cost & (2) *Different Conveyor Travel Path Elevations* concept has a pick conveyor travel path set a ¼ in higher than a take-away conveyor travel path and your pick and take-away conveyor frames assure that there is no gap between two conveyor travel paths. After a CO completion, a picker pushes a completed CO from a high pick conveyor across both conveyor frames onto a low take-away conveyor. Conveyor frames serve as smooth transfer surface and elevated pick conveyor frame serves as a guide rail for CO container travel on a take-away conveyor. To have a pick conveyor and take-away conveyor set at different elevations above a floor has no additional cost and is stated in your specifications.

PPL 18. With A Pick/Pass Concept Cycle Pickers To Different Pick Zones
With a pick/pass concept cycle pickers is a manual small item, GOH pick cart or trolley concept that minimizes a picker's non-productive walk time and reduces picker fatigue to improve picker productivity, rotates pickers to short walk sections and increases completed CO number. Cycle your pickers from your pick/pass 'A' fast moving high volume section allows a picker to rotate to a slow moving/low volume section that is requires less physical effort to complete pick transactions. With a push cart or trolley concept and picking from a slow moving/low volume section requires a long walks distance with an empty pick cart/trolley from your dispatch station to your most distant pick position. From a picker's most distant pick position, your picker routing pattern progressively directs your pickers through the pick aisles toward your pack stations. After a picker starts with an empty cart, a picker travels through the pick area and as a picker approaches your pack station, there is greater potential for a picker to move a full pick cart from a pick area to a pack station. After dropping a full cart/trolley in your pack station area, from a control desk to cycle a picker, a picker is given an empty cart/trolley with a CO pick instructions for 'A' fast moving high volume section that has a shorter walk to the first pick position.

PPL 19. Picker Uses A Glove
Employee picker use a glove is a manual small item pick concept to improve picker productivity and minimize sku damage. When a small item picker has to pick plastic bottles or plastic wrapped skus, there is potential damage from a sku to slip from a picker's hands. This is due to a sku exterior smooth and slick surface. With a pick/pass concept, to assure a CO ID on a container matches a pick zone CO ID a picker lifts a CO container. When lifting a plastic tote or new cardboard carton, there is potential for a picker to cut a hand but a glove minimizes injury possibility. In a small item pick concept and if your replenishment employee opens or cuts cartons, safety gloves are used to minimize employee injury.

PPL 20. Flag Each Pick/Pass Concept Pick Zone Start & End Pick Positions
Flag each pick/pass concept pick zone start and end pick position is used in a small item pick/pass concept that improves your picker productivity. In most high volume pick/pass concepts a pick line is separated into picker zones that have sufficient sku picks for a picker to match budgeted picker productivity and each pick zone has a

110

fixed start and end position. In a pick/pass aisle for each pick zone you use a different colored or numbered flag to identify a pick zone start and end position. Each flag extends down from a pick position top to the middle bottom and does not obstruct an picker walking in an aisle. Features are (1) allows a picker (especially new pickers) to easily identify a pick zone start and end pick position, (2) minimizes a picker non-productive walk and helps to determine no additional picks in a pick zone and (3) allows faster CO container transfer to the next pick zone.

PPL 21. Fixed Or Variable Pick Zone Length
Fixed or variable pick zone length are a small item pick/pass line length options that impact a picker productivity, pick line congestion and CO flow. On a pick line a pick zone is established by a picker start and end pick positions and determines a picker's pick position number and potential picks. Your pick line profile a pick number and sku volume influences a picker's ability to obtain budgeted pick rates. (1) Fixed Pick Zone means for each CO wave that a pick zone has the same start pick & end pick positions. If you do not rotate and re-profile your skus, there is potential for low picker productivity due to mixing 'A'/fasting moving skus adjacent to 'B' medium & 'C' slow moving sku means low hit concentration and density and increases walk distance between 2 picks. If you rotate your skus with a good sku profile, there is potential for high picker productivity due to 'A'/fast moving skus are adjacent to each other that means high hit concentration and density and minimal walk distance between 2 picks & (2) Variable Pick Zone has per each CO wave different start and end pick positions. If a pick zone length increases and becomes to long, a picker has low productivity due to increase walk distance between 2 picks.

PPL 22. Your Stationary Picker On A Cement Floor Use A Rubber Mat
A picker walking on a cement floor, a picker feels hard and rubber is soft/comforting. In a small item pick/pass aisle, horizontal carousel pick station, check station, pack station, returns process station or automatic pick machine replenishment aisle, a rubber mat on the floor surface improves employee productivity and reduce potential sku damage. If your pick/pass pick zone has a short walk distance (nomimal 5 ft long by 30/36 in wide aisle) or if your fixed pick station in front of a horizontal carousel, your picker is standing on a cement floor. Many studies have indicated that a hard cement floor lowers a picker productivity by an estimated 5% due to employee fatigue from standing on a cement floor. Rubber mat features are (1) in cold winter months, a floor is cold that is fatigues an employee that is reduced by a rubber mat, (2) in hot humid months there is potential for a floor surface to become moist that has potential for employee injury and is minimized by a rubber mat & (3) during a picked sku transfer from a pick position to a CO container, a dropped sku onto a cement floor has high potential for damage but is reduced with a rubber mat. It is noted that a wood surface between the floor & rubber mat improves a cushion feature.

PPL 23. Secure Your Pick Carton Flaps
Secure your pick carton flaps in a pick & sort cart and pick/pass conveyor is an option to improve picker productivity. Secure your pick carton flaps means that your pick carton top flaps are folded down onto a carton interior side walls or against a carton exterior side walls. With a pick and sort concept, a pick carton flaps folded down creates a smaller pick/sort position and with a pick/pass concept creates a lower elevation to transfer picked skus. You secure top flaps options are (1) fold flaps to a carton interior side walls. Features are (a) low cost and (b) requires packer double handling, (2) fold flaps on exterior side wall and secure with a rubber band. Features are (a) some additional cost & (b) requires packer to recycle, (3) fold picker side flap down onto exterior side & secure with a clip. Features are (a) some additional cost & (b) requires packer to recycle & (4) fold picker side flap down onto exterior side & secure. Features are (a) additional equipment cost & activity & (b) additional packer activity.

PPL 24. In A Pick Zone Use A Picker Clip For Your Picker's Active Customer Order Carton/Tote
In a pick zone use a picker clip for your picker's active CO carton/tote is a small item pick/pass with a pick train or pick cell concept that helps to improve picker to identify a CO carton/tote, improves productivity and minimizes errors (transfer a picker sku to a correct CO container). A CO container is constantly moving into a pick zone and moved over a pick line to a next pick zone or take-away conveyor. As a CO container arrives at a pick zone start, a picker attaches a pick zone clip that becomes a picker's active CO container. During a pick zone pick activity with a pick train concept or queue on a pick line, a picker clip serves to identify an active CO container from other CO

containers and helps to assure that CO picked skus are transferred to a correct CO container. After a CO completion, a picker transfers a pick zone clip from a completed CO container to the next CO container. A pick train & different pick zones, different colored clips are useful for new pickers.

PPL 25. How A Picker Walks In A Pick/Pass Aisle

How a picker walks in a pick/pass line pick zone/cell is as your picker walks between pick positions and a pick conveyor your reads a pick positions IDs and CO ID on a pick conveyor. As a picker walks in a 30 to 36 wide aisle between pick positions and a pick conveyor, a picker transfers skus from pick positions into a CO container on a pick conveyor and maintains your budgeted picker productivity with accurate transactions. During your pick activity, your picker matches a pick position ID (paper label or pick to light) to a CO ID container (pack slip/invoice clipped to a container or label attached to a container). With a paper document pick concept, a picker reads a sku pick position and quantity and looks and reads a pick position paper ID. With a pick to light pick concept, a picker reviews a pick bay to locate a CO ID on a pick zone light and for each CO sku pick quantity on an activated pick position light. Your picker walk options are (1) *Parallel Or Picker Faces A Pick Conveyor*. When a picker faces a pick conveyor and to complete a pick transaction, a picker is required to twist or turn for a look at the pick positions and for sku transfer into a CO container. Features are increased picker physical effort, picker turns to review pick positions & CO container, potential difficulty to a track CO container and potential to drop picked skus & (2) *Perpendicular Or Picker Faces A Pick Aisle*. With a picker perpendicular to a pick conveyor & pick positions, a picker simply turns their head to review required pick positions, easily to recognize a CO container & easy to transfer picked skus from a pick position into a CO container. Features are less picker physical effort, picker head turns to review pick positions & CO container, easier to a track CO container & less potential to drop picked skus.

PPL 26. How To Handle A Pick Position Empty Tote Or Pallet

How to handle a pick position empty tote or pallet is a statement that looks at your picker empty tote or wood/pallet handling options. After your WMS computer program receives a sku replenishment transaction completion to a pick position, your WMS computer program releases COs to your pick concept. In most pick concepts and with this approach a replenishment employee handles an empty tote. Tote handling options are (1) with a shelf/rack pick concept, a captive tote is transferred from a pick position to a temporary storage position that is at a shelf/rack top or bottom level position, (2) with a shelf/rack pick position, a tote remains in a position and is turned upside down or (3) with a flow rack pick position, a picker transfers an empty tote to non-powered conveyor, cart or holding position. A replenishment employee handles a full cart, removes totes from a conveyor or from a holding position 'A' fast moving and medium/high sku has a pallet flow lane pick position and has a wood pallet as a sku bottom support device. In a pallet flow rack pick concept and after sku depletion, a picker physically tilts an empty pallet onto a narrow meshed skate-wheel or roller return flow lane with two high side guards and is floor level. A picker pushes a pallet into a two high sided guard rail travel path that maintains a pallet upright as it flows to a forklift truck location.

Pick & Sort In Your Pick Aisle Ideas (PSIYPA 1 - PSIYPA 4)

PSIYPA 1. Manual Pick & Sort In Your Pick Area

Manual pick and sort in a pick area is a grouped CO pick and sort concept that is used in a small item warehouse to increase picker productivity and your completed CO number. When compared to a single CO pick concept, your picker productivity increase off-sets your picker's sort expense. After your computer program batches your COs into a pre-determined CO number per group (match your 4-wheel cart sort positions), for each pick/sort cart, it prints one pick & sort instruction/document and a batch CO pack slips/invoices. Each pick/sort cart is ID with your computer batch pick number. On a pick/sort document, for each batch each sku's pick position is printed down a page, across a page top is there are several columns. Each column starts with a sort location number, under a sort location number is a CO number and under each CO number is listed a CO sku quantity. Your sort location numbers are arithmetic from to required number (typically from 1 to 9 or 12). Your pick & sort cart positions are pre-numbered with a CO ID carton/tote into each position. Next, your picker places a CO pack slip/invoice into a corresponding CO sort position/cart/tote. At each pick position with a pick/sort cart and pick/sort instruction, a picker completes a bulk sku pick activity. Per your batch pick/sort instruction and from a sku bulk picked quantity a picker sorts a CO sku quantity to each CO location. Per your pick concept, for one batch cart one picker completes all pick transactions or one batch cart/tote is pushed from one assigned pick zone to another picker's assigned pick zone. After completion of all picks, a picker pushes a cart/tote to a pack area.

PSIYPA 2. Bulk Pick & Sort In The Pick Aisle Activity

Manual bulk pick & sort concept has your computer batches/groups your COs to match your pick cart sort position number, for each batch/group prints a special bulk pick & sort document and CO pack slips/invoices for each batch/group. After a picker arranges cartons/totes into each sort location and IDs each sort location, a picker travels to a pick position. With a bulk pick & sort document, a picker bulk picks a sku quantity. Per each CO sku quantity that is printed on bulk pick document, a picker sorts a CO sku quantity to each position. A pick & sort document lists each batch sku pick position and quantity and a CO sku quantity is listed under each CO ID. Features are (1) low cost, (2) some computer program cost, (3) cart with sort positions, (4) easy to train & (5) picker picks entire area.

Bulk Pick & Sort Instruction

Bulk Pick Batch Or Group A
Date
Picker Name

Pick Position	Sku Total Quantity	Customer Order Identification									
		111	212	233	241	365	376	437	418	599	610
A100	10	0	1	2	2	2	1	2	0	0	0
A110	20	2	4	1	1	2	2	2	2	2	2

PSIYPA 3. Secure Your Pick Carton Flaps (See PPL - 21 Page 93)

PSIYPA 4. Bulk Or 'En Masse' Pick 'A' Moving Single Skus

Bulk or 'en masse' pick 'A' moving single skus is a small item or GOH pick concept to improve picker and packer productivity and increase your completed CO number. To have a cost effective and efficient pick concept, your operation activities are (1) computer prints for a CO wave paper document single sku bulk or 'en masse' pick lists that are as a bulk pick instruction. Picked skus are delivered to an assigned pack station or fast pack line, (2) computer prints for each single sku quantity CO wave CO pack slips/invoices in the same sku sequence as on your paper bulk pick document sku print sequence, (3) at a CO and sku scan station, a picker delivers one sku piece for each bulk picked sku that appears on a picker's bulk pick list. This allows an employee to repetitively scan a sku to each CO and as required to insert each CO pack slip/invoice into a slapper envelop & (4) slapper envelopes are delivered to an assigned pack station or fast pack line.

Manual Bulk Pick, Sort & Final Pick Ideas (MBPSF 1 - MBPSF 6)
MBPSF 1. Manual Bulk Pick, Sort & Final Pick Small Items

Manual bulk pick & sort small items has your employee picker push a 4-wheel cart through storage/pick aisles. Manual bulk pick & sort small items requires an employee to have a printed document. Each bulk pick document shows pick position, bulk pick quantity, and sku description. At each sku pick position, a picker bulk picks a sku quantity and transfers a sku onto a cart holding position. In a sku sort area, you identify each sort position by a position ID that corresponds to your sku inventory ID. Your sort locations are shelves and deck standard pallet rack positions. To have all possible sort locations, your sort area has 5 levels per shelf bay and two shelf bays per digit. Sort location sequences are (1) sku first digit is a shelf bay and last sku digit is a shelf level, (2) sku first digit is a bay and sku second digit is the shelf level & (3) sku last digit is a shelf digit and next to last digit is a shelf level. A manual bulk pick, sort and final pick concept with CO pack slip/invoice improves your total employee productivity & higher CO completion number. Features are (1) requires a computer program to print bulk pick documents, (2) CO pack slip/invoice documents are used in your final pick activity & (3) easy to complete a pick check.

MBPSF 2. Manual Bulk Pick, Sort & Final Pick GOH Skus

Manual bulk pick & sort GOH skus has your employee picker push a 4-wheel cart with a load bar or trolley on a rail through your storage/pick aisles. Manual bulk pick & sort GOH skus requires an employee to have a printed document. Each bulk pick document shows pick position, bulk pick quantity, and sku description. At each sku pick position, a picker bulk picks a sku quantity and transfers a sku onto a cart or trolley hold position. In a sku sort area, you identify each sort position by a position ID that corresponds to your sku inventory ID. Your sort locations are carts with a load bar and trolley rail lanes. To have all possible sort locations, your sort area has 10 to 20 carts or 10 to 20 trolley capacity that has 1 or 2 carts/trolley per digit. Possible sort location sequences are (1) sku first digit is a cart or trolley and on a load bar last sku digit is arranged in arithmetic sequence from 0 to 9, (2) sku first digit is a cart or trolley and on a load bar sku second digit is arranged in arithmetic sequence from 0 to 9 & (3) sku last digit is a cart or trolley and on a load bar next to last digit is arranged in arithmetic sequence from 0 to 9. A manual bulk pick, sort and final pick concept with CO pack slip/invoice improves your total employee productivity and higher CO completion number. Features are (1) requires a computer program to print bulk pick documents, (2) CO pack slip/invoice documents are used in your final pick activity and (3) easy to complete a pick check.

MBPSF 3. Bulk Pick & Manual Sort & Final Pick By Sku

Bulk pick, transport, manual sort & final pick by sku concept is used in a multi-line/multi-sku small item or GOH warehouse to improve picker productivity and increase your completed CO number. When compared to a single CO pick or pick & sort concept, a bulk pick, transport, manual sort & final pick by sku concept has fewer picker trips that increase picker productivity and increases your CO number completed per day. Your picker productivity increase and completed CO number off-sets your sort expenses. To complete a bulk pick, transport, manual sort & final pick by sku activity, your computer program prints a bulk pick document that has each sku listed and in a pre-determined print sequence print your CO pack slips/invoices. Each CO pack slip/invoice indicates each sku WMS ID and quantity. In a sort section, shelves and decked pallet rack with position numbers are in a numerical sequence that allows your bulk sku pickers to sort skus to sort/pick positions and from the sort/pick positions permit your final CO pickers to complete CO picks. After a bulk picker with a sku, reads a sku WMS ID number, it serves as a sku sort instruction and sorts a sku to an appropriate position. From a sort/pick position & with CO pack slip/invoice as a CO final pick instruction that has a sku WMS ID number and sku quantity, a picker completes a CO final pick transaction.

MBPSF 4. Bulk Pick, Sort & Final Pick Custopmer Order Pack Slips/Invoices Preparation

How do you prepare your bulk pick & sort and bulk, sort and final pick CO pack slips/invoices is designed to improve your picker/pack productivity and minimize errors. With a bulk pick/sort to a CO carton/tote, a CO pack slip/invoice is placed into a CO carton/tote that is in a cart sort position. Most bulk pick & sort carts have 9 to 12 CO sort positions that requires your WMS computer program to batch COs into groups that have a CO number that matches your cart sort position number. To assure accurate CO pack slip/invoice handling, for each batch/group each batch number is included on each CO pack slip/invoice of a batch/group. With a bulk pick/sort to a CO carton/tote, a CO pack slip/invoice is placed into a CO carton/tote that is in a cart sort position. Features are (1) improves picker productivity, (2) matches your pick/sort activity to your cart sort positions & (3) improves CO pack slip/invoice control and accountability. With a bulk pick, sort and final pick concept, per your CO wave/group your WMS computer prints a bulk pick document in pick position sequence. Your CO wave/group CO pack slips/invoices are printed and sorted by sort position sequence (first digit, last digit) and each CO pack slip/invoice group is distributed to each sort position number. From each sort position, a final picker with a CO pack slip/invoice a CO completes final pick. If CO pack slips/invoices are randomly printed and distributed to sort positions, your picker productivity is low due to additional walk distance & time to the first pick position. Features are (1) improves packer productivity, (2) with pick, sort & final pick lowers pick instruction cost, (3) with pick, sort & final pick concept that has CO pack slips/invoices separated by sort location improves picker productivity & (4) improves CO pack slip/invoice control & accountability.

At each sku pick position, a picker bulk picks a sku quantity and transfers a sku quantity onto a cart hold position. In a sku sort area, you identify each sort position by a position ID that corresponds to your sku inventory ID number. For a sku sort activity, it appears on a sku ID label and for final CO pick activity, it appears on a CO pack slip/invoice document. Your sort locations are shelves and deck standard pallet rack positions. To have all possible sort and final pick locations, your sort area has 5 levels per shelf bay that provides 0 - 9 digits and two shelf bays per digit that provides 0 – 9. Possible sort location sequences are (1) MANUAL BULK PICK, SORT & FINAL PICK BY SKU LAST TWO DIGITS that has a sku first digit is a shelf bay with and last sku digit is a shelf level, (2) MANUAL BULK PICK, SORT & FINAL PICK BY SKU FIRST & SECOND DIGIT that a sku first digit is a shelf bay and sku second digit is a shelf level & (3) MANUAL BULK PICK, SORT & FINAL PICK BY SKU FIRST & LAST DIGITS that has a sku last digit as a shelf digit and next to last digit is a shelf level. A manual bulk pick, sort and final pick concept with CO pack slip/invoice improves your total employee productivity & higher CO completion number. Features are (1) requires a computer program to print bulk pick documents, (2) CO pack slip/invoice document is used in your final pick activity & (3) easy to complete a pick check.

EXHIBIT 7 - 4

BULK PICK SORT & CUSTOMER ORDER FINAL PICK DOCUMENT LOCATED BY CUSTOMER ORDER FIRST SKU DIGIT SEQUENCE AT EACH SORT/PICK POSITION

CUSTOMER ORDER PICK DOCUMENT BY CUSTOMER ORDER FIRST SKU DIGIT

0	1	2	3	4

SORT & FINAL ASSEMBLY POSITIONS

0	1	2	3	4
9	8	7	6	5

SORT & FINAL ASSEMBLY AISLE

9	8	7	6	5

CUSTOMER ORDER PICK DOCUMRNY BY CUSTOMER ORDER SKU DIGIT

AS FIRST & LAST DIGIT
100099   CUSTOMER ORDER PICK DOCUMENTS AT BAY 1
76452   CUSTOMER ORDER PICK DOCUMENTS AT BAY 7

AS LAST & NEXT TO LAST DIGIT
100099   CUSTOMER ORDER PICK DOCUMENTS AT BAY 9
76452   CUSTOMER ORDER PICK DOCUMENTS AT BAY 2

AS FIRST & SECOND DIGIT
850099   CUSTOMER ORDER PICK DOCUMENTS AT BAY 8
66452   CUSTOMER ORDER PICK DOCUMENTS AT BAY 6

Manual sort by sku concept has a numeric/digit ID on each sku and a computer prints a bulk pick document and CO pack slips/invoices. After pickers bulk pick skus arrive in a sort area, each bulk picked sku is transferred to a sort/temporary hold position. For maximum sku sort productivity, each sort location has numeric or digits that is related to a sku inventory numeric digits. Each sort location has two shelf bays with a total of 10 levels and each level has a numeric or digit ID. After all sku are sorted to the sort locations, a clerk verifies all bulk pick documents are returned to your control desk and CO final pick activity is able to start. Final pick activity occurs with a CO pack slip/invoice and into a CO carton/tote. For maximum final pick productivity, your computer arranges and prints your CO pack slips/invoice in a numeric/digit sequence. The sequence matches a specific CO pack slip/invoice first sku numeric/digit concept that permits your CO pack slips/invoices grouped & distributed to a sort position. The concept has a CO pack slip/invoice first pick in a sort position. A completed CO is transferred to a pack station or sent to a check station. Features are low cost with shelves/racks, easy to implement & train employees & low computer cost.

Sort instruction as a paper document or sku label instruction is required to assure an accurate sort activity, high sorter productivity and increase completed CO number. A sort instruction is a human/machine readable symbology that directs an employee or machine sort concept to transfer a sku from a sku group/travel path into a temporary sort/hold position. Per your sort concept, a sku identification is vendor or your receiving department with vendor approval applied to each sku.

Manual sort and final CO pick by sku digit designs with shelves, decked racks and pallet racks has sufficient positions for 0 – 9 digits that improve sorter/final picker productivity and increase completed CO number. The approach allows you to sort bulk picked skus by a sku ID label and with a CO pack slip/invoice sku identification to final pick COs. Per your sku size, for very small skus you have 10 shelf bays to provide 1 shelf bay for each digit 0 – 9 and for regular size skus you have 20 shelf bays to provide 2 shelf bays for each digit 0 – 9. To provide picker direction, each two bays has one digit and has numeric IDs that extend outward into the aisle from a first bay first post and a second bay last position and an ID is flat against a top shelf. In a typical layout your shelf bay is 4 ft wide with 2 posts that are I in wide. With regular skus, you have promotional and large size skus that have few skus, your design has a decked standard pallet rack bay opposite each 2 shelf bays and has a floor level and decked level. Ten shelf levels per two bays allows shelves for 0 – 9 digits. To provide picker direction, each shelf has one digit numeric ID that is in a shelf middle and on a first bay first post and a second bay last position. To match a 2 shelf bay span, your rack bay span is 8 ft 2 in C/C that equals distance between a rack bay two posts center lines. Deck your bottom hand stacked/decked standard pallet rack level has your bottom (floor) level skus hand stacked onto a deck instead of two pallets. To provide picker direction, each rack bay has one digit numeric ID that faces the aisle and the bay both posts and an ID is flat against the top load beam. A deck is a solid wood, harden plastic or metal member with 1 in high bottom full depth runners evenly spaced to assure minimal deck bow. When compared to hand stack onto 2 pallets, a deck concept increases vertical open space by a nomimal 4 ins and allows a rack bay entire area used for skus that increases the usable space by 8 to 12 ins or one standard carton width. Deck and runner cost is equal to 2 pallets cost. Standard pallet rack bays are located at your back to back deck rack rows and are positions for your promotional skus. Per your picker height, your rack bay design height & load beam arrangement has floor level for a 1 sku on a double stacked pallet or 2 levels for 2 skus.

Your sort by sku digit design assures that you have sufficient sort positions and cube capacity to handle your CO wave and permits a sorter/final picker pattern. To provide sufficient sort positions and cube your design has single or mix of standard shelves, deck racks or standard pallet racks. Your design options are (1) *Horse-Shoe* has only shelves and is used for very small skus. Shelves are arranged in a horse shoe shape with one shelf bay per each digit (0 – 9). As a sorter/final picker enters a horse-shoe, start is at a right side with four shelf bays (0 – 3), base with two shelf bays (4 & 5) and left side with four shelf bays (6 – 9), (2) *One Aisle Or Tunnel* has shelf bays with two per digit (0 – 9) on a right side and for each digit (0 – 9) a decked pallet rack bay with a C/C dimension to equal two shelf bays. A sorter/picker starts at a first shelf/rack bay and progressively moves to exit end and (3) *Two Aisles* has the first aisle shelf bays on an aisle left side with two per digit (0 – 4) on an aisle right side and for each digit (0 – 4) a decked pallet rack bay with a C/C dimension to equal two shelf bays and a second aisle shelf bays with two digit (5 – 9) and for each digit (5 – 9) a deck pallet rack with a C/C dimension to equal two shelf bays. For maximum space utilization and improve sorter/picker productivity, the shelf bays are on exterior and interior rack bays. Options are (a) to create large cube or high volume sku positions, on a back to back decked pallet rack rows is to have standard pallet racks and (b) to allow an employee early exit to have a middle turn aisle in a decked pallet rack row that requires two additional shelf bays.

MBPSF 5. Bulk Pick Document
Manual bulk pick, transport & sort small items has your employee picker push a 4-wheel cart through pick aisles. Manual bulk pick, transport & sort small items requires an employee to have a printed bulk pick document. Each bulk pick document shows pick position, bulk pick quantity, and sku description.

Bulk Pick Document

Bulk Pick Group
Date
Picker Name

Pick Position	Sku Description	Pick Quantity
C101	blue pen	20
D200	knife	5

MBPSF 6. Manual Bulk Pick, Transport, Manual Sort & Final Pick By Customer Order NUmber
Manual bulk pick, transport, sort and final pick by CO number is a small item idea that is used to increase your picker productivity and your completed CO number. When compared to a single CO pick concept, your picker productivity increase off-sets your sort expense. After your computer program batches your COs into a pre-determined CO number per group (match your sort positions), it prints one pick and sort instruction/label for each sku in a batch and print your batch CO pack slips/invoices. Your pick labels are printed in pick position sequence number and your CO pack slips/invoices are printed in an arithmetic sequence from a CO low number to a high number. With batch CO pack slips/invoices, a sorter employee writes each CO number on each cart/tote sort position that faces a sorter lane/aisle. Each sort aisle/lane is assigned to a batch and at each sort lane entrance is a batch color/digit ID. Per your pick, transport and sort concept, a CO carton/tote is placed into each position or a sort position is open (slide/chute) and places a CO pack slip/invoice into each CO sort position. On each batch pick label is printed a sku's pick position, CO number and other company required information. Each batch is assigned a color and batch digit ID, a batch colored tag and digit ID is placed onto each tote/carton/cart. As a picker travels with tote/carton/cart through all pick aisles, at each pick position a picker removes a sku, labels a sku and transfers a sku into a cart/tote/carton. After a cart/tote/carton is full or batch completion, a cart/tote/carton is transferred to a transport concept for travel to your sort area. In your sort area, each batch ID carton/tote/cart is pushed into an appropriate batch sort aisle/lane. As a batch cart/tote/carton moves through a sort aisle/lane, a sort employee removes a sku from a cart/tote/carton and matches a sku's CO number to a sort location CO number and a sku is transferred to an assigned CO sort location. Per your concept, sort location options are (1) one sort employee is assigned an entire sort aisle/lane or (2) sort aisle/lane is separated in sort zones with one employee is assigned to one sort zone. After all CO sku sorts, a packer removes a CO skus to a pack station and an empty tote is returned to your pick area.

Batched Customer Order Pick Ideas (BCOPA 1 - BCOPA 7)
BCOPA 1. Batched Customer Order Pick Activity
Batched CO pick activity is a small item or GOH paper pick concept that has your computer program group COs into pre-determined CO number per group. With a batched CO group, during one pick trip a picker picks for several COs that increases a sku hit concentration and density to increase your picker productivity and your completed CO number. It is your increased picker productivity that off-sets your additional batched picked sku sort labor and expenses. Your batched CO number is determined by your (1) manual pick & sort cart CO number and (2) mechanized sorter capacity that is based on (a) picker driven or your picker number and productivity rate or (b) active pack station number and productivity rate. After your computer program prints a (1) batched CO pick & sort document that directs an employee to bulk pick a sku quantity. Per a pick & sort document CO sku, your picker sorts from a bulk picked sku quantity into a CO location on a cart, (2) pick labels that has a (a) picker places a label onto a sku. A labeled sku is placed onto a belt conveyor travel path or in a tote that is transported to a sort station where an employee reads a sku sort label and sorts a sku into a CO location (b) labeled sku is inducted onto a sort conveyor for travel under a scanner that sends a message to a sort computer for a sku sort onto a CO location and

(3) with pre-labeled skus a paper pick document or RF device instructs a picker to transfer a pre-label sku quantity onto a belt conveyor travel path or in a tote that is transported to an induction station for sku transfer onto a sort conveyor for travel under a scanner that sends a message to a sort computer for a sku sorted onto a CO location.

BCOPA 2. Last Batched Picked Tote/Cart/Trolley Signal
Last batched picked tote/cart/trolley signal is a human readable code that is used on a batch pick tote/cart/trolley pick, transport, sort and final pick concept to signal a last picked sku in a batch. In your sort area, a last batch picked tote/cart/trolley signals to a sort employee/bar code scanner/RF tag reader that a batch is completed and your sort area supervisor signals that your next batch totes/carts/trolleys flow to the sort area. A last batch signals has a colored tag with a human/machine readable symbology.

BCOPA 3. Batch Pick & Sort Imbalance Plan
Batch pick & sort imbalance plan is your small item or GOH pick and sort/pack area plans to handle a batched pick/sort concept imbalance between your pick area and sort/pack area. An imbalance plan allows you to maintain your picker/sorter productivity and minimize errors. With a batched CO pick imbalance occurs between a pick area and sort/pack area, it creates an uncontrolled sku accumulation at a sort/pack area or there is insufficient pieces delivered to your sort/pack area. Your measures to minimize an imbalance situation are (1) for each CO wave, plan your picker and sorter/packer employee number. Your employee number is based on your picker productivity rate and your sorter/packer productivity rate that provides you with the proper employee number to assure a smooth customer order flow, (2) your pick tote, trolley, cart or conveyor travel path concept design number has a safety factor (extra quantity) to compensate for an imbalance and allows pickers to pick the next batch and maintain their productivity and your pick area design your have sufficient picked sku set-down area or queue conveyor lanes. If pickers pick a batch in advance, each next batch tote/cart/trolley/carton has a proper batch identification with a human/machine readable symbology and is placed in the set-down area. Some potential pick area set-down areas are (a) under or over a conveyor travel path and (b) wider aisle along a conveyor travel path, (3) in your sort/pack area (a) each mechanical sort location design has three windows (one window for present batch/second window for next batch/third window for next batch), (b) with manual sorted small items, have an additional sort lane with sort/pack locations, (c) additional tote/cart/trolley carton queue lanes or conveyor travel paths and (c) manual sort concept or a mechanical sorter is designed with sku re-circulation.

BCOPA 4. Your Batched Pick & Sort Customer Identification On A Label
Your batched pick sort CO ID on a label is used in a manual small item or GOH batched CO pick concept to improve picker/sorter productivity and minimize sort errors. After a picker applies a pick/sort label to sku, a labeled sku is placed into a tote, onto a belt conveyor or trolley for transport from a pick area to a sort area. In a sort area, an employee or mechanical scanner requires a sku label with a CO sort ID line of sight to complete a sort transaction. To assure maximum sorter productivity, your CO sort ID is printed as large as possible and is on a label front right and top section. CO sort ID location features are (1) easy to read and (2) first alpha character or digit on a label.

BCOPA 5. Batch Pick Onto A Belt Or Into A Carton/Tote For Manual Or Mechanized Induction
Batch pick onto a belt conveyor or into a carton/tote for manual sort or mechanized induction sort activity are a small item pick and transport options to assure good employee productivity and minimize sku damage. When your pick, transport and sort skus that are fragile, crushable, have sharp edges, heavy weight, can not have damaged edges or liquid skus, your picked skus are placed into a tote/carton. Totes/cartons are transported from a pick area to your sort/induction area. To assure empty totes/cartons are in a pick area, totes/cartons are transported to a pick area and strategically stacked in a pick area. Features are additional conveyor costs, tote/carton cost, queue areas, increased potential for a pick/sort label to remain on sku and protects skus. If your operation handles durable skus, your pickers place skus directly or transfers from a self-dumping cart onto a belt conveyor. A belt conveyor transports loose skus to your sort/induction area. Features are lower conveyor cost, no tote/carton cost, potential sku damage or lost pick/sort label and minimal queue capacity.

BCOPA 6. How To Control Your Batched Pick Activity

How to control your batch CO pick activity is a small item or carton method to assure that a batched and picker CO skus are released on-time from a pick area for transport to your sort/induction area. Features are to improve picker/sorter productivity, minimize errors and assure maximum completed CO number. In your pick area on scheduled batched CO picked sku release/control options are to have a (1) clock and batch release time that is printed on each pick label. Feature is relies on picker, (2) score board that shows an active batch for pick/release batch number and each batch number is printed each label. Feature is relies on picker and (3) clerk to issue batch labels to pickers. Feature is relies on a clerk that is additional control & cost. If you desire to maintain your picker activity with an imbalance between a pick and sort/induction area, in your pick area you design advance picked sku set-down area.

BCOPA 7. How To Identify Your Batched Pick Activity Last PIck

How to identify your batched pick activity last pick is a consideration for a small item batch pick warehouse to assure picker/sorter productivity, a smooth CO flow and minimize pick/sort errors. Your completed batch CO pick options are (1) if you use a tote/carton transport concept, a colored tote with a human/machine readable pick zone ID tag that is used to identify a last pick from a pick zone. In a sort/induction area, your sort/induction area collects tags until all pick zone tags are received that means a completed batch & (2) with a pick to conveyor concept, your last pick zone has a colored marked and human/machine readable ID on your last pick label. As each pick zone colored label arrives in a sort & induction area, each completed pick zone is listed until a sort/induction area collects all pick zone tags.

Horizontal Carousel Ideas (HC 1 – HC3)

HC 1. Mechanized Pick Small Items

Mechanized pick small items has your pick concept move pick positions to a pick station. At a pick station with paper document, RF device or pick to light pick instruction, a picker transfers/picks skus from a mechanized pick position into a CO container. A standard horizontal carousel has nomimal 50 basket stacks with 5 baskets per stack. A separated basket increases a basket sku capacity to 5 per basket and a rear sloped basket bottom with Velcro removable front reduces skus falling from a basket to the floor. At a pick station a stationary step ladder is used for an employee access to elevated positions. Pick concept options are (1) single COs, (2) bulk pick, sort and final pick and (3) bulk pick & sort. Your mechanized pick concept options are (1) *Pick From Single Horizontal Or Vertical Carousel* to CO cartons/totes. Features are (a) cost, (b) low picker productivity due to waiting time for carousel rotation and (c) minimal computer program cost, (2) *Pick From Multiple Horizontal Carousel* in a horse shaped layout to CO cartons/totes. Features are (a) higher cost, (b) higher picker productivity with a three carousel layout, carousel B & C rotate as a picker picks from carousel A, (c) for fast moving or large skus double pick positions and (d) additional computer program cost and (3) *Pick To A Horizontal Carousel CO Cartons/Totes* from a sku on a cart/conveyor. Features are (a) cost, (b) additional computer program cost and (c) carousel position matches your largest CO carton/tote.

HC 2. Horizontal Carousel Considerations

Horizontal carousel considerations are ideas to improve your picker productivity and increase your completed CO number. The ideas are (1) forward & reverse or 2-way travel that has a carousel carriers/baskets move in a forward & reverse direction past a pick/sort station. Features are increase computer program cost, minimizes potential picker non-productive time due to minimal waiting time for next sku or CO carrier/basket rotate & arrive at a pick/sort station, (2) carousel controls command a carousel to move an assigned carrier/basket to a pick station that is computer controlled that per your CO down load has your carousel rotate carriers/baskets with skus or COs to arrive at your pick/sort station. Features are maximum productive sku or CO basket/carrier rotation due to rotation that is based on sku or CO basket/carrier numerical sequence, maintains good picker/sorter productivity with no carousel move command activity, minimal non-productive employee waiting time & capable to command multiple carousels for maximum picker/sorter productivity, (3) 3 or multiple horizontal carousels service 1 pick/sort station. 3 carousel pick/sort station concept is designed with 3 horizontal carousel in a horse shaped pattern to service 1 pick/sort station that permits 1 picker/sorter employee access to 3 carousels. Carousels (1 & 2) have 'A' & 'B' moving skus with computer program potential for floating slot concept & carousel (3) has 'B' & 'C' moving skus. With family group or pairs skus are profiled by their volume to 1 carousel. Features are reduces non-productive pick waiting time due carousels 1 & 2 rotate as a picker completes sku pick/sort transactions from carousel 3 basket that is at a pick/sort station & (4) to access elevated positions with stationary ladder to permits a picker access to 1 – 3 carousel elevated positions,

HC 3. With An Open Carton/Tote Or Basket Use A Removable Front Barrier
A front barrier is used in a small item manual or mechanized pick concept on a vendor opened carton or pick position front to retain skus in a shelf, decked rack, carton flow rack or horizontal carousel basket pick position that improves picker productivity and minimized sku damage. After a vendor carton is prepared for pick position presentation, loose skus in a open front carton/tote or loose skus in a pick position, some times there is potential for skus to fall from a pick position or from a carton/tote open front. If skus fall from a pick position, there is non-productive picker time to return skus to a pick position or a sku falling to the floor damages a sku that creates need for special sku inventory adjustment or shortage. Some pick position barrier options are (1) with a smiley face master carton to insert a carton removed top in a carton open front, (2) with a captive tote to insert a carton removed top in a tote open front and (3) with skus stacked loose in a pick position or horizontal basket to use a Velcro attached plastic or fabric barrier. As a sku becomes depleted in a pick position, a cardboard barrier is save for reuse or thrown in the trash and a Velcro barrier is retain on a pick position/basket front.

Automatic Pick Machine Ideas (APM 1 - APM 6)
APM 1. Small Item Automatic Pick Machines
Automatic pick small item is a computer controlled pick machine that picks a single CO skus. Skus are transferred from a pick machine onto a cleated belt conveyor or into a CO carton/tote. When you profile an automatic pick machine, you allocate heavy and high cube skus at a pick machine pick pattern front/start and small or light weight skus at the patter end. To assure good pick rates and no stock outs, fast moving skus have two pick positions. Replenishments are made from a separate aisle and behind a replenishment aisle are skus ready reverse positions. Various automatic small item pick machines are (1) *S. I. Itematic* that from a pick device release skus onto belt conveyor for transport to a pack station slide. (2) *ROBO Pic* that from a cleated belt conveyor transfers/water falls a sku into a captive tote and (3) *A or H Frame* that from a pick sleeve releases a sku between two cleats on a belt conveyor for transport to water fall into a tote/carton.

APM 2. Automatic Pick Machine Gathering Belt Is A Cleated Belt
Cleated belt is used in a small item automatic pick machine as a picked sku gathering belt that transports a separated CO to a transfer station. A cleated belt is a belt conveyor with ¼ to ½ in high cleats that are attached full belt width and on 1 ft or pre-determined centers. After an automatic pick machine releases a sku, on a belt conveyor surface a sku is secured between two cleats. Cleats restrict a sku movement and becoming mixed with another CO skus. When using a cleated belt, attention is given to cleat clearance at a water fall transfer station.

APM 4. Pick Machine Gathering Conveyor Transfer In A Tote With A Cushion & Spring Loaded Bottom
An automatic pick machine gathering belt conveyor transfer into a captive pick tote with a cushion & spring loaded bottom is a small item automatic pick machine concept that is used to minimize sku damage as skus are transferred from a belt conveyor end for waterfall into a captive tote. With a standard waterfall/dump concept, an elevation change between a conveyor belt and container bottom is high and has potential to create sku damage or sku package edge damage. A captive pick tote with a spring loaded cushion bottom at a sku transfer location, an elevation change between a conveyor belt and container bottom is minimal and minimizes potential to create sku damage or sku package edge damage. As skus accumulate on a tote spring loaded bottom, skus collective weight depresses a tote bottom that creates additional space for skus.

APM 5. Automtic Pick Machine Gathering Belt Transfer Tilt Your Customer Order Carton/Tote
For automatic pick machine gathering belt transfer tilt your CO carton/tote concept is used in a small item automatic pick concept that has picked skus transferred from an automatic pick machine onto a belt conveyor travel path. At

a belt conveyor discharge end, skus are waterfalled/dumped from a belt conveyor into a CO container. With a standard waterfall/dump concept, an elevation change between a conveyor belt and container bottom is high and has potential to create sku damage or sku package edge damage. With a tilted container at a sku transfer location, an elevation change between a conveyor belt and container bottom is lowered and minimizes potential to create sku or sku package edge damage.

APM 6. Automatic Pick Machine Pick Pattern

Automatic pick machine pick pattern is a small item or GOH sku automatic pick machine release pattern that is from a pick position onto a powered conveyor travel path to complete a CO and minimize sku damage. With a GOH automatic pick machine concept, skus are released from pick lanes onto a powered conveyor travel for transport to a pack station or direct into a delivery truck for transfer to rope hooks. With a small item automatic pick machine, your sku release pattern is determined by your pick machine model. *With A S.I. Itematic Pick Machine*, sku pick positions are along a pick machine one side and skus are released from a pick lane onto a pick head for transfer onto a belt conveyor. To minimize sku damage on your belt conveyor & at your pack transfer station, your heavy skus are released first & light weight/fragile sku are released last. *With A ROBO Pic Machine*, skus are waterfalled from a pick belt conveyor into a container. To minimize sku damage, heavy skus are released first & light weight or fragile sku are released last. *With An 'A' or 'H' Frame Automatic Pick Machine*, sku release pattern is from a pick machine front, down 1 side, from a machine rear & down the other side to the front. Picked sku release pattern is onto a belt conveyor & control at a transfer/pack station is designed to minimize sku damage by your heavy skus are released first & light weight/fragile sku is released last.

GOH Pick Activity Ideas (GOHPA 1 - GOHPA 5)

GOHPA 1. Manual Pick GOH

Manual pick GOH has your picker push a 4-wheel cart or trolley through storage/pick aisles. Manual pick GOH requires an employee to have a printed document or RF device that shows a picker each CO sku. Each pick document shows pick position, pick quantity and sku description. A manual pick concept is used to pick single COs, bulk or 'en masse' picked skus for later sort and bulk pick and sort skus. Features are (1) easy to implement, (2) used with various pick concepts and (3) low equipment cost.

GOHPA 2. Pick GOH As A Single Piece Or 3 Piece Bundle

Pick GOH as a single piece or 3 piece bundle pick concept is used in a GOH warehouse that has a bulk or 'en masse' pick sku concept increases CO number and improves picker productivity. If GOH is bulk picked for retail store orders or for a pick, sort and final assembly concept, a 3 piece bundle pick concept has your computer program print pick instructions to show GOH bundle picks and single piece picks to complete a bulk pick transaction or retail CO. The approach improves picker productivity due to one GOH pick transaction has 3 GOH pieces instead of 1 GOH CO has one pick transaction that requires an employee to complete 3 pick transactions.

GOHPA 3. GOH Automatic Pick Machine

GOH automatic pick machine is a computer controlled concept that has a device that releases CO GOH skus onto a GOH take-away travel for travel to your pack area. If you have multi-line/multi-sku COs, your GOH concept has capability to transfer multi-line/multi-sku CO skus direct to a pack station or to a special consolidation area. For maximum efficiency GOH hangers are standard, match your manufacturer's specifications, each GOH has a unique identification and a sku overflow storage area. Your automatic pick machine concepts are (1) MTS, (2) 200 G and (3) Promech. Features are no employee activity means high productivity, high cost and to handle multi-line/multi-sku additional computer program costs or employee activity.

GOHPA 4. GOH SCAP

GOH SCAP concept means GOH sort, count and pick concept or is called a GOH GOLDEN highway. A GOH SCAP has one pick lane section or 2 pick lane sections. A GOH SCAP concept has 4-wheel carts or trolley rails that has each lane charge end face your receiving dock and discharge end permits travel to your pack area. A one pick lane section that allows skus transfer from your receiving dock to your GOH SCAP area and after your CO pick activity to transfer completed CO transfer to your pack stations and residual skus are transferred to your storage area. A two GOH SCAP concept has 2 pick lane sections for maximum flexibility and to handle a large GOH number. Prior to unloading a GOH delivery truck, your company purchase order indicates your sku number and quantity & sales date. Per your GOH SCAP design and GOH volume & GOH sales forecast and sales date, each GOH cart or trolley lane has 3 to 4 capacity. If your GOH quantity exceeds 1 SCAP design, you allocate overflow GOH skus to multiple cart/trolley lanes, to your other SCAP section or to warehouse storage positions. A GOH SCAP concept improves put-away productivity and picker productivity due to short travel distances and high sku hit concentration and density.

Trash Handling Ideas (TH 1 – TH 2)
TH 1. Trash Cartons Have No Flaps (Cut) Flaps
Trash cartons have no flaps has a replenishment or picker remove or fold-in a carton flaps as it sets in a pick position. No carton flaps features are (1) improves picker productivity due to unobstructed sku removal, (2) means easier employee trash handling to remove an empty carton from a pick position, (3) at a manual baler less time to prep a carton for a baler, (4) less complex transport or carton movement on a conveyor with fewer jams/hang-ups & (5) greater capacity in a trash container/conveyor travel path.

TH 2. Trash Removal Conveyor
Trash removal conveyor is a method to transport empty carton and filler material trash from a 'A'/fast moving pick area to a trash disposal area baler or container that assures good picker productivity and efficient trash handling. With a carton flow rack concept, your trash conveyor elevation is set at an elevation for easy picker (reach) transfer onto your trash conveyor belt. With a pick/pass concept, your trash conveyor starts at your first pick position ('A' fasting moving skus) and continues past all pick line pick positions (slow moving skus). The high to low pick volume approach assures that your 'A'/fast moving pick zone has an empty belt surface. Your trash conveyor picker (near) side guard rail is angled for easy picker transfer and far side guard rail is extra high to assure your tallest thrown trash cartons remain on a conveyor travel path. If require additional guard rail protection, you add fish netting above the far side guard rail to retain cartons on a conveyor travel path. Your trash conveyor width is designed for your widest carton, under side has a solid guard and you have an 'E' pull cord full length. To assure minimal carton hang-up and maximum carton capacity on a conveyor travel path, your replenishment employee removes a carton top flaps. To extend a trash conveyor length your options are (1) between two belt conveyor sections add a *Gap Plate Or Roller* that has the same surface elevation or (2) W*ater Fall* a front conveyor onto another conveyor. With both conveyor transfer options, at conveyor transfer locations your have angled photo eyes across the travel path that senses jams and sends a message to conveyor computer to stop conveyor belt.

Check Activities Ideas
General Check (GC 1 – GC 6)
GC 1. One Customer Order Or Multiple Customer Order Per Pick Tote
One CO or multiple COs per pick tote are your manual pick by paper, label or pick to light options that impact your packer productivity, completed CO number and computer program cube process. With one CO per pick tote, you have potential for lower picker productivity, increased CO containers on a travel path, good packer productivity and minimal WMS computer program CO process time. With two or more COs per pick tote has potential for you to increase picker productivity, reduce CO containers on a travel path, low packer productivity, increase your WMS computer cube program process time and cost and additional computer program cost for COs printed at your pack station. With a pick to light concept, additional & costly computer programming time & cost to have multiple COs into warehouse ID pick tote.

GC 2. Get Your Bad Apples
Get your bad apples is a computer program CO screen process to identify repeat customers with repeated returns & to suggest that your company have a supervisor manual check a CO or to suggest that your company cancel a CO. Get a bad apple is designed to minimize repeat CO returns that require (1) for you to complete a CO, to incur pick, pack & ship expenses that are not off-set with a sale, (2) additional labor & computer expenses to handle a customer order return & (3) to eliminate potential sku damage from your sku return process & activity. With your

customer return history & associated customer return expense and pick/pack/ship expense, your management has data for a decision to accept or cancel a CO for a customer who has repeat returns & minimize your future handling expenses.

GC 3. What Goes Out Bad Comes Back
What goes out bad comes back is a pack activity term that refers to a CO pack quality to minimize damage skus. To improve your customer service and reduce customer returns to reduce costs you assure your CO package has suffiicient filler material, properly sealed bottom and top flaps and clear customer delivery address.

GC 4. List Your Pick Activity Problems
In addition to assuring an accurate CO completion, your check activity lists the reasons that created a problem CO that reduces future CO problems. At your problem CO station, your supervisor identifies (1) each CO ID that identifies a specific pick line or section, (2) identifies CO problem such as (a) over pick, (b) shortage, (c) damage sku & (e) wrong sku that IDs potential picker problems. replenishment problems or vendor sku problems & (3) IDs package appearance & packer such as (a) label orientation, (b) tape strand number, (c) tape strand length, (d) filler material that creates package bow & (e) under filler material or not proper filler material that helps identify packer problems. If repeat employee errors occur, you have additional training or re-assign an employee to another activity.

GC 5. What Are Your Returns Reasons
Your returns reasons are a result from your pick and pack activity performance that do not match your CO service standards. Your r return reasons are (1) *Shortage* means that a customer did receive an order on-time but a CO picked, packed and delivered sku quantity was less than a CO pack slip/invoice sku quantity. A CO sku shortage means that a customer is dissatisfied with your pick & pack operation performance due to the fact a CO sku was not delivered on-time in a package. A shortage pick has your staff focus on your picker activity quality, (2) *Overage* means that a CO was received at a delivery address but a CO picked, packed and delivered sku quantity was more than a CO pack slip/invoice quantity. A CO overage means that a honest customer is dissatisfied with your pick & pack operation due to the fact a customer has to take time & expense for a sku return quantity to your pick & pack operation. An overage pick has your staff focus on your picker activity quality, (3) *Sku Damage* occurs when a CO is received at a delivery address & when a CO picked, packed & delivered sku quality is compared to a CO pack slip/invoice that an actual CO ID, picked, packed and delivered sku quality indicates that a sku is broken or not functioning sku. A CO sku damage means that a customer is dissatisfied with your pick/pack operation performance due to the fact a customer has to take time & expense and return a damage sku to your pick/pack operation and due to the fact that a customer did not received a CO good quality sku on-time. A damaged sku has your staff review your receiving/quality control, pack activity & filler material type, package seal type & quantity & vendor ready to ship carton quality & (4) *Incorrect Sku or Mis-Pick* occurs when a CO is received at a delivery address and when a CO picked, packed & delivered sku quality is compared to a CO pack slip/invoice that an actual CO picked, packed & delivered sku is not a CO sku. A CO incorrect sku means that a customer is dissatisfied with your operation performance due to the fact a customer takes time, expense and return an incorrect picked and delivered sku to your pick/pack operation and a customer did not received a correct sku on-time. With a sku or pick error has your staff focus on your picker activity quality that includes your replenishment activity.

GC 6. Package Appearance Is Important
Your package appearance is important to assure that a CO delivery address is in the proper location and that a package exterior appearance is per your company standard. A package with good exterior appearance is the first step to satisfy a customer. Good package appearance factors are CO delivery address label in the correct location, no package bow/bulge, no loose tape strands, carton top & bottom flaps sealed & no extra tape strands.

Check Activity Ideas (CA 1 - CA12)
CA 1. Computer Suggested (Problem Order) Customer Order Check
Computer suggested (problem) CO check concept has your CO process computer program to identify customers who have repeat returns. Your CO process computer program identifies a repeat return customer and suggests

that your pick/pack staff verify your CO pick and pack accuracy and sku quality. Per your pick and pack concept, each repeat CO is manual or mechanically transferred to a special check/pack station. At a special check/pack station, a staff member verifies a completed CO sku quantity accuracy & sku quality. After a check and pack activity, a completed CO package is transferred onto a take-away transport concept. Additional check expenses are off-set by reducing your CO return number and associated return process and sku return to stock expenses and potential sku damage.

CA 2. High Value Sku Check Activity
High value sku check is a computer suggested CO check concept that has your CO process computer program to identify CO with a high value sku. Your CO order process computer program identifies a CO with a high value sku and suggests that your pick/pack staff verify your CO pick and pack accuracy and sku quality. Per your pick and pack concept, each CO with a high value sku is manual or mechanically transferred to a special check and pack station. At a special check and pack station, a staff member verifies a completed CO accuracy and sku quality. After a check and pack activity, a completed CO package is transferred onto a take-away transport concept. Your additional check expenses are off-set by reducing your return number and assures a satisfied customer.

CA 3. 100% Check Activity
100% check activity is a check employee or automatic check machine concept that has each CO quantity or quantity/quality checked. Per your pick and pack concept, each CO is manual or mechanically checked a special check station or pack station. At a special check or pack station, a staff member or automatic check machine verifies a completed CO accuracy and sku quality. After a check and pack activity, a completed CO package is transferred onto a take-away transport concept. Features are high check labor expense and requires additional check station number. Your additional check expenses are off-set by reducing your CO return number and assures a satisfied customer.

CA 4. Random Check Activity
A random check activity concept is designed to have your checker randomly select CO containers to verify that picked sku quantity and quality match your CO pack slip/invoice sku quantity and quality. With a random concept, as picked CO containers leave your pick area, an employee or machine checker completes a check activity. Good COs are sent to your pack area and poor quality COs are transferred to a problem CO station. If your have a post pack random check activity, at a separate check station an employee verifies a CO container appearance match your company standard and picked/packed sku quantity and quality match your CO pack slip/invoice. Features are improves picker accuracy, assures accurate order and assures good checker productivity.

CA 5. Separate Check Activity Or Check/Pack Station Activity
Separate check station or check/pack station are two CO check options for your pick/pack operation. With a separate check station concept, after your pick activity, your completed COs are sent to a check station. At a separate check station, an employee or mechanized concept assures that a CO picked skus quantity and quality are per your company standard. Per your check station results, OK or all good COs are sent to a pack station and poor quality/not accurate COs are sent to a problem CO station. Features are (1) additional labor cost, (2) additional equipment, (3) completes a high CO number and (4) creates high packer productivity. A checker/packer concept has at a pack station, a packer verify a sku quantity and quality. If a check is OK, a packer completes a CO. If a CO has a problem, a packer transfers a problem CO pack slip/invoice with skus & ship carton/tote to a problem CO station. Features are requires additional queue prior to check/pack station, requires sufficient work table surface for a check activity, lower packer productivity & lower completed CO number/or you add work stations.

CA 6. Pre-Pack Check Or Post-Pack Check Activity
Pre-pack check or post-pack check activity are your two CO check options. A pre-pack check activity is completed after your pick area and prior to your pack area and verifies your CO picked sku quantity and quality match your CO pack slip/invoice sku quantity and description. A post-pack check activity completed after your pack activity and prior to your manifest area. Your post-pack check activity options are (1) package quality or appearance check that verifies your packer has sufficient tape strand (s) to secure a ship carton top flaps and sufficient filler material to

protect skus with no carton top bow or (2) picked sku quantity and quality check & package quality or appearance check. To maintain your CO package appearance standard, a post-pack check activity that opens a CO carton, requires a new ship carton & a new delivery label. The aspect requires a label printer at a post-pack check station.

CA 7. Pass A Problem Order, Problem Customer Order Or Poor Quality Station
A problem CO or poor quality sku station is shelf that is located in a check/pack area and is a very short walk distance for a checker/packer to transfer a problem CO. If your check/pack activity determines when compared to a CO pack slip/invoice that a CO container has a poor quality sku or sku quantity error, your company policy requires corrective action taken to assure an accurate CO. To maintain a checker/packer at a work station, when a problem CO occurs a checker/packer transfers a problem CO (skus, container & CO pack slip/invoice) to a problem CO shelf. The approach has a checker/packer remain at a work station & not have non-productive walk time to a pick area to correct a problem CO. A check/pack area supervisor corrects a problem CO and re-introduces a corrected CO to a check/pack station. Feature is increase check/packer productivity and increased completed CO check/pack number.

CA 8. Light Fixture Location
A check, pack and customer return process activity light fixture location improves check, packer and process employee productivity. At a manual activity station, a light fixture location is above a CO container on a work station table and at an elevation that allows an employee to read all CO container ID and sku descriptions. With a check weigh station, your light fixture lumens or brightness allows an employee to easily read a scales digital display.

CA 9. At A Check Station, Check Employee Sits Or Stands (See RS 11. Page 162)
CA 10. Where To Hold Your Customer Order Look-Up Table (See GRL 1. Page 157)
CA 11. Check Employee Stands On A Rubber Mat (See PPL 22. Page 110)
CA 12. Work Station Adjustable Legs Or Work Platform (See PT 1. Page 130)

Manual Check Activity Ideas (MCA 1 – MCA4)
MCA 1. Manual Quantity Check Activity
A manual quantity check activity has an employee compare a picked sku quantity to a CO pack slip quantity. For a manual sku quantity check concept have your CO process computer print a total sku on a CO pack slip/invoice. During your manual sku quantity check activity a total sku quantity is used by a checker as instruction. With the concept, your computer prints a CO total sku quantity in a clear and easy to recognize location on each CO pack slip/invoice. At a check or pack station, in a CO carton/tote a checker/packer counts an actual picked sku quantity and easily compares the actual count to sku total on a CO pack slip/invoice. Features are reduces an employee non-productive count time for skus on a CO pack slip/invoice.

MCA 2. Similar Skus With Different Colored Caps
Similar size skus with different colored caps is used in a manual sku quantity check activity to improve manual checker productivity. When you have mixed skus in a CO container, your checker uses a colored cap to assure that an actual sku matches a CO pack slip/invoice sku quantity due to the fact that your CO pack slip/invoice has a colored cap in a sku description. Feature minimizes your checker reading requirement, improves checker productivity and accuracy and has simple instructions.

MCA 3. Manual Check Or Total Sku Quantity On A Pack Slip/Invoice (See MCA 4 Page 125)

MCA 4. Manual Quantity & Quality Check
A manual quantity and quality check activity is completed prior to your pack area. A check activity has an employee compare a picked sku quantity to a CO pack slip quantity & a picked sku quality to a CO pack slip/invoice sku description. A sku quantity check options are have a (1) checker count each picked sku quantity in a CO carton/tote and compare each sku picked quantity to a CO pack slip/invoice quantity or (2) checker count a total sku quantity and compare an actual total sku quantity to a CO pack slip/invoice total sku quantity. An alternative to a count check concept is to have your checker bar code scan a CO ID and scan each sku WMS ID and sku quantity that are sent to your check computer program. Since your WMS computer has transferred your CO ID and sku ID

to your check computer, your check computer program compares each sku scan and quantity transaction to your computer CO sku quantity. To improve your check scan productivity your hand held scanners are elevated for easy sku scan transaction and default a scan transaction for one sku.

Check Bar Code Scanner Ideas (BCS 1 – BSC 9)
CBCS 1. Default Your Hand Held Scanner To One (See BCS 5. Page 18)
CBCS 2. Fixed Position Your Hand Held Scanner (See BCS 9. Page 19)
CBCS 3. Hand Held Scanner Multiple Light Beams Or Wide Light Beam (See BCS 9. Page 19)
CBCS 4. Use A Scanner Gun With Depth Of Field & Large/Tall Bar Code (See BCS 1. Page 17)
CBCS 5.   Re-Chargeable Battery Or Electric Battery Powered Hand Scanner (See BCS 2. Page 18)
CBCS 6.   Your Work Station Or Forklift Truck Scanner Has A Short/Long Cord (See BCS 3. Page 18)
CBCS 7.   Your Scanner Depth Of Field (See BCS 4. Page 18)
CBCS 8.   Delayed Or On-Line Transaction Update (See BCS 6. Page 18)
CBCS 9.   Human Symbology On Top/ Bottom Of Machine Symbology (See BCS 8. Page 19)

Mechanized Check Activity Ideas (MECA 1 – MECA3)
MECA 1. RF Tag Check
A RF tag check activity is a machine check activity that completes a sku quality and quantity check. With a RF tag check concept your WMS computer has transferred your CO ID and sku ID to your check computer. As a CO container with an RF tag ID and each sku with a RF tag ID arrives at your check station, a RF tag receiver receives a CO ID and each sku ID that is sent your check computer. Your check computer program compares each sku scan & quantity to your computer CO sku quantity. A RF tag check concept is a high tech 'check on-the-fly' check concept.

MECA 2. Stationary Scale Check
A stationary scale check concept is a sku quantity check concept that requires your staff to establish a weight variance between your actual and computer projected weight. This is very important with small size, liquid or powered skus, (2) assures each carton/tote size weight is entered into your computer program, (3) assure each sku actual weight is entered in your computer program and (4) per your CO process computer that your CO is cubed for a container. Your conveyor/scale computer has received each CO ID and weight for your CO wave. As your CO containers (cartons/totes) arrive at your scale station, an employee transfers onto a scale & cans a container CO ID that is sent to your scale computer. Also, your scale obtains a CO actual weight that is sent your scale computer. Your scale computer compares your actual CO ID (container) weight to your computer estimated CO ID weight. If your actual and computer projected CO weight variance is within your company allowance, your CO container is returned to the conveyor for travel onto a pack station. If your actual an computer projected CO weight variance is out of variance, your employee transfers a CO container onto your problem CO conveyor. Features are (1) handles a medium volume, (2) requires computer program cost, (3) requires a actual to computer weight variance & (4) accurate sku and container weight in your computer program.

MECA 3. Check On-The-Fly Or Mechanized Check
Check on-the-fly or mechanized check activity is considered a 100% CO picked sku quantity check concept. With a check on-the-fly concept, your staff (1) establishes a weight variance between your actual and computer projected weight. This is very important with small size, liquid or powered skus, (2) assures each carton/tote size weight is entered into your computer program, (3) assure each sku actual weight is entered in your computer program & (4) per your CO process computer that your CO is cubed for a container. Your conveyor/scale computer has received each CO ID and weight for your CO wave. As your CO cartons/totes leave your pick area on a conveyor travel path, a scanner reads a container CO ID that is sent to your conveyor/scale computer. With singulated container travel on a conveyor constant travel speed, a CO travels over an in-line scale that obtains a CO actual weight that is sent your conveyor/scale computer. Your conveyor/scale computer compares your actual CO ID (container) weight to your computer estimated CO ID weight. If your actual and computer projected CO weight variance is within your company allowance, your CO travels onto a pack station. If your actual and computer projected CO weight variance is out of variance, your conveyor/scale computer has your conveyor travel path divert a CO container onto

a problem CO conveyor. Features are (1) handles a high volume, (2) requires computer program cost, (3) conveyor cost, (4) requires a weight variance & (5) accurate sku & container weight in your computer program.

Pack Activities Ideas
General Pack Activity Ideas (GPA 1 – GPA 4)
GPA 1. Sort Or Pack Activity Warm Start
Sort or pack activity warm start improves your packer productivity and completed CO number. A pack activity warm start means that your pick activity queues picked COs prior to each pack station. To assure a pack activity warm start, your pick and sort activity starts prior to your pack activity. Your pick activity early start time is based on the time required to create a picked CO pack station quantity/queue. The time is based on your required completed CO number that is determined by your picker and sorter productivity and picker and sorter number. In most manual bulk pick and sort operations, your pre-start time is 1 hr to 1 hr 30 mn and in a manual bulk pick and mechanized sort operation, your pre-start time is 2 hr to 2 hr 30 mns.

GPA 2. Sort Or Pack Activity Cold Start
Sort or pack activity cold start lowers your packer productivity and completed CO number. A pack activity cold start means that your pick activity has no queued picked COs prior to each pack station. A pack activity cold start has your pick and sort activity start at the same time as your pack activity. Your pick activity same start time has no time to create a picked CO pack station quantity/queue. With no picked COs, your sort/pack employees are assigned to pick activity or other activity, features are non-productive employee reassignment and walk time between activity locations.

GPA 3. Know & Balance Your Pick, Sort & Pack Activity Productivity Rates & Employee Number
Know and balance your pick, sort and pack productivity rates and employee number is an operation plan that has a direct impact to assure your continuous CO flow and high completed CO number. Your pick, sort and pack activity rates are your budgeted productivity rate that were based on a projected sku volume and used to project your annual expense budget. With CO wave volume and activity productivity rates you determine your required employee work stations. From your day employee work schedule, you know your picker, sorter and packer number that is compared to your projected employee picker, sorter and packer number. For an on-budget operation, you assure your actual projected picker, sorter and packer number matches your budgeted picker, sorter and packer. If one operation activity has an employee number that exceeds your required employee number, there is potential for your CO flow to have uncontrolled queue or low completed CO number. With a CO wave plan, your operation has an opportunity to provide on-time customer service at the lowest cost.

GPA 4. How To Collect Your Sku Cube Dimensions
To collect your sku cube dimensions is an important activity that is completed by your receiving or QA department and sent to your WMS computer program. Based on your CO sku cube and available ship carton cube, your WMS computer program suggests a ship carton that improves packer productivity and reduces your filler material usage. Your sku cube dimension collection options are (1) *Vendor Cube Data*. Features are sometimes does not match your needs, low cost and requires clerk entry, (2) *Cube Platform* that is a three side platform with colored lines on each side. Each colored lines represent a ship carton interior cube. After your place a sku onto a platform its physical size is within a specific colored line group and it is preferred ship carton size for a sku. Features are low cost, easy to use, employee activity, requires entry into your cube program and best used for single line/single sku COs and for multiple line CO requires your computer program to add two carton sizes together for preferred carton size that has additional computer programming and cost and (3) *Automatic Cube Device* that has an employee place a sku onto a surface that moves a sku through a device tunnel. In the tunnel, a device obtains a sku external dimensions and weight that for computer entry are sent to your computer cube program. Features are accurate sku dimensions with weight, on-line computer program entry, does not require an employee and has a higher cost.

GPA 5. Promotional Skus To One Or Pre-Determined Pack Stations

Promotional skus transferred to one or pre-determined pack station is a concept that has a bulk picked sku (s) transferred one or selected adjacent pack stations. The approach permits your operation at a scan station, to pre-scan a sku ID to CO pack slips/invoices and deliver scanned CO pack slips/invoices to pack stations. Since your pack station are pre-determined and your know a computer suggested carton size, you can pre-make cartons that are delivered to pack stations. The exception is a pop-out carton that is formed by a packer. Features are high packer productivity & high completed CO number.

Pack Slip Ideas (PS1 – PS 4)

PS 1. Print Pack Slip With Delivery Label Or Pack Slip & Separate Print Pack Slip & Delivery Label

Print on one printer your CO pack slip/invoice with a delivery label or CO pack slip and label printed separately on two printers. A CO pack slip/invoice important data includes customer name, CO delivery address, sku description and quantity, price, other company information and is placed inside a CO container. A delivery label has your CO delivery address and your company's return address and is applied to a CO package exterior. Your print options are (1) both printed on one paper sheet has one printer complete a CO pack slip/invoice and delivery label on one sheet. Features are (1) some slight additional print time, (2) reduces risk of separation, (3) easier to control pack slip/invoice grouping by sku digit and (4) self-adhesive label makes the paper thicker and (2) printed on separate paper and printers that has one printer print your CO pack slip/invoice and another printer print your delivery label. Features are (1) additional paper supply items, (2) used in a bulk pick, transport & sort concept or pick & sort or pick into a CO container, (3) requires two print devices in a central office or pack station table and (4) used to print multiple page CO pack slip/invoice.

PS 2. Pre-Print Or Print On-Demand Customer Order Pack Slips/Invoices

Pre-print or print-on-demand CO pack slips/invoices and delivery labels are your options that assure CO documents are available for your pack activity. *Pre-Printed CO Pack Slips/Invoices* are printed and batched/grouped by each pack station in an office and distributed to each assigned sort/pack station. Pre-printed documents require your staff to create a CO wave/work day CO number and based on your active pack station (sort/pack station) number to batch or group COs for each pack station. To assure packer productivity and assure proper distribution, each pack station batch/group have a pack station ID. Features are requires one large capacity printer, print paper in an environmental controlled room, per your CO number requires a computer program to determine each pack station CO number and method to verify correct pack station distribution. *Print-On-Demand* occurs at a pack station and each pack station has a CO pack slip/invoice printer that is activated by a hand held scanner. A packer with a hand held scanner or fixed position scanner scans a captive tote warehouse ID or ship carton WMS CO ID that is sent to your printer computer. After a computer program activates a printer, a printer prints a CO pack slip/invoice and delivery label. Features are requires a scanner at each pack station, at each pack station and potential wait for print completion and if CO IDs are downloaded to a warehouse printer computer program, there is minimal print wait time.

PS 3. One Printer With Back-up Maintenance Or Two Printers

One printer with a vendor back-up maintenance contract or two printers are your central location (office) print options to print CO pick, pack & ship documents for on-time customer service and good employee productivity. One printer with a vendor back-up maintenance concept prints your CO pack slips/invoices & delivery labels. If your have a printer problem, your staff telephones your printer vendor for support/repair. Features are your past printer problem frequency and down-time length of time. Features are potential for a very cold pick or pack activity start, for past problems at other customer locations, vendor estimated travel and repair time, low printer cost and customer service below your standard. With two printers a problem with one printer you have a second printer to complete your print requirement and vendor repairs the disable printer. If your delivery label requires special label such as a carbon copy, you require a paper document printer for CO pack slip/invoice and a separate printer for a delivery label. Features are continued customer service standard, maintains your picker and packer productivity, higher cost with additional office space and determined by your print requirement.

PS 4. Identify Your Printer Problems

Identify your printer problems has your staff list each printer problem, frequency and length of time that provides data for your to improve your printer efficiency and minimize future printer down-time. If your are experiencing central office printer problems, your staff registers day of week printer problems, problem frequency, vendor repair time and parts, CO and line number that includes both pick and pack documents and paper quality. The information helps you to identify specific events that are repeaters.

Pack Slip & Gift Insert Ideas (PSI&G 1 - PSI&G 4)

PSI&G 1. Manual Or Mechanical Customer Order Pack Slip/Invoice Insert

Manual or mechanical CO pack slip/invoice insert activity are your options to assure that each CO container has a CO pack slip/invoice inserted in a package. Your CO pack slip/invoice insert location options are (1) *At Pick Area Entry* options are (a) pick one CO per container or bulk pick/CO sort concept that has your picker or picker/sorter transfer a CO pack slip/invoice into a CO container and (b) pick/pass concept that has an employee picker or machine transfer a CO pack slip/invoice into a package. Features are potential for CO pack slip/invoice to become lost, CO pack slip/invoice is a package bottom, high packer productivity and pre-printed pack slips/invoices, (2) *At A Sort Location* that has a sort employee place a CO pack slip/invoice into a CO assigned sort slide/chute, carton or tote. Features are less potential for CO pack slip/invoice becoming lost, pre-printed pack slips/invoices, with slide/chute sort position in a CO package pack slip/invoice is on sku top and packer uses CO pack slip/invoice to check picked skus & (3) *At A Pack Station* that has a packer transfer skus into a CO package & placed a pre-printed or printed on-demand pack slip/invoice on sku top. Features are pre-printed or print on-demand pack slips/invoices, less potential for CO pack slip/invoice becoming lost & lower packer productivity.

PSI&G 2. Fold Or Do Not Fold Customer Order Pack Slip/Invoice Into A Package

When your packer includes a CO pack slip/invoice in a carton, your CO pack slip/invoice options are to have a packer (1) *Fold Option* has a packer fold and place a CO pack slip/invoice inside a carton. The fold activity is a non-productive packer time and (2) *Do Not Fold* Option has a packer place a CO pack slip/invoice inside a carton that does not require non-productive packer time.

PSI&G 3 . Legend On A Pack Slip/Inovice To Indicate Insert Sales Literature

A legend or symbol on each CO pack slip/invoice is a concept that is a packer instruction for a packer to add sales literature to a CO container. After your company merchandising department completes a customer survey that customer after receiving one CO with a specific sku or month sales literature and with a second CO within the same time period do not desire to receive a second specific sku or mother's day sale literature, you have an opportunity to lower your company sales literature print expense and improve your packer productivity. With modifications made to your CO process computer program and determination of your CO number that has two or more COs and customer acceptance.

PSI&G 4. Insert Special Gift Or Sales Literature Into A Customer Order Package

Insert a special gift or sales literature into a CO package are activities that impact your picker or packer activity. Your special gift handling options are (1) *Create A Separate CO Wave* with a special gift sku in a pick position that has a picker complete a pick transaction. Features are sku appears on a CO pack slip/invoice with no charge, simple inventory control, track by your WMS computer program and allows a check activity to verify a special gift in a CO or (2) *Divert To Specific Pack Station* has all special gift WMS or warehouse CO IDs entered into your sort computer and each WMS or warehouse ID CO carton or tote is diverted to a specific pack station. At a pack station, a packer automatically transfers a special gift into a CO container. Features are (a) requires a mechanized sort concept, (b) your sort computer receives all CO IDs that require a gift and (c) assures smooth CO flow and your picker productivity. After you have completed a customer survey and conclude your repeat customers do not desire to receive a second or same sku or sales period sale literature, your CO process computer has a mark on a CO pack slip/invoice or delivery label that is in a easily recognized location and serves as a signal for a packer to include sales literature in a CO package. Features are (a) completed a customer survey, (b) computer program cost & additional process time, (c) additional packer training, (d) mark location on CO pack slip/invoice or delivery label & (e) lower sales literature usage means a lower advertising expense.

Pack Table Ideas (PT 1 – PT5)

PT 1. Work Station Adjustable Legs Or Work Platform

Adjustable legs or work platform are your work station options to improve your check, packer or returns employee productivity by assuring that a work station elevation matches an employee height. An employee work station height design factors are CO in-feed height, CO out-feed, empty tote out-feed height, work station height and employee height. Factors available for adjustment are your (1) work station height that adjusted by adjusting each work station height or legs to match an employee height but a work station height. Features are (a) improve employee productivity due to work station top allows employee to easily complete tasks and (b) low employee productivity die to potential difficulty for an employee to transfer a CO in-feed or out-feed and empty tote between a conveyor and work station surface and (2) raise your employee elevation by adding a wood platform under an employee work station stand area. With a wood platform, it raises a short employee to a height that allows an employee to transfer a CO in-feed or out-feed and empty tote between a conveyor and work station surface. Features are (a) platform height is variable and set to match each short employee height and provides a work station surface that reduces employee fatigue and cold feeling from standing on a cement floor.

PT 2. Pack Table Surface

Your pack table surface has sufficient are for your packer to complete a packer's activity. A pack table assures access to picked COs, packed CO take-away concept, trash container, cartons/bags and problem CO station. A table surface has space for handling a CO pack slip/invoice from a stack or printer, scan transactions, check picked skus with a 2 to 3 sku average, taper and carton make-up, fill material space and sale literature space. With a sort/pack activity, space includes sort activity.

PT 3. Light Fixture Location (See CA 8 Page 125)

PT 4. Rubber Mat Or Wood Floor (See PPL 22. Page 111)

PT 5. Pack Staton Shelves

Pack station shelves are a pack station idea that improves pack productivity and pack station space utilization. For best packer productivity, you set your first shelf elevation for your most frequent carton height with flaps up. From an elevated shelf a packer has a simple task to pull and transfer sheet filler material and sales literature into a CO. Features are shelf with structural straight to support paper and sales literature weight, shelf storage space for other ship supplies, used with a regular pack table and provides space for a large paper quantity.

Shippers Ideas (S1 - S10)

S 1. Ship Carton Secure Types & Selection Factors

Ship carton secure types and selection factors determines your CO package presentation and customer satisfaction. Carton secure material assures that your carton bottom and top flaps are sealed and provide sku security. Various secure types are (1) *Gummed Tape* to activate the glue a tape strand pass over a moist brush and a packer applies a tape strand to a carton flaps. Gummed tape machine options are manual operated, electric operated and heated water. Features are requires water supply, potential for packer to cut fingers on tape edge, potential sku damage for a packer to transfer glue from fingers onto a sku, down-time to replenish roll and requires flat work surface, (2) *Self-Adhesive Tape* has an employee or machine apply a plastic tape strand to a carton bottom or top flaps. Options are (a) manual concept that is best with spare tapers and tape rolls at a pack station, has good packer productivity, handles a wide carton size mix and multiple strands are easily applied to a carton, (b) total random machine taper has a higher cost, applies one tape strand, handles a small carton size range, requires floor space and electric supply, down-time to change a depleted roll and difficult with a narrow pre-delivery labeled carton, (c) fixed machine with manual adjustability has a highest cost, applies one tape strand, handles a small carton size range, requires floor space and electric supply, down-time to change a depleted roll and difficult with a narrow pre-delivery labeled carton, (3) *Machine Applied Plastic Bands* that has one or two bands in one direction or different directions that has some potential hang-up problems with a shoe sorter and down-time to replace depleted bands, (4) *Shrink Wrap* requires an electric supply and down-time to replace depleted bands, (5) Pop-Out Carton that interlocks a bottom carton flaps that lowers your tape expense and (6) *One Piece Solid Bottom Carton* that requires no packer activity but a carton form machine. Ship carton secure selection factors are (1) economics, (2) lead time, delivery and storage, (3) required space at a floor area and pack station, (4) employee or machine productivity rate, (5) ability to secure package, (6) customer acceptance and (7) time required to replenish depleted secure material.

S 2. Employee Or Computer Suggersted Carton/Bag Size
Employee or computer suggested carton/bag size are your packer ship carton/bag selection process that has an impact on your packer productivity, filler material usage and ability to track carton/bag usage. *Employee Suggested Ship Carton/Bag* has your packer look at a CO sku size & quantity and from their experience determine a ship carton/bag. Features are potential for extra filler material placed into a package and if a wrong is made-up and not used, low packer productivity. *Computer Suggested Carton/Bag* your computer program requires a package utilization factor, accurate sku exterior cube data and carton/bag interior cube data. From a CO sku quantity, a cube program determines the best carton size to match your CO cube and filler utilization factor. After a computer CO process, your computer prints a suggested carton/bag size on a CO pack slip/invoice or ship label. Features are higher packer productivity, lower filler material usage, requires sku and carton/bag dimension collection, cube program cost, some additional computer CO process time and from computer program files ability to track each ship carton/bag size usage.

S 3. Bag Or Carton Shipper
Bag or carton are your small item shipper options that assures a low cost shipper, properly protects a sku, present a delivery label to employees or scanners and encloses a sku in a shipper as your freight company delivers a CO. Your ship bag or carton selection factors are (1) sku protection, (2) pack employee productivity. When required to add sales literature and CO pack slip/invoice, a pop-out carton has good productivity, (3) container quantity storage at a pack station, (4) security to blend with other small size cartons/packages. A small size carton or pop-out carton matches your other ship cartons, (5) handled by your freight company such as conveyable and able to support other packages. Most freight companies have bags on one conveyor sort concept and cartons on another conveyor sort concept, (6) exterior surface holds your CO delivery label, (7) purchase cost. When compared to a bag, it is possible that a pop-out carton for light weight skus has a lower cost and reduces security and sku protection problems, (8) with void space in a carton, required labor and filler material, (9) customer acceptance and ability to use container for a return and (10) accept by your returns trash recycle program. A carton with filler material is easier to use as a return container. After your analysis & weight given to each factor, you determine the preferred small item shipper.

S 4. Bag Or Carton Delivery Label Window
Pre-printed label window with your return address on a ship container improves your packer productivity, reduces your CO delivery label print time, scan efficiency and enhances your CO package presentation. A label window is a preferred location for a CO ship label placement that assures maximum employee or bar code scanner/RF tag good read number. For easy employee instruction and to assure maximum area for a carton seal tape, a postage stamp label location on carton side wall or top exterior flap is preferred. The concept has an employee place a CO delivery address label in a pre-printed area on a carton upper right hand top or side surface. Part of a pre-printed label window includes your return delivery address for non-deliverable packages or customer refused packages. With your operation's return delivery address on a carton, it means that a CO delivery label requires less ink & paper space. Less CO delivery label paper space increases a combined CO pack slip/invoice print format flexibility & space for other items such carton size or include sales literature.

S 5. Pre-Print Your Return Address On A Ship Container Window
Pre-printed label window with your return address on a ship container improves your packer productivity, reduces your customer delivery label print time, improves scan efficiency and enhances your COr package presentation. A label window is a preferred location for a ship container CO ship label placement that assures maximum employee or bar code scanner/RF tag good read number. For easy employee instruction and to assure maximum area for a

carton seal tape, a postage stamp label location on carton side wall or top exterior flap is preferred. The concept has an employee place a CO delivery address label in a pre-printed area on a carton upper right hand top or side surface. Part of a pre-printed label window includes your return delivery address for a non-deliverable or customer refused package. With your operation's return delivery address on a carton, it means that a CO delivery label requires less ink & paper space. Less CO delivery label paper space increases a combined CO pack slip/invoice print format flexibility & space for other items such carton size or include sales literature.

S 6. Jewelry/Small Size Skus Use Pop-Out Cartons Instead Of Bags
Bag or carton are your small item shipper options that assures a low cost shipper, properly protects a sku, present a delivery label to employees or scanners and encloses a sku in a shipper as your freight company delivers a CO. Your ship bag or carton selection factors are (1) sku protection, (2) pack employee productivity. When required to add sales literature and CO pack slip/invoice, a pop-out carton has good productivity, (3) container quantity storage at a pack station, (4) security to blend with other small size cartons/packages. A small size carton or pop-out carton matches your other ship cartons, (5) handled by your freight company such as conveyable and able to support other packages. Most freight companies have bags on one conveyor sort concept and cartons on another conveyor sort concept, (6) exterior surface holds your CO delivery label, (7) purchase cost. When compared to a bag, it is possible that a pop-out carton for light weight skus has a lower cost and reduces security and sku protection problems, (8) with void space in a carton, required labor and filler material, (9) customer acceptance and ability to use container for a return and (10) accept by your returns trash recycle program. A carton with filler material is easier to use as a return container. After your analysis & weight given to each factor, you determine the preferred small item shipper.

S 7. Ship Carton Types
Two piece, regular, pop-out, chipboard, creased/slotted and notched cartons are your operation ship carton options. Each carton with tape assures a secured CO container and for manifest activity a CO delivery label is in the proper location. Your options are (1) *Two Piece Carton* is a CO container that has a bottom and matched top/cover. Each two piece carton size requires a from machine and cardboard sheet. Features are requires a packer to have both pieces, requires a strap secure method and during your transport activity, a lower transfer elevation and travel path window and requires top and bottom form machines, (2) *Regular Carton* is a 1 piece carton with bottom & top flaps. Prior to your pick or pack activity, an employee or machine forms & secures a regular carton bottom flaps with a tape strand. After a completed CO package, a packer or machine secures each carton top flaps. Features are requires a top and bottom tape labor and expense, with flaps up tall transport travel path window & a high elevation for sku transfer into a carton and available in a wide carton size mix, (3) *Pop-Out Carton* is a one piece carton with a performed bottom flap section. When a picker or packer presses a pop-out carton sides together, bottom flaps become interlocked to from a secured bottom. Features are minimal labor and tape expense, handles a light weight sku, assures high carton make-up employee productivity & with some cartons potential powered conveyor transport difficulties. (4) *Chipboard Carton/Box* is a two piece carton that is employee assembled and secured with tape or plastic bands. A chipboard handles light weight skus such as flatwear and has a low cost, (5) *Creased/Slotted Carton* is regular carton with pre-determined/vendor creases on the 4 side walls. If a CO skus create a void space inside a carton, with a knife a packer slides each side wall joint to the preferred crease that creates longer flaps. The flaps are folded & sealed to create a solid top. A creased carton increases carton flexibility, higher cost and reduces filler material usage/expense & (6) *Notched Carton* with a notched member at each side wall joint. If a CO skus create a void space inside a carton, with a lid extensions at each corner a packer pushes a lid downward inside a carton until a lid secures skus and each lid extension is locked into a notch. A packer tapes a carton top flaps. A notch carton increases carton flexibility, higher cost, lower productivity & reduces filler material usage/expense.

S 8. Pre-Made Cartons
Pre-made CO ship carton is a manual pack station activity that is used with a regular (one piece) top and bottom flap carton. For a carton make-up employee pre-made carton activity is a repetitive activity that means high carton make-up employee productivity. If your pack activity uses a pop-out carton, a pre-made carton concept is difficult to

justify. If your operation has a wide carton size mix, at a pack station it is difficult to have sufficient space for pre-made carton staging area. If your have a few carton sizes (4 to 5), at each pack station there is sufficient space for pre-made carton staging area.

S 9. Ship Bag Tpes & Selection Factors
Ship bag types and selection factors determines your CO package presentation and customer satisfaction. Bag material assures that your bag mouth is sealed and as a CO is shipped to a delivery address, it provides very small sku security. Various bag secure types are (1) *Plain Corrugated/Jiffy Bag* is available in a wide size range and has some water proof feature. Options are no padding, bubble sheet padding or rigid insert to protect a sku. A bag mouth is tape or staple sealed or self-sealed. Features are low cost, provide sku protection and customer can reuse for returns, (2) *Plastic Bag* has water proof feature and a self-seal mouth. Features are high cost, water proof protection, difficult to reuse for customer return & difficult to store a pack station & (3) *Sandwich Bag* is mechanized pack concept. The concept consists of two kraft paper sections that engulf and complete a 4 side seal of a sku with a CO pack slip/invoice and applies a CO delivery label. Features are handles a high concept, high cost and additional computer programming, requires floor area, high productivity with few employees. Ship bag selection factors are (1) economics, (2) lead time, delivery and storage, (3) required space at a pack station, (4) employee or machine productivity rate, (5) time to secure bag, (6) space for CO delivery label & (7) customer acceptance.

S 10. Pick/Ship Carton Size Variations
To provide maximum sku protection, maximum conveyor travel path & delivery vehicle utilization & minimum filler material usage, your operation carton size options are (1) *One Or Few Pick/Ship Carton Sizes*. Features are easy to control on conveyor travel path, requires additional filler material/expense, requires fewer make-up machines, minimizes computer cube program calculations/process time, fewer carton number per delivery truck, improved storage quantity at a pack station, easier to control inventory & less made-up carton storage space at a pick line entry or pack station or (2) *Mixed Or Wide Variety Pick/Ship Carton Sizes*. Features are less filler material/expense, potential conveyor travel path problems, additional made-up carton storage space at a pick line entry or pack station, greater carton number per delivery truck, greater carton make-up machine number, additional storage space & increases computer cube program calculations/process time.

Delivery Label Ideas (DL 1 – DL 3)
DL 1. Vendor Ready To Ship Or Slapper Label
Vendor ready to ship or slapper label is a pack concept that improves your packer productivity, increase completed CO number and decrease ship supply expense. A vendor ready to ship or slapper label concept components are (1) ship carton that has exterior structural wall strength, sealed flaps and exterior package markings assure sku protection and ship label/slapper label attachment & (2) slapper label that is an envelop with a self-adhesive backing, enclosed CO pack slip/invoice & sales literature and several windows for your (a) CO ID line of sight and delivery address, (b) sku ID & (c) sku pick position and your delivery company assures that their scanner reads a slapper label and label is not removed as it moves over the sort concept. For maximum use, your slapper label length and width and thickness that permits attachment to your maximum sku number. Your sku pick and slapper label options are (1) for high volume sku to bulk pick and have a sample sku ID pre-scanned to each CO ID and stuffed into an envelop. All completed envelops are delivered with the bulk picked sku to a fast pack line for slapper envelop to a sku & (2) for low volume sku at a pick position, with a slapper envelop a picker scans a sku ID and CO ID and a slapper envelop is attached to a sku.

DL 2. Customer Order Pack Slip/Invoice As A Slapper Envelop, Tape Or Wrap
CO pack slip/invoice as a slapper envelop, tape or wrap are two fast pack activity options to secure a CO pack slip/invoice onto a CO carton that increases your packer productivity and increases your completed CO number. A fast pack activity has a clerk pre-scan skus to a CO ID and CO pack slips/invoices are delivered to your fast pack line. Your secure options are based on your CO type, sku size, sku volume, customer acceptance, economics and freight company acceptance. *Slapper Envelop* has a CO pack slip/invoice & sales literature that are placed into an envelop with a self-adhesive back and is placed onto a carton exterior. Features are additional envelop cost, with

windows is used a pick instruction, envelop block some CO pack slip/invoice data and employee or machine applied to carton. *Tape* concept uses clear/transparent self-adhesive tape and has your pre-scanned CO pack slips/invoice folded and sent to a fast pack line. After a CO pack slip/invoice is placed onto a carton, tape is employee or machine applied to secure a CO pack slip/invoice onto a carton surface. Features are with CO pack slips/invoices on a carton surface have potential difficulty to assure accurate and high productive tape activity and CO pack slip/invoice folded face to have no important CO information. *Wrap* concept uses clear/transparent plastic sheet and has your pre-scanned CO pack slips/invoice folded and sent to a fast pack line. After a CO pack slip/invoice and sheet are placed onto a carton, an employee or conveyor directs each carton through a shrink wrap (heat) tunnel that has a plastic sheet secure a CO pack slip/invoice onto a carton surface. Features are with CO pack slips/invoices on a carton surface have potential difficulty to assure accurate activity, requires an electric heat tunnel and electric expense and CO pack slip/invoice folded face to have no important customer information.

DL 3. Peal-Off Label

A peal-off label is a pick and pack activity idea that improves packer productivity and when your CO ID on a pick carton does not match your CO ID/delivery label on a ship carton location, it allows you to place your CO ID in carton pick location and at your pack station to transfer a CO ID from a pick carton location to a ship carton location. A peal-off label has two self-adhesive labels. The first self-adhesive label is large and has a second (CO ID) self-adhesive label on its face and is applied to a carton pick location. A packer removes a CO ID label from the carton self-adhesive label and places a CO ID in a ship carton location. The first or large self-adhesive label remains on your CO carton or is removed and thrown in the trash. Features are satisfies both pick and ship label location requirements, slightly higher label cost, requires a packer activity and used with a separate CO pack slip/invoice and delivery label print concept.

Shipping Supplies Ideas (SS 1 – SS 4)

SS 1. Replenishment Ship Supplies Before & On Breaks

Re-supply your pack station ship supplies by a supply replenishment employee has a ship supply replenishment employee assure each pack station has sufficient ship supply quantity for your customer order wave CO number. Ship supply items are tape, special labels, filler material such as paper sheets, paper roll, bubble sheet or bubble glove. Your ship supply replenishment activity occurs during prior to your pack activity start-up. During pack activity breaks/lunch or other down times. When compared to a packer non-productive walk time to get ship item re-supply, replenishment employee activity means higher packer productivity & increase completed CO number.

SS 2. Re-Supply Your Pack Station Ship Supplies By Ship Supply Replenishment Employee

Re-supply your pack station ship supplies by a supply replenishment employee has a ship supply replenishment employee assure each pack station has sufficient ship supply quantity for your CO wave CO number. Ship supply items are tape, special labels, filler material such as paper sheets, paper roll, bubble sheet or bubble glove. Your ship supply replenishment activity occurs during prior to start-up. breaks, lunch or other pack station down times. When compared to a pack non-productive walk time to get ship item re-supply, a replenishment employee activity means higher packer productivity and increase completed CO number.

SS 3. Know & Where To Store Your Ship Supplies Safety Stock

Where to store your ship supplies safety stock is an idea that has your ship supply safety stock (from your historical data, you determine each ship supply most frequent or peak day usage & vendor lead time) in a non-vital area. Non-vital storage is not adjacent to your pack or pick area. Your non-vital storage options are (1) in your main remote dense storage location that does not require over-the road shuttle costs but requires sq ft & (2) in your off-site storage facility that requires shuttle cost & use dense storage concepts.

SS 4. Pack Station Ship Supply Reserve Locations

Pack station ship supply reserve locations is a concept that maintains packer productivity and assures a constant ship supply flow to your pack stations. Whenever possible there are sufficient floor level positions for each ship supply item that permits an employee quick access to a ship supply item for transport to a pack station. Between your two pack station rows, your ship supply reserve locations are (1) *Single Rack Row* that is two forklift truck aisle and one side protection netting on elevated positions. Feature is lowest space utilization due to two wide forklift truck aisles, (2) *Back To Back Rack Rows* that have two wide forklift truck aisles. Feature is poor space due to two wide forklift truck aisles & (3) *Single Off-Set Rack Row* that has one wide forklift truck aisle and one personnel aisle. A personnel aisle is adjacent to one pack station row and elevated positions have protective netting. Feature is best space utilization with one wide forklift truck aisle.

Tape & Tapers Ideas (TT 1 – TT 3)
TT 1. Hand Taper Or Machine Taper
Hand tape or machine tape a CO package are options that impact your packer productivity, CO flow and secured packages with self-adhesive tape strand. *Hand Tape* option has a pick line or packer transfer a CO sku transfer to a bottom sealed container and transfer a completed CO container onto a conveyor travel path. As a CO container travels on a conveyor travel path, prior to a tape machine a gap is pulled between 2 containers for tape machine entry. *Carton Under A Tape Machine* Control has one tape strand applied to a carton top flaps. Tape machines are available as (1) *Fixed Position* Or *Manual Adjustable Machine* that handles a narrow carton height range and has a higher tape carton rate and (2) *Random Machine* that places one tapes strand on a carton top flaps and handles a wide carton size range with a slight lower tape carton rate. With both machine tape machine types, your picker or packer CO delivery label placement on a carton top flaps and tape on a carton does not cover a label that creates potential CO ID read problem. Other features are one tape strand on each package, one time cost, requires an electric and/or air supply, down-time to replace an empty roll with a full tape roll and requires space to complete tape replacement and maintenance. A hand tape concept has a packer with a self-adhesive dispenser apply one or multiple tape strands per carton. At a pick line end or pack station, an employee applies a tape strand that does not cover a CO delivery label or after a tape strand placed onto a carton places a CO delivery label. Features are handles a wide carton size range, allows one or multiple tape strands per package, no warehouse space and at each tape station for maximum tape employee productivity spare tape dispensers.

TT 2. Gummed Or Self-Adhesive Tape
Gummed or self-adhesive tape are a CO container manual seal/tape options that secure a carton top & bottom flaps. *Gummed Tape* requires a water brush to activate tape. A gummed tape machine occupies a pack table surface and at each pack station requires a reserve bottle water supply. As a packer handles a moist gummed tape strand, there is potential for a gum adhesive on an employee hands to be transferred onto a sku and tape strand side to cut an employee fingers. If an electric tape machine is used an electric outlet is required at each pack station. As a gummed tape roll becomes smaller, a gummed tape strand becomes more difficult to handle and apply to a carton. *Self-Adhesive Tape* is used with a hand held tape dispenser. To tape a carton, a packer secures a tape strand end to a carton and moves a dispenser over a carton flaps. For maximum packer efficiency each pack station has spare tape dispensers and extra tape rolls. Features are used at any location, easier to handle a wide carton size mix and less potential employee finger cuts and glue damage to skus.

TT 3. Do Not Over Tape
How many tape strands and a tape strand length (extension over a carton two edges) is policy that is established by your company to assure secured carton surfaces. With a machine formed carton and top sealed carton there is one strand on bottom flaps and one strand on the top flaps. An employee formed carton has typically one tape strand on the bottom and top surfaces. For a heavy sku, most operations allow a packer to add 2 to 3 tape strands bottom and top flaps. Tape strand extension over a carton top or bottom edges assures that a tape strand is secured onto a carton. A CO carton with minimal and sufficient tape strands maintains your tape expense and assures that your best package presentation to customer for increase customer satisfaction.

Filler Material Ideas (FM 1 – FM 4)
FM 1. Employee Crushed Light Colored Paper Instead Of Gray Colored Paper, Peanuts & Recycle
Paper sheet or peanuts are popular package filler material that is used to fill voids in a CO container.

(1) *Peanut* is formed material that are employee hand or gravity/air blown through a funnel into a CO container. To complete a gravity/air blown fill activity, a packer positions a CO container for filler material transfer by lower a carton flap and assures a funnel is located over a container. With a tall carton, there is some difficulty to position a funnel inside a container. During filler material transfer, an employee spreads the filler material inside a container. If there is extra filler material in a container, your packer re-cycles extra filler material into the next CO container. A packer hand transfer option has a low packer productivity due a packer uses a scope to transfer peanuts from a container into a carton. Features are (a) at most pack stations, over-flow peanuts on the floor require clean-up that is non-productive employee time, (b) gravity/air blown concept has a higher cost & (c) requires large storage bag. Paper sheets are pre-cut sheets (full size & half size sheet) or packer cut from a roll and transferred as crushed paper into a container. Light green or blue colored paper is preferred. To assure maximum packer productivity, rubber fingers and paper sheets are located on pack table shelves. Features are (a) requires small storage area, (b) less messy & (c) packer crushes the paper.

(2) *Paper Roll Or Paper Sheets* are your paper filler material options for a packer to transfer a manual crushed paper sheet into a package. A paper roll concept has a paper roll that is horizontal or vertical to your fill station or pack table. With a roll, a packer pulls a paper from a roll and cuts a paper sheet from a roll. At a pack/fill with a horizontal paper roll concept, a paper roll has a cutter blade and a packer can easily reach a paper end. Features are assure paper roll length & width & weight is easily handled by your replenishment employee and to complete a replenishment and rod insert into a paper roll some fill/pack station down-time. A vertical roll paper concept has a paper roll that is located along a conveyor travel path or pack station in a location that allows a packer to easily reach a paper end, cut a paper sheet and crush/transfer into a package. Features are some cut/ripped paper sheets have jagged ends, after cutting a sheet some paper ends are difficult to reach assure paper roll length & width & weight is easily handled by your replenishment employee and to complete a replenishment and rod insert into a paper roll some fill/pack station down-time. Paper sheets are vendor delivery full size and half size sheets that are placed at a fill/pack station on a shelf or table surface. As requires a packer picks-up a sheet (s) and crushes/transfers a paper sheet into a package. Features are no jagged edges, replenishment has low down-time, two sheet sizes means maximum fill and replenishments are easily completed to a pack station. Plain or colored paper filler sheets are your options that use paper to fill voids in a CO container and protect skus & satisfy customers. *Plain Paper* has a gray or white color that have customers feel less satisfied with paper filler material. *Light Green Or Blue Colored Paper* have customers feel more satisfied with paper filler material.

FM 2. Filler Material Types & Selection Factors
Filler material fills a CO container void to protect skus as a container is transported to a CO delivery location.   In most operations, at a pack station an employee or machine adds filler material to a container. For filler material re-use/re-cycle at a returns station an employee removes filler material from a container and transfers to transport concept. Your filler material options are (1) crushed paper from a paper roll, paper sheets or machine, (2) manual or funnel transferred peanuts or peanuts in a bag, (3) cardboard chips, (4) air bubbles or bubble sheets, (5) cardboard cubes, (6) foam in a plastic bag or manual or machine foam in place, (7) meshed cardboard, (8) notched carton with lip insert and (9) sku enclosed on plastic on a cardboard sheet. Filler material selections factors are (A) economics, (B) lead time, delivery and storage, (C) required space at a pack station, (D) transfer into a container requirements, (E) ability to protect sku and fill voids, (F) customer acceptance and (G) re-cycle as filler material or trash.

FM 3. Do Not Overfill
Do not over fill is your packer standard to assure that your packers complete a CO package with proper presentation. Proper presentation characteristics are that filler material fills all void spaces to protect skus from damage and there is no convex bow to a package top surface. Features are good packer productivity, low filler material usage and improve customer satisfaction.

FM 4. Paper Roll Or Paper Sheets
Paper roll or paper sheets are your paper filler material options for a packer to transfer a manual crushed paper sheet into a package. *Paper Roll* Concept has a paper roll that is horizontal or vertical to your fill station or pack

table. With a roll, a packer pulls a paper from a roll and cuts a paper sheet from a roll. At a pack/fill with a horizontal paper roll concept, a paper roll has a cutter blade and a packer can easily reach a paper end. Features are assure paper roll length & width & weight is easily handled by your replenishment employee and to complete a replenishment and rod insert into a paper roll some fill/pack station down-time. A vertical roll paper concept has a paper roll that is located along a conveyor travel path or pack station in a location that allows a packer to easily reach a paper end, cut a paper sheet and crush/transfer into a package. Features are some cut/ripped paper sheets have jagged ends, after cutting a sheet some paper ends are difficult to reach assure paper roll length & width & weight is easily handled by your replenishment employee and to complete a replenishment and rod insert into a paper roll some fill/pack station down-time. *Paper Sheets* are vendor delivery full size and half size sheets that are placed at a fill/pack station on a shelf or table surface. As requires a packer picks-up a sheet (s) to crush/transfer paper sheet into a package. Features are no jagged edges, replenishments have minimal downtime, two sheet sizes means maximum fill & replenishments are easily completed to a pack station.

Pre-Pack Activity Ideas (PPA 1 - PPA 7)
PPA 1. How To Determine Your Pre-Pack Sku & Volume
To determined your pre-pack sku and volume you look at your sku history, projections or work with percentages, consider best for single line/single piece COs & with good control consider single line/multiple pieces & pairs

PPA 2. Pre-Pack Activity Timing Options
Your pre-pack timing options are (1) *Prior To Sku WMS ID* occurs when your vendor has not identified each sku, (2) *Post Sku WMS ID & Prior To Storage Put-Away* is completed by your employees & occurs between your receiving area & storage area & (3) *Post Sku Storage Put-Away & Prior To A Pick/Pack Activity* is completed by your employees & occurs between your storage area & pick area.

PPA 3. How To Store & Account For Pre-Pack Skus
Your pre-pack activity inventory accounting options (1) *New Sku WMS ID & New Sku ID & Quantity*. An employee deleted old sku WMS ID, old sku ID, sku quantity & enter new sku WMS ID & sku ID & sku quantity. During pre-pack your sku new count per pallet/cart is the same as your old count, requires new printed WMS & sku IDs & WMS scan transactions, easy to implement with your WMS program & assures proper ID handling, (2) *Existing Sku WMS ID Remains, New Sku ID & Sku Quantity*. An employee leaves WMS ID on a pallet/cart that is associated with an old sku ID & old sku quantity. Requires WMS scan transaction & program to delete old WMS ID relationship to a sku old ID & accept old WMS ID association with a new sku ID & sku quantity. During pre-pack your sku new count per pallet/cart is the same as tour old count, requires new printed sku ID & WMS scan transactions, potential problems to implement in your WMS program & assures proper ID handling, (3) *New Sku WMS ID, Existing Sku ID Remains & Sku Quantity*. An employee removes WMS ID from a pallet/cart that removes relationship to sku ID & quantity. Requires WMS scan transaction & program to delete old WMS ID relationship to a sku ID & quantity & accept new WMS ID & association with an existing sku ID & quantity. During pre-pack your sku new count per pallet/cart is the same as your old count, requires new printed sku WMS ID & sku ID & WMS scan transactions, minimal potential problems to implement in your WMS program & assures proper ID handling & (4) *Existing Sku WMS ID Remains & Existing Sku ID Remains & Sku Quantity*. An employee leaves WMS ID on a pallet/cart that is associated with an existing sku ID & sku quantity with no WMS transaction & WMS program problems. During pre-pack your sku new count per pallet/cart is the same as your old count, requires good employee sku handling

PPA 4. Pre-Pack Line
Pre-pack line is pack idea to improve your bulk/'en masse' pick and pack productivity and in the future to increase your completed CO number. Pre-pack line sequential stations are (1) carton make-up and as required bottom fill station, (2) carton open and sku & sales literature transfer station & (3) your last station options are (a) seal a pre-pack carton and transfer onto a pallet or cart or (b) transfer, stack & nest open ship cartons onto a pallet or cart.

PPA 5. Pre-Pack Sku For A Slapper Delivery Envelop/Label

Pre-pack sku for a slapper delivery envelop/label as a slapper is reference to your small item or GOH pick and pack concept for single line/single sku COs to improve picker/packer productivity and increase your completed CO number. Your pre-pack sku number is based on your historical sales for a promotional sku single line/single sku COs. A pre-pack activity has 1 sku that is placed into a sealed ship container. A pre-pack activity starts with a sku bulk picked and delivered to a fast pack line or regular pack station. All completed pre-packed cartons are sealed ship containers and placed onto a pallet with a WMS ID that is placed/scanned to a WMS ID position. Sku quantity and scan data are sent to a WMS computer program for update. After your COs are received, for single line/single sku, your WMS computer program allocates and suggests a pre-pack sku on a pallet for your pick activity. Your CO pack slips/invoices and 1 loose sku are sent to scan station. At a scan station, for each CO pack slip/invoice an employee completes a scan transaction that depletes a sku from inventory & attaches a sku to a CO. A slapper sku components are sku in a sealed ship container and CO pack slip/invoice (a) envelop with several windows. An employee places sales literature & a CO pack slip/invoice with a CO delivery address in one window. Other windows have a sku pick position and CO ID. A completed slapper envelop is self-adhesive attached or glued to a ship container or (b) your sales literature & CO pack slip/invoice are place on a sku with a CO delivery address facing-up that is sent through a shrink wrapped tunnel to seal a CO pack slip/invoice to a ship container.

PPA 6. Partial Pre-Pack

Partial pre-pack is a sku bulk pick and pack activity that improves employee productivity, provides a smooth CO volume and increases completed CO number. Partial pre-pack is a pack activity that uses a pack line layout and philosophy as a fast pack line. From your historical sales and merchandise sales plan, a few days prior to a sku sales promotion and during a low volume CO day, a partial pre-pack activity has a WMS ID sku placed from a master carton into a CO ship container that has sealed bottom flaps and as required bottom filler material and non-sealed top flaps. At a pre-pack line end, non-sealed cartons are stacked onto a pallet. Per your inventory policy and practice, a full pallet receives a new WMS ID and sku quantity count and for single line/single sku COs your WMS computer CO process program recognizes a pre-pack sku first. After your pre-pack sku quantity depletion, for single line/single sku COs, your WMS computer CO process program recognizes a standard non-pre-pack skus. When your operation receives a high CO volume for your CO final pack activity, your operation uses a fast pack line to complete COs. Prior to your CO pack line activities, at a scan station an employee pre scans a sku ID to each WMS CO ID, bulk picked partial pre-packed sku and pre-scanned CO pack slips/invoices are delivered to a pack line. On a pack line your activity stations are (1) transfer a partial pre-pack sku onto a conveyor, (2) as required add top filler material, (3) insert a CO pack slip/invoice and sales literature into a container and (4) add a CO delivery label onto a container, seal a container top flaps and transfer a completed CO container onto a take-away conveyor for transport to your manifest station. As an option at your pre-scan station each CO pack slip/invoice and sales literature are placed into a slapper envelop. A slapper envelop is attached directly onto a container sealed top flaps. When compared to a regular pick/pack activity concept, a pre-pack concept smoothes your CO work activity over days that maintains your employee productivity, CPU & handles a high CO number.

PPA 7. Complete Pre-Pack

Complete pre-pack is a sku bulk pick and pack activity that improves employee productivity, provides a smooth CO volume and increases completed CO number. Complete pre-pack is a pack activity that uses a pack line layout and philosophy as a fast pack line. From your historical sales and merchandise sales plan, a few days prior to a sku sales promotion and during a low volume CO day, a partial pre-pack activity has a WMS ID sku placed from a master carton into a CO ship container that has sealed bottom flaps and as required bottom filler material and sealed top flaps. At a pre-pack line end, sealed cartons are stacked onto a pallet. Per your inventory policy and practice, a full pallet receives a new WMS ID and sku quantity count and for single line/single sku COs your WMS computer CO process program recognizes a pre-pack sku first. After your pre-pack sku quantity depletion, for single line/single sku COs your WMS computer CO process program recognizes a standard non-pre-pack skus. When your operation receives a high CO volume for your CO final pack activity, your operation uses a fast pack line to complete COs. Prior to your CO pack line activities, at a scan station an employee pre scans a sku ID to each WMS CO ID, each CO pack slip/invoice with your sales literature are placed inside a slapper envelop and bulk picked partial pre-packed sku and slapper envelops (pre-scanned CO pack slips/invoices) are delivered to a pack line. On a pack line your activity stations are (1) transfer a completed pre-pack sku onto a conveyor and (2) transfer a completed CO container onto a take-away conveyor for transport to your manifest station.   When compared to a regular pick and pack activity concept, a pre-pack concept smoothes your CO work activity over days that maintains your employee productivity and CPU and handles a high CO number.

Fast Pack Activity Ideas (FPA 1 - FPA 4)
FPA 1. Fast Pack (Single Sku, Pairs Or Multi Skus)
For bulk/'en masse/ picked skus, a fast pack line sequential stations are (1) carton make-up and as required bottom fill station, (2) carton open and sku and sales literature transfer station and (3) CO pack slip/invoice insert, carton top flap seal and delivery label attachment station and transfer to a take-away conveyor. An option is to use a slapper envelop that contains a CO pack slip/invoice and sales literature. With a fast pack by sku concept, you sku determines your carton size and you have potential to change carton size for each sku. The approach has potential to have minimal non-productive time for carton size change.   When compared to a regular CO pick/pack activity, a fast pack concept improves picker and pack productivity and increases your completed CO number.

FPA 2. Use A Slapper Envelop
A slapper envelop is your small item or GOH pick concept that improves picker/packer productivity and increases completed CO number.   When a sku is received in a vendor ready to ship carton or you pre-pack a sku into a ship carton, your pick/pack activity has an opportunity to use a slapper label on single line/single COs.   For 'A'/fast moving skus, after your preparation employee with a sku sample and CO pack slips/invoices completes a sku association to a CO WMS ID, your preparation employee places a CO pack slip/invoice into a slapper envelop. In a slapper envelop window appears a CO pack slip/invoice CO delivery address. Bulk picked skus and sealed slapper envelopes are delivered to a pack station. At a pack station, an employee peals off a slapper envelop self-adhesive back or sends an envelope through a glue pot and places a slapper envelop with glue on to a ready to ship carton that is transferred onto a ship conveyor/pallet. With low or high volume skus, your preparation employee places a CO pack slip/invoice into a slapper envelop with 3 windows. One slapper envelope window has a CO WMS identification, second slapper envelope window has a sku WMS ID pick position and third slapper envelop window has a sku WMS ID. At a pick position, a picker with a hand held scanner completes a sku pick transaction & CO WMS ID scan transaction that attachs a WMS identified sku to a CO WMS ID and completes a pick transaction. After a slapper envelope self-adhesive back is removed & a slapper envelope is placed onto a vendor ready to ship carton. A labeled carton is placed onto a picked sku transport concept.   Prior to implementation, you verify that your freight company can handle a slapper envelop.

FPA 3. Fast Pack By Sku
Fast pack by sku is fast pack idea to improve your bulk/'en masse' pick and fast pack productivity and increase your completed CO number. A fast pack line sequential stations are (1) carton make-up and as required bottom fill station, (2) carton open and sku and sales literature transfer station and (3) CO pack slip/invoice insert, carton top flap seal and delivery label attachment station and transfer to a take-away conveyor. An option is to use a slapper envelop that contains a CO pack slip/invoice and sales literature. With a fast pack by sku concept, you sku determines your carton size and you have potential to change carton size for each sku. The approach has potential to have some non-productive for carton size change.   When compared to a regular CO pick/pack activity, a fast pack concept improves picker and pack productivity and increases your completed CO number.

FPA 4. Fast Pack By Carton Size
Fast pack by carton size is fast pack idea to improve your bulk/'en masse' pick and fast pack productivity and increase your completed CO number. A fast pack line sequential stations are (1) carton make-up and as required bottom fill station, (2) carton open and sku and sales literature transfer station and (3) CO pack slip/invoice insert, carton top flap seal and delivery label attachment station and transfer to a take-away conveyor. An option is to use a slapper envelop that contains a CO pack slip/invoice and sales literature. With a fast pack by carton size concept, you carton size is constantly replenished to your fast pack line and you change sku. With the concept there is less

non-productive time for carton change. When compared to a regular CO pick and pack activity, a fast pack concept improves picker and pack productivity and increases your completed CO number.

Captive Tote Zero Scan Ideas (ZS 1)
ZS 1. Zero Scan Your Captive Warehouse Identified Pick Tote
Zero scan your captive warehouse ID pick tote at your pack station is a packer activity that has a packer to complete a tote warehouse ID zero scan transaction and send it your warehouse and WMS computer program. After your computer program receives a captive tote warehouse ID zero scan transaction, your warehouse and WMS computer programs breaks a CO WMS ID to a captive tote warehouse ID that permits you to use your captive tote warehouse ID to become related to another WMS CO ID. If a packer does not complete a captive tote warehouse ID zero scan transaction and for another WMS CO a picker completes another WMS CO ID and captive tote warehouse ID scan transaction that is sent to your warehouse and WMS computer programs and associates a both transactions and a WMS CO ID to a captive tote warehouse ID. On pick line and pack area, you have two another WMS CO IDs that are associated to one captive tote warehouse ID and creates potential pick errors.

Carton Or Tote Delivery To Pack Stations Ideas (CTDPS 1 - CTDPS 6)
CTDPS 1. Divert Customer Order Carton/Tote To Pack Stations
Divert a CO carton or tote to a pack station has a conveyor travel path divert a CO pick tote/carton onto non-powered or powered conveyor travel path for transport to a pack table. From your pick area, your completed CO containers travel on a sort conveyor travel path that moves containers through your pack area and did not sort containers are re-circulated on a conveyor travel path. Each pack table conveyor travel path has a full lane photo-eye that sends a block message to your conveyor computer to stop/start container divert onto a lane. At each pack station, a pack table conveyor travel path discharges containers with packer assistance onto a pack table. Features are no packer physical effort, high cost, re-circulation assures constant CO container flow.

CTDPS 2. Packer Pulls-Off Carton/Tote To Pack Table
Packer pulls-off CO pick tote/carton onto a pack table has your completed CO containers travel on a powered zero pressure conveyor travel path from your pick area through your pack area. With a re-circulation conveyor travel path, your conveyor travel path is past each pack station and as a CO container travels past a pack station, a packer pulls-off a container from a conveyor travel onto a pack table. At each pack station, your conveyor travel path (top of roller) and guard rail elevation permits a packer to easily transfer a container to a pack table. If no re-circulation, an employee or mechanical divert device transfers completed CO containers onto a dead end conveyor travel path that services pack stations on both sides of a conveyor travel path. With a mechanical divert concept, each lane has a full lane photo-eye that sends a block message to your conveyor computer to stop/start container divert onto a lane. Features are some physical effort, low cost, re-circulation assures constant CO container flow and dead end conveyor concept to have maximum container available to pack stations, a pack station occupancy is started at the container lane end and pack stations are occupied to the divert location as the last pack station.

CTDPS 3. Customer Order Carton/Tote Decline To Pack Table
Divert a CO carton or tote to a pack station is used with your CO container is on highest elevation. The concept has a conveyor travel path divert a CO pick tote/carton onto a non-powered or powered decline belt conveyor travel path for transfer onto a powered roller conveyor travel path for transfer onto a pack table roller queue conveyor. With a right angle transfer device concept, prior to each right angle transfer is pop-up stop device to assure container transfer onto a pack table queue conveyor. With a curve conveyor travel path concept, each pack table queue roller conveyor travel path has a full lane photo-eye that sends a block message to your conveyor computer to stop/start container divert onto a lane. At each pack station, a CO container ID faces a packer and a pack table conveyor travel path discharges containers with packer assistance onto a pack table. Features are no packer physical effort, high cost, requires small sq ft area and re-circulation assures constant CO container flow.

CTDPS 4. Customer Order Carton/Tote Incline To Pack Table
Divert a CO carton or tote to a pack station is used with your CO container is on lowest elevation. The concept has a conveyor travel path divert a CO pick tote/carton onto powered incline belt conveyor travel path for transfer onto a powered roller conveyor travel path for right angle transfer onto a pack table roller queue conveyor. Prior to each

right angle transfer is pop-up stop device to assure container transfer onto a pack table queue conveyor. Each pack table queue roller conveyor travel path has a full lane photo-eye that sends a block message to your conveyor computer to stop/start container divert onto a lane. At each pack station, a CO container ID faces a packer and a pack table conveyor travel path discharges containers with packer assistance onto a pack table. Features are no packer physical effort, highest cost, requires small sq ft area and re-circulation assures constant CO container flow.

CTDPS 5. Complete Customer Order Take-Away Conveyor
A pack station completed CO take-away concept is your cart or conveyor that is used to transport a completed CO package from your pack area to your manifest station. A completed CO take-away concept assures a constant CO flow to your manifest station that assures good employee productivity and maximum completed CO number. Your options are (1) *4-Wheel Cart Take-Away Concept* has one or several load carrying surfaces and is located adjacent to a pack station. After a cart becomes full, an employee replaces a full cart with an empty cart and moves a full cart to your manifest station. Features are low cost, handles a low volume and creates surges at your manifest station, (2) *One Package Conveyor Travel Path* is a declined non-powered or powered skate-wheel or roller conveyor is used to move packages from your pack stations to your manifest station. Features are low cost, constant CO flow, handles a low volume and services few pack station number & (3) *Powered Zero Pressure Conveyor* that travels past all pack stations and has a top or roller that is set at an elevation to permit packer to easily transfer completed CO packages onto a conveyor travel path. Photo-eyes communicate conveyor travel path status to a conveyor computer that controls CO package flow from your pack area to your manifest station. Features are designed to handle a high volume, travels past all your pack stations, high cost and permits controllable queue.

CTDPS 6. Empty Tote Take-Away Conveyor Or Floor Stack
A pack station empty tote take-away conveyor or floor stack assure are your concept options that a packer moves empty totes from a pack table. *A Powered Conveyor Take-Away Concept*, your empty conveyor travel path is placed in a stack with your picked CO container and completed packed CO container travel paths. Empty travel path considerations are at the highest elevation it requires an employee to transfer totes at a high elevation and at the lowest elevation, it requires an employee to bend for tote transfer. Your empty tote final design is determined by your inbound/picked CO container travel path and completed CO container travel path windows (heights). Features are additional conveyor cost, constant empty tote flow and minimal employee effort. *An Empty Tote Floor Stack Concept*, a packer transfers empty totes to a tote stack that is located at a pack table end. When a tote stack obtains a pre-determined height an additional tote stack is started and an employee moves tote stacks from a pack area to a pick area. Features are low cost, additional packer effort, does not have a constant empty tote flow and requires another employee activity.

Bulk Pick & Sort Ideas (BPS 1 - BPS 12)
BPS 1. Manual Bulk Or 'En-Masse' Pick
Manual bulk or 'en masse' pick is a small item or GOH pick concept that is used to improve your picker productivity and completed CO number. After you establish your pick concept work day or CO wave CO number, your computer printer prints a manual bulk pick instruction. Your pick instruction options are (1) paper document or (2) pick labels. For each sku your bulk pick instruction directs a picker to pick a CO wave total sku quantity. A bulk pick concept increases a picker's hit concentration and density with at one pick position multiple sku quantity and minimal walk distance between two pick positions.

BPS 2. Bulk Or 'En Masse' Picked Sku Sort Or Batched Pick & Sort
Bulk pick or 'en masse' is a small item or GOH bulk pick and sort concept that is used to improve picker and sort productivity and high completed CO number. After you establish your pick concept CO wave or CO number, your computer program prints a bulk or 'en masse' that is your picker instruction. For each sku, a bulk pick instruction directs a picker to pick a grouped CO sku total quantity from a pick position that increases a high hit concentration and density and minimal walk distance between 2 picks to improve picker productivity. With a pick and sort concept, your bulk pick sku quantity is for grouped CO number that is 9 to 12 manual sort positions. With a bulk

pick, transport, sort and final pick concept, your bulk pick sku quantity is for a grouped CO number that is determined by your CO wave quantity and by your sku sort position capacity. With a bulk pick, transport, sort and pack concept, your bulk pick sku quantity is based on your manual sort CO sort positions.   With a bulk pick, transport, sort, final sort and pack concept, your bulk pick sku quantity is based on 50 pieces per CO sort position that is 16 to 25 COs and your CO sort position number

BPS 3. Your Manual Sort Types & Concept Selection Factors
Your bulk pick sku and sort concept types and selection factors determine your sort concept for your best bulk pick and sort concept cost and handling volume. Your manual bulk pick sku sort concept options are (1) *Bulk Pick & Sort To A Tote/Carton In Cart Temporary CO Sort/Hold Position*. As a picker/sorter moves through pick aisles, a picker/sorter completes each sku bulk pick and sort activity. Features are (a) with some computer programming low cost, (b) picker picks an entire pick area, (c) difficult to handle a large volume, (d) maximum CO sort locations are 9 to 12 and (e) sort is completed to a slide/chute, carton or tote, (2) *Bulk Pick Skus & Sort By Sku Digit To A Sort/Hold Position* and with a CO pack slip/invoice final pick CO skus from sort hold position. Features are (a) low cost with some computer programming cost to create a bulk pick document and separate CO pack slips/invoices by a sku digit, (b) increase picker productivity, (c) handle all CO sizes and (d) individual COs are delivered to a check or pack station & (3) *Bulk Pick Sku & Each Sku Is Labeled With CO ID* that are placed into a tote and sent to sort lane for sku sort to a CO ID sort position. Features are (a) some cost for computer program to create and print CO ID labels, (b) sort area determines your CO sort position number per batch, (c) difficult to handle large CO and (c) skus are sorted into a slide/chute, carton and tote for delivery to a pack station.

BPS 4. Manual Bulk Pick & Sort
Manual bulk pick & sort concept has your computer batches/groups your COs to match your pick cart sort position number, for each batch/group prints a special bulk pick & sort document and CO pack slips/invoices for each batch/group. After a picker places cartons/totes into each sort location and IDs each sort location, a picker travels to a pick position. With a bulk pick & sort document, a picker bulk picks a sku quantity. Per each CO sku quantity that is printed on bulk pick document, a picker sorts a CO sku quantity to each position.   A pick & sort document lists each batch sku pick position and quantity and a CO sku quantity is listed under each CO ID. Features are (1) low cost, (2) some computer program cost, (3) cart sort positions, (4) easy to train & (5) picker picks entire area.

BPS 5. Manual Sort By Sku Instruction
Manual bulk pick & sort small items has your employee picker push a 4-wheel cart through pick aisles. Manual bulk pick & sort small items requires an employee to have a printed bulk pick document. Each bulk pick document shows pick position, bulk pick quantity, and sku description. At each sku pick position, a picker bulk picks a sku quantity and transfers a sku onto a cart hold position. In a sku sort area, you identify each sort position by a position ID that corresponds to your sku inventory ID number. For a sku sort activity, it appears on a sku ID label and for final CO pick activity, it appears on a CO pack slip/invoice document. Your sort locations are shelves and deck standard pallet rack positions. To have all possible sort and final pick locations, your sort area has 5 levels per shelf bay that provides 0 - 9 digits and two shelf bays per digit that provides 0 – 9. Possible sort location sequences are (1) MANUAL BULK PICK, SORT & FINAL PICK BY SKU LAST TWO DIGITS that has a sku first digit is a shelf bay with and last sku digit is a shelf level, (2) MANUAL BULK PICK, SORT & FINAL PICK BY SKU FIRST & SECOND DIGIT that a sku first digit is a shelf bay and sku second digit is a shelf level & (3) MANUAL BULK PICK, SORT & FINAL PICK BY SKU FIRST & LAST DIGITS that has a sku last digit as a shelf digit and next to last digit is a shelf level. A manual bulk pick, sort and final pick concept with CO pack slip/invoice improves your total employee productivity & higher CO completion number. Features are (1) requires a computer program to print bulk pick documents, (2) CO pack slip/invoice document is used in your final pick activity & (3) easy to complete a pick check.

BPS 6. Manual Sort By Sku
Manual sort by sku concept has a numeric/digit ID on each sku and a computer prints a bulk pick document and CO pack slips/invoices. After pickers bulk pick skus arrive in a sort area, each bulk picked sku is transferred to a

sort/temporary hold position. For maximum sku sort productivity, each sort location has digits that are related to a sku inventory numeric digits. Each sort location has two shelf bays with a total of 10 levels and each level has a numeric or digit ID. After all sku are sorted to sort locations, a clerk verifies all bulk pick documents are returned to the control desk and CO final pick activity is able to start. Final pick activity occurs with a CO pack slip/invoice and into a CO carton/tote. For maximum final pick productivity, your computer arranges and prints your CO pack slips/invoice in a numeric/digit sequence. The sequence matches a specific CO pack slip/invoice first sku numeric/digit concept that permits your CO pack slips/invoices grouped & distributed to a sort position. The concept has a CO pack slip/invoice first pick in a sort position. A completed CO is transferred to a pack station or sent to a check station. Features are low cost with shelves/racks, easy to implement & train employees & low computer cost.

BPS 7. Sort Instruction As Paper Or Label Instruction

Sort instruction as a paper document or label instruction is required to assure an accurate sort activity, high sorter productivity and increase completed CO number. A sort instruction is a human/machine readable symbology that directs an employee or machine sort concept to transfer a sku from a sku group/travel path into a temporary sort/hold position. A sort document is computer controlled printed that shows a sku bulk pick quantity and each CO sku quantity & is used in a pick & sort concept. A sku or CO ID/label allows a picker and sorter to complete pick & sort activities. Per your sort concept, a sku ID is vendor applied to each sku and a CO ID is picker applied to each sku. Both sku ID concepts allow bulk picked skus & an employee/mechanical sorter to complete a sort transaction.

BPS 8. Manual sort & Final Customer Order Pick By Sku Digit Design With Shelf, Decked Racks Or
   Pallet Racks

Manual sort and final CO pick by sku digit designs with shelves, decked racks and pallet racks has sufficient positions for 0 – 9 digits that improve sorter/final picker productivity and increase completed CO number. The approach allows you to sort bulk picked skus by a sku ID label and with a CO pack slip/invoice sku ID to final pick COs. Per your sku size, for very small skus you have 10 shelf bays to provide 1 shelf bay for each digit 0 – 9 and for regular size skus you have 20 shelf bays to provide 2 shelf bays for each digit 0 – 9. To provide picker direction, each two bays has one digit and has numeric IDs that extend outward into the aisle from a first bay first post and a second bay last position and an ID is flat against a top shelf. In a typical layout your shelf bay is 4 ft wide with 2 posts that are 1 in wide. With regular skus, you have promotional and large size skus that have few skus, your design has a decked standard pallet rack bay opposite each 2 shelf bays and has a floor level and decked level. Ten shelf levels per two bays allows shelves for 0 – 9 digits. To provide picker direction, each shelf has one digit numeric ID that is in a shelf middle and on a first bay first post and a second bay last position. To match a 2 shelf bay span, your rack bay span is 8 ft 2 in C/C that equals distance between a rack bay two posts center lines. Deck your bottom hand stacked/decked standard pallet rack level has your bottom (floor) level skus hand stacked onto a deck instead of two pallets. To provide picker direction, each rack bay has one digit numeric ID that faces the aisle and the bay both posts and an ID is flat against the top load beam. A deck is a solid wood, harden plastic or metal member with 1 in high bottom full depth runners evenly spaced to assure minimal deck bow. When compared to hand stack onto 2 pallets, a deck concept increases vertical open space by a nomimal 4 ins and allows a rack bay entire area used for skus that increases the usable space by 8 to 12 ins or one standard carton width. Deck and runner cost is equal to 2 pallets cost. Standard pallet rack bays are located at your back to back deck rack rows and are positions for promotional skus that are very few skus. Per your picker height, your rack bay design height & load beam arrangement has floor level for a 1 sku on a double stacked pallet or 2 levels for 2 skus.

BPS 9. Manual Sort Instructions

Manual sort instruction indicates to picker/sorter or sorter a CO picked sku temporary hold/sort position. A manual sort instruction assures good sorter productivity and accurate sort activity. With a manual pick and sort concept, a paper document shows a bulk pick sku quantity and each CO sku quantity. Features are (1) limited to a cart/tote company temporary hold/sort position, (2) requires a computer program to batch COs per your sort positions, (3) difficult to handle a large CO quantity, (4) requires additional pickers who have potential to walk your entire pick area & (5) requires cart queue at your pick and pack stations. A manual applied self-adhesive label from a sheet or roll label is applied to a picked sku. Each label has a CO ID with other company required information and the pick labels are printed in pick position sequence. All picked and labeled skus are placed into a tote on conveyor travel path or directly onto a belt conveyor travel path that transports skus to a sort lane. In a sort lane each sku CO ID is matched to a CO ID sort position. With a match a sku is transferred to a CO ID sort position. Features are (1) each sku requires a CO ID, (2) per batch, your CO batch number matches your sort position number, (3) requires a batch computer program, (4) potential for sku to loose a CO ID and each label must fit onto all skus and (5) requires label print time & (3) pre-labeled/ID skus with a bulk pick document and CO pack slip/invoice concept has your vendor place a sku ID on each sku. CO skus are bulk picked with a paper document & sent to a sort area. In a sort area by sort ID digit, skus are sorted to sort/hold positions. After sku sort, a final picker with a CO pack slip/invoice that list each sku ID digits picks a CO. Features are (1) requires a bulk pick document, (2) requires a CO pack slip/invoice with each sku ID digits, (3) handles a large CO number and wide sku mix & (4) final pick into CO carton.

BPS 10. Manual Sort By Sku Digit Position Design As Horse Shoe, Two Aisle Or One Aisle
Your sort by sku digit design assures that you have sufficient sort positions and cube capacity to handle your COr wave and permits a sorter/final picker pattern. To provide sufficient sort positions and cube your design has single or mix of standard shelves, deck racks or standard pallet racks. Your design options are (1) *Horse-Shoe* has only shelves and is used for very small skus. Shelves are arranged in a horse shoe shape with one shelf bay per each digit (0 – 9). As a sorter/final picker enters a horse-shoe, start is at a right side with four shelf bays (0 – 3), base with two shelf bays (4 & 5) and left side with four shelf bays (6 – 9), (2) *One Aisle Or Tunnel* that has shelf bays with two per digit (0 – 9) on a right side and for each digit (0 – 9) a decked pallet rack bay with a C/C dimension to equal two shelf bays. A sorter/picker starts at a first shelf/rack bay and progressively moves to exit end and (3) *Two Aisles* has the first aisle shelf bays on an aisle left side with two per digit (0 – 4) on an aisle right side and for each digit (0 – 4) a decked pallet rack bay with a C/C dimension to equal two shelf bays and a second aisle shelf bays with two digit (5 – 9) and for each digit (5 – 9) a deck pallet rack with a C/C dimension to equal two shelf bays. For maximum space utilization and improve sorter/picker productivity, the shelf bays are on the exterior and rack bays are on the interior. Options are (a) to create large cube or high volume sku positions, on a back to back decked pallet rack rows is to have standard pallet racks and (b) to allow an employee early exit to have a middle turn aisle in a decked pallet rack row that requires two additional shelf bays.

BPS 11. Pick By Sku Digit For Customer Order Final Pick Instructions
Pick by sku digit your CO final pick instructions improve final picker productivity and increase CO number. Your final pick instructions are (1) *Pick By Light* for each CO requires a pick position progression through all pick positions. Feature with multiple pickers difficult to provide picker progression, high cost and additional computer programming, (2) *Separate Paper CO Pick Document* that lists each sku and quantity. Features are additional ink and paper print expense and computer programming and (3) *CO Pack Slip/Invoice* that lists each sku and quantity. Features are no additional ink or paper print expense and no additional computer programming.

BPS 12. Pick By Sku Digit For Your Customer Order Pack Slips/Invoices Preparation
Pick by sku digit your CO pack slips/invoices preparation that has an impact on your final picker productivity and increased completed CO number. Your CO pack slip/invoice group options are (1) *Random Sku Digit Sequence* that has your computer program print CO pack slips/invoices on a random bases. The approach has potential for your CO pack slip/invoice first/last sku digits mixed as CO pack slips/invoices are given to your final CO picker. Features are (a) low final picker productivity due to additional walk to the first pick position, (b) simple computer printer program and (c) low completed CO number or (2) *Grouped By Your CO Pack Slip* first or last sku digit sequence that has your computer program print your CO pack slips/invoices and each first or last sku digit CO pack slip/invoice group is placed to match shelf bay digit. Features are (a) high final pick productivity due to no walk distance/ time for transaction completion, (b) additional computer printer program & (c) high completed CO number.

Batch Pick & Sort Ideas (BTPS 1 - BTPS 11)

BTPS 1. Manual Batched Pick

Manual batched pick is a small item or GOH pick concept that is used to improve your picker productivity and completed CO number. Batched pick concept has your computer to separate a work day or CO wave CO number into pre-determined batches/groups. A CO number per batch is based on your picker and packer productivity rates and employee number. In a batched CO pick concept, each sku within a CO group are in pick position sequence. With multiple picks for one sku there is increase in your hit concentration& density that increases your picker productivity with minimal walk distance between picks.

BTPS 2. Manual Batched Pick, Transport & Sort/Pack

Manual batched pick, transport & sort/pack concept is designed to handle a large sku volume and large CO number. During your pick activity, skus are bulk picked into totes/cartons or onto a belt conveyor. Your sku physical, fragile, crushable and potential edge damage characteristics determine your tote/carton or belt conveyor transport concept. With a tote transport concept, your induction station is designed to handle and move full and empty totes. With a belt conveyor transport concept, your induction station has a decline slide for manual or automatic induction. Your pick, transport and sort/pack concept, your manual or mechanized concept design is based your projected work day sku volume, CO number, labor cost, available building space and sort/computer equipment/program cost.

BTPS 3. Your Customer Order Manual Sort Position Number Sequence

A CO manual sort position number sequence impacts your sorter productivity and reduces your sort errors and improves accuracy. Your manual CO sort position number sequence has your lowest number at a sort lane entry, through a sort lane progressively increases and has your highest number at a sort lane exit. If your sort lane has sort positions on an aisle one side, your arithmetic progression is by odd number for sort positions on an aisle left side and by even numbers for sort positions on an aisle right side. If your sort lane has sort positions on an aisle both sides, your arithmetic progression has odd number sort positions on an aisle left side and has even number sort positions on an aisle right side. Features are for maximum positions, sort positions have numeric digits, large as possible digits on a white or yellow background and in a constant sort position location.

BTPS 4. Manual Sort By Customer Order Identification

Manual sort by a CO ID sku concept has a alpha character or numeric/digit ID on each sku. For each sku, your CO process computer prints pick/sort label and for a CO, pack slip/invoice with CO ID, sku & quantity and other company required information. On each pick label is your pick position and CO ID in largest possible print and black alpha characters or digits onto a white label face. If possible a large bold and clear printed CO ID is in the right hand and upper label corner. In your sort area, your assure that a large bold and clear printed CO ID is on each sort position front and per your company CO pack slips/invoices are distributed to each sort position or to a packer. In your pick area, a picker goes to a pick position places a label onto a sku. A labeled sku is placed into tote or onto a belt conveyor surface and transported from your pick area to your sort area. In your sort area totes or skus are moved past all sort positions. Your sort positions are (a) slide/chute, (2) tote or (3) ship carton. Your sort area transport options are (1) an employee carriers a tote, pushes a tote on a non-powered conveyor or tote is moved over a powered conveyor surface and (2) a belt conveyor. A sorter removes a sku from a tote or belt conveyor surface, reads a sku CO ID and matches a sku CO ID to a sort position ID. With a match, a sku is transferred to a sort position. Sort lane options are (1) *One Sorter* moves a tote or with a belt conveyor over an entire travel path that difficult to obtain good sort productivity due to increased walk distance or (2) *Multiple Sort Zones*, after zone completion in a sort zone, a sorter moves a tote or belt conveyor skus to a next sort zone that is easier to obtain sorter productivity. When we compare tote & belt conveyor sort transport concepts, (1) both require re-circulation or decline to the floor or dump into a larger tote, (2) tote minimizes sku damagel, (3) tote travels over a skate-wheel or roller conveyor surface & (5) belt conveyor has potential sku ID removal & damage.

BTPS 5. Manual Sort Lane Design

Manual sort lane design has an impact on your sorter productivity and completed CO number. Based on your CO wave sort batch number, your sort area design has one sort lane or multiple sort lanes. One sort lane features are all batched pick totes are sent through one sort lane, difficult to handle a high volume due to wait time for packers to transfer sorted COs from sort positions to pack and less complex transport concept. Multiple sort lanes has at least three sort lanes. One sort lane is used for your active sort batch. Second sort lane has sort positions full of completed/sorted COs. Third sort lane is available for next batch sort activity. Features are additional sq ft area, additional computer programming cost to process batches, conveyor or transport concept requires a manual or fixed/adjustable divert device and improved sorter and packer productivity.

BTPS 6. Manual Sort For Entire Sort Lane Or A Sort Lane With Separate Sort Zones
Manual sort for an entire sort lane or sort lane separated into sort zones are manual sort lane sorter length design options that assure good sorter productivity and improves picked sku flow. *Sort An Entire Sort Lane* has one sorter with a tote start at a sort lane entrance, walk through a sort lane aisle and with a partial full or empty tote exit at a sort lane end. If at the last sort position, a tote has non-sorted skus, your tote is returned to a sort lane entrance for another sort lane pass. Features are with multiple sorters per aisle, potential sorter congestion and potential low sorter productivity due longer walk distances for a sort transaction. *Separate Sort Lane Into Short Sorter Zones* has a pre-determined sort position that are allocated to each sort zone. A sort zone is assigned to one sorter employee. A separated sort lane into short sort zones, has your sort zone front employee receive a tote and review/complete all sku sort transactions & pass tote to next sort zone. Colored or sort zone number banners/flags on each sort zone start & end positions and 50% full tote help improve sort zone employee productivity. Features are higher sort employee productivity due to short walk distance & required multiple sort employees.

BTPS 7. Manual Sort Positions Across & Over A Converyor Or Behind A Sorter Aisle
Manual sort positions across/over a conveyor or behind a sorter aisle are your manual sort position options. Sort across/over a conveyor travel path has an employee sorter aisle that is adjacent to a sort conveyor. On the conveyor travel path far side are CO sort positions. As a sort employee moves a tote over a conveyor travel path, a sorter employee transfers skus from a tote to a CO ID sort position. *Sort Positions Are 2 To 3 High Above A Sort Conveyor* travel path and as required to access a sort position a sorter moves a tote on a conveyor. Features are limited sort position number, sort positions have a number sequence, to complete a sort transaction makes a difficult reach across a conveyor and to access all sort positions, a sorter moves a tote. *Sort Positions Behind A Sorter Aisle* or on an aisle open side concept has a sorter aisle between a conveyor and CO sort positions. If a sorter moves a tote through an entire sort lane, totes on a conveyor travel path are moved by a sorter employee through a sort lane. With a sorter zone concept, a sorter employee walks perpendicular between a tote on a conveyor travel path and CO sort positions. After reading a sku CO sort number, a sorter matches a sku CO number to a sort position CO number and transfers a sku into a sort position. CO sort positions are 3 to 4 high sort positions and allows a sorter employee easy and quick access to all sort positions. Features are sort positions with a number sequence, increase CO sort position number per aisle and easy sorter access to all sort positions, minimal sorter reach effort. Hybrid sort lane design combines CO sort positions across/over a sort conveyor and behind a sorter aisle. Features are sort positions have a number sequence with odd number positions on an aisle on side and even number positions on an aisle other side and maximum sort position number per aisle.

BTPS 8. Manual Or Mechanized Sort Locations As A Chute, Carton Or Tote
Manual or mechanized sort location options are slide/chute, carton or tote that improve packer productivity, increase completed CO number, retain skus in a sort position and assure sorter/packer access to sort positions. Your rectangle shaped CO sort position has the narrow width face as your sort position open/front. This means that your slope, tote or carton long dimension is a sort position depth that creates maximum CO sort positions per ln ft. Each sort position has sufficient space on a structural member for CO ID, structural members are designed for maximum CO sku weight and sufficient clearance for a sorter to complete a sku sort transaction. A sloped slide/chute sort position has a solid bottom and side walls and a lockable solid/window door on a discharge end. With a 5 to 20 degree slope, a slide/chute bottom surface a smooth bottom surface with a low co-efficient of friction to assure sku flow. Your interior cube at ½ of a position height matches your largest CO cube that has a sort position slide/chute depth is an important dimension. Features are higher cost, packer uses a carton or tote for sku transfer from a slide/chute position to a pack table, requires a lockable discharge end door and packer makes-up a

ship carton. A tote sort position has a solid or angle bottom side runners as a bottom surface & has meshed between two runners. Meshed side walls assure that skus are retained in a sort position. A tote internal dimension (cube) is designed for your largest cube CO and requires a replenishment employee to place empty totes into sort positions. Features sort position set-up employee, improve packer productivity due to easy transfer a CO to a pack station and handles a wide carton mix and CO size. A carton in a CO sort position to minimize potential carton bottom bow, it requires a solid bottom surface and solid or meshed side walls. For maximum sort position space utilization you have your carton side walls that are secured with rubber bands. Your sort position width, length and height allows your largest carton size in a sort position with sufficient clearance for a sorter to complete a sku sort transaction. Features are sort position set-up employee, additional employee activity to secure carton flaps, improve packer productivity due to no carton make-up activity & easy to transfer a CO to a pack station, handles a wide carton mix and CO size.

BTPS 9. What Is Your Manual Or Mechanzied Sorter Travel Path Height
Your manual or mechanized sorter travel path height is a key factor that determines your sort station design/elevation and clear space between your ground floor and ceiling bottom structural support member, sort position number and sort productivity. *With A Manual Sort Concept*, from a tote on a conveyor travel path, your conveyor elevation minimizes a sorter reach/transfer sku to a sort position. Your conveyor travel path is determined by your average sorter employee height and tote side wall height. A lower conveyor travel path provides additional height for your sort positions. To provide a sorter easier access to a tote interior, an option is to tilt your sort conveyor travel path that has your tote travel on a 'V' shaped conveyor travel path. A tote side and tote bottom rides on a standard non-powered roller sections. Features are potential lower tote utilization, used with a tote transport concept, additional conveyor cost and requires employee to adjust totes. *Your Mechanized Sorter Conveyor* travel path elevation is determined by your selected sort manufacturer standard height to complete a sku induction on an elevated platform and your sort position slide/chute, tote or carton elevation. Your induction platform height has sufficient clearance for your sku in-bound transport concept, an employee to complete an induction activity and your sorter scanner to complete a top scan transaction.

BTPS 10. Account For Your Batch Last Picked Sku
Account for your last pick in a batch/group CO pick & pack activities assure accurate pack per batch and maintain packer productivity. In your pick activity, your picker attaches a last batch picked sku ID to a sku that signals to a packer that a batched COs skus have been picked and sent to a sort/pack area. After a pack area supervisor recognizes a batch last picked sku, a signal is sent to a pick area to start picking a next batched skus. Batch last picked sku options are (1) sku color coded label with human/machine readable symbology that is applied by a printer or picker, (2) tote color coded label with human/machine readable symbology that is applied by a picker and (3) batch last picked sku or tote symbology is read by a scanner.

BTPS 11. Sort & Pack Station
Sort and pack station is a sort chute platform and pack table surface has area for a small item warehouse with a mechanized sort concept that allows your final sorter and packer to complete a CO final check and pack activities. Your sort chute platform and pack table combined surface has sufficient space for a sorter/packer to complete a final sort for an estimated 25 COs with 50 to 75 pieces. To complete a CO final sort & pack activity, a final sorter/packer with a CO pack slip/invoice completes a final sku sort and to complete a CO pack activity.

Batched Pick & Mechanized Sort Ideas (BPMS 1 - BPMS 15)
BPMS 1. Batched Pick Mechanized Sort Batched Pick, Transport & Sort
A batched pick skus are placed onto a transport and sorter travel path. A mechanized sort conveyor travel path that directs picked & inducted sku past all sort locations. A sort travel path with no re-circulation is a straight line with a sort travel path all did not sort skus decline.

BPMS 2. Mechanized Sort Manual Or Automatic Induction Station

Manual or automatic sku induction are your sku transfer onto a mechanized sorter travel path options. With both concepts, prior to a sort conveyor scanner and divert position a sku is placed with a sku or CO ID/symbology facing upward (correct direction) for a bar code scanner to read the symbology and cause an inducted sku to divert onto a CO sort position. Both induction concepts have skus delivered to an induction station as loose skus on a belt conveyor and slide/chute or skus in totes on a low/zero pressure roller conveyor. *Manual Induction Station* an employee physically transfers a sku from a chute/slide or tote direct onto an empty sorter carrier. Features potential for low carrier utilization, in-feed belt and tote conveyor controlled by full & partial photo-eyes and on a platform multiple induction lanes requires a large sq ft area. *Automatic Induction Station* has an induction employee physically transfers a sku from a chute/slide or tote direct onto first short belt conveyor of a 4 short belt conveyor lane. Four short belt conveyors pull a gap between two skus. Fourth/last belt conveyor transfers a sku onto an sort empty carrier. Features are requires additional computer program & cost, assures high sorter carrier utilization and on a platform multiple induction lanes requires a small sq ft area.

BPMS 3. Mechanized Sort Tote Delivery To A Sku Induction Station
Tote delivery to a sku induction onto a mechanized sorter impact your sort capacity and sorter utilization. Manual or automatic induction has an employee transfer a picked sku from your transport concept (slide/chute or tote) onto an empty sorter carrier or onto the first belt conveyor of an automatic induction concept. With a powered conveyor belt and slide/chute concept, a slide/chute end is at a height for an induction employee to easily complete a sku transfer onto a sorter travel path. Features are (1) potential sku damage or label lose, (2) lower cost, (3) less sq ft space, (4) less employee physical effort and (5) no transport device return travel path. With a powered low or zero pressure conveyor and tote concept, your skus are delivered to an induction station. Your tote presentation or conveyor travel path options are (a) flat that has an employee reach over a tote side wall, into a tote and transfer a sku. Features are (1) increased employee effort, (2) tote side wall top that allows an employee access to a tote and (3) empty totes are stacked or placed onto powered transport concept (b) tote tilted that has an employee reach into slanted tote and transfer a sku. Features are (1) less employee effort, (2) tilted tote side wall top that allows an employee easy access to a tote, (3) additional conveyor cost to control tote travel to and from a tilt position, (4) mechanical device to tilt a tote & (5) empty totes are stacked or placed onto powered transport concept.

BPMS 4. Mechanized Sort How Many Reads
How many reads is a mechanized sorter concept that is designed to maximize your sort concept sort rate. Since your sort conveyor travel speed is at the fastest speed and from a top labeled package your scanner reads a package height with a wide mix and requires your scanner to obtain a good read. The maximum good read assures a sort conveyor has maximum utilization. An over-squared label (black bar height equals total black bars and white spaces width) and good quiet zones (white spaces between first/last black bar and white paper) are two options with minimal cost to improve your good reads. If your scanner reads the same bar code that is sent to your sort conveyor and there is no packer sort, after X good read number you have a your sort computer program to have a repeated bar code package diverted onto a problem CO lane. Feature improves your sorter capacity & utilization.

BPMS 5. Mechanized Sort Automatic Induction Side By Side
To assure sorter capacity, carrier utilization and induction platform utilization has your induction station that is located on a 13 ft elevated platform that is above your floor. An automatic induction concept has a series of short belt conveyor lanes for sku singluation and transfer onto sorter conveyor travel path. To achieve sku induction, an induction platform is on a mezzanine. Since a mezzanine has additional cost and with possible sprinklers and light fixtures under a mezzanine, a mezzanine has a high cost per sq ft. To minimize a mezzanine sq fr requirement, you place your multiple automatic induction conveyor lanes as side by side conveyor lanes. With this arrangement your assure that your conveyor travel path have maintenance access to conveyor travel paths.

BPMS 6. Mechanized Sort Single Or Dual Induction
Single or dual induction are a powered sort conveyor travel path sku induction design options. Sku induction on a sort conveyor travel path has a sku CO ID or sku ID machine readable symbology that is read by a bar code scanner. A scanner sends each CO ID or sku ID to your sorter computer program that activates a divert device that

moves a sku from a sorter travel path onto a CO divert/hold station. *Single Induction Concept* has one clean-out position, carrier re-set station, induction platform and bar code scanner that inducts and scans all skus. After scanning, a sorter computer program has all skus diverted to sort positions. Features are low cost, simple computer program/cost, sort conveyor travel is designed as a single/straight line or endless loop travel path and does not maximize your sort conveyor travel path. *Dual Induction Concept* is used on an elliptical endless loop or rectangle shaped sorter travel path. Each short or rectangle shaped sorter travel path end has a clean-out position, carrier re-set station, induction platform and bar code scanner. This means you have induction platform A and induction platform B. After scanning skus at induction platform A, a sorter computer program has skus diverted to sort positions between induction platform A and clean-out & carrier re-set prior to induction platform B and after scanning skus at induction platform B, a sorter computer program has skus diverted to sort positions between induction platform B and clean-out & carrier re-set prior to induction platform A. Features are higher cost, more complex computer program/cost, sort conveyor travel is designed as a endless loop travel path and maximizes your sort conveyor and increases your sort capacity by 85%.

BPMS 7. Mechanized Sort Single Scanner With Replacement Parts Or Dual Scanners
A single scanner on your sorter travel path with on-site replacement parts or dual scanners on a a sorter travel path are options to resolve your scanner problems with minimal down-time and maintain your sorter capacity. *Single Scanner* with on-site replacement parts has your operation purchase and maintains key and long lead time scanner spare parts on-site. When you have a scanner problem, your scanner spare parts are available to resolve your scanner problem in the shortest time. Features are shortest travel path to first sort position, lower cost, minimal sorter computer programming and cost and some down-time. *Dual Scanners* on your sorter travel path has two scanners that are adjacent to each other on a sorter travel path. If your front/first scanner has a problem, you switch your scanner activity to a second/back scanner and your sorter computer program automatically adjusts for the new sorter travel scan and travel to the first sort position distance. Features are added scanner cost, longer sorter travel path to first sort position and minimal sorter down-time.

BPMS 8. Mechanized Sort Sorter Travel Path
Your sorter travel path is a mechanized sort conveyor travel path that directs picked and inducted sku past all sort locations. A sort travel path with no re-circulation is a straight line that at a sort travel path all did not sort skus decline to the floor and are manually returned to your induction station. If your sort travel path has did not sort sku re-circulation, your sort travel path has did not sku return on a conveyor travel path to your induction station.

BPMS 9. Mechanized Sort Employee Protection & Noise Covers
Employee protection and noise covers are plastic formed section along both sorter travel path sides that improve employee safety and reduces noise level. After a sort travel path is installed, plastic covers and sides are attached to a sorter travel path support members.

BPMS 10. Netting
Netting is a power conveyor sorter travel path safety option that reduces employee injury and sku damage. Netting is more commonly referred to as fish net or fabric/plastic meshed net with openings between strands. With faster sorter conveyor travel path speeds, wide sku characteristic mix, some 90 degree curves and diverters to move sku from a sorter travel path, there is potential for a light weight, tall or smooth surface sku to slide from a sorter carrier onto the floor.

BPMS 11. Mechanized Sort Single/Straight Line Or Re-Circulation Sorter Travel Path
Single/straight line or re-circulation sorter conveyor travel path are your sorter conveyor travel path options that assure good space utilization and sku flow. *Single Line Sort Travel Path*, your picked skus travel past your induction station and sort stations and did not sort skus are accumulated at your sorter travel path run-out. A run-out declines to floor level, at a pre-determined times or full & partial full line controls have an employee physically re-introduce or physically sort the skus. Features are low cost, handles a low sku volume and small CO number and in a building with limited space. *Re-Circulation Sorter Conveyor Concept* has did not sort skus automatically re-introduce to an induction/scanner by a conveyor travel path that are. Features are higher sorter conveyor & controls cost, larger building space & designed to handle a large sku volume & CO number.

BPMS 12. Mechanized Sort To One Direction Or Two Directions

For improved space utilization, a mechanized sort concept sort from sorter travel path options are sort to one direction or two directions. One direction sort options are (1) *Down Direction* that are Bombay Drop and Flap Sorter & (2) *Side Direction* that are sliding shoe, brush sorter, ring sorter, moving vertical or horizontal belt or tilt tray. Both side directions include tilt tray.

BPMS 13. Mechanized Sort Full & Partial Sort Lane Controls

Full and partial sort lane controls are a mechanized sort travel sort lane devices that assure constant sku flow, minimizes potential sku/equipment damage. *Partial Sort Lane Control Device* is located in a sort lane middle (sides or bottom) and when blocked by accumulated skus, the device sends a message to a computer that activates an alarm (noise or light) that signals an employee to remove accumulated skus. *Full Sort Lane Control Device* is a sort line start section (sides) and when blocked by accumulated skus, the device sends a message to a computer that activates a sort conveyor travel path not to divert a sku onto a sort lane and travel on a re-circulation conveyor.

BPMS 14. Mechanized Sort Sort Lane Door With A Plastic Or Meshed Window

Sort lane door with a plastic window or meshed window is used on a manual or mechanized sort lane discharge door that improves packer productivity and minimizes sku damage. As your manual or mechanized sorter transfers a CO sku into a slide/chute sort lane, skus queue against a sort lane discharge door. A solid discharge door restricts a packer sort lane vision. A plastic or meshed window discharge door allows a packer sort lane vision and determines how a packer opens a door.

BPMS 15. Mechanized Sort Mechanized Tilt Tray Sort Lane Sort Location Has 3 Sort Lanes

Mechanized tilt tray sort location has 3 sort lanes to assure continuous CO flow and accurate sort activity (batched/group sku mix). Sort lane design options are (1) 3 sort lane allows 1 sort lane for your present/active batch sort, second sort lane for next sort batch and third sort lane for a safety factor and (2) 3 sort lane has two flippers that creates 3 sort lanes and each flipper is open or closed per the batch. Features are requires additional sorter program, wider sort lane and with a flipper has long sort lane.

Bar Code Scanning Ideas (BCS 1 – BSC 2)
BSC 1. Hand Scanner With Battery Or DC Electric Line (See BSC 2. Page 18)
BSC 2. Fixed Position Scanner At A Pre-Determined Elevation (See BSC 9 Page 19)

Manifest, Load & Ship Activities Ideas
General Manifest, Load & Ship (GMLS 1 - GMLS 7)
GMLS 1. When Does Your Customer Order Delivery Clock Start

When does your CO delivery clock start is an operation factor that improves customer satisfaction. When does your CO delivery clock start is the number of days that a customer expects to receive a CO delivery. Your CO delivery varies per industry and company. Various clock time starts are (1) after CO receipt by your host computer, (2) after your pick/pack WMS or host computer receives an approved CO and (3) after your pick/pack activity receives a CO.

GMLS 2. Cube Your Delivery Truck

Cube your delivery truck is a delivery truck load idea that improves direct load employee productivity and good delivery truck utilization. A direct load activity has CO packages travel from a sort conveyor into a delivery truck. In a delivery truck, a load employee off-loads packages onto a delivery truck floor. With a WMS computer cube program that suggests a CO carton size your WMS computer program has data to determine a package number per delivery truck. To cube a delivery truck your WMS computer program requires a delivery truck internal cube & your desire utilization and program to total your CO package cubes. After your sort/manifest computer obtains a desire package number, your sort conveyor does not transfer CO packages to a delivery truck, Features are minimizes load employee non-productive time to squeeze cartons into a delivery truck & accurate manifest list for each truck.

GMLS 3. Zone Skip By Cart, Pallet Or Truck
Zone skip is an operation with a freight company that has several terminals (spoke and wheel) and allows you to unitize CO packages for a specific zone onto a full delivery truck, cart or pallet. A full delivery truck, cart or pallet CO packages by-passes your operations freight company terminal sorter concept & driven to your CO local freight company terminal or carts/pallets are transferred onto your CO local freight company terminal delivery truck. With a delivery truck strategy & you have medium volume, with your freight company approval 20 ft long delivery trucks are load for a zone skip strategy. Features are low delivery cost & shorten CO delivery time or customer service.

GMLS 4. Ship Label On Top, Side Or Front
A package CO ID ship label placement options are carton top, side or front. A package CO ID location assures employee or bar code scanner line of sight for maximum good read and accurate scan transactions. If your warehouse operation uses a RF tag, to complete a package WMS CO ID good read, a RF tag sends a signal that is received by a receiver and does not require line of sight. Most catalog, direct mail and TV marketing operations, the most frequent location is on a package top or side that satisfies your operational and delivery company employee or bar code scanner requirements.

GMLS 5. Freight Delivery Truck Or Day Manifest Sent To Your Freight Company
Freight delivery truck or work day manifest that is sent to your freight company are company manifest list options. *Manifest By Delivery Truck* has your sort/manifest computer receive and keep separate for each delivery truck. After a delivery truck is considered full, you have your sort conveyor discontinue sorts to a delivery truck and you have your computer complete a manifest list that is sent your freight company, Features are requires good co-ordination between your loading employees and sort/manifest computer, possible for manifested/sorted conveyor remain on a divert lane, assures security to compare your company manifest list to a freight company scan transactions and additional computer program and costs. *Work Day End, Manifest By Work Day* delivery has your sort/manifest computer compile a manifest list for one work day at a work day end that is sent to your freight company. Features are if partial full trucks remain at your dock, at a freight terminal difficult to assure accurate manifest. But can be resolved by your work day ends with your last full delivery truck that is entered into your manifest computer, assures security to compare your company manifest list to a freight company scan transactions and simple computer program with standard cost.

GMLS 6. Manifest Transaction On-Line Or Delayed Update Transfer
Manifest transaction on-line or delayed update transfer to your WMS computer and freight company are your manifest list transfer options that assures an accurate manifest for a freight company truck. After each CO WMS ID passes a manifest bar code scanner, each CO WMS ID is sent to your WMS computer and is considered physically shipped from your facility. *On-Line CO WMS ID Scan Transaction* has your manifest scanner transfer direct to your WMS computer. Features are on-line ship data and your WMS computer with capacity to accept all transactions. Second on-line CO WMS ID has your manifest scanner transfer direct to your WMS computer and your freight company computer. Features are on-line ship data and your WMS computer with the capacity to accept all transactions, requires communication to your freight company and allows your freight company to improve delivery truck plans. *Delayed CO WMS ID Scan Transactions* are sent to a warehouse computer that holds/accumulates scan transactions in a file. At a pre-determined time or per WMS computer capacity, accumulated scan transactions are released to a WMS computer. Features are less complex WMS computer program, fewer transfer messages and lower WMS computer cost.

GMLS 7. Floor Stage Or Stage In Racks
Floor stage or stage in racks along a dock area walls are your dock area options to provide temporary unitized pallets in positions and carts on the floor level and supply item storage positions. If a delivery truck is not available at a dock, staging allows your operation to continue and hold manifest packages for a delivery truck arrival. *Floor*

Storage requires floor area, no cost and requires a pallet truck or forklift truck. *Racks Along Dock Area Walls & Above Dock Doors* provide positions that are accessed by a forklift truck. Features are improved space utilization, requires a forklift truck to access positions and first load beam elevation height allows cart storage.

Manifest Activity Ideas
Manual Manifest Activity Ideas (MMA 1 - MMA 2)
MMA 1. Manifest By Hand Held Scanner
Manifest by hand held scanner is manifest activity that has an employee bar code scan each package WMS CO ID. A manifest activity registers each package WMS CO ID as it leaves your operation. Per your freight company requirement your manifest scan transactions are transferred by a paper document, diskette or on-line from your operation to your freight company terminal. A manual bar code scanner manifest concept has at a separate manifest station or at a freight truck door an employee with a hand held scanner read each package WMS CO ID on-line or delayed to your freight company. Features are good employee productivity, minimal errors, accurate/on-line/delayed data transfer and low cost.

MMA 2. Manifest At A Scanner Or At A Delivery Truck Door
Manifest at your scanner or at delivery truck door (delivery truck entrance) are locations to accept a package WMS CO ID scan transaction. Sort and manifest read a CO ID bar code at a sort conveyor scanner location due to sort conveyor divert onto a travel path that transports CO package into a delivery truck. Features are (1) requires one scanner, (2) minimal employees and (3) accurate scan transactions. To identify a package CO ID read/manifest & load problem, you compare your WMS computer CO IDs and number to your scanner (actual) WMS CO IDs & number. If your travel path has packages fall from a travel path, a manifest option is to have an employee hand scan each package CO ID as a package enters a freight delivery truck. Features are (1) requires a second hand held scanner & additional manifest transfer time, (2) additional employee & (3) accurate scan transactions.

Mechanized Sort Activity Ideas (MSC 1 - MSC 16)
MSC 1. Mechanical Sort Concept Types & Selection Factors
Mechanical sort concept types and selection factors assure that your CO package is diverted from a sorter travel path onto an assigned sort lane. Various sort concepts are (1) *Active Sorter* with a powered induction station, conveyor travel path and mechanical device that pushes/pulls a CO package onto a sort lane. Various active sorters are (a) cross-horizontal or vertical moving belt that handles both bags and cartons, (b) pusher diverter that handles carton CO packages, (c) powered belt diverter, pop-up wheel, chain, roller, belt that handles carton CO packages, (d) ring sorter that handles bag CO packages & (e) rotating paddle, (2) *Active-Passive Sorter* with a manual induction station, powered sorter travel path that tips or plows a CO package onto a sort lane. Various active/passive sorters are (a) tilt tray that handles both bag and carton CO packages, (b) nova sort that handles both bag and carton CO packages, (c) tilt slat that handles carton CO packages, (d) gull wing that handles both bag and carton CO packages, (e) sliding shoe that handles carton CO packages, (f) flap sorter that handles bag CO packages or low profile carton CO packages, (g) plow diverter that handles carton CO packages, (h) brush sorter that handles bag or carton CO packages and (3) *Passive Sorter* with a anual induction station with a powered sorter travel path that uses gravity to move a CO package into a sort station. Sorter type is a Bombay drop that handles a bag package. Sorter selection factors are (1) economics, (2) available building area and height, (3) bar code presentation, (4) CO physical characteristics and volume, (4) required sort lanes and sort lane design, (5) required electric power and other utilities & (6) direct load or unitize station.

MSC 2. Side Or Overhead Bar Code Scan Packages
Side or overhead bar code scan CO packages are options for your CO package ID location as a CO package travels on your sorter travel path past your scan station that assure maximum bar code good reads and scan maximum package number. On a sort conveyor travel path a package CO ID assures a scanner line of sight to a CO ID and on a load conveyor an employee light of sight to a CO ID. *Package With A Side CO ID* on a sorter conveyor has a side scanner complete a scan transaction and package orientation on a load conveyor requires a package CO ID face your load/unitize employee. Features are shorter scanner depth of field, potential fixed

scanner device that has a lower cost, potential lower picker/packer productivity due to it requires a CO ID that is placed on a package in a specific location and on some occasions low load/unitize employee productivity, due to a package with a CO ID not facing in the proper direction requires an employee to turn a package. *Package With A Top CO ID* on a sorter conveyor has an overhead scanner complete a scan transaction and all packages orientation on a load conveyor has each package CO ID face your loading/unitize employee. Features are longer scanner depth of field, potential moving beam scanner device that has a higher cost, higher picker/packer productivity due to it a CO ID is placed on a package top in any location and assures good load/unitize employee productivity, due to a package with a CO ID facing in the proper direction.

MSC 3. Employee Or Mechancial Induct (See BPMS 2. Page 147)
MSC 4. Manual Or Automatic Induction (See BPMS 2. Pager 147)
MSC 5. Straight Or Endless Loop (See BPMS 11. Page 149)
MSC 6. Single Or Dual Induction (See BPMS 6. Page 148)

MSC 7. Dual Induction For Separate Sort /Load Lanes
Dual induction for separate sort/load lanes is a sorter design concept that permits sorter flexibility.   With a top labeled CO ID package dual induction allows your sorter to handle both bags and cartons, side by side sort/unitize lanes, increased sort lane number. With dual induction, after your first induction station (A) CO packages are sorted to lanes and travel past a clean-out sort lane to assure each all CO packages are sorted and past a carrier re-set station that prepares a carrier for the next induction station (B).   After your first induction station (B) CO packages are sorted to lanes and travel past a clean-out sort lane to assure each all CO packages are sorted & past a carrier re-set station that prepares a carrier for the next induction station (A).   Features are requires top label packages, improves space utilization, maximizes sort utilization, permits zone skip and additional sorter & computer cost.

MSC 8. Separate Or Combined Mechanized Sort For Bags Or Cartons
Separate mechanized sort for bags or cartons has an operation use separate sort concept or dual induction for bags and carton that assure maximum sort and minimize package damage. With bags or cartons on sorter conveyor travel path, there is a wide CO package size, height, shape and weight difference. If bags and cartons are placed on the same sorter conveyor travel path, potential problems are with some sort concepts, low profile packages are not sorted by the sort device, difficult to assure a scanner light of site to all packages CO IDs, some bag and small size packages are difficult to convey and some carton packages are heavy weight and bags packages are low weight. *Separate Sorter Concepts* for bags and cartons, each sort concept is designed to convey and sort each package type. Features are additional sorter and conveyor costs and additional floor space. A hybrid (dual induction and separate sort location concept) sort concept sorts both bags and cartons. *Dual Induction & Separate Sort Locations* Concept has bags inducted on one scan/induction station (A), sorter completes all bag sorts prior to clean-out and re-set station and sorter carriers are ready to receive cartons and cartons are inducted on another scan/induction station (B), sorter completes all carton sorts prior to clean-out & re-set station and sorter carriers are ready to received bags.

MSC 9. No Customer Order Identification, No Read Or No Data
No read or no data is a manifest scanner activity that improves your security to have only packages with an actual CO ID entered into your manifest file and do not ship from your operation. A no read means that your manifest scanner did not get a good read and a no date situation occurs as a package CO ID is read by a scanner. A scanner sends each CO ID to a sort computer that compares a scanned CO ID to a WMS computer CO IDs that are in the files. If a manifest scanner does not get a good read, your warehouse sort computer does not add a CO ID to its manifest files and the package with a no read is divert to a special divert location & is not shipped from your facility. When a sort/manifest computer does not obtain a match, your sort computer diverts a package with no data is diverted to a special location.

MSC 10. Canceled Customer Order

Canceled CO is a manifest activity that improves your security to assure valid CO packages are send from your operation. After your WMS computer transfers a canceled CO WMS ID to your sort/manifest computer, your warehouse manifest computer file creates a canceled CO message for a specific CO WMS ID. After your sort conveyor or hand held scanner completes a CO WMS ID that is sent to your sort/manifest computer, your computer sends a cancel CO message to a hand held scanner or sort/manifest computer to transfer a WMS CO ID package onto a cancel CO sort lane that restricts a package from being shipped from your facility. Your warehouse staff assures that a canceled CO skus are transferred to a WMS ID pick-able position.

MSC 11. Delivery Date Sort

Delivery date sort is a sort activity that has your sort conveyor computer program receive CO package with a specific delivery date and to have a CO package diverted to sort lane and assure on a specific date that a CO package is transferred onto a ship conveyor. The strategy improves your customer service. After a sort computer program receives a delivery date CO ID and receives a scanner induction message (CO ID), a sort computer program has a delivery date CO ID/package diverted from a sorter onto a specific sort lane. At a sort lane, an employee physically and scans a CO ID onto a WMS ID temporary hold position that is sent and update in your WMS computer program. On the required delivery date, your WMS computer program lists all CO IDs for shipment. On a hand held scanner display screen or paper document, an employee transfers each delivery date CO ID/package onto your re-circulation conveyor for travel to your induction station that manifests & ships a date CO ID/package.

MSC 12. Did Not Sort Or How Many Times A Package Travels Around A Mechanical Sorter

A did not sort occurs on a mechanized sort conveyor with a CO package that is scanned, not sorted at an assigned location and is re-scanned. A did not sort package occurs due to a sort lane full condition or problem and creates re-circulation that lowers your sort conveyor utilization or completed sort numbers. An option to remove a did not sort package from a sort conveyor is to have sort conveyor computer program to register a package WMS CO ID X number times (did not sort) and to have your sort conveyor computer to activate a sort device for package sort/transfer onto a did not sort lane. Your package is manual manifest scanned and transferred to a delivery truck.

MSC 13. How To Get Good Scanner Reads

How to get good scanner reads is a mechanized sorter concept that is designed to increase your sorter utilization or sort rate. Since your sort conveyor travel speed is set at the fastest travel speed and your scanner reads a top labeled package height with a wide mix and direction of travel, your bar code scanner is required to obtain maximum reads. Your maximum good reads result from over-squared label (bar code height equals total bar bars & white spaces width), good quiet zones (white space between a label first and last black bars and label paper edges and assures your package heights are within your scanner depth of field.

MSC 14. Control Your Carton Travel On Your Sort Lane Decline Conveyor Travel Path

Control your carton travel on your sort lane decline conveyor assures controlled carton travel and minimizes damage. After your carton divert onto a sort lane, there is potential for fast carton travel over a decline conveyor travel path and to have a heavy carton crash and push a light weight carton onto a queued carton. Your carton control options are (1) *Tilt Your Roller Conveyor Travel Path* that has carton slide against the low side guard. A carton side rubbing against a side guard slows your carton travel speed. Features are low cost and slows heavy and light weight cartons, (2) *Restrict Pre-Determined Rollers Turning* on your decline roller conveyor travel path that momentarily restricts or slows carton travel. Features are low cost and slow heavy and light weight cartons and (3) *Plastic Stripes* above a decline roller conveyor travel path and extend downward to a pre-determined height to come in contact with a specific carton height and slow carton travel. Features are low cost and slow tall carton travel.

MSC 15. Over & Under Sort Conveyor Travel Path

Over and under sort conveyor travel path is used with an endless loop sorter travel and in a building dock area with limited space. An over & under sorter conveyor travel path has after an induction station, a sorter travel path travel at a pre-determined elevation past all sort lanes, completes a 360 degree turn, makes an elevation (higher or lower) change to return travel to an induction station & makes an elevation change prior to an induction station. Features are elevation is per sorter manufacturer, fits into a building & sort lanes are unitize stations & direct load concept.

MSC 16. Side By Side Sort/Unitize Lanes
Side by side sort/unitize lanes are used in a unitized onto a cart concept that provides maximum unitize positions, good sorter productivity, good space utilization and maximum sorter utilization. A side by side sort concept is a closed loop sorter travel path that on the travel outward from an induction platform a sorter diverts top labeled CO packages onto one sort lane and after a sorter travel path 360 turn/second induction station that on the return travel to the first or induction station a sorter diverts top labeled cartons onto another sort lane. A second sort lane directs cartons over a sort lane curve and onto a sort lane that is adjacent to the first sort lane. Each sort lane has photo-eyes that stop/start a sorter divert device. Features are some additional conveyor cost, extra unitize stations and top labeled CO package.

Load Activity Ideas (LA 1 – LA 9)
LA 1. Unitize Onto A Cart At A Conveyor End Or Side
Unitize onto a cart at a conveyor end or side are your unitize options that assure package flow and good unitize productivity. Your conveyor travel path between your sort conveyor and unitize conveyor has photo eyes that start/stop sort conveyor divert devices. If your operation has few delivery locations or ship sort locations or sorted at your freight company terminal, *Unitize At Your Conveyor End* assures good employee productivity and space utilization. Features are requires less sq ft area, requires sufficient space between dock door and conveyor end for employee work station, cart (s) & travel aisle, maximum sort/conveyor lanes per ln ft. If your operation has multiple sort or ship sort locations and your freight company zone skips by your freight local terminal sending a full cart direct to a another freight company terminal, *Unitize On Your Conveyor Side* improves your customer service and lowers cost. Features are provides a greater sort locations along a unitize conveyor, provides fewer sort lanes, additional cost, requires two employee work stations, carts and aisles space between two unitize conveyor lanes, requires on-time empty transfer to a unitize conveyor lane.

LA 2. Load Conveyor Queue Or Where Is Your Sort Conveyor Travel Path
Load conveyor queue or where your sort conveyor travel path is design idea that is used to assure good loader employee productivity and package flow. Load conveyor queue is low or zero pressure conveyor travel path that is located prior to your direct load conveyor or unitize station. If your loading or unitize activity does not match your load/unit activity, a queue conveyor section provides temporary hold area for scanned and sorted CO packages and with a surge to one sort lane reduces potential did not sort/re-circulation. Your sort conveyor travel path speed (250 to 300 ft pr hr) is faster than your direct load conveyor travel speed (65 to 80 ft pr hr), there is potential for CO package queue. Load/unitize conveyor queue travel path options are (1) sort conveyor travel path above your load doors, divert lanes extend toward your dock area rear wall, make a 360 degree turn onto a decline & queue conveyor section for travel onto a direct load conveyor or unitize station. Features are provides maximum queue, additional cost and ceiling structural designed for conveyor load support & (2) sort conveyor travel path is along your dock area rear wall, divert lanes extend toward your loading doors & decline to a load conveyor and unitize station. Features are minimal queue, low cost & ceiling designed for conveyor load support.

LA 3. Unitize Or Direct Load
Unitize or direct load are an operations CO package load/ship options to assure package flow and good loader productivity. After your manifest and sort activities, your unitize or direct load activity is determined by your freight company requirements and assures each CO package is transferred onto a freight company delivery truck. *Unitize Activity* occurs on your dock area with empty carts or pallets located along a sort lane and has an employee transfer CO packages onto a cart or pallet. Your dock space design allows empty carts/pallet placed at a unitize station and full carts/pallets transferred onto a freight company truck. Features are permits CO package sort by a freight company criteria that permits a low volume operation to utilize zone skip, additional space for unitize stations and cart/pallet storage area or use a freight company truck that uses a dock position, each dock position requires a

dock device to bridge a gap between dock and delivery truck and a dock light and matches your freight company delivery requirement. *Direct Load Activity* has CO package travel on your sort lane onto a fixed position or mobile conveyor travel path that extends into a freight company truck. In a freight company truck, an employee transfers CO packages onto a freight company truck floor or onto another package. Direct conveyor travel path concepts are belt, roller or skate-wheel conveyors. Features are permits CO package sort by a freight company criteria that permits a high volume operation to utilize zone skip, space for extendable or fixed position direct load conveyor that means less required dock space, electric outlet and a dock light.

LA 4. Light Your Delivery Truck (See DAE 1 Page 27)

LA 5. Load On The Floor, 4-Wheel Cart Or Pallet
Load your CO packages onto a delivery truck floor, in 4-wheel carts or on pallets are delivery truck loading options that assures full delivery trucks, maximum load productivity and minimal package damage. *Floor Load Concept* uses an extendable conveyor travel path for an employee to transfer CO packages from a conveyor travel path onto a delivery truck floor or another package top. CO packages are stacked to your load employee's highest reach. Features are maximum delivery truck utilization, difficult to ship bags, requires longest load time, to load and unload requires an extendible conveyor with a cost, bottom package of stack has potential damage and requires a high volume for zone skip with 20 ft trucks offer an opportunity. *4-Wheel Cart Concept* has an unitize employee place CO cartons/bags from a unitize station into a cart cavity. Full carts at a unitize station are employee pushed into a delivery truck and an empty cart is transferred to a unitized station. Features are packages secured into a cart cavity, empty carts require a staging area or are pushed from a delivery truck onto an unitize area, added cart cost, lower delivery truck utilization due to wheel and truck door clearance space requirements, each dock requires dock leveler/board and requires an employee to load/unload carts. *Pallet Concept* has an unitize employee place CO cartons/bags from a unitize station onto a pallet. Full pallets at a unitize station are employee with a pallet truck or forklift truck are transferred into a delivery truck and empty pallets are transferred to a unitized station, Features packages are some pallets are secured into a cart cavity, empty pallets require a staging area or are transferred from a delivery truck onto an unitize area, very low cost, lower delivery truck utilization due to low pallet height that does occupy the entire space, each dock requires dock leveler/board and requires an employee with a pallet truck or forklift truck to load/unload carts.

LA 6. Captive Freight Company Trucks
Captive freight company truck means your freight company has dedicated delivery truck to transfer your company packages from your operation to their terminal and used to bring customer returns or empty trucks to your operation. A captive truck strategy with your freight company approval, you install roller or skate-wheel conveyor travel path along each delivery truck left side as a truck is at a dock. With a level non-powered roller conveyor travel path allows packages loaded/unloaded between a delivery truck and dock area conveyor. With a level non-powered skate-wheel conveyor travel path allows packages loaded onto a delivery truck from your dock area conveyor. If skate-wheel conveyor is used to unload a delivery truck, there is potential skate-wheel damage from carton placement onto a conveyor. Features are some additional cost, improve loader/unloader productivity and less extendable dock conveyor length and cost.

LA 7. Direct Or Fuild Load Options
Direct or fluid load options assure that your CO package is transported from a divert lane into a delivery truck. Inside a delivery truck, an employee transfers a CO package from a conveyor travel path onto a delivery truck floor or another package. Various direct load concepts are (1) non-powered manual nesting or retractable and extendible skate-wheel straight or flexible conveyor travel path. The concept is with lockable/unlockable rear wheels mobile between docks, handles carton CO packages and has a low cost, (2) non-powered manual nesting or retractable and extendible roller conveyor travel path. The concept is with lockable/unlockable rear wheels mobile between docks handles carton CO packages and has a low cost, (3) manual & electric powered nesting or retractable and extendible skate-wheel conveyor travel path, (4) manual & electric powered nesting or retractable and extendible skate-wheel conveyor travel path, (5) mobile position & electric powered nesting or retractable and

extendible powered belt conveyor travel path. The concept services multiple/2 docks, handles bag and carton CO packages and has a high cost, (6) fixed position & electric powered nesting or retractable powered belt conveyor travel path. The concept services one dock, handles bag and carton CO packages and has a high cost & (7) electric powered extendible or retractable belt conveyor with a fixed support for a belt conveyor. The concept services one dock, handles bag & carton CO packages with a high cost.

LA 8. With Fixed Direct & Pallet Truck Loading Set Conveyor To The Side
With mixed direct and pallet truck load activity, you set your direct load conveyor to a delivery truck side that permits loading flexibility and improves loader productivity. With a mix CO package load concept, your dock area direct load conveyor location permits a conveyor to extend into a delivery truck and allows a pallet to travel over a dock leveler into a delivery truck. For maximum dock flexibility, your direct load conveyor is set on your dock in a location that allows your extendible conveyor to run along a delivery truck right side as you face a truck at your dock.

LA 9. Off-Load A Manifested & Loaded Customer Order Package
Off-load a manifested and loaded WMS CO ID package is a ship dock activity that assures an accurate manifest for loaded WMS CO ID packages on a delivery truck. After a manifested WMS CO ID package is physically placed into a delivery truck, a WMS CO ID package is considered shipped to a customer.   With a full delivery truck at your dock and your warehouse staff requires to place other WMS CO ID packages onto a delivery truck, your warehouse staff removes manifested and loaded WMSCO ID packages. To assure an accurate manifest of WMS CO ID packages, your staff off-loads and hand scans each off-loaded WMS CO ID package. Each WMS CO ID package scan transactions is transferred to your WMS computer that removes each CO WMS ID from a manifest list.   To track off-loaded WMS CO ID packages, each WMS CO ID package is scanned and physically transferred to a WMS ID temporary hold position that is updated in a WMS computer file.

Returns Activity Ideas
General Return Ideas (GRI 1 – GRI 5)
GRI 1. Where To Hold Your Customer Order Look-Up Table
Where to hold your CO look-up table assures a returns process employee good productivity. To complete a return, a process employee requires quick and accurate access to your CO detail information that includes CO ID number, sku description, sku quantity, manufacture lot number and date. Your CO look-up table location options are in your (1) *Host Computer* that is not preferred due to difficult to have on-time access from a host computer completing other department activities and security issues. But is used to access old COs, (2) *WMS Computer* is a preferred computer after you complete a survey for time period that determines your returns life cycle or day number after a CO manifest for a r return received at your returns process station. Life cycle determines a day number for COs that are retained in your WMS computer and reduces your WMS computer look-up time. If an old return is received at a process station, your returns employee accesses your host computer. Features are good returns productivity & host computer has fewer transactions or (3) *Warehouse Computer* that is not preferred due to security issues.

GRI 2. Know Your Customer Order (Most Important Your Promotional Skus) Return Life Cycle
Know your return life cycle or time improves your space utilization, employee productivity and returns flow. Your returns quantity varies from medium volume to high volume. In a returns process area, return to stock and return to vendor temporary or final sort area requires a WMS ID position for each sku. To assure good space utilization and good employee put-away productivity, good sku location strategy is to associate a sku volume with a sku position. To assist a returns process manager sku location strategy, a manager uses each sku return history or sales as the location criteria. From the sales history, important factors are (1) promotional skus that are allocated to a large sort position and is close to your process station and (2) after a sku sales the day number such as 30, 60 or 90 days and associated sku return volume or percentage that are allocated to a regular sort position. Feature assures a position has capacity to handle a large sku quantity.

GRI 3. FIFO Customer Order Returns
FIFO return sku rotation is a return process sku concept to assure that your oldest skus are picked first for new COs. In a return to stock sort or temporary hold position, skus with different return processed dates are mixed in a one WMS ID position and it is difficult to assure an accurate FIFO sku rotation. A macro FIFO rotation is to have all

returned skus in one WMS ID position transferred to another temporary hold or permanent pick position and sku transfer date becomes a sku received date in your WMS computer inventory control program. New returned skus are accumulated in another WMS ID position & in your WMS computer inventory program are considered as the newest skus.

GRI 4. How To Record Manufacturer Lot Number

To record a manufacturer lot number in your returns process activity is difficult to track a specific manufacturer lot number. A black box approach assures good returns employee productivity and provides inventory tracking. A manufacturer lot number is a unique sku ID that indicates a manufacturer's specific date & production facility. Since returns occur random & could have numerous manufacturer lot numbers, it is very difficult to identify specifics. With mixed manufacturer's lot number skus in a returns process flow, it is preferred to associate a manufacturer's lot number to a CO ID at a pack station or as a sku is package for a return to vendor pick activity.

GRI 5. Know & Track Your Customer Return Reasons

Track and know your returns reasons are important factors that assist you to reduce your future return package number. Return reasons help your determine where your operation needs improvement. Your returns reasons are a result from your pick and pack activity performance that do not match your CO service standards. Your return reasons are (1) *Shortage* means that a customer did receive an order on-time but a CO picked, packed and delivered sku quantity was less than a CO pack slip/invoice sku quantity. A CO sku shortage means that a customer is dissatisfied with your pick & pack operation performance due to the fact a CO sku was not delivered on-time in a package. A shortage pick has your staff focus on your picker activity quality, (2) *Overage* means that a CO was received at a delivery address but a CO picked, packed and delivered sku quantity was more than a CO pack slip/invoice quantity. A CO overage means that a honest customer is dissatisfied with your pick & pack operation due to the fact a customer has to take time & expense for a sku return quantity to your pick & pack operation. An overage pick has your staff focus on your picker activity quality, (3) *Sku Damage* occurs when a CO is received at a delivery address & when a CO picked, packed & delivered sku quality is compared to a CO pack slip/invoice that an actual CO identified, picked, packed and delivered sku quality indicates that a sku is broken or not functioning sku. A CO sku damage means that a customer is dissatisfied with your pick/pack operation performance due to the fact a customer has to take time & expense and return a damage sku to your pick/pack operation and due to the fact that a customer did not received a CO good quality sku on-time. A damaged sku has your staff review your receiving/quality control, pack activity & filler material type, package seal type & quantity & vendor ready to ship carton quality & (4) *Incorrect Sku or Mis-Pick* occurs when a CO is received at a delivery address and when a CO picked, packed & delivered sku quality is compared to a CO pack slip/invoice that an actual CO picked, packed & delivered sku is not a CO sku. A CO incorrect sku means that a customer is dissatisfied with your pick/pack operation performance due to the fact a customer takes time & expense and return an incorrect picked and delivered sku to your pick/pack operation and a customer did not received a correct sku on-time. With an incorrect sku or pick error has your staff focus on your picker activity quality that includes your replenishment activity.

Customer Return Label Ideas (CRL 1 – CRL 2)

CRL 1. Customer Returns Label On Your Customer Order Pack Slip/Inovice

Returns label on your CO pack slip/invoice assures smooth returns arrive at your preferred warehouse dock position and provides a customer with a return label with an accurate human readable address/bar coded face. Your pre-printed returns label provides you or freight company with ability to pre-sort returns to your preferred process section that is achieve by your returns label has your CO most important sku to your operation. Examples: combination CO with jewelry, GOH or specific sku. Feature assures a sku flows to your process section that is designed to handle the sku and minimizes in-house transport costs.

CRL 2. One Return Address Or Several Return Addresses

One return address or several return addresses are your printed return address label on your CO pack slip/invoice options. One return Address, your freight company sort concept has all your return packages that are sorted and delivered onto 1 delivery truck. At your unload dock, all return packages (GOH, jewelry, BIG/UGLY, food and hard goods) flow to your first process station or over your sort concept to process stations. Your one return address returns flow has each process station handle high value and other skus. With some sku classifications such as jewelry or GOH your process employee requires additional skills and you mix high value skus with low value skus. If your WMS computer creates a separate return address label for each single CO sku classification or for a high value sku classification in a combination CO. *Deparate Return Label* for each sku classification, your returns are separated by your (1) freight company onto separate carts, pallets or delivery truck or (2) your return sort conveyor, sorts each sku classification to specific sort lanes/process stations. Features are (1) less complex and improve process employee productivity & (2) skus flow as group for increase transport and sku sort activities.

Returns Dock Ideas (RD 1 – RD7)
RD 1. Freight Company Pre-Sort
Freight company pre-sort concept has your freight company per each returns label to sort packages onto one sort lane for load onto a delivery truck, carton or pallet that is delivered to your company assigned dock. Per your pre-printed returns label, a freight company pre-sort activity separates returns by GOH, jewelry/high value, Big/ugly and regular cartons. When your freight company sorts specific returns onto a delivery truck, carts or pallets, there is high potential for improved returns flow. Since your GOH and jewelry returns require special quality control skills, it improves your returns process employee productivity. Since Big/ugly sku physical characteristics do match your regular returns transport concept, big/ugly skus require a special transport concept. Features are improves returns employee productivity and assure good sku flow.

RD 2. Your Returns Dock Arrangement
Dock door arrangement has your freight company returns trucks spotted/parked at a specific dock door to improve your unload employee productivity, assure good returns flow and increase space utilization. If your returns are floor stacked and unloaded onto a mobile belt conveyor or skate-wheel or roller extendible/retrackable conveyor for maximum dock door flexibility your unload conveyors traverses between 2 or 3 dock doors. If your operation has three dock doors and your returns are delivered on 4-wheel carts, pallets or containers, you use a three dock door arrangement. A three dock door arrangement has one dock door used for active unload activity, second dock door is scheduled for your next returns truck and third dock door is used for empty cart, pallet or container load activity.

RD 3. After Unload You Have Queue
After your returns packages are unloaded from your delivery truck you have a queue section that is prior to your first returns process work station. The queue section assures good unload employee productivity, returns flow and truck dock turn. With a conveyor unload concept, you have zero or low pressure accumulation conveyor between the unload conveyor and first work station. With a cart, pallet or container unload concept, you have floor staging area between your dock area and first returns work station. To assure proper cart, pallet or container control you have painted parallel lines on your floor to indicate a staging lane.

RD 4. Between Your Unload Area & Next Work Station Provide Queue
Between your unload area and next work station (open/dump or returns process station) provide queue for your return packages that assures sku flow and good employee productivity. Your carton unload and transport concept is a powered conveyor travel path, you provide low/zero pressure roller conveyor travel path between your dock conveyor and your open/dump or returns process station. If your carton unload and transport concept is 4-wheel carts and pallets, you provide dock staging floor area, pallet racks along your walls or back to back racks in your floor staging area. The pallet rack bottom load height is set at an elevation to allow full carts/pallets through a rack bay and your protect your rack upright posts. All queue concepts provide queue for an imbalance between a slow returns process stations and your unload productivity rate.

RD 5. Age Customer Returns In Your Staging Area
Age returns in your returns staging area assures a FIFO (first-in first-out) returns rotation or flow through your process area. Proper returns rotation maintains company returns policy and assures customer satisfaction. FIFO returns concept has your oldest or dated returns processed first. If your returns operation receives bulk or floor loaded on a delivery truck, your delivery company, yard control or dock supervisor tracks the oldest delivery truck and schedules the oldest truck at the next vacate dock. If returns are on carts, on pallets or in containers, each

cart, pallet or container receives a human readable and color coded date tag with a color for each week day.   To assure FIFO returns rotation, dated carts, pallets or containers are grouped together with a first-in first-out flow to a vacate process station.

RD 6. Racks In Your Returns Staging Area

Racks in your returns area is an idea to improve space utilization. Since a returns process area is in a building area with a normal ceiling height, there is an opportunity to place racks along walls and above conveyor travel paths. The positions are considered return supplies, return paper document and returned sku temporary hold storage positions. If your customer returns are delivered on carts or pallets and you do not use powered equipment to move carts or pallets, back to back racks in a staging area provides additional storage positions. To optimize space utilization, a first load beam permits an employee to move a full cart or pallet under rack bays. A first load beam has 6 ft 6 in to 7 ft clear space from the floor surface.   To protect rack posts, post protectors are place in each rack post front.

Returns Separation Before Process Station Ideas (RS 1 – RS11)

RS 1. Separate Your Customer Returns By BIG/UGLY, Carton Or Small Carton

Separate your returns by big/ugly, carton or small carton has your freight company or sort concept (after unload) to separate your returns by a sku physical characteristics that improves your employee productivity and assures good sku flow. Sku separation concept matches a sku to your returns process section that is designed to handle a sku volume, sku size or returns process employee is skilled to check a sku quality and assures a cost effective and efficient process.

RS 2. Separate BIG/UGLY Skus From Other Skus

Separate big/ugly skus from other skus is returns process activity that has your returns unload or open employee separate your big/ugly skus from other skus that improves process employee productivity and sku flow. Your returns activity handles a wide sku mix, your process options are (1) *All Skus Or Sku Mix* is processed through any process station. When all skus or sku mix is sent to one process station, a process employee has potential to handle a big/ulgy sku at a process station that is designed to handle medium size skus. With a large sku at a process station, a process employee has low productivity due to handle and process a large sku that requires a process employee to walk around and move a large and disposed sku and (2) *Separate Your Big/Ugly Skus* from your other skus flow to other process stations that handle small and medium size skus.   When you design a process station with a sku in-flow and out-flow layout to handle large skus, there is smooth returns flow due to your process station work area and equipment are designed to match your sku size.

RS 3. High Value Sku Separation

High value sku separation is a returns idea that improves your returns process productivity, assures good sku flow and improves security. If your operation handles expensive items such as jewelry and your COs are sent with a pre-printed returns label with a separate address, it separates your high value returns from returns with other skus. During your freight company customer returns sort and flow to your operation, your high value sku returns are delivered to your jewelry operation.

RS 4. Customer Non-Deliverable Separated To One Process Station

Customer non-deliverable separated to one process station has your freight company or your returns sort concept separate/sort CO non-deliverable packages to one process station that improves process employee productivity due to quality is good and constant return flow due to no credit issues. A non-deliverable CO is a CO package that was not accepted by a customer and by your company return delivery label return address is sent back to your returns operation. Also, your company package seal is not broken. Most occurrences skus are in return to stock or have good quality. If your delivery/freight company sorts the non-deliverable that are delivered to your operation in bulk or in a separate container, on a pallet or cart or your returns sort conveyor diverts a non-deliverable package to one process station. Feature allows on process station to improve productivity & processed returns due to minimal inspection time.

RS 5. Transport Your Customer Order Return Package To Your First Process Station

Transport your return package to your first process station improves returns employee productivity, reduces sku damage and assures returns sku flow. Your returns transport concept is determined by your return package open location. Your options are (1) *Open At Your Returns Process/Sku Disposition Station* that has your return carton or bag package travel direct from a delivery truck to a process station. With closed returns packages, your transport options are (a) powered belt or roller conveyor travel path that assure a constant one-way flow and additional cost with stop/start controls and (b) 4-wheel with shelves that has an employee move carts, move empty carts to unload dock and requires floor space and (2) *Open/Slice Your Packages At An Open Station* for transport to returns process station, your transport options have controlled sku travel and provide queue at each return process station. Options are (a) powered roller conveyor travel path that have medium size carton and small size carton on a tray to assure good travel and CO pack slip/invoice inside a package, (b) 4-wheel carton with shelves/netting that has an employee move carts, move empty carts to unload dock and requires floor space.

RS 6. Your Process Returns (Open & Dispose) Completed At One Station

When you process returns (open & dispose) at one process station all your returns activities (open, dump filler material, credit process & dispose) are completed at one work station. The return process has return packages delivered to your process stations. At each process station, a highly trained and high wage rate employee completes skilled activities that include credit process and sku quality inspection and unskilled activities that include package open & filler material dump. One station concept has a high unit cost and under productive employee who completes both skilled and unskilled activities.

RS 7. Return Package Open & Dump Filler Material Or Process Employee Completes All Activities

Return package open and dump filler material at a separate work station or at a return process station are your options that improve and assure good sku flow. If your returns process concept has a return process employee open a return container and dump filler material into a trash transport concept, a returns process station employee to completes all return activities. Features are (1) multiple returns process employee tasks at one work table that has an employee use a cutting knife to open a package/empty container transport concept and from a package to dump filler material into a trash concept and to assure customer credit approval/sku disposition that make a complex work station, (2) potential employee cutting injuries, (3) skilled and trained employee completing simple, repetitive and non-skill activity, (4) possible separate trash handling concept & (5) possible separate filler material handling concept. If your returns process concept has a separate package open and filler material dump station and separate returns process station for customer credit approval/sku disposition, it is a more production line design operation. With the concept, each station completes repetitive activities such as open/dump and credit approval/sku disposition. At a package open and dump station an employee works with safety gloves and cutting knife to open each package, dump filler material into a transport concept and transfers skus/CO pack slip/invoice in a return container that is placed onto a transport concept. At a returns process station, an employee completes customer credit approval/sku disposition and a return container is transferred onto a transport concept and disposed sku is transferred onto a transport concept. Features are (1) improves employee safety and productivity, (2) at each open/dump station, separate filler material and at each process station, empty return container and disposed sku transport concepts that a less complex work station, (3) open/dump station completes repetitive and non-highly skilled activity, (4) at a process station employee completes highly skilled activities of credit approval and sku quality check to improve employee productivity & accurate transactions & (5) assure constant returns & disposed sku flows.

RS 8. You Process Returns Flow Through Several (Open, Transport & Dispose) Stations

When you process returns with skus flow through open/dump station, over a transport path and disposed (credit and sku disposition) station has your return activities separated at unskilled and skilled employees. With (open & dispose) at one process station all your returns activities (open, dump filler material, credit process & dispose) are completed at 1 work station. Your first return station has an unskilled employee open packages and dump filler material and transfer open packages onto a cart or conveyor travel path for transport to your process station. At each process station, a highly trained and high wage rate employee completes skilled activities that include credit process, sku quality inspection and sku pre-sort/transfer onto a transport concept or unskilled activities that include package open and filler material dump. The returns process has a continuous return and sku flow.

RS 9. Customer Return Problem Station
A problem return sku station is shelf that is located in a returns process area and is a very short walk distance for a process employee to transfer a problem r return. If your return process activities are (1) matches a CO WMS ID to your WMS computer CO ID, (2) assures each sku quantity matches a WMS ID CO quantity sku error and (3) determines a sku quality and disposition status. If a process employee has a problem with a return, your company policy requires additional action taken to process a return. To maintain a process employee at a process station, when a problem return occurs a process employee transfers a problem return (skus, container and CO pack slip/invoice) to a problem station shelf. The approach has a process employee remain at a process station and not have non-productive wait or walk time to a supervisor to review a problem return. A return process area supervisor resolves a problem return and re-introduces a corrected return to a process station. Feature is increase returns process employee productivity and increased completed return number.

RS 10. How To Handle Leakers & Sharpe Edge Skus (Damage Sku Scrap) At Your Process Station
Damage sku scrap at your process station is a returns activity idea to reduce sku damage, assure inventory control and improve employee productivity. In your returns sku flow, a damaged sku (sharp edge or leaker) moves beyond your process station, there is potential for additional/other sku damage, additional employee sku handling and employee injury. To minimize potential damage sku problems and assure accurate inventory, each process station has a scrap sheet for a process employee to place each damage sku printed disposition WMS ID. At a work day end each scrap sheet with a sku disposition label is sent to an office for WMS inventory update. To reduce sku damage & employee injury, each station has a solid container for leakers & a solid container for sharp edge skus.

RS 11. At A Returns Process Station, Returns Employee Sits Or Stands
At a returns process station do your returns employee sit or stand are your employee option that assures an employee complete all return process activities and good productivity. If your employee sit on a stool your stool options are to use a (1) *Low Level Chair* that has your returns process employee have increased non-productive time to get-up from a chair, reach a returns package from a conveyor, sit in a chair and complete a sku disposition, get-up front a chair and transfer a disposed sku onto a take-away concept and (2) *High Level Chair* that has your returns process employee have minimal non-productive time to reach a returns package from a conveyor, lean against/sit on top of chair and complete a sku disposition and transfer a disposed sku onto a take-away concept.

RS 12. Hand Held Scanner Default To One (See BSC 5 Page 15)
RS 13. Hand Held Scanner Muliple Light Beams/ Wide Light Beam (See BSC 4 Page 15)
RS 14. Fixed Position Your Hand Held Scanner (See BSC 1 Page 15)
RS 15. Hand Held Scanner With A Direct Electric Not A Battery (See BSC 2 Page 15)
RS 16. Light Fixture Location (See CA 8. Page 93)

Trash Handling Ideas (TH 1 – TH 2)
TH 1. Re-Cycle Trash
Handle your re-cycle trash is handling/transport concept that collects and transports re-cycle trash from each open/dump or returns process station to your trash re-cycle concept. When designing an open/dump or returns process station, you assure a collection and constant trash removal concept or your activity station will become clogged that lowers your employee productivity and slow returns flow. Your re-cycle trash concept options are determined by your re-cycle trash volume and type. Your options are (1) *Carton* includes (a) overhead belt conveyor that is set at an elevation for an employee to easily transfer a carton onto a conveyor travel path and is adjacent to your work stations. At each work station, a side guard is angled type with a high far side guard or has a saw-tooth design between two work stations. If a higher far side guard requires additional height (handle extra tall cartons or double stack cartons) you add fish or meshed netting between a side guard and ceiling/overhead support member. At conveyor merge locations, you have stop/start photo-eyes to minimize jam problems. Features are handles high volume, assure constant flow, travel path is available to all process stations, requires minimal employee effort and high cost that is set at an elevation for an employee to easily transfer a carton onto a conveyor

travel path and is adjacent to your work stations, (b) overhead conveyor with flat tray at a pendant end that is set at an elevation for an employee to easily transfer a carton onto a flat tray and travel path is adjacent to your work stations. Features handles medium volume, assure constant flow but an empty carrier/tray is not available to every work station, travel path is past all process stations, requires an employee effort and high cost and (c) overhead conveyor with hooks/clasps on a pendant that is set at an elevation for an employee to easily transfer a carton onto a hook/clasp and travel path is adjacent to your work stations. Features handles medium volume, assure constant flow but an empty hook/clasp is not available to every work station, travel path is past all process stations, requires an employee effort and high cost, (2) *Loose Peanut Filler Material* includes (a) air blower/vacuum and tunnel/tube that is set at an elevation for an employee to easily transfer a peanuts into access opening and tube/tunnel travel path is adjacent to your work stations. Blowers or vacuum concept assures peanuts flow into a container bag for transfer to pack stations. Features handles high volume, assure constant flow is available at every work station, travel path is past all process stations, requires little employee effort, potential maintenance problems and high cost (b) solid or small meshed opening 4-wall container has a meshed opening top and the container sets on a pallet or has fork openings for pallet truck or forklift truck handling. An option has a plastic bag that inserted into the interior. After an open employee opens a package and dumps the sku and peanuts onto the meshed top that allows peanuts to full through meshed openings into a container. Features separate package open activity, handles small volume, moved by a pallet truck or forklift truck, requires floor or rack storage positions and requires an employee to transfer peanuts into a peanut re-cycle concept & (3) *Crushed Paper, Meshed Cardboard & Bagged Filler Material* has an open employee remove bags from a return package and transfer the bags into a container and has a size handled by an employee or has fork openings for pallet truck or forklift truck handling. Features separate or combined package open activity, handles small volume, moved by an employee, pallet truck or forklift truck, requires floor or rack storage positions and requires an employee to transfer peanuts into a peanut re-cycle concept.

TH 2. Non-Recycle Trash
Handle your non-re-cycle trash is handling/transport concept that transports re-cycle trash from each open/dump or returns process station to your trash non-re-cycle concept. When designing an open/dump or returns process station, you assure a collection & constant trash removal concept or your activity station will become clogged that lowers your employee productivity & slow returns flow. Your non-re-cycle trash concept options are determined by your non-re-cycle trash volume (usually very low) and type. For damaged filler material or non-standard package material your option is a four wall container or plastic bag that is strategically located at an open/dump or returns process station.

Disposed Sku Sort Ideas (DSS 1 - DSS26)
DSS 1. What Is Printed On Your Sort Or Disposed Labels
What is printed on your RTS, RTV and other sku sort or disposition labels serves as an instruction for employee or mechanical presort or final sort activity that improves returns employee productivity, assures accurate sku sort and inventory control. Rturned sku disposition label options are (1) return-to-stock/pick position options are (a) "RTS", (b) QA inspection or (c) sku with an existing sku ID. If a label is blank it is easily ID by a returns process employee. if an sku with a blank label or a QA inspection label is sent to a customer, there is less customer concern, (2) return to vendor with "RTV", (3) damaged sku with a "D", (4) outlet store ("OS") or company store ("CS"), (5) retail or jobber with a "J", (6) charity with a "C", (7) rework with "RW" and (8) spare parts with "SP".

DSS 2. Transport Your Disposed Skus To A Temporary Sort & Hold Position
Transport your return package from your process stations to a temporary sort and hold position improves returns employee productivity, reduces sku damage & assures returns sku flow. Your returns transport concept is determined by your return disposed sku volume and sku type. Your options are at your returns process/sku disposition station that has your skus are transferred as (1) *Loose Skus On A Powered Belt Conveyor* that has skus travel from each process station at a slow travel speed past your temporary sort positions. To assure continuous sku flow your 'did not sort' skus are transferred from your sort belt conveyor into a large tote or onto a belt conveyor re-circulation travel path. Features are does not allow pre-sort sku travel, potential sku damage/hang-up, difficult to

handle a wide sku mix or label removal, additional stop/start controls and additional employee handling or additional floor space and (2) *Skus That Are (a) Pre-Sort Into A Tote Or (b) Non-Sorted/Mixed Skus Into A Tote*. Zero/low pressure roller or skate-wheel conveyor travel path or on 4-wheel shelf cart moves from your process stations to your temporary sort location. Features are additional tote cost, handles a wide sku mix, minimizes sku damage & tote has handles and empty totes/carts are returned to process station.

DSS 3. BIG/UGLY Disposed Sku Pre-Sort Rack Layout
BIG/UGLY disposed sku pre-sort layout that is designed to handle your RTS & RTV disposed BIG/UGLY sku for improved returns employee productivity, assures accurate sku sort and inventory control. For maximum efficiency & cost effectiveness, you have separate RTS and RTV sections that allow each position with greater capacity and minimal in-house transport to a final sort location. Your pre-sort rack layout is determined by your final sort concept design and sort instruction. Your pre-sort layout has your inbound/non-disposed return skus arrive on 4-wheel carts/pallets at returns process station side and disposed skus are transferred onto a 4-wheel cart for transfer to a pre-sort position. Your pre-sort position options are 4-wheel carts or pallets that are arranged in a horse pattern that has a short travel distance or straight line that sort position progression is easy to follow. Your pre-sort instruction options are (1) *By Sku Inventory Code* with your skus sorted to each pre-sort position by sku first digit or last digit that has allows faster final sku sort activity and requires your final sort section to have same sort instruction, (2) *Mixed Skus* that decreases your final sku sort productivity or (3) *Vendor Name* as individual vendor that allows fast final sku sort and a vendor with multiple skus that requires additional time for consolidation has mixed vendor names that are group by specific alpha characters A - E, F - J, K - O, P - S & T – Z that minimizes your final sku sort travel distance & has lower final sku sort productivity.

DSS 4. Very Small Sku & Small Sku Pre-Sort Shelf & Rack Layout (See BPS 10 Page 143)
DSS 5. Manual Disposed Sku Pre-Sort By Sku First & Second Digits (See MBPSF 10 Page 114)
DSS 6. Manual Disposed Sku Pre-Sort By Sku First & Last Digits (See MBPSF 10 Page 114)
DSS 7. Manual Disposed Sku Pre-Sort By First Two Digits (See MBPSF 10 Page 114)
DSS 8. Manual Temporary Sort Design With Shelf, Decked Racks & Racks (See MBPSF 10 Page 114)
DSS 9. Manual Temporary Sort Area Design As Horse-Shoe, 2 Aisle & 1 Aisle (See BPS 10 Page 143)

DSS 10. Pre-Sort Disposed Skus Into A Temporary Pick Position By Sku Or Mixed In A Tote
Pre-sort disposed skus into a temporary pick position by sku or mixed skus into tote impacts your employee productivity, space utilization and assures disposed skus in a pick position. *Sort By Dku* has one sku in one pick position that is scanned to your WMS computer program and becomes available for sale/COs. Features are large pick position number and sq ft area, additional time to complete a deposit transaction due to sorter travel past skus in other pick positions that is minimized with a narrow and deep pick position container, slow transfer time to potential multiple trips to same pick positions and good picker productivity, *Mixed Skus In A Tote* has multiple skus in one pick position that has each sku WMS ID & pick position WMS ID scanned and sent to your WMS computer program for skus to become available for sale/Cos. Features are requires small pick position number and sq ft area, minimal to complete a deposit and scan transaction, lower picker productivity due to increase search time to find sku that is reduced with sku separation in a tote.

DSS 11. Manual Or Mechanized Pre-Sort Disposed Customer Return Skus
Manual or mechanized sku pre-sort disposed return skus are your options to assure accurate sku sort and good sku flow. Both sort concepts require that each sku has a sku ID and each sort position has an ID. A sort concept design parameters and selection factors are (1) returns sku volume, (2) sku physical characteristics such as crushable, fragile, sharp edges, heavy or light weight, cube or length, width and height, (3) most frequent, average or peak sku number, (4) available building sq ft, (5) cost includes computer programming, (6) labor requirements, (7) final sort labor and cost and (8) time require for sku to become available for sale.
  Manual Sort Concept has disposed skus loose on a belt conveyor or in totes on roller conveyor travel through a sort lane. After a sorter matches a sku ID to a sort position ID, a sku is transferred to a sort position. Per your sort concept, the sort position is a non-pick-able position or pick-able position. If sorted to a pick-able position, a scan transaction is sent to your WMS computer program. The sku and pick position is up dated and sku becomes

available for sale/COs. Also, if your WMS computer program receives a sku scan transaction and a sku was previously scanned to a WMS ID position, a hand held scanner display screen shows a sku previous WMS ID position. Features are (1) low cost, (2) employee activity, (3) sort to a pick position or non-pick-able position, (4) handles a wide sku mix, (5) additional computer programming and cost & (6) completed for all sku types.

Mechanized Sort Concept has disposed skus travel under a scanner and each sku ID is sent to your sort computer. Your sort computer assures that a sku is diverted to a sort position that has other ID skus (mixed skus in on sort position). After sort completion, skus are sent to pick area as skus sorted to an individual pick position or as mixed skus in a tote in a pick position that requires a sku and pick position ID scan transactions sent to your WMS computer for sku and pick position update and available for sale/Cos. Features are (1) independent sort concept that is a stand alone sort concept with a high cost, requires space and utilities, available any time, handles a large volume and some skus (crushable/fragile/heavy/sharp edge) are restricted or (2) combined picked sku and returns sort concept that has your returns skus sorted when your picked skus are not sorted or when not available for CO sku sort activity. Features are requires available time that is difficult during peck activity periods, potential double sku handling and added sort computer programming.

DSS 12. Returned To Stock (RTS) Disposed Sku Sent To A Non-Pick-able Or Pick-able Position
Customer disposed RTS sku sent to a non-pick-able or pick-able position are your options to have skus in a WMS ID position. When a disposed sku is placed into a *Non-Pick-able Position*, it means that a sku is not entered into a WMS ID pick position and a sku is not available for sale/CO. A disposed sku is placed into a WMS ID *Pick-able Position*, a sku & pick position IDs & quantity are sent to a WMS computer program that updates a sku status as available for sale/CO and are potential to reduce CO back orders or out-of-stock sku.

DSS 13. Return To Vendor (RTV) Sku By Sku Inventory Code Or Vendor Name
Return to vendor (RTV) sku pre-sort options are designed to improve returns employee productivity, assure good sku flow and inventory tracking. Your options are (1) *Sort By* (a) *Inventory Code* that has your sorter employee use a sku inventory digit as a sort instruction to a position. Inventory code options are (*) sku first digit as a shelf bay and last digit as shelf level, (*) sku first digit as a shelf bay and second digit as shelf level (*) sku last digit as a shelf bay and next to last digit as shelf level or (b) *Vendor Name* that has each vendor name assigned to a pre-scanned WMS ID position that after a sorter employee scans a sku ID a WMS program communicates on hand held scanner a sku WMS ID position. Features are same a mixed sku tote concept due one vendor has potential to multiple skus in your inventory. If multiple skus in one tote, a reader is referred to mixed skus in one tote in this section (2) *Single Sku To A Position* that has each RTV sku or has one tote for one vendor. As a sort employee enters a vendor return aisle & scans an sku bar code/RF tag with a RF device & if a RTV sku was previously scanned to WMS ID position, a hand held scanner shows that previous a sku. Features are each sku has a position, large final sort area, low put-away employee productivity, vendor return sku easier and quicker consolidation & accurate inventory & (3) *Mixed Skus By Inventory Code Or Vendors In 1 Tote* that has RTV skus presorted return vendor mixed skus in a tote. As a sort employee transfers the tote to a storage position & per a WMS program, a final sort employee completes position and tote or each RTV sku scan transactions that are sent to a WMS computer. Features are minimal position number, smaller final sort area, improved put-away employee productivity, slower & more difficult sku consolidation for a vendor shipment & potential sku inventory control problems.

DSS 14. Pre-Sort Disposed Skus At Your Process Station Or Separate Temporary Hold Position
Pre-sort disposed skus at your process station or separate temporary hold position is a returns activity to improve good returns employee productivity and assure good sku flow. After a process returns employee disposes a customer returned sku, a disposed sku flow options are move to a final sort area as (1) *Wide Mixed Skus In A Tote* that requires sort employee to travel through all aisles. Features are low final sort employee productivity due to skus are randomly available to a sort employee, if mixed skus are placed into a WMS ID position, there is good employee put-away productivity and low pick employee productivity or (2) *Pre-Sorted Skus In A Tote* have a returns process employee pre-sort disposed skus by a pre-determined criteria. If a process employee pre-sorts skus, sku WMS ID digits are a sku sort instruction. A process station has sufficient sort containers for your sort criteria. Full pre-sort containers are sent to a final sort area with pick-able positions for a low volume operation. If a process

employee sends loose mixed over a belt conveyor travel path or in totes to a pre-sort station, at a pre-sort station there are sufficient containers to handle your sort criteria & full pre-sort containers are to final sort area with pick-able positions. Features are handles a high volume, pre-sort & final sort area & additional employee activity.

DSS 15. Manual Or Mechanical Pre-Sort Return To Stock & Return To Vendor Skus
Manual or mechanical pre-sort return to stock and return to vendor skus are options to complete separate skus into smaller and more manageable groups for your final sort activity has a constant sku flow and high employee productivity. Your pre-sort concept requires a human/machine readable WMS sku ID, sku travel path from a process station to a pre-sort area and pre-sort sku positions. *Mechanical Sort Concept* has all disposed skus travel from your process stations to an induction station, under a scanner device continue travel on a sort conveyor and to divert onto a sku assigned sort position. After a full sort location or at pre-determined times a final sort employee transfers skus from a pre-sort position to a final sort area. Features are (1) one time high cost, fewer sort but some induction employees, difficult to handle a wide sku mix that includes heavy, crushable, fragile or edge skus and requires a high volume. *Manual Pre-Sort Concept At Your Process Station* all disposed skus are pre-sort in separate containers by return to stock and return to vendor skus and containers are transported to a pre-sort area. In a pre-sort area, employees at pre-sort station sort skus into return to stock positions and return to vendor positions/containers. From each container, pre-sort employee uses a sku WMS ID or disposed label as a pre-sort instruction. Features are (1) designed to handle any volume, requires some additional sort employees, low one-time cost, handles a wide sku mix with minimal sku damage and reduces sort employee walk distance and time.

DSS 17. Pre-Sort Disposed GOH Rail Layout
Pre-sort disposed GOH rail layout permits a returns employee at a returns process station or in a pre-sort area to separate disposed GOH skus by a sku inventory digit (first or last) that improves sorter productivity and assures good sku flow and a disposed GOH sku is transferred to a pick-able position. GOH pre-sort layout has a 4-wheel cart with a load bar or on a rail, a trolley with a load bar. A 4-wheel cart/trolley rail layout has four lanes with 3 carts/trolleys per lane and 2 aisles between lanes that allows cart/trolley and sorter travel. With a trolley concept sufficient drop switches for trolley travel through each aisle and full trolley transfer onto a main travel rail. Each cart/trolley has a digit (0 – 9) for your sort by sku primary digit and on each cart/trolley load bar has ID sliders for (0 – 9). Per your GOH return volume, your layout is expanded to have 2 carts/trolley primary digits that have 20 to 24 carts/trolleys and 3 aisles between lanes that allows cart/trolley and sorter travel. With a trolley concept sufficient drop switches for trolley travel through each aisle & full trolley transfer onto a main travel rail. A cart/trolley has a digit (0 – 9) for your sort by sku primary digit & on each load bar has ID sliders for (0 – 9).

DSS 18. Carton, GOH OR BIG/UGLY Final Sort Rack Layout
Carton, GOH or BIG/UGLY sku final sort layout that is designed to handle your RTS & RTV disposed carton, GOH or BIG/UGLY sku for improved returns employee productivity, assures accurate sku sort and inventory control. For maximum efficiency & cost effectiveness, you have separate RTS and RTV sections that allow each position with greater capacity and minimal transport to a final sort location. Your final sort rack layout uses standard pallet rack positions that are in single deep or back to back rack rows with elevated positions for storage. Each rack row has a sort position progression that is easy to follow. Your sort instruction has your (1) *Sku Inventory Code* as (a) sku first digit as a rack row and last digit as rack bay, (*) sku first digit as a rack row and second digit as rack bay & (*) sku last digit as a rack row and next to last digit as rack bay or (2) *Vendor Name* as individual vendor that allows fast final sku sort and a vendor with multiple skus that requires additional time for consolidation has mixed vendor names. Your rack rows has specific alpha characters A - E, F - J, K - O, P - S & T – Z with the final alpha characters per rack row to be determined by your number per alpha character. Example rack row has A – E and each bay within a rack row has each vendor name that progresses from A through E.

DSS 19. GOH Temporary Sort Cart & Rail Layout
Manual GOH sku temporary sort cart or rail layout has your employee push a 4-wheel cart with a load bar or trolley through sort cart and rail layout. Manual returned GOH sku sort requires each GOH sku to have a disposed label with a sku inventory ID number. After a sorter picks a sku from a cart or trolley and reads a sku ID and transfers a sku onto a cart or trolley temporary hold position. In a sku sort area, you identify each sort position by a position ID

that corresponds to your sku inventory ID. Your sort locations are carts with a load bar and trolley rail lanes. To have all possible sort locations, your sort area has 10 to 20 carts or 10 to 20 trolley capacity that has 1 or 2 carts/trolley per digit. Possible sort location sequences are (1) *Sku First Digit Is A Cart/Trolley & On A Load Bar Last Sku Digit* is arranged in arithmetic sequence from 0 to 9, (2) *Sku First Digit Is A Cart/Trolley & On A Load Bar Sku Second Digit* is arranged in arithmetic sequence from 0 to 9 and (3) *Sku Last Digit Is A Cart/Trolley & On A Load Bar Next To Last Digit* is arranged in arithmetic sequence from 0 to 9. A manual returned GOH sort by sku ID number to a cart or trolley improves your total employee productivity, sku flow and increase sorted returned GOH number and higher CO completion number. Features are (1) requires a computer program to print disposed label with sku ID number, (2) floor area for carts and trolleys and (3) transfer full carts or trolleys to final sort/storage area.

DSS 20. Pick-able Or Non-Pickable Sku Sort Position
A sku non-pick-able position is a return area position that holds returned and processed WMS ID skus that are available for sale (CO pick activity). With a sku quantity in a pick-able position, for your next CO your WMS computer directs a pick transaction from your returns temporary or final sort pick-able position. Features are (1) concept to fill back ordered skus & (2) sku picked from a pick position, it reduces a sku quantity that is transferred to storage position. A non-pick-able position means that a WMS identified sku in a position is not available for sale or COs. Some non-pick-able positions are pre-sort positions that are required for controlled sku flow.

DSS 21. Very Small Item Final Sort To Shelf Or Horse Shoe Layout (See BPS 8. Page 143)
DSS 22. Medium Size Sku Final Sort To Shelf & Rack Layout (See BPS 8. Page 143)
DSS 23. Temporary Pick Position (See DSS 12 Page 165)

DSS 24. Sort Disposed Skus To Your Temporary Pick Positions
Sort disposed skus in your temporary pick positions has your returns disposed sku sort employee transfer and scan a sku to a WMS ID temporary pick position that assures good returns employee productivity and provides inventory tracking. By your sku sort concept (by sku first or last as primary or bay ID and sku second or next to last digit as shelf ID or a separate position), each sku transferred is updated in your WMS inventory as in a pick-able position. This means that the sku is available for your next CO, back order CO or out-of-stock CO. If picked for a CO from a pick-able position, it means less skus for transfer to a position in your pick area & your oldest skus are picked first.

DSS 25. Return To Vendor (RTV) Sku Final Sort By Sku Inventory Code Or Vendor Name
Return to vendor sku final sort improves RTV employee productivity, assure good sku flow & inventory tracking. Your options are (1) sort instructions that are the same as pre-sort instructions (a) inventory code or (b) vendor name, (2) single sku to a position & (3) mixed skus by inventory code or vendors in 1 tote.

DSS 26. Sort Return To Vendor Or Retail/Discount Store Skus Into Square Front Cartons
Sort return to vendor or retail discount store skus into a squared front carton that increases your sort employee productivity. With the concept, each WMS ID sku position has a squared front carton. A squared front carton has a front side cut half way down, folded down to a front and secured with tape. On a front section is attached a WMS ID peal-off label that permits WMS scan transaction completion. With a half open carton front, an employee easily & quickly transfers skus into a carton. With a full carton, a peal-off label is removed and carton flap folded down & placed into a proper location for a sku WMS ID. Aa carton with taped top flaps , a carton is ready to ship.

Pick Sorted Skus Ideas (PSS 1 – PSS4)
PSS 1. Customer Order Pick From Temporary Pick Position (See DSS 12 Page 165)

PSS 2. Final Sorted Sku Reverse Or Consolidated Pick Activity
Final sorted sku reverse or consolidate pick activity is a returned, processed and disposed sku activity that has after vendor or company approval for an employee pick skus from WMS ID temporary and permanent positions. Skus are prepared for return to vendor, sent to a company store or third party retailer. For maximum picker productivity, your WMS ID positions have a numerical sequence.

PSS 3. How To Package Your Return To Vendor Or Retail/Discount Store Skus

How to package your return to vendor or retail discount store skus is to assure skus are contained in a package and minimizes your costs. Since your return to vendor or retail discount store package is not sent to a regular customer, your container does not require your company log on its exterior. With the criteria, your company purchases your carton vendor second (manufactured) ucartons, bad printed cartons or cartons with a plain exterior.

PSS 4. Move-Out Aged Customer Return Final Sorted Skus

Move-out aged return final sorted skus is an idea to improve space utilization, employee processed sku put-away productivity and inventory control. From your company sku sales history and returns life cycle, you determine number of days that a sku quantity is returned by customers. The information provides you with number of days after a sku sales for the vast majority is returned to your operation. A WMS program computer indicates WMS ID skus that have a 30, 60 or 90 day life cycle and end date and each WMS ID sku temporary hold position that has not had a put-away transaction for a pre-determined time period. With a computer printed list an employee assures that there are sufficient vacate temporary hold positions and ID each position with no put-away transactions. To assist in the aged process, your sku returns label has a return process date or each position has transaction sheet for your put-away employee to list the last return date. Per your company policy, aged skus or skus with no transactions are placed into sealed and WMS ID containers that are scanned and placed into a remote WMS ID position. All transactions are updated in your WMS computer.

Operation Or Specific Activity Review

Your total or specific warehouse activity review ensures your activity is meeting your company objectives. The objectives are (1) ensures that your activity is achieving your budget cost and CO service standard, (2) assures that your activity expense or cost savings matches your economic justification & (3) shows the relationship between handled COs/piece volumes to your activity expenses.

Activity Review Measurement Basics are (1) keep it simple to collect your activity productivity data, (2) cost effective, (3) timely to have work Day 1 results collected, analyzed and develop your work Day 2 game plan, (4) consistent standard with your measurement factors changes are made with your management and employee agreement and (5) determine your unit of measure.

Activity Non-Financial Review Factors are your activity results that do not have a direct impact on your activity operational expenses. Your non-financial factors are (1) activity accuracy, (2) on-time CO delivery, (3) none or minimal employee overtime, (4) none or minimal sku or equipment damage, (5) no or minor employee injury or accident free days and (6) positive customer comments.

Activity Statistical Review Methods in addition to your activity non-financial review factors allows you to rank your activity performance, to compare your activity present year results to last year results and to compare your activity to another company activity. The statistical review methods are

Dollar Cost Measurement Review method compares your activity actual expense dollars to your budget expenses. From your annual approved budget you obtain your activity annual, quarter, monthly, or weekly activity expense dollars and from your finance department you obtain your actual activity expense for a similar time period. Your actual and budget dollar expense/cost comparison allows you to review your total activity or specific activity budget/actual dollar variance. Features are minimal calculations, finance department supported figures, able to track and compare to past or another company activity results, show an impact on new I T computer program, activity equipment or CO download, provides an insight where your staff has an opportunity for improvement & capital investment.

Dollar Cost Per Unit, Piece Or Customer Order (CPU) is a common activity review. It requires your day, week, month, quarter or annual activity expense and total pieces or COs. To calculate, your activity cost per piece or CO, your activity expense is divided by your pieces or COs. Your CPU comparison is completed for (1) your activity handled pieces or units, (2) your completed COs or (3) combined activities. Features are easy to calculate, able to compare to past year or another company, able to determine expense impact from a change & used an expense impact from additional CO or pieces.

$$\frac{\text{Activity Operating Dollar Expense}}{\text{Total Units, Pieces Or Customer Orders Handled}} = \begin{array}{l}\text{Dollar Cost Per} \\ \text{Unit, Piece Or Customer} \\ \text{Order Handled}\end{array}$$

Activity Expenses As A Percent To Sales Dollars has your activity expenses divided by your associated activity skus sales dollars. Since your activity skus sales dollars vary over time, your activity expenses as a percent to sales dollars can vary.

$$\frac{\text{Activity Operating Dollar Expense}}{\text{Total Sales Dollars}} = \begin{array}{l}\text{Dollar Cost As A} \\ \text{Percentage To Sales}\end{array}$$

Activity Pieces, Units Or Customer Orders Handled Per Employee Hour (UPH) is another common review factor. To calculate your UPH has your activity pieces or COs divided by your activity employee total work hours. Your UPH cost comparison is completed for (1) your activity handled pieces, (2) your completed COs or (3) combined activities. Features are easy to calculate, able to compare to past year or another company, able to determine impact from a activity change and used to determine an additional activity or shift from additional COs or pieces.

$$\frac{\text{Activity Total Units, Pieces Or Customer Orders}}{\text{Total Warehouse Or Warehouse Activity Direct Hours}} = \frac{\text{Unit, Piece Or Customer Order}}{\text{For An Employee Hour}}$$

Activity Labor Ratio shows your employee total work hour number that was assigned to your pick line as a percentage of your operation's total employee work hour number. You calculate by dividing your pick line employee total work hour number by your operation's total employee work hour number. Features are easy to calculate, shows the relationship your pick line hours to your total operation hours and impact of re-allocating another department employees (receiving, QA or returns) to your activity.

$$\frac{\text{Activity Total Employees}}{\text{Total Warehouse Or Warehouse Activity Employee Number}} = \frac{\text{Activity}}{\text{Labor Ratio}}$$

Customer Order/Delivery Cycle Time is the time your activity requires to complete a CO. Your CO cycle time calculation options are (1) time for your CO activity instruction print start time to your CO ship time. The time shows total time that is required for your I T computer to print CO print instructions (pack slip/invoice & delivery label) and to have a CO manifested and loaded onto a delivery truck and (2) time for your CO entry to your pick line and arrival at a manifest and load onto a delivery truck. The time shows your activity actual time to complete a CO. Features are helps your staff determine additional employee number (part-time/re-locate employee) to complete new CO number.

$$\frac{\text{Total Time Required To Move An Order From A}}{\text{Storage Or Pick Position To Your Ship Door}} = \text{Customer Order/Delivery Cycle Time}$$

Activity Storage, Pick Or Returns Position Ratio has your occupied position number divided by your total activity position number. The results shows your activity vacate position number and opportunity to add 'B'/medium moving skus in half high or narrower position.

$$\frac{\text{Total Occupied Storage Or Pick Position Number}}{\text{Total Available Storage Or Pick Position}} = \frac{\text{Position}}{\text{Ratio}}$$

Storage, Pick Or Returns Area Aisle Space Potential Ratio Storage Or Pick Area Aisle Space Potential Ratio has two components (1) theoretical concept aisle space and (2) actual or current aisle space.

$$\frac{\text{Total Actual Square Feet For Product To Product Aisle Width}}{\text{Total Theoretical Square Feet For Product To Product Aisle Width}} = \frac{\text{Potential Aisle}}{\text{Space Ratio}}$$

Equipment Utilization Ratio is used for your activity machines, you divide your actual machine used hours by your capital justification hour number. It shows a machine available machine capacity and good time to complete preventive maintenance.

$$\frac{\text{Total Number Of Actual Storage/Pick Transactions For A Given Time Period}}{\text{Number Of Storage/Pick Transactions For A Given Time Period}} = \frac{\text{Total Theoretical}}{\text{Ratio}}$$

The Author

David Mulcahy is a speaker, a consultant, a magazine contributing author and the author or co-author of multiple essential reference books on warehouse management including: *Warehouse Distribution & Operations Handbook, Materials Handling Management, Order Fulfillment And Across The Dock Operations Concepts, Designs And Operations Handbook, Eaches And Pieces Order Fulfillment Design And Operations Handbook A Supply Chain Logistics Program For Warehouse Management.*

While working with the AMWAY Corporation, Mr. Mulcahy participated as a project manager for the design, build, install and start-up for order fulfillment operations in Japan, Korea, Taiwan, New Zealand, Australia, China, UK, Italy and Germany. These include 'pick to light' concepts as well as wire guided VNA storage vehicles with tall racks.   He was also involved with the re-model for Spain, Netherlands, Mexico, Canada and European Central Warehouses.

As a QVC project manager Mr. Mulcahy was involved with the remodel of QVC's Germany operation to increase storage capacity, improve picker, sort and packer productivity (UPH) and lower operational expenses (CPU) and in QVC's Japan operation to optimize off-site storage activity, improve space utilization, lower CPU and improve picker, sort and packer productivity (UPH). In the QVC Japan operation, the results of Mr. Mulcahy's efforts helped QVC Japan to achieve a positive cash flow within 3 years of startup. For both QVC Germany and Japan operations, Mr. Mulcahy was a key associate in completing site selection and overall warehouse operation design with a Carton and Pallet AS/RS, GOH trolley-less, tilt tray sorter, pick to light, customer returns conveyor concepts and extensive conveyor network and the WMS program written functional specifications.

For Peter J Schmitt, Buffalo, NY, Mr. Mulcahy consolidated two warehouse operations into one facility, improved the facility maintenance and sanitation rating to the top in the region and improved space utilization.

For A & P Tea Co., Dallas, TX Mr. Mulcahy consolidated a small item warehouse into the main warehouse, improved picker productivity and delivery truck utilization.   Improvements resulted in raising the division's operational ranking from number 26th to 6th nationally.

Most recently Mr. Mulcahy has also provided his services for the non-profit community.

Mr. Mulcahy received his MBA from the University Of Dallas, Texas. In 1981 Mr. Mulcahy designed a multi-layer case selection concept that won a 1981 Materials Handling Institute award at that year's Material Handling Show.